HEGEL'S

Undiscovered Thesis-Antithesis-Synthesis Dialectics

HEGEL'S
Undiscovered Thesis-Antithesis-Synthesis Dialectics

What Only Marx and Tillich Understood

LEONARD F. WHEAT

Prometheus Books

59 John Glenn Drive
Amherst, New York 14228–2119

Published 2012 by Prometheus Books

Cover background pattern © 2004 Dover Publications
Cover design by Grace M. Conti-Zilsberger

Inquiries should be addressed to
Prometheus Books
59 John Glenn Drive
Amherst, New York 14228—2119
VOICE: 716—691—0133
FAX: 716—691—0137
WWW.PROMETHEUSBOOKS.COM
16 15 14 13 12 5 4 3 2 1

Library of Congress Cataloging-in-Publication Data

Wheat, Leonard F., 1931–
    Hegel's undiscovered thesis-antithesis-synthesis dialectics : what only Marx and Tillich understood / by Leonard F. Wheat.
        p. cm.
    Includes bibliographical references and index.
    ISBN 978-1-61614-642-9 (cloth : alk. paper)
    ISBN 978-1-61614-643-6 (ebook)
    1. Hegel, Georg Wilhelm Friedrich, 1770–1831. 2. Dialectic. 3. Hegel, Georg Wilhelm Friedrich, 1770–1831. Phenomenologie des Geistes. 4. Hegel, Georg Wilhelm Friedrich, 1770–1831. Einleitung in die Geschichte der Philosophie. 5. Marx, Karl, 1818–1883. 6. Tillich, Paul, 1886–1965. I. Title.

B2948.W468 2012
193--dc23

                                                                              2012025638

Printed in the United States of America on acid-free paper

CONTENTS

PREFACE

The genesis of this book dates back to 1956, when I was preparing for my doctoral oral exams at Harvard. I was scared to death that I would be asked to give an example of one of Hegel's dialectics. Having searched in every available textbook and having found nothing but the usual abstract descriptions of thesis, antithesis, and synthesis, I felt helpless. Fortunately, nobody asked the dreaded question. And, as I now realize, I needn't have worried: no potential interrogator—this includes the noted professor who taught the course I took in medieval and post-medieval political theory—could have answered it either. In fact, although I didn't find this out until fifty years later, the year I got my degree (1958) was the year Gustav Mueller wrote his revolutionary, and until now widely endorsed, article declaring that the formerly universal belief that Hegel used thesis-antithesis-synthesis dialectics is just a "legend."

A second graduate school development initiated a slow train of events that would lead me to an understanding of Hegel. Two of my friends were auditing a course taught in Harvard's Divinity School by Paul Tillich, the noted Protestant theologian who was one of only five faculty members honored with the top-of-the-line title University Professor. My friends were baffled by Tillich's abstruse language and impenetrable concept of God, and they were surprised by his negative attitudes toward a wide range of Christian beliefs. Tillich's liberalism piqued my curiosity and stuck in my mind. There it sat for a half dozen or more years.

Then one day, while browsing through some publisher's closeout books on sale, I came across a copy of Walter Kaufmann's *The Faith of a Heretic*. I bought it. In it I found Kaufmann attacking Tillich for using ancient formulations of belief to express his own lack of belief. Although Kaufmann had no idea what Tillich meant in calling God "being-itself," Kaufmann clearly (and correctly, as I later discovered) saw Tillich as an atheist who was reinterpreting every doctrine of Christian mythology to give it nonsupernatural content.

Now my curiosity was really piqued. I decided to gain a firsthand acquaintance with Tillich's thought. An arbitrary but lucky choice from among

Tillich's many popular-style books led to my reading *The Courage to Be*. It quickly became apparent that Tillich was indeed hostile to Christian supernaturalism—the afterlife, divine moral codes, all the other contents of religious tradition, and the "ultimate concern" of Christians (obviously God). Then the bombshell: "the negation of the negation." My academic background in political science and economics enabled me to instantly recognize those words as Marx's phrase for dialectical synthesis—specifically, for the replacement of capitalism (the "negation," or antithesis, of feudalism) by communism. (I didn't learn until much later that "negation of the negation" was first used by Hegel, from whom Marx borrowed it.) I now knew that Tillich was practicing dialectics. And three pages later, when Tillich spoke of "the God above God," it was apparent that he had constructed a hidden dialectic moving from (1) a *thesis* of Yes to God and to the supernatural in general to (2) an *antithesis* of No to God and to the supernatural in general to (3) a *synthesis* that combines Yes to God with No to the supernatural. The dialectic thus moved from theism (Yes, affirmation) to atheism (No, the negation of the Yes) to espousal of a *nonsupernatural* God (a *higher* Yes, the negation of the No), soon rephrased by Tillich as "the God *above* the God of theism." The question became: what is this cryptically described God above the God of theism?

I read more books, both by and about Tillich. It didn't take long to figure out that the God above God was humanity. The evidence came from many directions and included two other dialectics. One was (1) thesis: God (the believer's source of wisdom), (2) antithesis: man (the atheist's source of wisdom), and (3) synthesis: God = man. The second dialectic was (1) thesis: revelation (the product of God), (2) antithesis: reason (the product of man), and (3) synthesis: revelation = reason (the product of God = the product of man, which means God is man). An especially telling piece of evidence was Tillich's insistence that the "norm" for a systematic theology should be "Jesus as the Christ"—the Jesus of mythology, contrasted with the real historical Jesus. According to Christian theology, cited by Tillich, Jesus as the Christ was "fully God and fully man," not half God and half man. Only if God is humanity is that possible.

Reading the books about Tillich, I soon realized that the many authors who had written books or commentaries supposedly explaining Tillich's thought recognized neither Tillich's use of Hegelian dialectics nor the identity of the God above God. Tillich was variously interpreted as a theist, a panentheist, a pantheist, and a mystic. Many of those who considered Tillich a theist seemed to think the God above God was merely nonanthropomorphic—an amorphous spirit, not a person with arms and legs who sits on a throne in heaven, not Genesis's anthropomorphic prototype of whom man is the physical "image." Others apparently thought the God above God was just friendlier and more loving than the nasty, punitive, homicidal Old Testament God, supposedly "the God of theism." Only Kaufmann and Alasdair MacIntyre recognized Tillich's unqualified antisupernaturalism.

I decided that another book about Tillich was needed. So I proceeded with the necessary research. I poured over the three volumes of Tillich's *Systematic Theology*, read all the rest of Tillich's books and Robert Tucker's *Philosophy and Myth in Karl Marx*, and struggled with Hegel's *Phenomenology of Mind* (the Baillie translation). Tucker's book familiarized me with Hegel's and Marx's concepts of self-alienation, or self-estrangement, and thereby enabled me to recognize Tillichian self-estrangement and reconciliation. Tillich's books, in turn, clarified many of Hegel's ideas, most notably (*a*) the relationship of Christian mythology's concept of separation and return (union-separation-reunion) to Hegel's—and Marx's—dialectics and (*b*) the movement from potential essence (potential unity, Yes) to actual existence (actual separation, No) to actual essence (actual unity, a higher Yes). My research led to the publication of *Paul Tillich's Dialectical Humanism: Unmasking the God above God* (Johns Hopkins Press, 1970). More to the point, it also led to a basic understanding of Hegel's dialectics and Marx's dialectical materialism.

But at that point I still thought Hegel's dialectics were common knowledge among philosophers and political scientists. So that information, which in any case barely scratched the surface of Hegel's vast repertoire of dialectics, went on the shelf. Marx was another matter. I now realized that the base-superstructure dialectics of Marx that I had been taught in graduate school and had read about in several books was not the genuine Hegelian dialectics of Marx's dialectical materialism. Maybe someday, when I had time to do some more research and writing, I would write an article about Marx's dialectics. But other interests and obligations put that project on the back burner, more or less forgotten.

Time passed. I wrote a few books and articles relating to my professional field of economics. In 1997 I retired. During the next ten years, a couple of unprecedented, highly detailed, marvelously complex, intertwined triple allegories—one in film, one in literature—engaged my attention. These led to two more books. One was about Stanley Kubrick's film *2001: A Space Odyssey*, deservedly ranked among the ten greatest films of all time by the British Film Institute. The other interpreted Philip Pullman's multiple-award-winning *His Dark Materials* fantasy trilogy, with its cleverly disguised story of the warfare between knowledge (symbolized by golden "dust" that drifts down from the sky) and religious superstition (symbolized by mind-devouring "specters"). Interestingly, Kubrick's film and Pullman's trilogy both symbolically depict the death of God, something we also find in Hegel's *Phenomenology*. But Hegel and Marx still failed to attract my attention.

Then one day Marx came to mind. I decided to see if the Wikipedia articles on Marx and dialectical materialism could use some editing and improved accuracy. As expected, neither article had more than a highly abstract explanation of Marx's historical dialectics: Marx's actual thesis-antithesis-synthesis dialectics and their underlying concepts were apparently still unknown. I also found, however, that Wikipedia forbids editing and revisions that add original ideas and material to its articles. So I kept my hands off the two Marx articles; as of this writing they remain incomplete and inaccurate. My attention turned to Hegel. Maybe the articles on Hegel and dialectics could use some help. Since I still thought Hegel's dialectics were well understood by academicians, I wasn't deterred by worries about originality. Then came the dawn. The Wikipedia articles on Hegel and on dialectics described dialectics only in terms of the same abstractions that frightened me in graduate school. In fact, the article on dialectics, far from providing even one concrete example, denied that Hegel used the thesis-antithesis-synthesis formula! And it again misconstrued Marx's dialectical materialism.

I decided to write a journal article explaining Hegel's and Marx's dialectics. That task required consulting a vast number of books and essays on Hegel's and Marx's thought. I needed to verify that my insights and ideas were original and to learn whether Hegel's related concept of Spirit was understood. I found that what I learned in college was now universally repudiated: those authors who had anything to say about dialectics either expressly denied that Hegel used the thesis-antithesis-synthesis formula or reinterpreted Hegelian dialectics beyond recognition. I also learned that more than half the authors who were willing to venture an opinion about Spirit had the misconception that Spirit is a supernatural entity, partly theistic (i.e., pan*en*theistic, or both transcendent and immanent) in most interpretations. These authors were taking Hegel's references to "God" literally! The other authors, presumably unacquainted with Tillich and the close parallelism between Hegel's thought and Tillich's, had their own misconceptions about Spirit, although they did recognize that Spirit is nonsupernatural. I was also able to verify that Marx's thesis-antithesis-synthesis dialectics were universally unrecognized, except in the abstract. And in delving deeper into primary sources—Hegel's own writing—I discovered that there was far more to Hegel's dialectics than I had realized: dialectics everywhere, including four different outline levels of *Phenomenology of Spirit* and three outline levels of *The Philosophy of History*.

I tried writing that journal article, but my product was wholly unsatisfactory. There was simply too much material for an article, even if I threw out the material on Marx. I could not leave so much unsaid; I could not leave so many specific, but hidden and unrecognized, dialectics unidentified and unexplained. So I scrapped the article and wrote this book.

Chapter 1

DIALECTICS DENIED

More than two centuries have elapsed since 1807, when G. W. F. Hegel published his first major—and most famous—work, *Phenomenology of Spirit*, a.k.a. *Phenomenology of Mind*. The philosophy presented in this work and in Hegel's later posthumously edited history lectures, *The Philosophy of History*, is noted for its mystifying dialectical method. Hegelian dialectics is said to revolve around three progressive stages of development: (1) a *thesis*, which is an idea or concept, (2) an *antithesis* (anti-thesis), an opposite idea that contradicts the thesis, and (3) a *synthesis*, a climactic idea that somehow combines the thesis and the antithesis, or the best parts of them, into a sort of compromise, reconciliation, or previously unperceived identity. Yet to this day, none of the innumerable Hegel interpreters who have written in English or whose works have been translated into English—and, from powerful indirect evidence, none of the untranslated European interpreters either—has more than a superficial, nonsubstantive understanding of what a thesis-antithesis-synthesis dialectic is. No author has presented even one accurate example, taken from *Phenomenology of Spirit* or *The Philosophy of History*, of a sequential thesis-antithesis-synthesis dialectic. (The static triads of Hegel's *Logic* have been called "dialectical" in different senses but do not qualify as thesis-antithesis-synthesis dialectics.) To make matters worse, for the past half century it has been fashionable to deny that Hegel really used thesis-antithesis-synthesis dialectics. Writing in 2007, Verene provides an accurate, up-to-date assessment of the prevailing attitude among scholars toward the moribund idea (which I intend to resuscitate) that Hegel uses thesis-antithesis-synthesis dialectics: "No first-rate Hegel scholar speaks of Hegel having a dialectic of thesis-antithesis-synthesis."[1]

THE NATURE OF THE PROBLEM

It is true that a few of Hegel's *labels* for specific dialectical stages—for example, "Oriental despotism" as a history thesis—have been offered. But nobody has recognized the antithetical *concepts* that particular pairs of thesis and antithesis labels represent. Neither has anyone shown how or where Hegel merges the two members of any pair of opposing concepts into a synthesis. The thesis-antithesis conceptual pairs include the following:

1. universal and particular
2. one and many
3. union and separation
4. essence and existence
5. divine and human
6. inner and outer
7. in itself and for itself
8. potential and actual
9. unconscious and conscious
10. artificial (man-made) and natural
11. God and man
12. Father (God, heaven, divine, man-made) and Son (Jesus, earth, human, natural)
13. God in heaven and God incarnate
14. abstract and concrete
15. theology (revelation) and philosophy (reason)
16. God (divine ruler) and monarch (human ruler)
17. independence and dependence
18. freedom (release from superstition) and bondage (enslavement by superstition)
19. truth and falsehood
20. natural (physical) law and psychological (mental) law
21. moral (societal) law and natural (personal) impulses
22. inner law ("of the heart," personal) and outer law (societal)
23. predator and victim

24. subject and object
25. internal (self) approval and external (societal) approval
26. theory and practice
27. validity and invalidity
28. woman (family, divinity) and man (state, humanity)
29. divine law and human law
30. morality (moral law) and human nature (natural behavior)
31. conscience (inner law) and morality (outer or societal law)
32. identity (one) and nonidentity (many)
33. thought (an idea, intangible) and substance (something physical, tangible)
34. one ruler and many rulers
35. one ruled territory and many ruled territories

In some of these thesis-antithesis pairs, the thesis concept is combined with either "unconscious" ("unconscious union") or "potential" ("potential union"). The antithesis concept is, in turn, combined with "conscious" ("conscious separation") or "actual" ("actual separation"). Double opposition between a two-part thesis and a two-part antithesis results. Perhaps, given this clue, you can already anticipate the format many of Hegel's syntheses use.

Some of the above concepts have been discussed in the literature, but not in the context of thesis-antithesis-synthesis dialectics, identified as such. Where particular concepts have been discussed, they have often been treated incidentally, without particular emphasis on those concepts and without their being labeled "thesis" and "antithesis." And no synthesis has been identified. Nor has anyone explained the several formats a Hegelian synthesis can use. Moreover, nobody has recognized how Hegel based his thesis-antithesis-synthesis formula on Christian theology's two "separation-and-return" (union, separation, reunion) doctrines. In fact, thirteen interpreters—I'll get to them shortly—explicitly deny that Hegel's thought really is dialectical in a thesis-antithesis-synthesis sense, because neither these interpreters nor any of the hundreds of other interpreters they have collectively consulted have been able to deduce and assemble specific Hegelian dialectics. Other interpreters have indirectly denied the existence of thesis-antithesis-synthesis dialectics by defining "dialectics" as meaning something else. That "something else" has typically been either (*a*) the static triads found in Hegel's *Logic*—being, nothing, and becoming is the usual example—or (*b*) a clash between two different viewpoints, not reduced to concepts, that Hegel supposedly never merges into a clearly articulated synthesis.

I base these statements on a survey of the writings of (*a*) 190 authors of books, book chapters, book introductions, and articles explaining Hegel's philosophy and (*b*) an additional 56 authors of material on the dialectician Karl Marx (not counting 13 Marx authors also on the Hegel list). Most of the surveyed authors read German and cite German-language studies. Yet none of these 246 authors understands concretely, not just abstractly, what a sequential thesis-antithesis-synthesis dialectic is, even after doing an independent literature survey and independently analyzing Hegel's or Marx's writing. For example, Stern, in his book *Hegel and the* Phenomenology of Spirit (2002), lists in his bibliography 167 Hegel interpreters whose works he consulted and who, in turn, did their own literature surveys, bringing the number of directly and indirectly surveyed authors into the high hundreds. The works Stern cites include 13 written in German and 3 in French. If the 167 authors surveyed by Stern included in their own surveys and average of just 2 additional authors not on the survey list of Stern or the list of one of his other surveyed other authors, Stern would have indirect coverage of $2 \times 167 = 334$ additional Hegel interpreters, or direct and indirect coverage of 501 authors. Yet neither in his own survey nor in his own highly detailed analysis of *Phenomenology* has Stern found a triad such as (1) predator, (2) victim, and (3) predator = victim (Hegel's *Faust* dialectic) whose concepts he can identify and whose synthesis (e.g., Faust, a predator who becomes a victim in the *Faust* dialectic) he can clarify. Like many others, Stern mistakenly regards Hegelian dialectics as nothing more than an abstraction—opposing viewpoints, imprecisely defined and not necessarily opposites, whose opposition Hegel never satisfactorily resolves in a recognizable synthesis that incorporates both the thesis and the antithesis or parts thereof.[2] If none of my 246 authors and none of the literally hundreds if not thousands of other Hegel interpreters they have directly *and indirectly* surveyed has ever been able to identify in Hegel's thought a genuine thesis-antithesis-synthesis dialectic, then it is virtually inconceivable that some other author, the many German authors included, has provided the missing insights.[3]

Conceivably, some of the early post-Hegelians—the so-called Right Hegelians and Left (or Young) Hegelians—did understand Hegel's dialectics. One of the left Hegelians, Karl Marx, definitely did. But any such understanding among the other post-Hegelians has vanished. It probably never existed. Be that as it may, the only writers I have encountered whose works do reveal a solid understanding of Hegelian dialectics are Marx, Marx's collaborator Frederick Engels, and Paul Tillich. (I'm not entirely sure about Engels.) But these philosophers, dialecticians themselves, have not tried to explain Hegelian dialectics. Their understanding is revealed largely in the dialectical formats they use in their own philosophies, analogical formats that reveal a secure grasp of Hegel's dialectics. Tillich does provide some additional detail concerning dialectics, most notably (*a*) the relationship of dialectics to Christianity's two separation-and-return myths, (*b*) separation's being an antithesis and return's being a synthesis, and (*c*) the existence of an original identity—alluding to a thesis—of the one and the many (many separated objects) to which Hegel so often refers.

I emphasize that I refer only to the sequential triads of *Phenomenology* and Hegel's *Philosophy of History*, not to the static triads of Hegel's *Logic*, most of his other later writings, and parts of *Phenomenology*. (A very few of Hegel's dozens of dialectics do not display thesis-antithesis time sequence.) The sequential dialectics describe both the Spirit's approach to self-realization over time and history's unfolding over time. Findlay accurately summarizes and paraphrases Hegel: "*Time* . . . is the form of this self-realizing process. Until Spirit reaches the end of the requisite *temporal* process it cannot achieve complete self-consciousness."[4]

THE LITERATURE: DENIAL OF DIALECTICS

Before examining the abortive efforts of some authors to identify true dialectical triads in Hegel's thought, we need to be aware that almost all Hegel scholars who mention dialectics now deny that such triads even exist.

I have already commented that it has become fashionable to deny that Hegel uses thesis-antithesis-synthesis dialectics. The thirteen interpreters mentioned earlier who deny that Hegel's writing contains any dialectics are Mueller, Kaufmann, Young, Wilkins, Maker, Solomon, Wood, Pinkard, Dove, Crites, Fox, Beiser, and Verene.[5] Mueller was the first to reject the formerly popular idea that Hegel uses dialectics. Ever since Mueller propounded his thesis, new authors have been jumping on the Mueller bandwagon. Still other authors, such as Forster,[6] ascribe dialectics to Hegel but reinterpret the concept so that dialectics no longer means thesis, antithesis, and synthesis. To many authors, a "dialectic" is nothing more than a section or subtopic of *Phenomenology*. Consider what the following skeptics have to say.

Mueller. Gustav Mueller (1958) wrote an article that marks the beginning of a wave of skepticism about Hegel's dialectics. This wave is now rolling into its second half-century. The article's title, "The Hegel Legend of 'Thesis-Antithesis-Synthesis,'" states Mueller's conclusion: Hegelian dialectics is just a legend. Mueller writes that "Hegel's peculiar terminology and style" have produced several legends. "The most vexing and devastating" of these "is that everything is thought in 'thesis, antithesis, and synthesis.'" Mueller begins by attacking Stace, who, after trying and failing to show that Hegel used dialectics, excused Hegel's failures as "irregularities." But, says Mueller, "the actual texts of Hegel not only occasionally deviate from 'thesis, antithesis, and synthesis,' but show nothing of the sort." Mueller goes on to argue that Hegel used the three terms together only once. The first Hegel biography, he argues, does not mention thesis, antithesis, and synthesis. More telling, "the very important new Hegel literature of this century has altogether abandoned the legend." How did the "legend" originate? Mueller says it originated in a "very popular" 1843 book by Heinrich Moritz Chalybäus, professor of philosophy at the University of Kiel. Chalybäus, referring to Being, Nothing, and Becoming as "the first trilogy," applied the thesis, antithesis, and synthesis labels to the three concepts. Marx took up and spread the terminology. Mueller concludes: "Once the Hegel legend was established, writers of textbooks in the history of philosophy copied it from their predecessors."[7] An obvious fault of Mueller's analysis is that he is looking in the wrong place— Hegel's *Logic*, which is where Stace looked—for dialectics. He should have looked in *Phenomenology* and in *The Philosophy of History*. Ironically, Mueller was right about Hegel's *Logic*: it has no dialectics.

Kaufmann. Kaufmann, in his book *Hegel: A Reinterpretation* (1965), is particularly forceful in denying that Hegel used dialectics. Kaufmann cites Mueller and repeats Mueller's argument that Hegel didn't use the terms "thesis," "antithesis," and "synthesis" together to identify stages in an argument. (Kaufmann doesn't realize that Hegel generally used other terms such as "moment," "factors," "negation," "second realization," and "third stage" to identify dialectics.) But Kaufmann's indictment of the idea that Hegel used dialectics is largely original. He begins: "Whoever looks for the stereotype of the allegedly Hegelian dialectic in Hegel's *Phenomenology* will not find it. What one does find on looking at the table of contents is a very decided preference for triadic arrangements. . . . But these many triads are not presented or deduced by Hegel as so many theses, antitheses, and syntheses. It is not by means of any dialectic of that sort that his thought moves up the ladder to absolute knowledge."[8] (*Phenomenology*'s table-of-contents triads actually include four hidden dialectics.) Beyond the table of contents, Kaufmann says Hegel's master and servant fable comes closer to dialectics—I will show in chapter 4 that it actually is a dialectic—but he sees no identifiable dialectical stages in the fable or elsewhere in *Phenomenology*. Continuing: "Hegel's later works are different in many ways from his first book, but . . . his dialectic never became the ritualistic three-step it is so widely supposed to be."[9] In these later works, "the organization . . . becomes neat to a fault—triads everywhere (but not theses, antitheses, and syntheses)."[10] Kaufmann vehemently—and incorrectly—attacks the idea that Hegel's philosophy of history is dialectical. (It actually has ten dialectics.) Kaufmann's conclusion about whether Hegel has a dialectic: "there is none."[11]

Young. Young (1972) develops the proposition that Hegel's dialectic is not thesis-antithesis-synthesis but is instead simply thesis and antithesis, repeated over and over. There is no synthesis. Or, as he puts it, "The dialectic method is essentially based upon a principle of negativity"—the opposition between two concepts. Developing his analysis, Young writes: "Even a superficial survey of the passages in Hegel's writings in which dialectic is made the subject of explicit discussion will reveal a surprising fact. Hegel does not define dialectic in terms of the triadic movement from thesis through antithesis to synthesis. . . . The dialectic, in his view of it, is more immediately related to the antithetic than to the synthetic aspect of his method."[12] It would seem that, if Young is correct, Hegel's reference in *Phenomenology*'s Preface to "the triadic form" that "has emerged" as a new "Science" must refer to either something other than dialectics or to something with no synthesis in its triad.[13] Does "triadic form" really mean "binary form," which is what Young implies? And why did Young settle for a *"superficial* survey"? Superficial effort, superficial conclusions.

Wilkins. One of those who deny that Hegel used dialectics, Wilkins (1974), is notable for his focusing on Hegel's *Philosophy of History*, where Hegel's use of a three-level hierarchy of triads—ten triads altogether—is conspicuous, even if the dialectical content of those triads requires deciphering. Wilkins is content to paraphrase Mueller: "The legend or myth has grown that Hegel's philosophy was a tightly deductive system with an almost impenetrable technical vocabulary, and a system in which a dialectic of 'thesis-antithesis-synthesis' predominated. According to this legend or myth, everything in the world . . . was held by Hegel to be deducible from his system and explainable in terms of the thesis-antithesis-synthesis formula."[14] Wilkins exaggerates the "legend": I seriously doubt that anyone ever claimed that Hegel said "everything in the world" can be explained by dialectics. But that doesn't matter. What does matter is that Wilkins gives us another voice explicitly denying that Hegel used thesis-antithesis-synthesis dialectics.

Maker. Picking up where Mueller left off, Maker (1982) argues at great length that "Hegel does not have a 'dialectic method.'"[15] According to Maker, Hegel's *Phenomenology*, his *Science of Logic*, and his *Encyclopedia* each employ a different understanding of "dialectic," none of which amounts to thesis-antithesis-synthesis. Since *Phenomenology* is the only volume of these three that concerns us, I will focus on his *Phenomenology* discussion. Maker writes, "The dialectical-phenomenological method of the *PhG* [*Phenomenology of Geist*] of 1807 is no method at all."[16] Instead it is a long, tedious (my word) discussion of consciousness. (Maker is totally unaware of the unconscious thesis stage that precedes consciousness.) Consciousness, according to Maker, advances through various forms that are not theses or antitheses and finally arrives at Absolute

Knowing, which is a dialectical synthesis but which Maker does not recognize as such. The nature of this synthesis is explained in chapter 3.

Solomon. Solomon (1983) begins his chapter 1's section on "Hegel's Method: Dialectic" by saying, "I will be arguing that Hegel *has no such method*—at least not in the *Phenomenology*. . . . What we do get in the *Phenomenology*, that might warrant if not deserve the name 'dialectic,' is a metaphor. . . . It is the idea of the universe as, in some sense, a living process, growing according to its inner rules and potentials."[17] Hegel's so-called dialectic, he says, is not "thesis-antithesis-synthesis"; instead it is "the process of discovering the limitations of various 'forms of consciousness.'"[18] Indeed, "this image of consciousness in self-transformation is the key to the *Phenomenology* and its 'dialectical' method."[19] (Here Solomon goes astray by failing to notice that consciousness is the antithesis of—the opposite of—unconsciousness, which is part of the thesis stage of Hegel's overarching dialectic.) The basic "pattern of the 'dialectic' of the *Phenomenology*" is "an attitude of [1] confidence, then [2] confusion, withdrawal, desperation, or doubt; finally [3] a new reconciliation and confidence." But: "This pattern of three should not be interpreted as 'thesis-antithesis-synthesis.'"[20] A final point: "The pattern of Hegel's strategy can also be described in terms of an over-all tendency, at every stage, to move from the particular to the general."[21] (This is untrue. Hegel's overarching *Phenomenology* dialectic moves from [1] universal, which means general, to [2] particular to [3] universe composed of particulars: separation and return. Most of Hegel's other dialectics don't use general and particular as concepts, although the antithetical concepts divine and human, sometimes used, reflect general and particular, or one universal divinity [sometimes Spirit, sometimes God] and many particular humans or, more broadly, "objects.")

Strangely, in another part of his book Solomon mentions in passing, but overlooks the significance of, something Hegel wrote in an 1800 fragment. In this fragment Hegel provides what Solomon calls an "obscure" discussion of "the union of opposites."[22] That is an obvious description of a dialectical synthesis: a union of opposites is a *synthesis* of opposites, the opposites being a thesis and an antithesis. Had Solomon latched on to this clue and searched for opposites and their syntheses, he could have found them in *Phenomenology*. Finding them would have simply entailed keeping an open mind regarding

Mueller's "legend" conclusion while looking for concepts that can generally be reduced to one or two words—specifically, the thirty-five pairs of concepts listed at the beginning of this chapter.

Wood. Wood (1990) is the next interpreter to explicitly deny that Hegel uses dialectics. What he has to say, however, is pretty much a regurgitation, enhanced by sarcasm and other inflammatory language, of what Mueller wrote: "The regrettable expounding of this theme [reconciliation of contradictions] . . . through the grotesque jargon of 'thesis,' 'antithesis,' and 'synthesis' began in 1837 with Heinrich Moritz Chalybäus, a bowdlerizer [*sic*] of German idealist philosophy, whose ridiculous expository devices should have been forgotten along with his name. This triad of terms is used by both Fichte and Schelling, though never to express . . . Hegelian ideas. . . . The use of Chalybäus's terminology to expound the Hegelian dialectic is nearly always an unwitting confession that the expositor has little or no firsthand knowledge of Hegel."[23]

Pinkard. Pinkard (1994) begins much as Wood does, but without the sarcasm. He refers to "the ongoing myth (started by the deservedly forgotten Heinrich Moritz Chalybäus) of Hegel's system as consisting of some oddly formal triumvirate of 'Thesis, Antithesis and Synthesis' (terms that Hegel himself never [*sic*] uses and that also completely mischaracterize his thought)."[24] Hegel's dialectic, as described by Pinkard, is much the same progression of negatives that Young and Solomon described earlier:

> A reflective form of life [consciousness] takes such and such to be authoritative reasons for belief and action; those types of reasoning then generate within their own terms skeptical objections against themselves (as Hegel puts it, they generate their own "negation"); that form of reflective life, however, turns out to be unable to reassure itself about what it had taken as authoritative for itself; the new form of reflective life that replaces it and claims to complete it, however, takes *its* accounts of what *for it* have come to be authoritative reasons to be that which was necessary to successfully resolve the issues that were self-undermining for the older form of life; but this new reflective form of life in turn generates self-undermining skepticism about its own accounts, and the progression continues.[25]

Pinkard sees nothing he would call a synthesis in this trail of events. The basic flaw in his analysis is its failure to reduce those "reasons" and "forms" to simple one-word and two-word concepts. No wonder he can't find any syntheses. Also, I wonder why Pinkard thinks "Hegel himself never uses" the terms thesis, antithesis, and synthesis is a reasonable argument, given that Pinkard himself acknowledges Hegel's use of "negation," an obvious substitute for "antithesis." (Hegel also uses many other substitute terms.) And surely Pinkard is familiar with the Hegel-Marx-Tillich phrase "negation of the negation"—negation of the antithesis—which refers to the synthesis stage, which replaces the antithesis.

Dove. Dove (1998) writes that "the notorious triad: thesis-antithesis-synthesis" commands attention "not only because it misrepresents Hegel, but because Hegel's *Phenomenology of Spirit* was probably the *first* philosophical treatise whose method was radically and consistently non-dialectical."[26] Expanding on this point in a note, Dove says that "Ivan Iljin was, so far as I am aware, the first to develop the insight that 'Hegel, in his philosophical method, was no dialectician' (Ivan Iljin, *Die Philosophie Hegels als kontemplative Gotteslehre* [Bern: A. Francke Verlag, 1946], 126). Iljin's argument, persuasive though it is, does not focus on the *Phenomenology*, but deals rather with Hegel's authorship as a whole."[27] Would it be unreasonable to suggest that, since Iljin gives short shrift to *Phenomenology*, Dove should have substituted some of his own original analysis of *Phenomenology*?

Crites. Crites (1998), in his preface, very quickly writes off the idea that Hegelian dialectics employs thesis, antithesis, and synthesis: "Perhaps no philosopher has ever been so ill-served by standard summary interpretations as Hegel has. . . . The familiar mechanical three-step, for instance (thesis-antithesis-synthesis, a formula he never used), is a dead caricature of everything Hegel ever meant by dialectic."[28] Like so many other interpreters, Crites refers to Hegel's dialectic from time to time but usually seems to mean nothing more than the ill-defined structure of *Phenomenology*; he never clarifies what he means. Well, at one point he does say this: "The life of reason capable of comprehending its movement he would call *dialectic*."[29] But whatever that means, it isn't the three-step. In fact, late in his book Crites describes a four-step dialectic: "The dialectical 'moments' of this *fragmentary* existence [Spirit's many 'localizations and historical episodes'], Hegel says, 'are *consciousness*, *self-consciousness*, *reason*, and *spirit*—spirit, that is, as immediate spirit, that is not yet the consciousness of spirit.'"[30]

Fox. Fox (2005) is somewhat less emphatic in denying Hegel's use of dialectics but nonetheless succeeds in delivering the same point. He writes: "It is regularly (but erroneously) supposed that wherever Hegel discerned opposing tendencies he posited a 'thesis' and an 'antithesis,' which yield ground eventually to an all-embracing 'synthesis.' This is an unfortunate caricature." Not only is this picture unfortunate, it is "ironic," because Hegel himself "denounced such recipes as 'lifeless schemas' and as examples of 'monotonous formalism.'"[31] It is erroneous to suppose that "whenever the evolution of knowledge or belief is viewed dialectically, this automatically entails that an irreversible shift from some position to its opposite is taking place." Fox identifies this "error" as "attributing a thesis-antithesis-synthesis structure to Hegel's method of reasoning."[32]

I am forced to comment that Fox's research on this point is sloppy. The "lifeless schema" Hegel denounces is that of Kant, who is explicitly named; Hegel says that "since then"—since Kant—dialectics "has, however, been raised to its absolute significance" and has become a "Science" (the emphatic capitalization is Hegel's).[33] Fox also errs in suggesting that "the evolution of knowledge or belief" that occurs in *Phenomenology* and *The Philosophy of History* typically does not entail a "shift from some position to its opposite." The fact is that the shift typically *is* to an opposite position: from the first member to the second member of one of the thirty-five thesis-antithesis pairs vertically listed earlier in this chapter.

Beiser. Whereas thesis-antithesis-synthesis dialectics is undeniably a methodology for presenting ideas and developing a philosophy, Beiser (2005) says, "Hegel utterly opposed having a methodology." Beiser then proceeds to abstractly redefine thesis-antithesis-synthesis dialectics out of existence. "When Hegel uses the term 'dialectic' it usually designates the 'self-organization' of the subject matter, its 'inner necessity' and 'inherent movement.'" This summation is highly ambiguous, but the context makes it clear that Beiser thinks dialectics is nothing more than the forward movement, development, or progression of thoughts, ideas, or concepts that display "conflicting tendencies" or "contradictions"; the conflicts and contradictions entail disagreement or difference but not necessarily thesis-antithesis style oppositeness. Dialectics has no specific form or structure. Most important, Beiser sees in dialectics no element of synthesis. "So we can talk about Hegel's dialectic after all, . . . provided that we see it as nothing more than an a posteriori summary of the formal structure of his investigations."[34]

Verene. In four places Verene (2007) denies that Hegel uses thesis-antithesis-synthesis dialectics. First, he explicitly endorses Mueller's "legend" thesis.[35] Next, he says "Hegel's dialectical method, like Socratic method, is not properly a method." Why not? Because "it [the misnamed 'method'] concerns *two* moments as Hegel describes it, not three," and "consciousness never unifies them or synthesizes them."[36] Later, discussing the Hegelian concepts "in-itself" and "for-itself," Verene writes: "If we were to call the in-itself a 'thesis' and the for-itself an 'antithesis,' we could *not* go on to call the in-and for-itself a 'synthesis.' The constant conjunction of two moments is not a synthesis" (my italics). Accordingly, "the standpoint of absolute knowing is the realization that there is no synthesis of the two moments of knowing."[37] Finally, defining the German *dialektik* in a "Hegel's Terminology" appendix, Verene has this to say: "Hegel's dialectic is unlike dialectic as it is commonly understood. . . . Hegel never describes his own dialectic as having the form: *thesis-antithesis-synthesis*."[38] For Verene (and many other interpreters), a Hegelian dialectic is simply the conflict between two opposing viewpoints or concepts (those "moments"), a conflict that has no resolution.

Other Authors. Though not denying that Hegel uses dialectics, other authors as well as some of the above ones render the concept lifeless by removing its heart, lungs, and brain—the thesis, antithesis, and synthesis. Many of these authors use the word "dialectic" to refer to whatever section of Hegel's *Phenomenology* they happen to be discussing. For example, sixteen authors refer to "the master and slave dialectic" or use similar words.[39] Master and slave really is a thesis-antithesis-synthesis dialectic—I explain this dialectic in chapters 3 and 4—but these authors don't recognize it as such. They are simply referring to the topic of the moment. One of the authors, Beiser, is so undialectical in his interpretation of what he calls "the dialectic" of "lordship and bondage" (master and slave) that he describes not three stages but six.[40] Still other authors think a dialectic is just a movement from one idea to a contradictory, but not necessarily opposite, idea. There is no synthesis, except that some interpreters hold that a long series of misnamed two-stage thesis-antithesis "dialectics" culminates in a final synthesis in the form of Spirit's self-realization at the end of *Phenomenology*. Even this final "synthesis" is not a true synthesis: the long chain of supposed theses and antitheses provides no single thesis and single antithesis that a synthesis could combine, and no interpreter even attempts to show that self-realization combines an identified thesis concept and an identified antithesis concept from a preceding chain.

The misuse of "dialectic" and "dialectics" is pervasive; the abundant discussion of these terms, and the accompanying affirmations (sometimes just implicit) that Hegel uses dialectics, do not refute my assertion that Hegel's genuine thesis-antithesis dialectics remain unrecognized more than two hundred years after the 1807 publication of *Phenomenology*. McCumber comments that the interpretations of Hegelian terminology are "unimaginably diverse." He elaborates: "In the beginning of the 1980s, at a symposium on Hegelian dialectic and formal logic, Jaako Hintikka counted over twenty different senses given to 'dialectic' by the participants alone."[41] A 2010 essay collection edited by Limnatis, the unifying topic of which is "Hegel's Dialectic," has essays by thirteen authors. These focus specifically on what the authors call dialectics. But in the book's introduction, the editor defines dialectics not as thesis-antithesis-synthesis but as "a way of thinking" where "in all cases the reference is to antithetical, oppositional, or contradictory arguments or features."[42] Three characteristics of this description epitomize the universal misunderstanding of what a Hegelian dialectic is. First, the "antithetical" or "oppositional" features are not identified as opposites; they are simply different or in conflict, whereas in a genuine Hegelian dialectic the antithesis is the opposite of the thesis. (One contributor, Brinkmann, does speak abstractly of two "opposites"; but he does not identify them as thesis and antithesis, falsely claims that one is "stronger" than the other, fails to recognize the thesis and antithesis concepts [universal and particular] Hegel alludes to in the "Force and Understanding" material Brinkmann bases his discussion on, and is unable to provide concrete dialectical examples of Hegel's amorphous abstractions ["moments," "opposites," "self-identical," "self-sundering"].

Brinkmann, like so many others, is discussing his own cloudy redefinition of Hegelian dialectics, not the real thing.[43]) Second, in the Limnatis description (mirrored in the various essays), there is no synthesis, no combining of an initial pair of opposite concepts into a third concept that includes both of the first two, or parts thereof. Third, the opposing entities are described as "arguments," whereas Hegelian theses and antitheses are not arguments; they are simple concepts such as one and many, conscious and unconscious, and divine and human. We see that in the year 2010, thirteen Hegel specialists, all of them presumably well versed in the Hegel literature and focusing on the topic of dialectics, are really discussing something other than thesis-antithesis-synthesis dialectics.

THE LITERATURE: FALSE EXAMPLES OF DIALECTICS

Among those authors who don't deny that Hegel uses dialectics are some who try to provide examples, taken from Hegel, of thesis-antithesis-synthesis dialectics. These supposed examples seek to overcome a basic problem with expositions of Hegel's thought. The problem: just about everyone having even a superficial acquaintance with Hegel understands the general or abstract— but not the specific or concrete—format of the dialectical triads attributed to him. The general format is thesis, antithesis, and synthesis. These three stages usually—*always*, in the case of Hegel's history dialectics—occur in chronological sequence, but there are exceptions. The words "affirmation" (Yes), "negation" (No), and "negation of the negation" (a double negative is an affirmative, a higher Yes) are sometimes used in referring to the dialectic's three stages. For example, "negation of the negation" is used in reference to syntheses by all four of the dialectical technique's outstanding users—Hegel,[44] Marx,[45] Engels,[46] and Tillich.[47] It is usually claimed that the synthesis becomes the thesis of a follow-on dialectic, which leads to a long stream of subsequent dialectics, but in fact only one of Hegel's syntheses becomes the thesis of a follow-on dialectic.

You would think that, given the abstract understanding of what a dialectic is, there exists somewhere in the Hegel literature a concrete example of a dialectic, an example found in Hegel's work. By concrete, I mean an example that doesn't simply label each stage but (1) shows the thesis *concept* or concepts, the substance behind the label, (2) shows the antithesis concept or concepts, which must be the opposite of their thesis counterparts, and (3) shows how the thesis and antithesis concepts are combined in a synthesis that really synthesizes. The concepts must be precise words, usually just one or two, not general descriptions of subject matter. A thesis concept (a word or two) and an antithesis concept must be combined in the synthesis. That's what synthesis means: a synthesis is the result of putting together, assembling, or combining parts. Synthesis is the opposite of analysis, which means taking something apart and looking at the pieces. (In the field of literature, professors like to substitute "construct" for "synthesize" and "deconstruct"—a horribly pretentious word—for "analyze," but the general idea is the same.)

No such example of a Hegelian synthesis, a combining of parts—concepts—taken from a thesis and its antithesis, exists. When students and scholars search in textbooks and in more focused and detailed analyses of Hegel's philosophy for even one concrete example of a thesis-antithesis-synthesis dialectic, no genuine example can be found. All we have are false examples. Below are some that I have found.

Supposed Examples from Hegel's Logic. Quite a few interpreters, most notably Hartmann[48] and Forster,[49] have reinterpreted dialectics as a method embodied in the hierarchical system of triads found in Hegel's *Logic*. *Logic*'s many triads have been cited as examples of dialectics, but these triads lack the element of sequence; they are just static triads. Even worse, as Stace and Findlay have pointed out, many of these *Logic* triads have arbitrary if not nonsensical antitheses and syntheses, and a few "triads" have two or four parts instead of three.[50] Take a look at the fold-out chart inside the back cover of Stace's book. Labeled "Diagram of the Hegelian System," the chart shows a multitude of hierarchically arranged static triads. (The hierarchy is laid out sideways, with its peak—"The Idea," or all reality—on the left.) The two uppermost terms in each triad (e.g., transparency and refraction) are supposedly antithetical; the third (e.g., color) is supposedly their resolution. But ask yourself these questions:

- Is art the opposite of religion? Why not atheism, philosophy, or science? Is religion the opposite of art, which is man-made (*arti*ficial)? Why not nature—that is, naturally occurring things? Is philosophy the synthesis of art and religion (subjective fields)? Why not culture or the humanities?

- Is painting the opposite of music? Why not cacophony or silence? Is music (esthetically and emotionally based) the opposite of painting (also esthetically and emotionally based)? Why not science (empirically and rationally based)? In what sense is poetry a synthesis of art and music?

- Is sea the opposite of atmosphere? Why not vacuum? Is atmosphere the opposite of sea? Why not land? Is a continent the synthesis of sea and atmosphere? Why not planet?

- Is a vegetable organism the opposite of a terrestrial organism? (Most vegetable organisms *are* terrestrial.) Why not an atmospheric or oceanic organism? Is a terrestrial organism the opposite of a vegetable organism? Why not an animal organism?

- Is a monarch the opposite of an executive? Why not a maid, a clerk, or a committee? Is an executive the opposite of a monarch? Why not a serf or legislature? And is a legislature a synthesis of a monarch and an executive? Why not an English style constitutional monarchy with a king *and* a prime minister (executive)?

- Is "repulsion and attraction" a synthesis of one and many? Why not *Phenomenology*'s syntheses: "one composed of many" and "universe composed of particulars"?

- Is cohesion the opposite of sound? Why not silence? Is sound the opposite of cohesion? Why not slipperiness or repulsion? Is heat a synthesis of sound and cohesion?

- Is cognition the opposite of life? Why not death? Is life the opposite of cognition? Why not ignorance, misunderstanding, or confusion?

- Is taste the *opposite* of smell? Or is taste—like tactile feeling, vision, sight, and hearing—merely a *different* sense?

- Is refraction the opposite of transparency? Why not opaqueness? Is transparency the opposite of refraction? Why not straightening (of something bent)?

- Is substance the opposite of cause? Why not effect? Is cause the opposite of substance? Why not spirits, thought, or mind (intangible things)?

- Is chemism the opposite of mechanism (an object with moving parts)? Why not a partless object—a spoon, a ball, or a monolith?

- Is civil society (many) the opposite of family (several)? Why not a person (one)? Is family the opposite of civil society? Why not a lawless, barbarian tribe?

- Is representation the opposite of intuition? Why not observation or reason? Is intuition the opposite of representation? Why not misrepresentation or direct participation?

- Is the moon the opposite of "light—the solar center"? Why not darkness, Pluto, or outer space? Is the sun the opposite of the moon? Why not earth, the body in gravitational-centrifugal balance with the moon?

And so it goes in Hegel's *Logic*. Yes, a few of the triads, like the one coming up, do have opposites, and two of them have real syntheses. But in contrast with the generally sequential triads of true thesis-antithesis-synthesis dialectics, these few are static triads, and they swim in a sea of other triads that lack antitheses or syntheses—and sometimes aren't even triads. Calling *Logic*'s triads "dialectics" requires a reckless imagination. Whatever Hartmann and Forster may think, we should not call these triads dialectics.

Being-nothing-becoming, the first triad from Hegel's *Science of Logic*, is often cited (for example, by McTaggart, Findlay, C. Taylor, Singer, and James) as an example of a thesis-antithesis-synthesis dialectic.[51] If rearranged chronologically into the sequence (1) nothing (or nonbeing), (2) becoming, and (3) being, those three elements could serve as *labels* (not concepts) for the stages of Hegel's basic dialectic from *Phenomenology*. In that dialectic, Absolute Spirit progresses from (1) an embryonic thesis stage in which the Spirit has no mind (humans haven't arrived yet, so no mind = nonbeing of Mind) through (2) an antithesis stage of flawed consciousness—humans have arrived with their flawed minds—to (3) its fully developed synthesis stage, where Absolute Spirit comes into *being*. But how absurd it would be to use *Logic*'s 1-2-3 order (being-nothing-becoming) and call those three stages (1) being (Spirit *before* humans arrive and Spirit's Mind comes into being?), (2) nothing (Spirit *after* humans arrive?), and (3) becoming (Spirit after it has *become* Absolute Spirit?). In more detail, the problems of using being-nothing-becoming as an example of a dialectic that elucidates Hegel's thought are these:

1. Hegel's Spirit really begins in a prehuman era that might loosely be called "nothing": neither conscious Spirit (antithesis) nor Absolute Spirit (synthesis) exists yet. So "nothing" would describe the thesis (nonexistence), not the antithesis. To make the "example" even worse, Absolute Spirit does not really start from a stage of nothing—nonexistence—but from a stage of nascent or embryonic being consisting of physical reality (nature) without mental reality, that is, without human minds to serve as Spirit's Mind. There is no "nothing" in Spirit's evolution. And neither does being precede nothing. Only in the last stage of the dialectic does Absolute Spirit come into being.

2. After humans arrive, Spirit acquires its Mind and goes through a developing stage of self-estrangement, Hegel's real antithesis. Self-estrangement might be described as "becoming," a sort of fetal stage. So "becoming" would be the antithesis—the middle stage—of Hegel's basic *Phenomenology* dialectic, the macrodialectic discussed in my chapter 3. In fact, in each of the first two sentences of the final paragraph of *Phenomenology*, Hegel treats "Becoming"

as not the synthesis but as a descriptive label for the *antithesis*—the middle stage—of his macrodialectic! And in the paragraph's third sentence, Hegel says Becoming is followed by "fulfilment." Near the end of the paragraph, fulfilment takes the form of the "Absolute Knowledge" produced by self-realization. Absolute Knowledge, not Becoming, is the dialectic's synthesis. Yet "being-nothing-becoming" makes "becoming" the synthesis, the last stage. That contradicts becoming's role in *Phenomenology*. Becoming can certainly serve as a *label* for the middle stage, but it can't be the middle stage *concept*; it can't serve as the antithesis. The reason: becoming is not the opposite—the antithesis—of nothing. The concept being is the opposite of nothing, or at least of nonbeing. If becoming is the opposite of any concept, that concept is retrogression, decline, evanescence, or decay.

3. Spirit finally matures into Absolute Spirit, which is the real synthesis of Hegel's basic dialectic. This outcome might be described loosely as "being." But the sequential dialectic of being-nothing-becoming dialectic treats being as the thesis, not as the synthesis. The "example," if used to represent the "divine life" of Spirit, is a mess.

My point, once again, is that *Logic*'s static triads cannot serve as examples of thesis-antithesis-synthesis dialectics. Hegel does provide examples—all sorts of examples. But those examples must be found elsewhere—in *Phenomenology* and in Hegel's *Philosophy of History*. Hegel's interpreters have not found those examples.

McDonald's Supposed Examples. My point about *Logic*'s triads requires further elaboration, because McDonald's detailed and complex analysis of those triads might otherwise be offered as a refutation of that point. McDonald has prepared a diagram of "The Hegelian System." It consists of twenty-two circles. They are arranged in five hierarchical levels with a single circle at the apex. Each circle contains a *Logic* triad that is supposedly a dialectic and that McDonald has selected from *Logic*'s much larger number of triads. Each circle except the one at the apex feeds into (via a connecting arrow) another circle at the next level above it. Another twenty-four circles, not shown in the diagram, send out dotted-line arrows that feed into those circles in the diagram that have no incoming arrows from other circles shown in the diagram. Every circle in the diagram except the six on the bottom level has three arrows feeding into it. Solid-line arrows come from circles that are shown, dotted-line arrows from circles that are not shown. Each of the three thesis-antithesis-synthesis concepts within each displayed circle has one incoming arrow pointing to it, but the concept pointed to is never the same as any of the three in the lower-level circle from which the arrow comes. Smaller internal arrows within each circle show that the thesis "contains and gives birth to" the antithesis. The thesis enters the synthesis via the antithesis, which transports the thesis to the synthesis. The diagram purports to show how *Logic*'s more important dialectics are related and how they converge on the apex dialectic, whose alleged "synthesis" is Spirit. Oddly, Absolute Spirit, treated as the synthesis of a second-level circle, feeds into Spirit, treated as the synthesis of the apex circle, whereas in *Phenomenology* Spirit actually precedes Absolute Spirit. Spirit evolves into Absolute Spirit at the climax of Spirit's "divine life," where Spirit undergoes "self-realization."[52]

But the main problem with McDonald's diagram is that it fails to demonstrate that any of the triads are what McDonald says they are, dialectics. All the diagram does is show that *Logic*'s triads are arranged hierarchically, something that Stace previously showed in more detail. Take the art-religion-philosophy triad, supposedly a thesis, an antithesis, and a synthesis. The fact that art contains religious elements (e.g., Madonna paintings, Michelangelo's mural on the ceiling of the Sistine Chapel) hardly makes religion the antithesis or opposite of art; it merely establishes a small overlap between art and religion. Likewise, the fact that some philosophy has religious content (e.g., the divine right of kings, Nietzsche's "God is dead") doesn't make philosophy a synthesis of art and religion; it merely establishes a small overlap between religion and philosophy. We might also observe that philosophy overlaps politics (Machiavelli), economics (Marx), history (Hegel), and education (Dewey). But that doesn't mean philosophy is a four-way synthesis of politics, economics, history, and education. Neither does it mean that history is the antithesis of politics or economics or education, nor does it mean that education is the antithesis of economics.

McDonald, like so many others, simply does not understand the Hegelian concepts of thesis, antithesis, and synthesis. Black-white-gray is a dialectic (although it does not use a format that Hegel uses). White is the antithesis (opposite) of black, the thesis. Contrary to McDonald's ideas, black, the thesis, does not "contain" any white; it is the total absence of white. Gray is a synthesis (combination) of black and white; you get gray by combining black and white and nothing else. Gray does not get its black indirectly, via white, which supposedly originates in black. Instead, black enters directly into the synthesis, as does white. If you mix white paint with black paint to get gray paint, the black does not come indirectly from the white. The schematic arrow runs directly from white to gray.

Findlay's Supposed Example. Findlay does try—but fails—to provide such an example. It comes from *Phenomenology*. (At least he is looking in the right place, not in *Logic*.) The supposed example is a wildly inaccurate assertion about a "main triad" of "his [Hegel's] Dialectic." Findlay claims that "the *Phenomenology* has a main triad whose members [thesis, antithesis, and synthesis] are (A) *Consciousness*, (B) *Self-consciousness* and (C) *Reason*."[53] This "main triad" consists of the three main headings of Hegel's table-of-contents outline. Findlay's claim that these headings form a dialectic is rife with errors:

- The *Phenomenology*'s real "main triad"—its overarching dialectic—actually has *unconscious* (without the *ness*), not *consciousness*, as the thesis. And unconscious is really paired with a second thesis concept, union, so unconscious is just half of the real thesis, which is unconscious union. I develop this point in chapter 3.

- Far from being the thesis, *consciousness*—really just "*conscious*"—is the antithesis in Hegel's main dialectic. And again, this concept is really just half of a conceptual pair, conscious separation. Regarding the true status of "conscious" as part of the antithesis, note that conscious is the opposite of its thesis counterpart, unconscious. And separation is the opposite of union.

- Self-consciousness, the alleged antithesis, is not the opposite (anti-thesis) of consciousness, the alleged thesis. Instead self-consciousness is just a special form of consciousness, a subheading of consciousness. The true opposite of consciousness is unconsciousness, which is not among the three concepts Findlay cites.

- Self-consciousness is actually the synthesis of Hegel's "main dialectic." It is the state that arrives when Spirit becomes Absolute Spirit—when consciousness of separation ("self-alienation") changes to consciousness— awareness—of unity ("self-realization").

- Self-consciousness, falsely described as the opposite of consciousness, is simply the result of Spirit's climactic act of becoming conscious that the external "objects" it sees (in its guise as "subject," a human observer's mind) are really itself, Spirit, because every particular thing in the universe is essentially Spirit.

- "Reason," which Findlay treats as different from self-consciousness, is actually defined by Hegel as the Spirit's achievement (via Hegel's mind) of self-consciousness (awareness that both subject and object are one entity, Spirit): "Self-consciousness is Reason."[54] And: "Reason is the certainty of consciousness that it is all reality."[55] So reason is just an alternative label for self-consciousness, or at any rate an advanced state of self-consciousness.

- Even if we go by Hegel's peculiar definition of reason, reason per se cannot by any stretch of the imagination be viewed as a synthesis of consciousness and self-consciousness. What opposites are merged? How?

Singer's Supposed Example. One interpreter, Singer, turns from *Phenomenology* to Hegel's *Philosophy of History* for a supposed non-*Logic* (nonstatic) example of a dialectic. Singer offers what he thinks is an example of a history dialectic. He writes that, in Hegel's *Philosophy of History*, a vast dialectical movement extending from the Greek world to the present governs world history. But the supposed dialectic is not Hegel's real "immense" history dialectical movement, his overarching history dialectic. (Hegel actually has *two* overarching history dialectics—one for freedom, one for monarchy; both use the same three periods.) Hegel's real dialectic doesn't begin with Greece; it begins with China. Hegel's real dialectic advances from (1) Oriental despotism to (2) Greco-Roman slave-based societies to (3) Germanic monarchy. (The foregoing are Hegel's *labels*, not to be confused with the thesis-antithesis-synthesis *concepts* behind the labels.)

Singer, in falsely claiming that Hegel's main historical dialectic begins with "the Greek world," says Greece represents "customary morality." Customary morality is morality based on custom, as opposed to codified law. He identifies this customary morality as "the *thesis*." The supposed antithesis of "customary morality" is "independent thought," brought to fruition in Germany during the Protestant Reformation. Independent thought is "the antithesis." But Singer is wrong. The Greco-Roman era is really Hegel's antithesis period. That period is not where the Reformation occurs. Neither is the Reformation a separate, antithetical historical period in Hegel's own analysis. Instead, the Reformation and independent thought—freedom of thought—belong to Hegel's synthesis period, Germanic monarchy. Martin Luther was a German monk, and the Germanic states of northern Europe were where Protestantism not only began but was concentrated in Hegel's day.[56]

Singer continues: "The synthesis in the overall dialectical movement is the German society of Hegel's time, which he saw as . . . an organic community . . . [that preserves] individual freedom because it is rationally organized."[57] But, although Germanic *monarchy* (not "German *society*") is the synthesis period in one of Hegel's two overarching history dialectics, Protestantism is one of the monarchy's definitive characteristics, not the substance of a preceding "Reformation" dialectical period. In this respect, Singer completely misses—doesn't even mention—the transition from the "bondage" (Hegel's term) that preceded the synthesis period. That bondage was Greco-Roman slavery. (In another of Hegel's history dialectics, a subdialectic covering a shorter period, the bondage is the suppression of free thought by the medieval Catholic Church, which Hegel despised.)

Still another problem is that Singer fails to show, and it would be impossible to show, that Greek-style "customary morality" from the thesis is brought into the Germanic monarchy synthesis. In 1794, shortly after the Germanic monarchy period came into full bloom, codified law—the Prussian General

Civil Code—was introduced in Hegel's Prussia. The monarchy came into full bloom, according to Hegel, only about a half century earlier: Frederick II (Frederick the Great, who ruled Prussia during 1740–86) was "the ruler with whom the new epoch [Germanic monarchy] enters actual reality, in which the real interest of the state achieves general recognition and highest justification."[58] So codified law was, along with Protestantism and monarchy, a definitive characteristic of the Germanic monarchy period. My point is that Prussian law was *codified* law, not Greek-style customary law; there was no synthesis of customary law and Protestant free thought. Singer apparently does not understand the concept of synthesis, for he makes no effort to show how his supposed thesis ("customary law") is brought into the synthesis ("individual freedom"). As far as he is concerned, a Hegelian dialectical synthesis is simply the third stage of a triad, nothing more; it does not draw upon the thesis and the antithesis for its content. Singer's "example," in short, is inaccurate from beginning to end. It is not an example of a Hegelian dialectic. It is not even a narrower example of a Hegelian synthesis.

Strathern's Supposed Example. An absurd "example" of a dialectic is that provided by Strathern. It is this:

> Thesis: Universality
> Antithesis: Particularity
> Synthesis: Individuality[59]

This mislabeled "dialectic" actually gets off to a good start. Universality and particularity really are ways of expressing the thesis and antithesis of Hegel's main dialectic, the macrodialectic that I explain in chapter 3. The example's problem is its horribly misconceived synthesis. Individuality is not a synthesis of universality and particularity; individuality is a *synonym* for particularity. Individuality and particularity are the same thing—individual or particular elements that constitute the general or universal category.

In Hegel's real universal-particular dialectic, the synthesis is "universe composed of particulars." This synthesis can also be expressed as "universe = particulars." Hegel's Spirit is, to greatly oversimplify, the universe—all reality. When this is understood, Spirit is seen as a universe composed of particulars. The particulars are the individual parts that constitute the universe—planets, clouds, prairies, rivers, weeds, pebbles, birds, deer, humans, shops, ships, and shirts.

Although Strathern does not give the source of his "example," he could try to defend it by showing it comes from Hegel's *Logic*.[60] The problem with that defense is that this triad's appearance in *Logic* does not make it a dialectic. It is just a triad. I showed under the "Supposed Examples from Hegel's *Logic*" subheading that the *Logic* has lots of triads whose third members are not true syntheses. Individuality is not a synthesis of universality and particularity. Rather than including universality, it is antithetical to universality.[61]

Tucker's Near-Miss Example. Tucker is the one interpreter who comes close to providing a thesis-antithesis-synthesis example. I mentioned in connection with both Hegel's *Logic* and Findlay's false example that primal unconsciousness is a salient feature (one of two such features) of Hegel's basic *Phenomenology* dialectic's thesis. (*Phenomenology* has many other dialectics, but the basic one overarches the entire book.) Tucker, alone among Hegel's interpreters, names "primal unconsciousness" in connection with what seems to be the basic dialectic's thesis. But then he abandons this concept. And there are other problems, many of them. Part of the difficulty is that Tucker presents, in three different places, three partly conflicting descriptions that seem intended to refer to Hegel's overarching *Phenomenology* dialectic, the basic dialectic I call the macrodialectic. The three descriptions are these:

1. Tucker first says, "God [Spirit] passes from primal unconsciousness in the form of nature to ultimate self-consciousness in the person of historical man."[62] This is an accurate but vague general description of the dialectic. As far as I know, it is the only description that recognizes "primal unconsciousness" as what at least seems to be the thesis. The problems are that (*a*) Tucker does not identify "primal unconsciousness" as a dialectic's thesis, (*b*) a paired second thesis concept, union (of all the particulars in the universe), is missing, (*c*) the antithesis stage is entirely missing, and (*d*) the synthesis, "self-consciousness," does not name any thesis or antithesis concepts that are combined. In Tucker's exposition, self-consciousness is just a

label—accurate but still only a label—for the third stage. In Tucker's reference, it neither contains nor synthesizes concepts.

2. Two pages later, Tucker draws a contrast between nature and man, calling them "two different grades of spirit." He elaborates: "[1] Nature is externalized spirit that is unconscious of itself as spirit; it is the 'unconscious.' [2] Man, on the other hand, is spirit in the act of becoming conscious of itself as spirit. . . . [3] In the process of becoming in terms of knowledge, finite self-conscious spirit overcomes its finitude and rises to the plane of absolute self-conscious spirit."[63] By again pairing "nature" with "unconscious," Tucker seems to imply that item 1 is the thesis. Item 2 fails to recognize that man, like nature, is not conscious of himself as spirit. Item 3 undeniably describes Spirit's synthesis stage. But if I am correct in interpolating [1], [2], and [3] to identify thesis, antithesis, and synthesis, we have some serious problems. I will discuss these in a moment.

3. Twelve pages later Tucker offers his third version: "In the well-known triadic formula, [1] the given world-form or creative self-objectification of spirit is the 'thesis,' [2] the world apprehended by the knowing self as an alien and hostile object is the 'antithesis,' and [3] the world repossessed by the knowing self as a mental content is the 'synthesis.'"[64]

The three descriptions have too many flaws to provide us with an example of a dialectic. The one important and accurate detail is "primal unconsciousness." Tucker certainly deserves tentative credit for spotlighting primal unconsciousness. But we quickly run into problems and contradictions. These problems and contradictions amount to abandonment of the idea that "primal unconsciousness" is part of the thesis. Starting with the thesis, let's see what those problems are.

1. Nature in its prehuman state indeed is where primal unconsciousness is found. The trouble is, Tucker hasn't said unconsciousness belongs

to a dialectical thesis. And when Tucker later does say "thesis," the description ("creative self-objectification of spirit") says nothing about unconsciousness. Indeed, it implies consciousness.

2. In Tucker's second description of the dialectic, which does mention unconsciousness, the concept of unconsciousness suddenly changes. The concept is now spatial rather than temporal: "Nature is externalized spirit that is unconscious of itself as spirit; it is the 'unconscious.' Here Tucker is comparing Spirit in its role as an observer in spatial location A with Spirit in its role as an observed external object in location B. He is contrasting a person, who is the observer and who does have consciousness, with external "nature," which he says is unconscious. In truth, both are Spirit, the "essence" of everything that exists. But what we now have is a spatial concept of unconsciousness, whereas Hegel's true concept of unconsciousness is temporal. Unconsciousness exists in time before consciousness (man's mind) comes into existence.

3. In attributing unconsciousness to external nature (the spatial concept) instead of to a time period before humans appeared on earth, Tucker forgets that humans are part of nature. It is not nature per se that is unconscious in Hegel's real dialectic; it is nature as it once existed before humans arrived on earth. So when Tucker identifies nature with the externality that is observed by a human observer after humans arrive, he fails to notice that external nature has gained consciousness: externally observed nature now includes conscious human beings, humans other than the one who is the observer. Nature is therefore now conscious, or at least partly conscious, not unconscious.

4. When Tucker says "unconscious of itself as spirit," he is not using "unconscious" in the sense of lacking a conscious mind, which is what Hegel means by unconscious. Tucker is instead using unconscious in the sense of *unawareness*. Consciousness, a conscious human mind, is present. But the mind isn't aware that the external objects it sees are essentially the same as itself. The human is unaware that both it and

the external objects Tucker is calling "nature" are essentially Spirit. Spirit is their essence.

5. "Primal unconsciousness," from Tucker's first description, is hard to reconcile with "externalized spirit that is unconscious of itself as [unaware that it is] spirit." The second phrase describes Hegel's antithesis, not his thesis. It is in the antithesis stage that Spirit is unaware that ("unconscious of the fact that") the external objects it sees are itself, Spirit. Hegel's Spirit in the thesis stage is internalized, not externalized; it does not and cannot perceive external objects. Why? In the primordial state of nature, before man arrives, no human mind exists to perceive external objects and misinterpret them as "alien." Spirit therefore exists only in its unseparated, non-self-alienated state of universality, or oneness.

6. "Primal unconsciousness" is even harder to reconcile with "creative self-objectification," described as the "thesis" fourteen pages later. An unconscious, prehuman Spirit can't be creative. Neither can it falsely "objectify" itself—treat itself as "alien" natural objects, things other than itself. It is therefore almost a certainty that Tucker's reference to "primal unconsciousness" is a reference to what is really Hegel's antithesis period, the period in which an observing "consciousness" is not "conscious" (aware) that the "object" it observes is itself, Spirit, because both consciousness and the object are Spirit.

7. Describing the thesis as a "given world-form" and a "creative self-objectification of spirit" leaves me scratching my head. If that's a thesis, what could its antithesis—its opposite—possibly be? What is the opposite of a "given world-form" or "creative self-objectification"?

8. "Self-objectification" seems to mean that Spirit, using the mind of a human observer, misinterprets itself as a separate object, something apart from itself. Spirit objectifies (treats as an alien object) itself. But that is something that happens in the antithesis stage of the dialectic,

not in the thesis stage. So Tucker's third description, the only one that actually says "thesis," is plainly inaccurate.

The above eight objections relate to the dialectic's thesis, as described by Tucker. We now move on to the antithesis. Tucker says the "antithesis" is "the world apprehended by the knowing self as an alien and hostile object." That is a superficially accurate description of what happens in Hegel's real antithesis. But the description reveals no antithetic characteristics when compared with the descriptions of the thesis. What in the thesis is the opposite of "apprehended as alien"? To make matters worse, I see in Tucker's description of the thesis the very same thing he places in the antithesis. The "self-objectification" Tucker places in the thesis surely is the act of "the knowing self" (observer) apprehending the external "world" as "an alien and hostile object." The "knowing self" objectifies itself, the external object. Instead of making the antithesis the opposite of the thesis, Tucker has made both the same!

I should add that Hegel's real thesis has no apprehension. In the basic dialectic's thesis stage there are no humans around to apprehend anything. A further problem, extremely minor, is the word "hostile." In the real antithesis, the world—or at least objects within it—is indeed apprehended as alien, but "alien" has no connotation of hostility. "Alien" is simply a matter of misinterpretation: Spirit, using the mind of man, thinks external objects that are essentially itself—Spirit—are objects that are *not* itself but, rather, alien. Alien simply means "other than itself."

Tucker's synthesis, which involves a repossessed world, doesn't say what it means to repossess the world. When and in what sense was the world ever possessed in the first place? When was it lost? A related problem is that the synthesis does not square with the thesis. The thesis says nothing about an earlier possession. And there is no showing that conceptual opposites are united in the synthesis. There aren't even any conceptual opposites to unite. Similarly, "overcomes its finitude and rises to the plane of absolute self-conscious spirit" fails to refer to anything in the thesis or in the antithesis. Tucker hasn't said "finitude" is a characteristic of the antithesis (although finitude actually is a characteristic of the antithesis); neither has he said what finitude means. (It actually means being a finite—limited—particular of the universe, especially a human being, as contrasted with the "infinite" or unlimited Spirit, which includes every finite thing in the universe.)

TILLICH: GENUINE EXAMPLES OF THESIS-ANTITHESIS-SYNTHESIS DIALECTICS

To further clarify what I mean by the literature's lack of concrete examples, I will cite four genuine, concrete examples of dialectics from the philosophical theology of Paul Tillich. Tillich's dialectics is basically a matter of putting new wine in old Hegelian wineskins. The examples accordingly illustrate Hegel's three main dialectical formats. Old formats, new content. Each format is defined by the manner in which the synthesis is achieved or expressed.

- Tillich calls his thought "neo-dialectical" and "dialectical realism."[65] He describes this as "thinking" that "moves through 'yes' [affirmation] and 'no' [negation] and 'yes' again [a higher yes, the negation of the negation]."[66] To understand the allusions you must know from other sources that Tillich, a closet atheist-humanist, embraces a "God above the God of theism."[67] This "God above God" happens to be a nonsupernatural God, humanity.[68] The initial Yes combines (A) a Yes to Christianity's supernatural God of theism and (B) a Yes to supernaturalism in general. Then the No comes along: the thinker becomes an atheist, the antithesis of a theist. His No unites (C) No to the God of theism and (D) No to supernaturalism in general—the antitheses (opposites) of A and B. Finally, the thinker becomes a humanist who returns to Yes, a Yes to "God." But the new Yes affirms a *higher* God ("*above* the God of theism"). This Yes, the synthesis, combines (A) Yes to God, from the thesis, with (D) No to supernaturalism, from the antithesis. The result is a *nonsupernatural* God. That God happens to be humanity, a figurative God not openly identified by Tillich. (The identity of "God" must be deduced from lots of clues.) The thinker separates from and returns to God—separation and return, the basic theme of dialectics. The dialectic's format: (1) thesis: A + B, (2) antithesis: C + D, (3) synthesis:

A + D. In this format, the synthesis combines one concept from the two-part thesis with one from the two-part antithesis. Summary:

> Thesis: Yes to God + Yes to supernaturalism
> Antithesis: No to God + No to supernaturalism
> Synthesis: Yes to God + No to supernaturalism
>   (= Yes to the nonsupernatural God)

Tillich provides his own summary of this dialectical process, confirming that it does entail thesis-antithesis-synthesis dialectics. "True being [the God above God]," he says, "must be discovered under the surface. . . . This discovery is made through a process of preliminary affirmations [of God and supernaturalism], consequent negations [of God and supernaturalism], and final affirmations [of the God above God]. It is made through 'yes and no' or *dialectically*" (my italics).[69] The God above God is the "Yes above the Yes and No of life and of truth."[70]

- A second Tillichian example of the format having two-part stages uses Hegel's basic potential-actual format. (In chapter 3, I describe this format and its derivation in detail.) This second dialectic follows the same Yes-No-Yes pattern. In the thesis stage of theism (Yes to God), man is potentially united with God. But the union is not actual, because the God man worships is the wrong God, the false God of theism. The thesis becomes a combination of two concepts: potential + union (of man and God). In the antithesis stage of atheism (No to God), man separates from God. Note that separation is the antithesis—the opposite—of the thesis's concept of union. We now have a two-concept antithesis: actual + separation. In the synthesis stage of humanism, man returns to God (Yes to God). But the God he "returns" to is not the original God. It is a higher God, humanity. The synthesis borrows "actual" from the antithesis and "union" from the thesis. Summary:

> Thesis: potential + union (of God and man)
> Antithesis: actual + separation (of God and man)
> Synthesis: actual + union (of God and man)

- The same thought progression is described in a dialectic that moves from theology to philosophy to Tillich's philosophical theology, a synthesis of philosophy and theology. Theology treats God as the source of Truth; philosophy treats man, God's opposite (antithesis), as the source of Truth; and Tillich's thought combines the two sources— God and man. The resulting dialectic flows from a *thesis* of God (one being) to an *antithesis* of Man (many beings) to the *synthesis*, God = Man (one = many). This synthesis redefines God as humanity. Abstractly stated, the dialectic is (1) thesis: A, (2) antithesis: B, and (3) synthesis: A = B. This A = B format is Hegel's second format. The synthesis reveals that the antithesis is the thesis in disguise. Summary:

> Thesis: God (one being)
> Antithesis: man (many human beings)
> Synthesis: God = man (the true God, the one humanity = many
>   human beings)

The above dialectic, in turn, can easily be transformed into a particular version of Hegel's third basic dialectic: (1) *one*, from "one God," (2) *many*, from "many humans," and (3) *one composed of many* (equivalent to one *and* many). A variation of this one-composed-of-many format is "universe (Tillich's humanity, Hegel's Spirit) composed of particulars (Tillich's human beings, Hegel's subject and objects)." Summary:

> Thesis: one (God)
> Antithesis: many (humanity)
> Synthesis: one composed of many (one God composed of many
>   human beings)

Hegel uses these three formats with his overarching *Phenomenology* dialectic and several of its variants. I refer to the macrodialectic that doesn't reach a synthesis until the end of the book. But *Phenomenology* has more than two dozen shorter dialectics, some of which use other synthesis formats. One of these other formats has as its synthesis A + B, or thesis + antithesis, which is really a slightly broader concept than "one composed of many." Some of the other formats are quite imaginative. One of these has a synthesis that uses a masked actor in Greek comedy. The actor alternately wears and removes a divinity mask, thereby alternating between two roles—divine (mask on) and human (mask off), or thesis and antithesis. The actor, who plays both roles, is the synthesis. Another format likewise uses one person as the synthesis: Faust, who begins as a predator but becomes the victim of Mephistopheles, represents both the thesis and the antithesis—predator and victim. (In chapter 4, I describe the mask dialectic and the *Faust* dialectic in more detail.)

The failure of the Hegel literature to provide genuine examples of dialectics points to a deeper problem: none of Hegel's hundreds of expositors has recognized Hegel's three main dialectical formats, presented above in the Tillich examples. For example, no expositor has been able to get from the recognized concept of self-estrangement (failure of "subject" to recognize external "objects" as itself, Spirit) to the concept of "many" (Spirit separated into many particulars), *explicitly identified as a dialectical antithesis*. To make matters worse, most expositors (Baillie, Stace, and Pinkard are exceptions) don't even mention the prehuman stage of natural history that provides the thesis concept of "one," or unconscious union (i.e., potential union, unrealized union).

Chapter 2

DIALECTICS AFFIRMED

The now-almost-universal skepticism about the idea that Hegel uses thesis-antithesis-synthesis dialectics of a dynamic (nonstatic) sort runs afoul of overwhelming evidence that Hegel does practice thesis-antithesis-synthesis dialectics. Among the most powerful pieces of evidence are Hegel's soon-to-be-revealed actual dialectics: the overarching macrodialectic that spans the entire length of *Phenomenology*, a Preface dialectic, four disguised table-of-contents dialectics hidden among a larger number of triads, twenty-two microdialectics employed in the march of consciousness, and ten history dialectics. That's thirty-eight dialectics, not counting many variants of particular dialectics. But before we get to the highly persuasive evidence of the macrodialectic, other evidence must be considered. This evidence shows that Hegel directly and indirectly affirmed his use of thesis-antithesis-synthesis dialectics. First, the text of *Phenomenology* is full of dialectical terminology—references and allusions to dialectics, theses, antitheses, and syntheses. Second, one passage in the Preface praises dialectics, even while saying it has been misused by Kant; a second unmistakably describes a thesis-antithesis-synthesis dialectic; and a third alludes to Spirit's dialectical movement. Third, *Phenomenology*'s Introduction offers a detailed, if guardedly worded, description of one version of Hegel's overarching macrodialectic. Fourth, the first primary heading of the text, (A) "Consciousness," has three subheadings (I, II, and III) that provide a hidden thesis-antithesis-synthesis perspective (I = universality, II = particularity, III = universe composed of particulars) for Hegel's analysis of consciousness. Below, after explaining ten especially important thesis-antithesis pairs used by Hegel, I will analyze the evidence from the four sources just named.

ANTITHETICAL CONCEPTS

One reason previous interpreters have not found in Hegel's writing the thesis-antithesis-synthesis dialectics that to me are remarkably obvious is that the first ten of the thirty-five antithetical conceptual pairs introduced in chapter 1 have been either overlooked or underinterpreted. The ten pairs are

1. universal and particular
2. one and many
3. union and separation (separation = "estrangement" or "alienation")
4. essence and existence (existence = appearance)
5. divine and human ("God" and man)
6. inner and outer (unseen and seen)
7. in itself and for itself
8. potential and actual
9. unconscious and conscious
10. artificial and natural

The first four pairs, and to some extent the next three, are different ways of saying the same thing; they are more or less interchangeable. Let's examine the details.

1. Universal and Particular. "Universal and particular" means essentially the same thing as the well-known combination "general and particular." That combination, in turn, is similar in meaning to "abstract (vague) and concrete (specific)." Universal, however, often (not always) has a more specific meaning than general. Hegel's Spirit—here I oversimplify—embraces and thus unites all reality, the entire universe. Spirit includes our physical universe and everything in it. Tillich, who understood Hegel better than any other philosopher did, could therefore write that Hegel's Spirit "is the essence of every species of plants and animals, of the structures of the atoms and stars, of the nature of man in which his [Spirit's] innermost center [mind] is manifest."[1] This "essence" is not metaphysical; it is simply a mental concept, Spirit. Tucker, who displays at least limited understanding of Hegel's dialectics, agrees. He says Spirit's self-realization is its "awareness of itself as the whole of reality."[2] This awareness materializes in the mind of man. Man's mind is where Spirit's "innermost center is located"—meaning that man's collective mind is Spirit's Mind.

Hegel confirms this conclusion by saying, "Reason is [when self-realization is reached] the certainty of consciousness [a person's mind] that it is all reality."[3] He later repeats this theme in his first sentence following heading VI, "Spirit": "Reason is Spirit when its certainty of being all reality has been raised to [recognized by a human mind as] truth."[4] Baillie has no difficulty comprehending what Hegel means: he states that "the Absolute [Spirit] is the totality of all reality" and that, as such, Spirit contains "a multiplicity of [narrower] universals [limited general categories, such as animals]."[5] But, in Hegel's usage, "universal" almost always refers to the physical universe—stars, mountains, cows, frying pans, fences, and so on. "Universal" therefore includes everything in the universe. Most important, it includes ourselves, we whose minds are Spirit's Mind—its only Mind. Spirit has no independent, transcendent mind.

Every universal (or general) category consists of particulars, the individual items that constitute the universe. The universe of flowers consists of ladyslippers, chicory, spiderworts, tulips, daylilies, and countless other flower varieties; each variety is another universe consisting of billions or trillions of individual plants. Particularity comes into play in *Phenomenology* because man has a perceptual problem. (This problem is the subject of the second subheading, "Perception," under *Phenomenology*'s first main heading—heading A, "Consciousness.") Man looks around and sees all sorts of external "objects"—other persons, robins, boxwoods, rainbows, houses, apples, cookies, toys, lampposts, haystacks. These particulars are all Spirit: everything is Spirit, including the observer, called "consciousness," "subject," or "the I." But the observer, who like all humans is essentially Spirit, does not recognize the objects as Spirit, that is, as itself. Spirit (the observer) instead perceives the external things as separate objects—separate from each other and separate from itself, Spirit. Spirit, observing the world though the mind of man (itself), thus regards all external things as "alien" objects, objects that are not itself. ("Alien" has no negative or prejudicial connotation.) In Hegel's words, "what it [Spirit] does *not* know is that this [perceived] . . . object . . . is *its own self.*"[6] Consequently, Spirit is self-alienated or self-estranged—separated from itself.

Things that are *essentially* one universal entity, the universe or Spirit, become *existentially* many things, many particulars.

2. One and Many. As just noted, the universe is one—one universe—whereas the particulars are many. So the second conceptual pair, "one and many," means roughly the same thing as "universal and particular." A qualification concerning "many" is that, when Hegel is discussing Christianity's Trinity, "one" is God in his pre-incarnation state (thesis) and "many" is really just two—God in heaven and God incarnate (Jesus) on earth. Spirit's task is to recognize that the one and the many are the same thing—one entity composed of many particulars. Spirit is the one entity, the universal (general) category that embraces the many particulars of the universe, which are also Spirit.

3. Union and Separation. "Union and separation" focuses on how the one and the many are perceived or not perceived. In its unconscious, pre-human state of nature, Spirit has no human mind with which to perceive external objects, so "all reality" is united as the universe. Two stages later, in its essential state of Absolute Knowledge (the dialectical synthesis), Spirit belatedly becomes aware that it (now in its guise of the mind of Hegel) is one entity, a universe; this is a second state of union. But in its existential (misperceiving) state of separation, the in-between antithesis stage, Spirit thinks whatever it senses (sees, hears, smells, tastes, or feels) is a separate object; hence Spirit is existentially separated, estranged, or alienated from itself. That is man's existential predicament, coming up next. Man remains in this state of self-estrangement throughout the entire book, until Spirit acquires Absolute Knowledge in the last paragraph of *Phenomenology*. When Spirit acquires Absolute Knowledge, it becomes Absolute Spirit, thereby tipping its hat to the metaphysical concept of "the absolute"—even though Spirit is not really metaphysical.

4. Essence and Existence. "Essence and existence" has two sets of meanings. In the first, essence is the way things *ought to be*. Specifically, Spirit ought to be aware, through the mind of man, that it is all reality—everything in the universe. Existence is the way things *actually are*. Spirit, perceiving and interpreting with the minds of individual men, sees external "objects" and mistakenly thinks the objects are things other than itself, Spirit. Spirit, unaware that it is all reality, the divine, thinks it is nothing more than whichever human being is doing its thinking at a particular time and place. Spirit's need is to make the way things ought to be (essence) identical to the way they actually are (existence). Existence becomes essence when Spirit achieves self-realization, self-consciousness, self-awareness—when Spirit becomes Absolute Spirit.

Tillich, describing his own essence-existence philosophy, which is based on Hegel's, summarizes these polar concepts: "Estrangement points to the basic characteristic of man's predicament. Man as he exists is not what he essentially is and ought to be."[7] Tillich's man ought to be aware that he is God, and Hegel's Spirit ought to be aware (through the mind of man) that it is the universe, all reality. That's another way of saying that man is unaware that he is worshipping the wrong God; he needs to realize that *he* is God, or (in Hegel's case but not Tillich's) at least part of God (Spirit). In another passage, Tillich reaffirms the "ought to be" of essence: "In so far as man's existence has the character of . . . estrangement, a double consideration is demanded, one side dealing with man as he essentially is (and ought to be) and the other dealing with what he is in his self-estranged existence (and should not be)."[8]

In the second set of meanings, essence and existence is another way of describing union and separation. Essence is a state where the universe, hence Spirit, is united, just one entity. Essence can be (1) potential or (2) actual. Potential essence describes Spirit's unconscious, prehuman state, wherein man's conscious mind (Spirit's Mind) is not yet available to perceive the many separate objects that constitute reality. In this primal state, the thesis, Spirit is potentially united in the sense that it isn't separated: no human mind is available to separate it into all the particulars that constitute the universe. Actual essence, the synthesis, is the state wherein Spirit, after a long stage of conscious separation into particulars (self-estrangement), becomes aware, through the comprehending mind of Hegel, that it is all reality. Existence is the middle stage, the antithesis. It is the state that prevails until the last chapter, and really the last paragraph, of *Phenomenology*. It its existential state, Spirit is separated from itself through its failure to recognize itself (external objects) as itself (the Spirit-observer); Spirit perceives itself as many rather than as one. Hegel lays out the problem: "The Unhappy Consciousness [Spirit in its antithetical state of self-estrangement] itself is the gazing of one self-consciousness into [at] another, and itself is both, and the unity of both is also its *essential* nature. But it is not as yet explicitly aware that this is its essential nature, or that it is the unity of both" (my italics).[9] Existence "is not as yet" what it ought to be, essence. When Spirit eventually returns to itself from its state of self-estrangement, "Spirit has made its existence identical with its essence."[10] Spirit has now become Absolute Spirit.

When Hegel speaks of "the gazing of one self-consciousness into another," his statement is misleading. The statement is true in cases where the object gazed at is another human: humans are self-conscious. But the statement is not true when the observed object is inanimate, as is usually the case. Inanimate objects are not self-conscious.

You can see that Hegel was the original existentialist philosopher. His philosophy revolves around concern about the plight of man, who is (among other things) the Unhappy Consciousness. The plight of man is that he doesn't know who he is—doesn't know that he is the divine. He mistakenly thinks an imaginary rational, self-conscious, omnipotent, supernatural being named God is the divine. This mistaken belief separates him from the true divine, himself. (Paul Tillich's so-called existentialist philosophy is almost identical. The only difference is in the details of who the divine is—a deified *universe* [hence including a deified humanity] in Hegel's case, more narrowly a deified *humanity*—nothing else—in Tillich's case. For both philosophers, an alternative way of expressing the "plight of man" is that he worships the wrong God. And for both philosophers, the wrong God is the God of Christian theism.)

5. Divine and Human. "Divine and human," repeats the "one and many" theme. In Christianity, Judaism, and Islam the divine is one—one rational, self-conscious, omnipotent supernatural being. Although polytheistic religions, such as Greek and Hindu religion and some forms of Buddhism, had or have many deities, Hegel ignores them and treats "divine" as conceptually equivalent to one. In Hegel's philosophy, Spirit is the divine and is likewise just one entity, the universe. In short, "divine" represents the concepts of "one" and "universal." Human, on the other hand, refers to humanity. Humanity is conceptually equivalent to many: there are many humans, billions in fact. It follows that, in places where Hegel is describing conflict or contrast between a divine and a human orientation or point of view, he is simultaneously alluding to the antithesis between universal and particular, between one and many, between union and separation, and between essence and existence.

6. **Inner and Outer.** "Inner and outer" is yet another way of conceiving one and many. If I see a tree, I see only what is visible and material—the trunk, the bark, the branches, the twigs, the leaves, and maybe some buds, blossoms, nuts, or fruit. I don't see what Hegel regards as the hidden inner essence of that tree; I don't see what is invisible and nonmaterial. I don't see Spirit. Spirit is the *concept* that unifies into one entity the many things that differ on the outside but are identical inside. Here things get a bit complicated, because "Spirit" can be used in two different senses. In chapter 3, I will show that Hegel defines Spirit as a four-part physical-and-mental entity whose physical side is the entire universe and everything in it. Spirit in that sense is not precisely what inner refers to. Instead, inner refers to the *concept* of Hegel's Spirit. There is nothing physical about a concept; concepts—ideas—are intangible, nonmaterial. Spirit, viewed as a concept, is the universality of everything in the universe. As such, Spirit is the unifying essence of everything in the universe. Everything is *essentially*, but not visibly, Spirit. Spirit is not literally inside of everything, because Spirit is just an idea, a concept, not something material. But it is inner in the sense that it is hidden from sensory perception, just as something material that is literally inside something else (something opaque) is hidden.

Hegel says: "Spirit is alone Reality. It is the inner being of the world."[11] "Inner," in other words, points to Spirit, the conceptual essence of everything, as the "pure" or "actual" form of reality. Spirit is "supersensible," not perceivable by the senses. The outer, the antithesis of inner, is whatever the senses, particularly sight, can perceive. "Outer" implies that the book is being judged by its cover. The perceived object is being judged—really misjudged—by what is visible. But it ought to be judged by its invisible inner essence, Spirit.

Both inner and outer are characteristics of the so-called objects that "subject" or "consciousness" sees. Spirit is self-estranged, estranged from itself, because, when subject (Spirit) sees external objects (also Spirit), subject sees only the "outer" of each object. Almost all objects differ in their outer appearance, so subject concludes that the objects constitute a huge cast of particulars—*many* particulars. But in truth, what subject sees is itself. Subject's "inner" essence is Spirit, and each object's "inner" essence is also Spirit: both subject and object are Spirit. They are *one*. Everything in the universe is part of the one, Spirit. Spirit is a *synthesis* of one and many. It is one composed of many.

7. In Itself and For Itself. The confusing terms "in itself" and "for itself" are deliberately obfuscatory ways of expressing abstractly all the preceding pairs of meanings. That which is "in itself" is (*a*) universal—encompassing everything—rather than particular, (*b*) one rather than many, (*c*) unified, either potentially or (when combined with "for itself") actually, (*d*) the essence of every particular thing in the universe, (*e*) the divine, (*f*) "inside" of everything in the sense of being intangible and thus invisible, and (*g*) Spirit in a conceptual sense rather than the physical universe. "For itself" has the opposite meanings. That which is "for itself" is (*a*) particular, (*b*) a particular member of the "many" category, (*c*) perceived as a separate "object," (*d*) related to the state of existence rather than essence, (*e*) not divine, but not necessarily human either, (*f*) endowed with a visible exterior, and (*g*) material, hence perceivable by the senses.

Another distinction, and really the most important one, is that "in itself" relates to a dialectic's thesis, whereas "for itself" relates to a dialectic's antithesis. Hegel can thus refer to "the antithesis of being *for itself* and being *in itself*."[12] "Antithesis" does not in this context mean the second stage of a dialectic; it means the oppositeness of the thesis and the antithesis. The "in itself" is an observed object's inner essence; the "for itself" is the object's misleading outer appearance. When the two phrases are combined as "in and for itself," Hegel is describing a dialectical synthesis, which combines the thesis and the antithesis (or else the best parts of them). Hegel often uses the word "mediate" and its variants to describe the combining of a thesis and an antithesis in a synthesis. So when he says that "individuality [the status of being a particular object], which [when it] exists *in and for itself*, . . . contains the antithesis of being *in itself* and being *for itself* effaced [erased] within its own . . . mediation,"[13] he is saying that, in the synthesis, the opposition between the thesis and the antithesis is eliminated by the synthesis's function of mediation. "In and for itself" reconciles or mediates "in itself" and "for itself." Here the "in itself" and the "for itself"—abstract terms—are whatever thesis and antithesis Hegel is discussing.

The "in" of "in itself" helps us remember what "in itself" refers to, namely, universality, or the unifying concept—Spirit—found *in* everything. But the "for" in "for itself" seems arbitrary. Tillich provides an illustrative word that you might find easier to work with when Hegel says "for itself." Tillich says that in the "highly dialectical structure" of "the self [observer] having a world to which it belongs," the concept of "individuality" expresses the meaning of "for itself."[14] Individuality is a synonym for particularity; individuality refers to the many particulars that constitute the world. The observer regards these as particulars because they differ on the outside, that is, in their appearance or existence. The "world" Tillich refers to is his own God, humanity, and the individuals are human beings. But the "individuality" concept also applies to Hegel's "world," the universe, where almost all the particulars are nonhuman.

"In itself" and "for itself" are widely misunderstood, for two reasons. First, "in itself" in some contexts relates to Spirit's thesis stage of unconsciousness, the existence of which nobody has recognized. Second, the word "for" in "for itself" cannot on its face be recognized as referring to a visible ("outer") characteristic. I like to think of "for itself" as short for "for itself to see," referring to the particularizing outer characteristics of an observed object.

An example of the general misunderstanding is Forster's incorrect explanation. He says "the contrasting pair of terms 'in itself' and 'for itself' is used to mark two different distinctions in Hegel: (i) the distinction between merely being ('in itself') and being aware that one is ('for itself'), and (ii) the Aristotelian distinction between being potentially ('in itself') and being actually ('for itself')."[15] Regarding the first alleged distinction, "in itself" does *not* mean "merely being," or existing. Spirit exists—has being—in all three stages of Hegel's overarching dialectic; "in itself" relates only to the thesis stage, where "in itself" stands alone, not combined as "in *and* for itself." And "for itself" does not mean being aware that one is. On the contrary, "for itself" relates to the antithesis stage, self-estrangement, in which Spirit is *not* aware that it is the essence of everything in the universe, hence is *not* aware that it is Spirit.

Forster's second distinction has some truth but is largely false. "In itself" is related to the thesis stage of potential union and in that sense is related to "being potentially." But Forster does not recognize that Hegel uses thesis-antithesis-antithesis dialectics; even less is he aware that a thesis stage of unconsciousness exists. He thinks potentiality, or "in itself," is something that accompanies estrangement, which (unknown to him) is the dialectic's antithesis stage. And that idea is flat-out wrong. "Potential" is a thesis concept, not an antithesis concept. A further implication of Forster's interpretation is that "potentially" becomes "actually" ("for itself") when Spirit achieves self-realization—when the dialectic's synthesis materializes. But the truth is that "for itself," when not combined with "in itself" ("in *and* for itself") relates to the antithesis stage of estrangement. There Spirit is "*actually* self-estranged" through the failure of an observing subject to recognize itself (Spirit) in external objects.

Beiser also misinterprets "in itself" and "for itself." He writes, "The term 'in itself' (*an sich*) means not only [*a*] by itself, apart from its relations to other things, but also [*b*] something potential, undeveloped, and inchoate."[16] The first half of that definition, because it is too abstract, is correct only if "by itself" is understood to mean general or universal. The second half of the definition is correct insofar as "in itself" generally refers to the thesis state of potentiality. But Beiser overlooks an important qualification: "in itself" means an actual state when it is combined with "for itself" ("in *and* for itself"). Beiser next writes, "The term 'for itself' (*für sich*) means not only [*a*] something self-conscious but also [*b*] something that acts for ends and that has become organized and developed."[17] Now Beiser is thoroughly wrong. That which is "for itself" is a particular observed object that is misperceived by the observer ("subject") as something other than the observer, whereas both are Spirit. It is the subject, not the observed object, that has consciousness (unless the object is another human). And this consciousness is self-consciousness only when "subject" finally realizes that the observed "object" is itself, the subject. Furthermore, the state of being "for itself" has absolutely nothing to do with actions, ends, or being organized or developed. The observed "for itself" object might be a block of salt. It actually is a block of salt in Hegel's chapter on perception. A block of salt has no mind, therefore has no "ends," isn't "something that acts"—it just sits there waiting for deer to come along—and is neither "organized" nor "developed."

A third interpreter, Baillie, gets things right, although he misses the thesis-antithesis connection. In his 1910 "Translator's Introduction" to *Phenomenology*, he says one feature of the concept of "the Absolute" (Spirit) is "its bare, concentrated universality, the notion [concept] 'in itself.'" Universality is, of course, the state of being one, unified—the thesis concept. Baillie then correctly says "for itself" has a meaning that "is the sheer opposite of the first," or "externalization"—the opposite of inner and the opposite of universality. "For itself," he says, means "*out* of itself." "On the outside" is a better way of putting it, but "out of itself" is close enough. The outside of anything is the part that is visible. And since the outsides of objects differ from one object to another, the related concept of particularity—the opposite of universality—is implied. Moving on, Baillie says "the third aspect of the notion [concept] of the Absolute is the explicit union of the first (pure universality) and the second (pure difference) in a *synthesis*," which is "in and for itself" (my italics)."[18] Baillie actually says "synthesis." He understands.

8. Potential and Actual. In "potential and actual," we have antithetical concepts that are related to yet substantively different from the seven preceding pairs. The foremost problem of interpretations of Hegel to date is their failure to recognize that Spirit moves from a thesis stage of potential universality (or union, or essence, the state of being one) to an antithesis stage of actual particularity (or separation, or existence, the state of being many). Stated otherwise, the problem is the failure of interpreters to recognize the dialectical format, illustrated in chapter 1 with the first Tillich dialectic. That dialectic runs from (1) thesis: A + B to (2) antithesis: C + D to (3) synthesis: C + B. The synthesis borrows one concept, B, from the two-part thesis and one concept, C, from the two-part antithesis. In the Hegelian macrodialectic's application of this format, A is potential and C is actual; the goal is actual union, as contrasted with potential union—actual essence as contrasted with potential essence. Hegel therefore writes that "the third moment" (third stage of a dialectic) is where Spirit achieves "a knowledge of itself . . . as it is both *in essence* [from the thesis] *and in actuality* [from the antithesis], or *in and for itself*."[19]

Tillich and Baillie help clarify the potential-actual dichotomy. Tillich puts it this way: "Actual being is the true expression of potential being . . . [and] is realized only *after estrangement* [separation, the antithesis]" (my italics).[20] In

Tillich's thought, this means that man, who is God but doesn't know it, is actually estranged from God because he thinks God is a separate being who lives in heaven. But "if he were what he essentially is [God], if his potentiality [of becoming 'the infinite,' God] were identical with his actuality [his being finite, man], the question of the infinite would not arise."[21] Translation: If man recognized himself, humanity, as God, questions about God would not arise.

Baillie comes remarkably close to getting the point when he writes: "Looking at the process [of Spirit's maturation] as a growth from a lower to a higher degree of articulation of the nature of the whole [Spirit], it is spoken of as a process [of advancing] from 'potentiality' to 'actuality.'"[22] Unfortunately, Baillie fails to combine potentiality with B in a dialectical thesis, actuality with D in an antithesis, and actuality with B in a synthesis. He, like Forster, thinks *estrangement* is the state of potentiality. Had he ruminated at greater length on what Hegel meant in his Preface by "give actuality to the universal,"[23] Baillie might have unlocked the door to Hegel's thought.

9. **Unconscious and Conscious.** "Unconscious and conscious" is basically synonymous with, or rather a special case of, "potential and actual." "Unconscious" refers to an early state of nature, before man exists. Man's mind is Spirit's Mind, Spirit's only Mind. So without man and man's minds, Spirit exists—the universe exists—but as yet has no Mind. Without a mind, Spirit cannot have consciousness. Without consciousness, Spirit cannot perceive the "alien" external objects it mistakenly thinks are separate from itself: there can be no state of separation, or self-estrangement. And without self-estrangement, Spirit is unified, unseparated; it "lives" in a state of unconscious unity. It displays the thesis concept: universality.

This unconscious unity is merely potential unity, potential essence. To become actual, the unity must be consciously recognized. Recognition of Spirit's essential unity must await the arrival on earth of man. This unconscious-conscious dichotomy is the foundation on which Hegel's overarching dialectic, the macrodialectic, rests. It will therefore be developed in much more detail in chapter 3. For the moment, all we need to know is that (*a*) unconscious is equivalent to potential and (*b*) conscious is equivalent to actual. But whereas unconscious always refers only to the thesis stage, or unconscious (potential) union, conscious can refer to either the antithesis or the synthesis: it can refer to either conscious (actual) separation or conscious (actual) union.

10. Artificial and Natural. Hegel has two dialectics in which the thesis is "natural" and the antithesis is "artificial." One dialectic is hidden in a trio of table-of-contents headings; the other is hidden in Hegel's *Philosophy of History*. In both dialectics, "natural" is actually right out in the open, explicitly stated (though not identified as a thesis). "Artificial," in turn, is hidden in plain sight—in the word "art." All art is man-made. And anything man-made is artificial. Artificial is, of course, the antithesis of—the opposite of—natural.

In Hegel's dialectics, natural alludes to two things. First, it carries the implication that Spirit, as all reality, includes all of nature. (Artificial bears the complementary implication that Spirit also includes all artificial objects in the universe; Spirit goes beyond the Spinoza-Schelling concept of the absolute as something limited to nature.) But the main allusion is to Jesus, viewed as one of two manifestations of God. According to Christian theology, Jesus was God incarnate, God in the flesh. This version of God was natural. Jesus was a real, natural human being. The God-man Jesus, in addition to being God incarnate, was the Son of God—the second member of the Trinity. So "natural" alludes to Son in "Father, Son, and Holy Spirit."

Artificial, in addition to alluding to the inclusion of artificial objects in the concept of Spirit, alludes primarily to God's other form, God the Father. Hegel was an atheist. He didn't believe in God. To him, God was a creation of the human imagination, a product of what he called "picture-thinking." Since God—the imaginary God in heaven—is something created by man, he is artificial.

You can see where this is leading. Transpose Son and Father to put them in their proper Trinitarian order and you get a dialectic that runs from Father (artificial) to Son (natural) to Holy Spirit (unites artificial and natural). The Holy Spirit's job is to do what spirits do best: they possess people (e.g., to cause "Holy Rollers," or Pentecostal sect members, to roll around on the floor and speak in tongues). By possessing Jesus, the Holy Spirit united Father and Son in a synthesis. In this Trinitarian story, Father in the thesis stage is potentially one in the sense of a union of parts, but he is not actually one because there is not yet a Son to unite with. Then the Son comes along. He represents actual separation: the Father is in heaven, and the Son is on earth.

How do we combine (1) potential + union and (2) actual + separation to get (3) actual (from the antithesis) + union (from the thesis)? Easy: we call out the Holy Spirit. God's Holy Spirit possesses Jesus (right after Jesus is baptized), creating an *actual union* of the artificial (the Father) and the natural (the Son).

What is the point of this dialectical story? It is this: Hegel's Spirit is a synthesis of natural and artificial. The "natural" is man, the most important part of Spirit—the part that provides Spirit with its Mind. Man, in turn, represents the concept "human." The "artificial" is God, a man-made entity, the creation of man's imagination. God represents the concept "divine." The synthesis of natural and artificial is therefore a synthesis of human and divine. This synthesis is another way of saying "man is God." In Tillich's thought, man—humanity—is all there is to God. But in Hegel's thought, man is just the essential part of God (Spirit), the part Hegel is particularly concerned with deifying. Hegel is espousing a pseudotheology of humanism.

DIALECTICAL TERMINOLOGY

We are now ready to look at the several ways in which Hegel affirms his use of thesis-antithesis-synthesis dialectics. The evidence begins with dialectical terminology. Hegel's frequent terminological allusions, and occasional outright references, to theses, antitheses, and syntheses provide solid evidence that he is practicing dialectics. Kaufmann argues that Hegel "never once used these three terms [thesis, antithesis, and synthesis] together to designate three stages in an argument or account in any of his books."[24] But Hegel actually did use the terms "antithesis," "synthesis," "negation" (a synonym for antithesis), and "negation of the negation" (a widely recognized alternate label for synthesis). Whether he used these terms together, and whether he used "thesis" with them (he didn't), is irrelevant. What is relevant is that Hegel referred explicitly to his use of dialectics. And he made it clear that he meant thesis-antithesis-synthesis dialectics. He did this by using a wide variety of substitute terms to identify the three dialectical stages. Below are Hegelian terms, taken from Baillie's translation of *Phenomenology*, that either refer or allude to the three-stage process and to the individual stages (page references in parentheses).

- **Dialectics:** "dialectical movement" (123, 247), "dialectic process" (142, 154, 158, 176, 180), "the dialectic" (151), "triple process" (256), "the triplicity" (107), "three moments constitute the life of spirit" (765), "three moments" (767), "the complete succession of forms" (137), "the process of negation [antithesis] and mediation [synthesis]" (153), "the two factors [thesis and antithesis]" (402).

- **Thesis:** "primitive stage" (88), "first stage" (111, 625), "first moment" (590), "first realization" (693), "the positive element [Yes], viz., the universal" (190, 552), "unrealized [potential] essence" (550), "essence [potential]" (145), "[the] universal" (191, 261), "universality" (395, 656), "moment" (388), "it's previous state" (564), "the family [from *Antigone*], as the *inner* indwelling principle of sociality operating in an *unconscious* way [my italics]" (468). (In this wordy last example, the words "inner" and "unconscious" allude to the first members of the thesis-antithesis pairs inner-outer and unconscious-conscious.)

- **Antithesis:** "antithesis" (205, 367, 391, 423, 562),[25] "negation [No]" (137, 154, 165, 608), "the negative factor" (105), "the negative element" (386), "principle of negation" (565), "second attitude" (259), "second moment" (572), "second realization" (694), "stage of perception [consciousness, or conscious separation]" (180), "moment" (388), "self-estranged" (506, 511), "self-alienated notion" (591), "estrangement" (551), "alienated" (251), "middle term" (230), "the extreme of individuation [particularization]" (327), "the particular" (191, 261), "appearance [existence, contrasted with essence]" (145), "existence" (55), "something opposed [No opposed to Yes]" (564).

- **Synthesis:** "synthesis" (272, 482), "synthetic unity of the first two propositions [thesis and antithesis]" (626), "synthetic connection" (765), "negate thereby the negation" (156), "union" (482), "unification" (794), "third stage" (262, 555, 765), "third attitude" (263), "third realization" (694), "third moment" (793), "reconciling affirmation [terminal Yes of Yes-No-Yes]" (679), "actual real essence" (550), "actualizing the universal" (94), "attains the form of universality" (795), "essence [actual]" (55), "mediating term uniting inner [universality] and outer [particularity]" (343), "has got rid of the opposition between universal and particular" (191), "formal universality of all the component individuals" (499), "comes back ['returns' in Miller's translation] to itself from this state of estrangement" (96), "mind has made its existence . . . one with its essential nature" (97), "the actual self-consciousness of Absolute Spirit" (461), "union" (482).

Kaufmann and Pinkard may have believed that "thesis," "antithesis," and "synthesis" are the only terms Hegel could have used to refer to the three stages of a dialectic. But they were ignoring the obvious: Hegel is deliberately obscure. He deliberately conceals his message, which is essentially a message of atheism—a message that would get him banned from his profession if it became known. The message: The mind of the divine is not the mind of an omnipotent, omniscient supernatural being named God; it is the mind of man, and the divine is conscious of itself (self-conscious) only to the extent that individual humans recognize themselves as Spirit, the divine. Kaufmann knew this, for he said of Hegel that "his religious position may be safely characterized as a form of humanism."[26] Humanism is, of course, a form of atheism—disbelief in the God of theism—and is typically full-blown atheism, contrasted with pantheism and deism.

To expect Hegel to come right out and say "X is a thesis," "Y is an antithesis," and "Z is a synthesis" is to expect way too much. Kaufmann himself wrote: "The whole style of the *Phenomenology* is such that the student and scholar are almost bound to ask themselves: What is the man talking about? *Whom* does he have in mind? Indeed—and this is crucial—the obscurity and whole manner of the text are such that these questions are almost bound to replace the question of whether what Hegel says is right."[27] In the light of these words, Kaufmann is being nonsensical when he argues that Hegel's rare use of the terms antithesis and synthesis constitutes evidence that Hegel did not use "Hegelian dialectics." The simple truth is: Hegel didn't want to be understood, except perhaps by a few followers who were sympathetic to his atheist-humanist convictions.[28] In order not to be understood, Hegel generally used oblique and frequently opaque terminology in place of "thesis," "antithesis," and "synthesis."

This point, that Hegel generally avoided using "thesis," "antithesis," and "synthesis" in order to make comprehension difficult, is of utmost importance. It bears further elaboration. Solomon convincingly explains why Hegel chose to keep his meanings obscure (by, among other means, not saying "thesis," "antithesis," and "synthesis"). During 1793–99 Hegel wrote but didn't publish his highly critical, sometimes scathing and contemptuous, early manuscripts on Christianity. But around 1800 Hegel abruptly softened his criticism of Christianity and, at the same time, began expressing it guardedly rather than openly. His previously clear writing became the ambiguous, hard-to-comprehend language for which he is now famous. Solomon's explanation:

> Hegel had seen Spinoza's *Ethics* condemned in Germany. He had seen Kant, whom he considered to be unquestioningly orthodox, censured and censored by the narrow-minded regime of Frederick Wilhelm II. He had seen Fichte dismissed from the University at Jena for views that were (incorrectly) construed as atheistic. Is it only coincidence that the year of Hegel's "great conversion," 1800, is also the beginning of his professional philosophical career, and that the writing of the *Phenomenology* (1806) is simultaneously the time of his first professorship?[29]

Elsewhere, Solomon answers the question he poses in the last of the sentences just quoted: "Hegel really did have a secret, and . . . it has been well kept. The secret, abruptly stated, is that *Hegel was an atheist*. His 'Christianity' is nothing but nominal, an elaborate subterfuge to protect his professional ambitions in the most religiously conservative country in northern Europe."[30] In short, Hegel had to keep his atheism a secret in order to win the professorship he sought at the University of Jena, where he wrote *Phenomenology* and where he was a mere unsalaried *Privatdozent*. The same consideration applied to potential professorships elsewhere if his Jena ambitions fell short. Were Hegel's true beliefs about God and Christianity to become known, he would be unemployable.

PHENOMENOLOGY'S PREFACE

Phenomenology's Preface has three places where Hegel affirms his predilection for dialectics. First, he enthusiastically endorses the thesis-antithesis-synthesis dialectical format partially developed by Kant and refined by Fichte. Second, he provides a general description of a dialectic that is, in fact, his macrodialectic, the dialectic that culminates in Absolute Knowledge in the last paragraph of *Phenomenology*. Third, he cryptically refers to the Spirit's dialectical movement.

The "Triadic Form" as Science. In a widely quoted paragraph, Hegel unmistakably refers to the thesis-antithesis-synthesis triad of Kant and Fichte; he even mentions Kant by name. While criticizing the uses to which Kant, and possibly Fichte, put dialectics, Hegel leaves no room for doubt that he approves the basic concept. Hegel begins: "Of course, the *triadic form* must not be regarded as scientific when it is reduced to a lifeless schema, a mere shadow, and when scientific organization is degraded into a table [Kant's table] of terms. Kant rediscovered this triadic form by instinct, but in his work it was still lifeless and uncomprehended."[31] Hegel is saying that the concept of dialectics is good. What is bad is the way dialectics was used by Kant—used merely to construct a table.

Hegel next describes properly used dialectics. "Since then [since Kant] it [the dialectic triad] has been raised to its absolute significance, and with it the true form in its true content has been presented, so that the Notion of Science has emerged." The "science" in question is not what you and I would call science; it is the dialectical thought patterns that characterize Hegel's philosophy. What counts, though, is that Hegel is praising the sort of dialectics that "has emerged" in his *Phenomenology*. Conceivably, "has emerged" is anticipatory and self-adulatory, alluding strictly to what follows in Hegel's book. Findlay thus paraphrases Hegel as saying that "neither he [Kant] nor his successors"—this would include Fichte—"have been able to give it [dialectics] life."[32] That would mean it's up to Hegel to give life to dialectics. But Kaufmann says Glockner thinks Fichte and Schelling are the ones being praised for raising dialectics to the level of science, although Kaufmann himself "would reserve the praise for Fichte and the critique for Schelling."[33] Whatever the truth, the essential fact is that Hegel is praising, not denigrating, dialectics.[34]

Beiser disagrees. Referring to the passage in *Phenomenology*'s Preface, he grossly misinterprets what Hegel says:

> Hegel did praise "the triadic form" that had been rediscovered by Kant, . . . but this is a reference to the triadic form of Kant's table of categories, not a method of thesis-antithesis-synthesis. . . . Hegel never used Kant's method of exposition of thesis and antithesis. It has been said that this method was used by Fichte and Schelling, and then by extension wrongly attributed to Hegel; but it corresponds to nothing in Fichte or Schelling, let alone Hegel.[35]

Beiser is terribly confused. Refer to the Preface lines I quoted. Hegel is *not* praising Kant's table; he is criticizing it, calling it "a lifeless schema." The praise is for Kant's *rediscovery* of dialectics and for post-Kantian dialectics. Next, Beiser's endnote cites Kaufmann as his authority for the final sentence above. But in the Kaufmann reference cited, Kaufmann interprets Hegel's Preface remarks as meaning dialectics "was again raised to 'absolute importance' by Fichte [not Kant] who made much of theses, antitheses, and syntheses."[36] And in a companion volume, Kaufmann points out that Fichte went beyond Kant's table, which never displayed the word "synthesis." Specifically: "Fichte introduced into German philosophy the three-step of thesis, antithesis, and synthesis, using these three terms. Schelling took up this terminology; Hegel did not."[37] Despite Beiser's protests, the fact remains that Hegel, in his Preface, praises dialectics, saying it has been raised to "absolute significance" and has attained the status of "science." How can Beiser interpret that as meaning Hegel was not enamored with dialectics?

In what amounts to anticipatory rebuttal of Beiser, Findlay joins Kaufmann and Glockner in disputing the idea Hegel didn't borrow his dialectics from Fichte and Schelling: "Hegel did not really borrow his triadic scheme from Kant: it had already been read into Kant by Fichte, who had grounded the Kantian categories in the relations of the Ego to the non-Ego, and who also treated these relations in a series of threefold movements, a *thesis* being confronted by a contradictory *anti-thesis*, and both being combined in a *synthesis*. . . . The terms 'thesis,' 'antithesis' and 'synthesis,' so often used in expositions of Hegel's doctrine, are in fact not frequently used by Hegel: they are much more characteristic of Fitche."[38]

The Preface Dialectic. Three paragraphs later in his Preface, Hegel alludes to thesis, antithesis, and synthesis and to separation and return as essential features of his method, which he calls science. Separation and return is the dialectical movement from Yes to No, then back to Yes; and from union (potential) to separation, then back to union (actual); and from essence (potential) to existence, then back to essence (actual). Several pages earlier Hegel told how "Spirit . . . becomes alienated from itself and then returns to itself from this alienation."[39] Hegel now writes, "The movement of a being [Spirit] that [1] immediately is, consists partly in becoming [2] an other than itself [a misinterpreted external "object"] and . . . partly in [3] taking back into itself this . . . [externalized] existence of itself into a [new] moment [dialectical stage]."[40]

Let's analyze that sentence. The "being" that "immediately is" before "becoming" something else is Spirit in its potential (unconscious) union stage, the thesis. It simply *is*. "Becoming an other than itself" refers to the overarching macrodialectic's antithesis, separation or self-estrangement—the "becomes alienated from itself" stage. Here Spirit, through previously nonexistent human minds, falsely perceives external objects (including other humans) as things "other than itself." But in truth they are itself, Spirit. Their "outer" materiality may be "other," but their "inner" reality is Spirit. Moving on to the synthesis, Spirit advances by "taking back into itself" the external objects. It does this by recognizing that the objects are really itself. They become part of itself, hence are taken "back into itself." The new "moment" that results from this advance is the synthesis, wherein Spirit has advanced from actual separation ("other than itself") to actual union ("back into itself").[41]

In the next sentence, Hegel writes: "In the former movement, *negativity* is the differentiating and positing of existence."[42] In a dialectic, there are two movements: (1) from thesis to antithesis and (2) from antithesis to synthesis. The "former movement" is thus the first, the movement from thesis to antithesis. "Negativity" describes the antithesis; it is the No in the Yes-No-Yes (affirmation, negation, negation of the negation) triad. "Differentiating" means the antithesis differentiates the Spirit as "subject" (observer) from Spirit as "objects" (the external things that "subject" observes). Spirit becomes differentiated—separated—from itself in the antithesis stage. "Positing of existence" alludes to an alternative formulation of the dialectic: potential essence, actual existence (appearance), and actual essence. In the antithesis, the Spirit falsely posits the existence of something external that is not itself. "Existence" is appearance, that which appears to be but really isn't. The perceived objects appear to be things other than the observer—separate objects—but in essence they are really the observer, the subject, who (like the objects) is Spirit.

Hegel continues: "In this return into itself, it . . . [ar]ranges itself as a moment having its own place in the whole."[43] The first thing to note here is the word "return." Hegel is alluding to the Christian concept of separation and return, on which dialectics is based (more about this later). That allusion is one more indication that Hegel is talking dialectical talk. Spirit returns to itself in the third stages of these two dialectics: (1) unconscious union, conscious separation, and conscious union—separation from and return to union—and (2) potential essence, actual existence, and actual essence—separation from and return to essence. The other thing to note is that "this return" is a "moment," which is a word Hegel sometimes uses as a synonym for "stage." A moment is a stage of a three-stage dialectic. The return is "a moment having its own place in the whole" because it is a stage having its own place (third place, stage three) in the three-stage dialectic, which is "the whole."

The verb "ranges" is grotesque in this context, but the fault is Miller's, or perhaps a typesetter's, not Hegel's. Whether or not "ranges itself" is a good literal translation of the German word, it certainly is not acceptable English idiom; it has no English meaning in this context. It may be, therefore, that "ranges itself" is a typo and was intended to be "arranges itself"— still awkward but not grotesque—although elsewhere a different interpreter (Sibree) has Hegel saying, in a different work, that "methods may be ranged under three heads."[44] The misuse of "ranges" explains my bracketed *ar* interpolation, which changes "ranges" to "*ar*ranges." Baillie translates the phrase as "appoints itself;"[45] Kaufmann says "assigns itself."[46] Better still would be "makes itself into," "converts itself into," or simply "becomes." (In today's language, "morphs into" would do the trick.) Hegel is saying that when Spirit returns to where it started—the state of union or essence—it thereby departs from the antithesis and moves on to the synthesis stage ("moment") of the overall ("whole") dialectic.

I am not the first to recognize that the sentences interpreted above describe a thesis-antithesis-synthesis movement. Kaufmann, in his commentary on his translation of the text of Hegel's Preface, is forced to concede that Glockner said the same thing: "Glockner summarizes this sentence and the preceding one by saying: 'Hegel describes the three-step: thesis, antithesis, synthesis' (II, 460)."[47] I had not read Kaufmann's comment when I wrote the preceding four paragraphs; I arrived at the same conclusion independently.

Kaufmann, who denies that Hegel uses dialectics, tries to explain away Glockner's conclusion by saying that Glockner, in another work, writes that Hegel mentions thesis, antithesis, and synthesis together only once, namely, in his lectures on the history of philosophy. But all that shows is that Hegel preferred his own hard-to-decipher terminology to the lucid thesis-antithesis-synthesis terminology of Fichte. With help from Solomon, I explained the reason for this preference—fear of being fired for atheism—under the "Dialectical Terminology" heading.

Spirit's Dialectical Movement. The penultimate paragraph of *Phenomenology*'s Preface begins with this gem: "I hold that Science exists solely in the self-movement of the Notion."[48] What Hegel calls "Science," modestly spelled with an uppercase S, refers of course to his method of exposition. As we shall see in increasing detail in the analysis that follows, that method is the thesis-antithesis-synthesis dialectic. "Self-movement" refers to the dialectic's method of progression. It is Spirit itself that is moving itself—moving itself from thesis to antithesis to synthesis. How does it do this? With its Mind, which is the minds of humans. In Hegel's overarching macrodialectic, the first of the two movements (the movement from thesis to antithesis) takes place when Spirit's Mind comes into existence. Since Spirit's Mind is the mind of man, Spirit's Mind comes into existence when man comes into existence. That is when the first movement takes place. Spirit moves from unconscious union (thesis) to conscious separation (antithesis). Spirit becomes separated from itself when a human mind (Spirit) mistakenly concludes that a perceived "object," which like all objects is Spirit, is something "other"—other than itself, Spirit.

The first movement, the movement from thesis to antithesis, has now occurred. But man's mind is at first inadequate for the second movement, the movement from antithesis to synthesis. For tens of thousands of years, man's mind is too weak to recognize that the external things it sees are itself. Socrates, Copernicus, and Newton all prove inadequate for the task. Then Hegel is born (1770). Thirty-some years later his now-mature mind, the most important part of Spirit's Mind, happens on the eureka moment. Hegel suddenly realizes that all reality is essentially Spirit. That means Hegel is Spirit. It also means that everything around him is Spirit. Everything he sees, hears, smells, tastes, or feels is Spirit. This is the moment of self-realization. Spirit, through Hegel's mind, realizes that itself is everything, and that everything is one. The particulars are the universal, Spirit. This self-realization is the second and last "self-movement of the Notion [concept]." It is the movement from antithesis (the "notion" that external objects are separate things, not the observer) to synthesis (the "notion" that external objects are *not* separate things, that they are the observer's own self).

To avoid misleading anyone, I must now add that Hegel does not really "suddenly realize" that all reality is essentially Spirit. What really happens is that Hegel decides to create the philosophical concept of Spirit and to define Spirit as all reality. And the decision isn't sudden. The concept of Spirit seems to have evolved from Schelling's concept of nature over a period of several years.

PHENOMENOLOGY'S INTRODUCTION

Having thrice affirmed in his Preface that he is using thesis-antithesis-synthesis dialectics, Hegel reiterates this fact in *Phenomenology*'s Introduction. At the end of the Introduction, Hegel actually says—in his customary convoluted, obscurantist language—that he is using thesis-antithesis-synthesis dialectics. I have already mentioned that one version of Hegel's overarching macrodialectic moves from (1) potential (unconscious) essence to (2) actual (conscious) existence to (3) actual (conscious) essence. In the antithesis, "existence" refers to appearances, to what things *seem* to be but are not. In the synthesis, Spirit's (Hegel's) mind realizes the truth: both the subject (observer) and the objects seen—the objects that previously seemed to be varied "alien" items—are Spirit. Not only are all the objects really unvaried because all are essentially Spirit, the subject too is Spirit. So subject and objects are one; they are not separated after all. When this truth becomes the new "appearance," appearance and truth become identical. Hence existence (appearance) and essence also become identical.

And this is almost exactly what Hegel says in the penultimate sentence of his Introduction: "In pressing forward to its true existence [truth], consciousness [Spirit's mind] will arrive at a point . . . where appearance [existence] becomes identical with essence."[49] In other words, the dialectical synthesis of essence and existence (potential essence and actual existence) is essence = existence. Hegel is describing the dialectical synthesis that takes place in his macrodialectic. In this synthesis, "consciousness [the subject-observer] itself grasps . . . its own essence."[50] The result is this dialectic: (1) potential + essence, (2) actual + existence, and (3) actual (from the antithesis) + essence (from the thesis).

By grasping the true essence, consciousness "gets rid of its semblance of being burdened [1] with something alien, [2] with what is only 'for it,' and [3] [with] some sort of 'other.'"[51] Here the words "gets rid of" unmistakably allude to what is left behind when the synthesis is achieved. What is left behind by any dialectic's third stage, the synthesis, is the dialectic's second stage, the antithesis. Lest there be doubts about this point, Hegel reinforces it with the three enumerated identifiers of what consciousness gets rid of. First [1], it gets rid of "something alien." The reference is to the state of self-alienation—the antithesis—that precedes the synthesis. The objects subject sees are no longer alien things, things separate from itself, but instead are itself, subject. Both subject and objects are now recognized as Spirit.

Second [2], "for it" is part of Hegel's standard "in itself," "for itself," and "in and for itself" triadic language. The phrase "in itself" flows from Hegel's concept of prehuman unconscious essence. In this concept there is no perception of anything external, because there is no mind with which to perceive anything external. Since there is no external reality, everything is *inner*. "In itself" means inner. This "in itself" condition is the state of pure universality, the absence of separation or alienation. Baillie thus calls "in itself" the concept of "bare concentrated universality."[52] But this is just potential (unrecognized) universality, the thesis stage. The phrase "for itself" relates to the second stage, the antithesis. There Spirit acquires a conscious mind (man has evolved) and perceives external objects. The external objects are *outer*, or outside of itself. From "for itself," consciousness moves on to "in and for itself." This new concept is obviously a combination of "in itself" and "for itself"—a combination of the thesis and the antithesis. "In and for itself" thus describes the dialectical synthesis. To quote Baillie, this "third aspect [the third stage, 'in and for itself'] . . . is the explicit union of the first (pure universality) ['in itself'] and the second (pure difference) ['for itself'] in a synthesis."[53] Conclusion: when consciousness "gets rid of . . . [2] what is only 'for it,'" consciousness is leaving behind the "for itself" dialectical stage, the antithesis, and moving on to "in and for itself," the synthesis.

Third [3], the synthesis finds consciousness getting rid of "some sort of 'other.'" The "other" is the external objects that consciousness previously—in the antithesis stage—thought were things *other than itself*, sometimes called "otherness." In the synthesis, consciousness realizes that those "other" (external) things aren't really other things. They are itself, Spirit. My point is that the three-item "burden" consciousness "gets rid of"—[1], [2], and [3]—in the synthesis is the antithesis, the state of self-estrangement. Though he doesn't use the word "antithesis" here, Hegel is saying that his thought uses antitheses as well as syntheses.

Does Hegel also allude to the thesis stage? He does. Three paragraphs earlier he says that "this dialectical movement" contains "a moment [stage]" that "is the essence or the in-itself."[54] Both "essence" (potential essence here) and "in-itself" ("pure universality") describe a dialectic's thesis stage. And both terms refer to Spirit, the essence of everything real.

Additional words by Hegel pull the dialectic together. One of the problems we encounter when reading Hegel is his habit of giving a word or phrase different meanings in different contexts. "Object" is such a word. It usually means something external to "subject," something subject perceives as separated from itself. But in the words I am about to quote, Hegel uses "object"—along with "notion"—to refer to stages of a dialectic. He says "our knowledge of the first object [the thesis]" contains "untruth."[55] The untruth, which Hegel does not identify, is that nothing but pure universality, the "in itself," exists. The truth is that particularity, the "for itself," also exists: Spirit is a universe composed of particulars, one composed of many. Next, Hegel says "our experience of the untruth of our first notion [the thesis] comes by way of a second object [the antithesis or second stage] which we come upon . . . externally."[56] "Second" alludes, of course, to the dialectic's second stage. And "externally" alludes to the external things that subject, or consciousness, sees when man arrives and Spirit attains consciousness. The external things are perceived as "other"—things other than the perceiving subject.

"The new object [the antithesis] shows itself to have come about through *a reversal of consciousness itself.*" These words confirm that the "new object" is an antithesis. An antithesis is the opposite—loosely speaking, a "reversal"— of the thesis. "The succession of experiences through which consciousness passes" is plainly the thesis, the antithesis, and the synthesis.[57] The result is "a scientific progression," a dialectic. But this dialectic "is not known to the consciousness that we are observing."[58] In particular, consciousness fails to apprehend "what is in and for itself," Hegel's term for dialectical synthesis.[59] Can anyone doubt that Hegel is describing a dialectic?

In case there is doubt, Hegel supplies even more information. This information fits the concept of a dialectic. The "new object" or second stage of the "scientific progression" is "an untrue mode of knowledge."[60] That means the new knowledge is untrue: the knowledge that everything is par- ticularity, that the external world is just a collection of alien objects, is untrue. Those words fit the description of a Hegelian antithesis. Antitheses are untrue, although they do contain elements of truth. Because these ele- ments of truth are present, the "new knowledge"—the antithesis—"must not be allowed to run away into an empty nothing [a complete falsehood]."[61] Instead it must be preserved in "a result which contains what was true in the preceding knowledge."[62]

Reading between the lines, we can see that the "result which contains what was true in the preceding knowledge" is the dialectic's synthesis. The "preceding knowledge" includes both the thesis and the antithesis. And "what was true" in them is both (1) the "essence" part of "potential + essence," the thesis, and (2) the "actual" part of "actual + existence" (or "actual + appear- ance"), the antithesis. Combining "actual" and "essence" gives us (3) "actual essence." This result is "a new pattern of consciousness . . . for which the essence is something different from what it was" previously.[63] What is different about the new "essence"? Originally, in the thesis stage, it was *potential* or unconscious essence. Now it is *actual* or conscious essence. Spirit has completed its "task," which has been "to give actuality to the universal."[64] The dialectic has moved from Yes (affirmation) to No (negation) back to Yes (negation of the negation)—separation and return. But the second Yes (to essence) is a higher Yes, actual essence rather than potential essence. This Yes gives "actuality" to the universal, which is Spirit.

Hegel's "higher Yes"—the actual Yes that is higher than the potential Yes—provides the prototype for Tillich's Yes-No-Yes dialectic, described in chapter 1. In Tillich's dialectic the initial Yes is a Yes to the God of theism and the "higher Yes" is a Yes to "the God *above* the God of theism," humanity. Hegel's Yes-No-Yes is also the prototype for one of Marx's historical dialectics, which will be described in detail in chapter 5. In Marx's dialectic, the initial Yes is a Yes to primitive communism, and the higher Yes is a Yes to final communism. Primitive communism is only potential essence, because it is associated with poverty resulting from primitive methods of production (hunter-gatherer methods); final communism is actual essence, because it is associated with wealth resulting from advanced methods of production (factory methods, waterwheels, and steam engines).

In summary, the Introduction's dialectic takes two forms:

Thesis: potential + essence   Thesis: in itself
Antithesis: actual + existence   Antithesis: for itself
Synthesis: actual + essence   Synthesis: in and for itself

PHENOMENOLOGY'S PART A: CONSCIOUSNESS

Part A of *Phenomenology*, "Consciousness" (the first primary heading), consists of forty-six pages devoted to silly, pretentious, contrived problems of concern only to people who live in ivory towers. Hegel's pontificating on these nonproblems is the sort of claptrap that makes down-to-earth people either groan or chuckle. What Hegel writes about "Sense Certainty" and "Perception" was surely part of the inspiration for Karl Popper's assertion that "there is so much philosophical writing (especially in the Hegelian school) which may justly be criticized as meaningless verbiage."[65] Popper's scarifying description of much of what goes on in philosophy certainly provides a perfect fit for Hegel's "Consciousness" meanderings. Popper observes that "every philosophy, and especially every philosophical 'school,' is liable to degenerate in such a way that its problems become practically indistinguishable from pseudo-problems, and its cant, accordingly, practically indistinguishable from meaningless babble."[66]

All Hegel has to say about what he pretends is his subject matter under "Sense Certainty," the first of the three "Consciousness" chapters, could be said in a few clearly written sentences. Even those sentences could be dispensed with. They would do almost nothing to advance the exposition. What Hegel is vaguely implying, but is unwilling to say, can be said in the following words (mine): "We cannot comprehend anything in the external world, or even comprehend ourselves, unless we realize that the external world and everything in it *is* ourselves, Spirit. Spirit is the hidden essence of everything in the external world—and of ourselves." Beyond that substantive conclusion, Hegel is formulating a dialectic. That dialectic is what concerns us.

Part A consists of three sections: (I) "Sense Certainty: or the 'This' and 'Meaning,'" (II) "Perception: or the Thing and Deception," and (III) "Force and the Understanding: Appearance and the Supersensible World." These three sections form a dialectic: section I is the thesis, section II is the antithesis, and section III is the synthesis. Kaufmann is therefore wrong when he writes that "these many triads [found in *Phenomenology*'s table of contents] are not presented or deduced by Hegel as so many theses, antitheses, and syntheses."[67] Hegel even tells us, unmistakably, that Kaufmann is wrong. *Hegel does this by saying in pellucid language that Sense Certainty, Perception, and Understanding form a "dialectical movement."* Here are Hegel's words (taken from his subsequent discussion of skepticism):

> The activity of skepticism . . . exhibits the *dialectical movement* [Hegel's italics] which Sense-certainty, Perception, and the Understanding each is.[68]

Four of those table-of-contents triads, including this one, do form dialectics. The problem is, the stages of the dialectics (except for the natural-artificial dialectic) can't be recognized by the table-of-contents labels Hegel gives them. It is concepts hidden behind the labels that create the dialectics. Sections I, II, and III of Part A respectively examine from the perspectives of thesis, antithesis, and synthesis the things we are consciously aware of. The basic dialectic of Part A takes this form:

> Thesis: Universal (or Universality)
> Antithesis: Particular (or Particularity)
> Synthesis: Universe = Particulars (or universe composed of
>   particulars)

By substituting equivalent concepts for the above ones, you can create four additional dialectics. The above dialectic plus the four additional ones are the dialectics derived from the first five "antithetical conceptual pairs" discussed under this chapter's first heading, "Antithetical Concepts." The second dialectic:

> Thesis: One (one universe)
> Antithesis: Many (the many particulars the universe comprises)
> Synthesis: One = Many (one universe composed of many particulars)

When you aggregate the many particulars into the one universal entity, you get the concept of union. And when you view the particulars as individual entities, you get the concept of separation. This gives us a third dialectic:

> Thesis: Union
> Antithesis: Separation
> Synthesis: Union of separate parts (particulars)

When Hegel speaks of essence and existence, the fourth pair of antithetical concepts, union is the essential state or ideal state, essence. Separation is the existential or actual state, existence. When Spirit, using Hegel's mind, ultimately realizes (self-realization) that the many particulars previously perceived as separate entities are actually one unified entity, Spirit, the ideal (essential) state becomes the actual (existential) state. The result is a fourth dialectic:

> Thesis: Essence (ideal)
> Antithesis: Existence (actual)
> Synthesis: Essence = Existence (ideal = actual)

The fifth dialectic advances from the abstract concept of universal to the concrete concept of divine. Just as there is one universal entity, there is but one divinity in Judeo-Christian (and Islamic) religion—and in Hegel's pseudotheology. And both because human is the opposite of divine and because humans are the most important of the particulars that constitute the divine (Spirit), human becomes the antithetical concept. A fifth dialectic results:

> Thesis: Divine
> Antithesis: Human
> Synthesis: Divine = Human

I could go on to show how these five dialectics evolve into additional dialectics based on the ten antithetical conceptual pairs discussed at the beginning of this chapter. Take the tenth pair, artificial and natural, for example. In Hegel's opinion, the "divine" or "God," is an artificial (man-made) entity, a product of the human imagination or "picture-thinking." The opposing concept, human, represents the concept "natural": all humans are products of nature rather than being man-made. So "Divine = Human" is equivalent to "Artificial = Natural." This dialectic, by the way, alludes to the Johannine doctrine holding that Jesus was God incarnate: God (an artificial being) = Jesus (a natural human being). Ergo, God = man (humanity).

These dialectics, particularly the first, are the foundation on which Part A of *Phenomenology of Spirit* is built. Part A is nothing more than an incredibly overblown dialectic in which the thesis is universal (Section I), the antithesis is particular (Section II), and the synthesis is universe = particulars, or universe composed of particulars (Section III). Section III is subject to this qualification: the synthesis of the Part A dialectic doesn't get beyond the bud stage. We see the bud start to open, but it never reaches full bloom, because Hegel is saving the blossom for the last pages of his book. Still, the full-bloom dialectic formed by Sections I, II, and III is recognizable.

I. Sense Certainty. Sense certainty is analogous to, but not the same as, a nearly mindless underground grub's coming into contact with something. The grub's primitive mind is dimly aware of the presence of an external "This." But the grub knows nothing about the This. Although other external objects exist, the grub is conscious of only the one it is in contact with at the moment. From the grub's standpoint, the one external object is all the externality there is. Hence the object is perceived as a universe, the whole of external reality, instead of as one member of a set of particulars that constitute a universe. Since particulars are out of the picture, we can say that the grub's sense certainty analogically represents the thesis point of view in a dialectical context where the thesis is "universal."

Hegel goes through some monstrous reasoning to reach the same conclusion: "So it is in fact the universal that is the true [content] of sense certainty."[69] He later repeats this conclusion: "The truth of sense-certainty . . . is . . . it . . . is a Here out of other Heres, . . . i.e., it is a universal [one]."[70] Hegel doesn't do an especially good job of supporting this point. His argument seems to be that things that are merely sensed but can't be differentiated from each other all seem to be the same thing. This argument hardly fits a human observer. Human observers might not be able to distinguish between two virtually identical objects, such as identical teacups or identical twins. But human observers can always see or otherwise sense the presence of many different external objects. And this isn't true only of human observers. The same can be said of mammals, reptiles, amphibians, birds, and fish and probably even of post-larval insects and arachnids.

That doesn't matter, however. What does matter is what Hegel is trying to say, or perhaps trying not to say in any understandable way. He is trying to say that mere sense perception fails to differentiate one object from another. Objects that are merely sensed have no "properties" or characteristics—these come up for discussion in the next section—that allow the perception of particularities. So instead of particulars, all we get is the universal, many objects that *seem* to be just one. That is why the truth of sense certainty is that "it is a universal."

And that conclusion is really the whole point of "Sense Certainty." The universal is the true content of sense certainty. Hegel is simply establishing the thesis of a dialectic. That thesis is "universal." Everything else is so elementary, so axiomatic, that it need not be said. The "everything else," the supposed purpose of the analysis, is arguments purporting to show that sense certainty falls well short of complete knowledge of whatever is sensed. But nobody needs to be told that mere awareness of the presence or existence of something external does not constitute the whole truth about that something. The truth, yes, but not the whole truth. Anyone who thinks there is anything profound or even worth saying under the "Sense Certainty" needs to rethink his or her intellectual standards. To repeat, the real purpose of Hegel's discussion of sense certainty is to establish the thesis—"universal"—of his dialectic. The next section, "Perception," will establish the antithesis, which is "particular."

Well, I must concede that the sense certainty discussion does have a second purpose, a more substantive one. That purpose is to dance around the notion that mere perception overlooks the true essence of the object sensed. The object's—any object's—essence is Spirit. So let's consider a few other details of Hegel's discussion. Sense certainty is knowledge "at the start" or "immediate knowledge," the sort of undeveloped, undetailed, unenriched knowledge associated with first contact.[71] Consciousness is aware that the object is there. But consciousness knows the object "only as a pure 'This,'" something apart from the perceiving consciousness, who is the "pure 'I.'" This knowledge, mere "certainty" that the "This" exists, "proves to be the most abstract and poorest *truth.*" Why is this "truth" so poor? Because "all that it says about what it knows [senses] is just that it *is*; and its truth contains nothing but the sheer *being* [existence] of the thing."[72] The *essence* of the thing—Spirit—remains unknown, unrecognized.

Hegel goes on for twenty more paragraphs explaining why primitive "sense certainty" knowledge is inadequate. Many commentators seem to find this sort of pretentious meandering highly intellectual, even though ambiguous, hard to interpret. My own reaction is: "Good grief!" Even persons of well below average intelligence know that simple awareness of the existence of something is an extremely superficial form of knowledge. Why is Hegel dragging us through all these pseudointellectual maneuvers? And why have all of

Hegel's commentators except Popper been afraid to say that Emperor Hegel is wearing no clothes?

The conclusion reached in the last paragraph of "Sense Certainty" is this: "If nothing more is said of something than that it is 'an actual thing,' an 'external object,' its description is only the most abstract of generalities."[73] That's the same thing he said in the second paragraph, where he called sense certainty "*the most abstract* and poorest *truth*." At that point he should have quit and moved on to "Perception."

What Hegel is driving at, but has no intent of actually saying, is simply this: whereas the "pure This" (perceived object) and the "pure I" (perceiver) are one and the same—both are Spirit—mere sense certainty is only *potentially* aware of this fact. Awareness of both the This and the I embodies the potential for awareness that these two aspects of reality are really one. But actual awareness that the two are one is a long way off. Hegel does in fact say, not in the "Sense Certainty" section but in the last paragraph under "Perception," that "sense certainty is unaware that the empty abstraction of pure being [Spirit] is its essence."[74] But that is just a hint; "pure being" is undefined. Since Hegel isn't ready to come right out and say that the fatal flaw of sense certainty is its unawareness that both the "I" and the "This" are Spirit, he should skip his obfuscatory analysis.

The discussion of sense certainty degenerates into such foolishness—the idea that some humans can't differentiate between different objects perceived by the senses—that I suspect he may not be talking about humans at all. Whether he knows it or not, Hegel isn't describing an "I" who resembles a real person. He's describing a mythical person, a metaphorical mentally challenged Eve who can't tell Adam from an apple, a serpent, or a fig leaf. I therefore suspect—just a suspicion—that he is alluding not to a human consciousness but to his concept of soul.

Hegel calls the earliest stage of animal life "soul." Soul is a nonsupernatural aspect of life, not to be confused with theology's supernatural soul. "The soul . . . is at first sentient only, and not yet freely self-conscious"—another way of saying it belongs to a *prehuman* organism.[75] Soul is an aspect of "animal life" and entails merely the capacity for "feeling."[76] This preconscious stage is like "the dreaming of one asleep" and comes before the "stage" in which Spirit "awakes and receives its consciousness in Man."[77] I like Stace's description: "The natural soul is an even thinner abstraction than bare sensation. It does not exist, at any rate, in man. It might perhaps be said to exist in an amoeba."[78] The soul's salient characteristic, Stace observes, is that "there is for it nothing external to itself."[79] That is, there is no awareness of external "objects." So there is no separation of the universe into subjects and objects. Soul, then, is a late phase of Spirit's primitive, prehuman stage, the unconscious state of nature.

Baillie, who doesn't realize he is describing a dialectical thesis, comes close to implying that this early stage, prehuman life, displays *unconsciousness*: "Experience, with which the *Phenomenology* deals, is rooted in the distinction between subject {a human observer} and object {whatever is observed}. This distinction, however, arises in the 'evolution' of mind out of an earlier stage {the thesis} of life. . . . Before the stage of consciousness {the antithesis of unconsciousness} there is life and there is soul, but neither of these as such involves the distinction between subject and object {i.e., the aforementioned separation of Spirit into a multitude of subjects and objects}."[80] This means that "before . . . consciousness" there is no separation ("distinction"); there is union or universality. This is unconscious union or potential union, pure universality without any particularity.

We see that, regardless of whether Hegel is thinking of incredibly ignorant human beings or soul in his discussion of sense certainty, he is describing the thesis stage of a dialectic. The earlier quotation from Hegel about sense certainty bears repeating: "The truth of sense-certainty . . . is . . . it is a universal." Sense certainty is a universal if it belongs to a human who is unable to perceive the existence of more than one This. And it is still a universal if it belongs to soul, perhaps in the form of Stace's amoeba. As such—as a universal—sense perception represents the thesis stage, universality. Indeed, sense perception is a thesis from two perspectives if Hegel is talking about soul: soul belongs to Spirit's unconscious stage, which is clearly the thesis stage. The conclusion is inescapable: section I of Part A is basically a ploy for smuggling in a dialectical thesis, potential universality. Section II will follow with the complementary stage, the antithesis, which is actual particularity. Note that (*a*) actual is the opposite of potential and (*b*) particularity is the opposite of universality.

A final point reinforces my conclusion that the sense perception discussion amounts to little more than a dialectical thesis, potential universality. The "This" is one item; "This" is singular (one), not plural (many). The concept "one," we have seen, is simply an alternate way of saying universal. There is one universe; there are many particulars. The fact that "This" means one emphasizes the point that "the universal . . . is the true [content] of sense certainty." It is this concept, universality, that identifies sense certainty as a thesis: Hegel's basic dialectic departs from a thesis of *potential* universality and returns to a synthesis of *actual* universality. Under the next heading, "Perception," Hegel begins by discussing a "Thing," again singular, but then describes how one "Thing" becomes differentiated from "other Things."[81] We then see that the sense certainty discussion leads to a contrast between (*a*) one This or one Thing, a universe, and (*b*) many things, particulars. That is a contrast between a thesis and an antithesis—between universal and particular and between one and many. This one-many contrast is further evidence that "sense certainty" has a hidden meaning: thesis.

II. Perception. In moving on to Part A's section II, "Perception," Hegel advances from the thesis perspective of "universal" (one) to the antithesis perspective of "particular" (many). The perceiver is no longer like a grub or an amoeba, no longer unable to distinguish one external object from another. Finally we are dealing with real human beings. Hegel spends another twenty-one long paragraphs intellectualizing on why (*a*) awareness of the existence of many particular objects and (*b*) awareness that the particulars have properties that differentiate them from each other still falls short of what consciousness needs to know. The "I" ("subject," "consciousness") first tries to describe objects according to their properties—color, taste, shape, specific gravity, and so on. This approach runs into problems, as do other approaches. The biggest problem is one Hegel doesn't mention: nobody needs to be told that every object has properties or characteristics—observable details—that differentiate it from other objects.

Meanwhile, a common thread running through different parts of the analysis needs highlighting. That thread is particularity. The discussion of perception relates to a multiplicity of objects. Those properties of "the Thing" (any observed object) give it a character that "distinguishes it from all others," that is, from "other Things."[82] This object is white, cubical, and salty; that one is green and gray, vertical, and leafy. Now the observer, "I," can perceive that there are many different "Things," many particulars. We see that this section of Part A, "Consciousness," is about particularity. The subject matter is the antithesis of the dialectic that runs from "universal" to "particular" to "universe composed of particulars." "Sense certainty" developed the universal perspective: potentially universal, potentially one. We are now looking at consciousness from the antithesis perspective. And the real purpose of the section on "Perception" is not to reach a conclusion—Hegel reaches no conclusion—but to create the antithesis of a dialectic. That antithesis is the opposite of "potentially one." The opposite of "potentially one" is "actually many." Or, to use a different pair of antithetical concepts, we have the opposition between a thesis of "potentially universal" and an antithesis of "actually particular."

Hegel's analysis of perception makes no meaningful substantive progress until it reaches the last paragraph. There he says the concepts he has been playing with "are powers [why call them powers?] whose interplay is . . . often called 'sound common sense.'" This so-called common sense is what Hegel chooses to call "perceptual understanding." We immediately sense that "common sense" is being used disparagingly. Knowledge that physical objects have properties or characteristics is still elementary. It doesn't get us very far—anyhow, not far enough.

We aren't surprised, therefore, that Hegel goes on to say that perceptual understanding "takes them [perceptions] for the truth and is led by them from one error to another." These errors—contrived errors—are the subject matter of the preceding paragraphs of the subsection. The errors result because our perceptual understanding "fancies that it [what we think we understand] has always to do with wholly substantial *material* content" (my italics). The implication: we fail to understand that the real essence of both the universal and the particular is something *nonmaterial*, intangible, rather than something material or tangible. That real essence happens to be Spirit. But Hegel isn't going to tell us this. He still has no intention of saying what consciousness really needs to know, namely, that the truly essential characteristic of the perceived objects is not that they differ from one another but that they *don't* differ. They are all the same. All are Spirit. But all Hegel is willing to say is that "when common sense [incorrectly] separates what is essential from what is supposedly unessential [the Spirit within objects] . . . it . . . convicts *itself* of untruth."[83] Clear as mud, as the saying goes.

To replace the mud with transparent glass, Hegel would need to declare that he is making a distinction between essence ("potential essence," the thesis) and existence ("actual existence," the antithesis). "Perception" is a variant of, or perhaps I should say a derivative of, "appearance." And appearance, in the context of dialectics, implies deception: things are not what they appear to be. Man's "existential predicament" is that he cannot distinguish between mere appearance (existence) and truth (essence). So appearance is more or less a synonym for existence, the opposite of essence. Hegel's discussion of perception thus serves to establish "actual existence" as the antithesis of potential essence. Actual existence is the same thing as actual separation—perceived (untrue) separation, or separateness of the observer and the observed. In the antithesis, what is potentially one, a universe, becomes actually many, a multiplicity of separate objects, particulars.

III. Force and the Understanding. We move on to section III, "Force and the Understanding." This heading alludes to dialectical synthesis; the analysis has shifted to the synthesis perspective. The word "force" ostensibly refers primarily to Newton's law of gravity, published in 1687. But "force" also covers other invisible physical forces such as magnetism, centrifugal force, and electricity. Gravity pulls two objects together; so does magnetism. By analogy, a nonmaterial "force" pulls thesis and antithesis together into a synthesis. Solomon writes that, in Hegel's day, "'force' had become a metaphor for any below-the-surface activity which could be used to explain movements and transformations."[84] That means, though Solomon doesn't notice this (he denies that Hegel uses dialectics), that "force" could be used as a metaphor for dialectical synthesis. And that is how Hegel uses the term.

In Hegel's thought, a nonmaterial dialectical force—Spirit—causes thesis and antithesis to merge. The underlying idea is that both Newtonian gravity and the dialectical force are nonmaterial and invisible, not to mention tasteless, odorless, silent, and unfeelable. These characteristics contrast with the materiality and visibleness of whatever is perceived in the context of "Perception." So dialectical Force, the analog of gravity, has the potential to overcome the fatal weakness of Perception—unawareness of the noncorporeal Spirit, which is just a concept, an idea. "Understanding," for its part, is the hoped-for result of the synthesis: awareness that the particulars perceived in the "Perception" chapter constitute the "Universal" sensed in the "Sense Certainty" chapter—that is, awareness that everything is Spirit. Unfortunately, the synthesis we are about to view fails to bring about full understanding.

In his first paragraph, Hegel presents the problem he is now going to emphasize. Consciousness "does not recognize itself" as a certain "object" that he calls the "unconditioned universal."[85] "Unconditioned" apparently refers here to the universal's not being subject to the condition that it excludes spiritual reality, the mind and its concept of Spirit. In contrast, the conditioned universal of sense certainty and perception is subject to the condition that only material reality is included.[86] (Not being subject to a certain condition is the meaning Tillich, who is imitating Hegel, gives to "unconditioned." When Tillich refers to his dialectical God, humanity, as "the unconditioned," he means that when humanity—"the God above the God of theism"—is conceived of as God it is not subject to the condition that certain elements of humanity, such as Jews or non-Jews, are excluded from the concept of God. Those gods, such as the Old Testament God, that include or serve less than all of humanity are "demonic" or "idolatrous.") Consciousness must remove this unwarranted perceptual condition to arrive at Understanding. Consciousness must recognize that objects have spiritual as well as material content. Consciousness must understand that it, the "I," is all the other particulars in the universe—the Things—because it and everything else are Spirit.

The contrast between materiality and spirituality—between physical (outer) and conceptual (inner)—is what Hegel is referring to in the "Force" section's subtitle, "Appearance and the Supersensible World." Ostensibly, the supersensible world—a world beyond the senses—refers to the invisible world of gravity and other physical forces. Hegel wants us to think he is discussing scientific themes popular in his day and already discussed by Kant, Leibniz, and Schelling. But his real concern is a different invisible world. This is the mental world of human thought, the world of concepts or ideas. "Appearance" is the world of perception, the topic of the preceding section.

Force represents progress toward Understanding in two ways. First, it overcomes the worst flaw of both sense certainty and perception. That flaw is their focus on mere appearance and on directly observable, material (physical) characteristics—"outer" characteristics—of objects. Magnetism's effects can be observed—iron filings can be moved around by a magnet—but magnetism itself is invisible, nonobservable, nonmaterial. The mind, the thing that sense certainty and perception overlook, is likewise invisible, nonobservable, non-material. The mind is the essence of Spirit. And Spirit, viewed narrowly as the mind in the context of force, is what will eventually undergo self-realization, thereby uniting subject and objects into the universe.

The second way in which force represents progress toward understanding is this: force, viewed in the abstract, has the capacity to pull things together. Consider the force known as gravity. Gravity pulls two bodies together. Analogically speaking, that's the same thing a dialectical synthesis does: it pulls the thesis and the antithesis together. It is also the same thing Spirit's mind can do when it undergoes self-realization. The dialectical synthesis will result when the mind pulls the thesis and the antithesis together. The many will then become one. As Hegel explains things, gravitational attraction really consists of two forces: the gravity of body A pulling on B and the gravity of body B pulling on A. This is one of two meanings Hegel has when he writes: "These two Forces exist as independent *essences*; but their *existence* is a move-ment of each [body] towards the other" (my italics).[87] Note (*a*) the presence of Hegel's essence and existence—thesis and antithesis—pair and (*b*) that essence is moving from existence (appearance) toward actuality. Actuality in the case of real gravity is "actual union" (contrasted with "potential union") in the form of a collision: "their substances . . . collapse unresistingly into an undif-ferentiated unity."[88]

By analogy, dialectical synthesis results from a dialectical force—the mind—that causes thesis and antithesis to collapse into an undifferenti-ated unity; they become one. When Hegel mentions the "movement of each toward the other," he is speaking ambiguously. "Each" alludes not just to two gravitationally attracted bodies but to each of the first two stages of a dia-lectic—the thesis and the antithesis. Hegel is hinting—still just hinting— that Understanding will eventuate when we perceive that dialectical forces are at play. We will then recognize the macrodialectic in which the invisible Spirit moves from unconscious union (universality) to actual separation (particularity) to actual union (a universe composed of particulars). To requote some words from the Introduction, "consciousness will arrive at a point . . . where appearance [actual separation] becomes identical with essence [actual union]."[89] When we perceive this, we will understand that we are not only each other and but are also everything else we sense or perceive. Everything is Spirit. The many are one. The particulars constitute the universe.

Anyone who doubts that Hegel is referring primarily to dialectical synthesis and not to gravity should more carefully consider what "undifferentiated" means when Hegel says two things merge into "undifferentiated unity." With rare exceptions, two objects that gravity causes to collide do not become "undifferentiated." If I drop a hammer on a rug, the hammer and the rug remain distinctly different things. The chief exception occurs when one liquid is poured into another. Red paint poured into an equal volume of blue paint produces purple paint. But even with liquids, differentiation may remain: when oil is poured into water, the oil floats to the top. What happens in gravity-caused collisions differs sharply from what happens in dialectics. When a thesis and an antithesis merge into a synthesis, they lose their separate identities; they become an "undifferentiated unity." "Undifferentiated unity" describes not gravity but dialectics.

A bit farther on Hegel introduces the "supersensible world," which is also the "true world." He vaguely implies that the "inner truth" he is talking about is Spirit, but ostensibly the "inner truth" is just gravity, the physical essence. The ambiguously described force is "the *absolute universal* which has been purged of the *antithesis* between the universal and the individual [particular]."[90] Once you realize that Hegel is talking dialectical talk ("antithesis," oppositeness), it's easy to see he is describing a dialectical synthesis: the synthesis unites potential essence with actual existence (antithetical concepts), making them one, actual essence. The supersensible world, the concept of Spirit, will be realized as actual or conscious essence when the conscious mind of Hegel—Spirit's Mind—realizes that he and everything else in the universe are one entity, Spirit. Spirit is the "world" or "World-Spirit," terms that Hegel uses as synonyms for the universe.

The deliberately ambiguous, seemingly nonsensical statements Hegel makes in paragraphs 161 and 162 (Miller translation) illustrate how he attempts to confuse us. What he says is uninterpretable unless you know in advance that he is describing two dialectics. Given that (1) the preceding "Consciousness" material about "Sense Certainty" introduces "universal" as a *thesis* and (2) the material about "Perception" introduces "particular" as the *antithesis* of "universal," we can infer that (3) the "Force and Understanding" *synthesis* is "universe composed of particulars"—equivalent to one composed of many, and also equivalent to God (one) composed of humans (many). The dialectic becomes

> Thesis: universal (one, the "infinite")
> Antithesis: particular (many, the "finite")
> Synthesis: universe composed of particulars (one composed of many; infinite = finite)

This dialectic has a closely related two-concepts-per-stage form that employs the opposing concepts "potential" and "actual." This dialectic is

> Thesis: potentially united (potential + union; Yes to unity)
> Antithesis: actually separated (actual + separation; No to unity)
> Synthesis: actually united (actual + union; Yes—a *higher* Yes—to unity)

If this second dialectic looks familiar, that is because it is also one of Tillich's. It was used in chapter 1 to illustrate the dialectical format in which the synthesis borrows one concept from the thesis ("union" in this case) and one from the antithesis ("actual" in this case).

Now let's see if we can make sense of what Hegel is saying. He speaks of "two distinguished moments." "Moment" is a word Hegel uses in several senses but usually as a synonym for "stage." A stage is a stage of a dialectic: first stage = thesis, second stage = antithesis, third stage = synthesis. The temporality of "moment" alludes to the time sequence in which the stages, moments of time, occur. In the two paragraphs I now discuss, Hegel tries to mislead us into thinking that the "supersensible" (invisible) "force" he is describing is a natural force such as gravity or electricity or magnetic polarity, whereas the force is actually dialectical attraction. Or, to be more precise, force is the invisible *concept* of Spirit that unites the one and the many in a dialectical synthesis (one composed of many). Hegel's mentioning "positive and negative electricity" as "moments" in this context is simply an attempt to deceive us by making us think he is discussing physics. But "positive" really alludes to "Yes," the thesis; "negative" really means "No," the antithesis. Tillich, you will recall, calls his thought "dialectical realism." He describes dialectics as moving from Yes to No, then back to Yes—a higher Yes. A dialectic starts with one concept or one pair of concepts ("affirmation"), advances to the opposite concept or two opposite concepts ("negation"), and then *returns* to a higher version of the first concept or conceptual pair ("negation of the negation"). The higher version incorporates the second concept or one of its two parts. The "two distinguished moments," then, are the thesis and the antithesis of a dialectic.[91] Hegel is talking about a thesis-antithesis-synthesis dialectic, not physics.

In this context, Hegel refers to Spirit as "what is selfsame." He says this "selfsame" or "self-identical" entity, which happens to be Spirit, is something whose "essence is unity." His hidden meaning is that Spirit, *in its essential state* ("essence"), is unified, one composed of many, or a universe composed of particulars. The one self, Spirit, becomes identical to the many particulars it comprises. This essential state of self-identity is the dialectic's synthesis. The synthesis is where the antithetical state of disunity—separation into perceived particulars—is transformed into the essential state of unity. But before Spirit's essential state arrives, Spirit "sunders itself into two," two parts. (The third part hasn't arrived yet.) The sundering is the transition from thesis to antithesis. And the two parts are the thesis and the antithesis. These parts—parts of a dialectic—can be described by either of the two dialectics presented above. In one dialectic the two parts are "universal" and "particular"—equivalent to union and separation. In the other dialectic they are "potentially united" and "actually separated."[92]

Alluding to the dialectic's synthesis, Hegel then says that "the *unity* . . . is in fact itself one of the two moments [the two preceding stages of the dialectic]." He means that unity is also the thesis stage, which is "one of the two [preceding] moments." Both the thesis and the synthesis represent unity. The thesis's unity, however, is *potential* unity—contrasted with the *actual* unity of the synthesis. Hegel then adds that the potential unity of Spirit in its thesis stage "has an antithesis within it." Here Hegel is using "antithesis" not as a reference to stage two but as a reference to the particulars that must be present for unity to exist: there can be no union of particulars unless particulars exist. Particularity is, in turn, antithetical to unity.[93]

In stage two of the dialectic, the "selfsame" (meaning Spirit) "sunders" itself into two."[94] The "two" are the two concepts—universal and particular—that now exist where previously (thesis stage) there was only one. Hegel also uses "sunders" in a different sense when he describes stage two as an act of "self-sundering."[95] The antithesis is where Spirit sunders itself—breaks itself into particulars. It does this by acquiring a Mind, something it lacked in the thesis stage. That is why it was unified: it had no Mind with which to perceive all the particulars it comprised. The Mind Spirit acquires in stage two is the collective mind of humans, who were not present in the primordial, prehuman stage of nature—stage one. Spirit's newly acquired Mind perceives all sorts of "objects." The objects are really itself, Spirit, but in stage two Spirit misconstrues the objects as "alien," things other than itself. Poor Spirit. It is now self-estranged, self-alienated. Universality (thesis) has been replaced by particularity (antithesis).

Estrangement is overcome when Hegel's mind, the truly cerebral part of Spirit's Mind, arrives on the scene. This is the third "moment," the moment "of *becoming self-identical*."[96]

Hegel, hence Spirit too, experiences self-realization. Hegel, a "self" wearing the mask of "subject" and the costume of "consciousness," realizes that he and every "object" or "self" he sees are identical. Every self is identical to every other self, because every self is Spirit. The many are one! The particulars constitute the universal. Actual unity replaces actual separation.

What do these two highly abstract dialects describe? Spirit is a fictitious entity invented by Hegel—he knows it is fictitious—for the purpose of developing a philosophy that secretly endorses atheism. Spirit is really nothing more than an arbitrary—and radical—redefinition of God. Hegel occasionally calls Spirit "God" so as to imply supernaturalism and thereby prevent readers from recognizing his atheism. In doing so, Hegel is *pretending* to present insights into God's true nature. But this is sheer hypocrisy: Hegel doesn't

believe in God. He is really making things up. And he knows it. To oversimplify (the details will come in chapter 3), Spirit is all reality or the universe,
including artificial (man-made) material objects such as works of art. Spirit is
in no sense supernatural. It has no transcendent mind like that of the God of
theism. It is not metaphysical entity. And it is "within" everything only as a
philosophical concept or idea.

Hegel is telling a story, pure fiction rather than an exposition of esoteric knowledge. In this story Spirit undergoes a metaphorical "life." Spirit
advances from (1) potential essence, where this essence is unity that exists in
the prehuman state of nature, to (2) actual existence, where Spirit acquires its
Mind from newly arrived humans and misperceives all external "objects" as
things other than itself—they are really itself, Spirit—to (3) actual essence,
where Spirit, still thinking with its human minds (its only Mind), suddenly
realizes that those external "objects" are really itself. Everything is Spirit! The
invisible *concept* of Spirit (not a metaphysical "substance" or "essence" within
everything) is the hidden inner essence of everything, the "force" that unites
the many into one.

Stage three, the synthesis, is where Spirit realizes the "truth": it is all
reality, the universe or "world." This realization is self-realization. Self-
realization is the attainment of "Absolute Knowing, or Spirit that knows
itself as Spirit."[97] Absolute Knowing transforms Spirit into absolute Spirit.
Since absolute Spirit, like its earlier nonabsolute form, is "God"—albeit just
a figurative God—and since humans are the most important of the "particulars" that constitute Spirit, man becomes God. (Humans are the most important particulars because they provide Spirit with its Mind.) And there you
have Hegel's hidden message of atheism: God is man. The supernatural God
invented by humans—the artificial (man-made) God—does not exist.

Remarks in paragraph 164 of the "Force and Understanding" material
confirm the foregoing interpretation. Hegel says that, in stage three (implied),
"infinity itself becomes the *object* of the Understanding." In Hegelese, infinite
and finite are synonyms for God and man, although finite can also stand for any
nonhuman "object" or "other." So the quoted line amounts to a statement that,
when Spirit attains self-realization (also called self-consciousness), man finally
understands God: man finally understands that *he*, not a supernatural being

in heaven, is God. This stage three situation displays "that which contains no difference, or *self-consciousness*." By this Hegel means that, when self-consciousness or self-realization is achieved, "consciousness" (hence Spirit) realizes that there is "no difference" between itself and every observed object. All are Spirit. Consciousness of external objects is therefore consciousness of one's self, or *self*-consciousness. Hegel actually says this: "It is true that [in the synthesis stage of the dialectic] consciousness of an 'other', of an object in general [any object], is itself necessarily *self-consciousness*." When "consciousness" ultimately recognizes that every "other" it sees is *itself*, Spirit, this recognition is a *"necessary advance* from the previous shapes of consciousness for which their truth was a Thing, an 'other' than themselves." This means that, in the merely conscious (not yet self-conscious) stage of self-estrangement, or the antithesis stage of the dialectic, whatever consciousness saw (or otherwise sensed) was misinterpreted as something other than itself—something other than Spirit. When the ordinary consciousness of stage two becomes the *self*-consciousness of stage three, this final development is a "necessary advance." The advance from stage two (antithesis) to stage three (synthesis) completes the dialectic.

The next paragraph concludes Part A, "Consciousness," without our having achieved any real progress toward "Understanding." All we have are vague hints buried in obfuscatory gibberish. The hints assume we already know that Hegel is alluding to dialectical activity, and more specifically to the two dialectics I presented. Hegel's final paragraph merely rephrases the problem of reaching "Understanding." That problem is now posed as a what's-behind-the-curtain riddle. "We see that in the *inner* [mental] world of appearance, the [consciousness's] Understanding in truth comes to know nothing else but appearance."[98] ("Appearance" is a synonym for "existence," which in turn describes the dialectic's antithesis stage of separation, or self-alienation. Existence is the opposite of essence. So Hegel is saying that we haven't yet reached the synthesis, which is essence.) Those words restate the idea that Spirit, the inner reality of the conscious observer, doesn't know that the material (outer) reality it thinks is all reality isn't really all reality. Appearance omits the nonmaterial reality, Spirit (but ostensibly gravity, whose presence Hegel implies in order to mislead us). Appearance is the metaphorical "curtain" that blocks our view of the inner world, the conceptual world of Spirit.

Now some nonsense: "It is manifest [that's the nonsense] that behind the so-called curtain which is supposed to conceal the inner world [Spirit], there is nothing to be seen unless *we* go behind it ourselves." And "it is evident [how so? to whom?] that we cannot without more ado go straightaway behind appearance."[99] As a matter of fact, Hegel could, if he wanted to, take us straight to the truth: that Spirit awaits us behind that curtain. The reason Hegel asserts, falsely, that we can't do what Dorothy and Toto did—go straight past the curtain to the Wizard—is that Hegel wants to escort us through twenty-one more thesis-antithesis-synthesis dialectics ("more ado") that begin eight pages later with the master-and-slave dialectic. (These twenty-one don't count the Introduction's dialectic, which is the first microdialectic.) Hegel is at heart a puzzle maker. He has deluded himself into believing that only by forcing us to practice by solving a lot of little dialectical puzzles can he give us the skill needed to solve the big puzzle. The big puzzle is an unmentioned maze, the macrodialectic, that lies behind the curtain and that, if properly navigated, will lead us to Absolute Spirit.

Chapter 3

SPIRIT, UNCONSCIOUSNESS, THE MACRODIALECTIC, AND FREEDOM

In this chapter I will open the metaphorical doors to (1) Hegel's Spirit, (2) Hegel's thesis-antithesis-synthesis dialectics, and (3) Hegel's eccentric concept of freedom. These doors have never before been opened. Hegel's most important dialectic encompasses the entirety of *Phenomenology of Spirit*. I call this dialectic the macrodialectic, because it takes 493 pages in Miller's translation to reach its conclusion. "Macrodialectic" differentiates this overarching dialectic from shorter dialectics: the Preface dialectic (chapter 2), the Introduction dialectic (chapter 2), four much shorter table-of-contents-heading dialectics (chapter 4), twenty-two even shorter microdialectics (chapter 4), and ten history dialectics (chapter 5). In the present chapter, I first explain Hegel's concept of Spirit, a complicated four-part, two-level concept no previous interpretation has recognized. Next, I discuss the Christian-theology-based concept of separation and return, which is the foundation on which the dialectical superstructure is erected. Then I show how Hegel uses Christianity's Trinity to symbolize both separation and return and the three stages of his macrodialectic. I go on to explain the macrodialectic itself, its underlying concept of Spirit's prehuman unconscious (mindless) state of union, the macrodialectic's twenty-seven variants (not to be confused with the twenty-two microdialectics), and the concepts these variants embody. Finally, I discuss *Phenomenology*'s misunderstood concept of freedom and its dependent relationship to the implied concept of bondage—bondage to the imaginary Judeo-Christian God symbolized by the master of the master-and-slave parable.

SPIRIT: A NONSUPERNATURAL PHYSICAL-MENTAL "ORGANISM"

Hegel's philosophy revolves around the Spirit (*Geist*). To fully understand the macrodialectic, you must understand what Spirit is. Such understanding will be facilitated if you first understand two other things. First, Spirit is neither metaphysical (as I once believed) nor in any other sense supernatural;[1] it is not pantheistic, panentheistic, theistic, or deistic, and neither is it something with which a mystic can commune. Second, it is closely analogous to Paul Tillich's nonsupernatural "God above the God of theism," which is analogically based on Hegel's Spirit and has both a physical and a mental side, each of which has a universal (general) and a particular feature. In the following three subsections, I will examine both of these characteristics and then explain Hegel's concept of Spirit.

A Nonsupernatural Spirit. Roughly half of those Hegel interpreters who have arrived at an intelligible interpretation of Spirit have concluded that Spirit is either a pantheistic concept or a panentheistic concept. Pantheism is popularly viewed as the belief that God is either nature or the universe. But this view is false. "God is nature" is not a belief. It is a *definition*, really a redefinition. It is an arbitrary definition of God used by timid souls who no longer believe in God but are afraid to admit they are atheists. When someone says God is nature, that person is using an unnecessary and misleading word to say what is really meant: "I don't believe in God."

Properly understood, pantheism is the doctrine that there exists *within* everything in nature an impersonal metaphysical "substance" or "essence" that binds the particulars together into the whole. Spinoza's pantheism is a possible example, although I have my doubts that Spinoza really attached to "substance" the metaphysical or mystical meaning usually attributed to it. For amplification of my point that "God is nature" is a definition and not a belief, I again turn to Paul Tillich, who understood Hegel better than did anyone else. Tillich also happens to be a well-read, comprehending scholar of philosophy and theology. He describes what pantheism really means:

> Pantheism does not mean, and never has meant, and never should mean that everything that is, is God. If God is identified with nature (*deus sive*

natura), it is not the totality of natural objects which is called God but rather the creative power and unity of nature, the absolute substance which is present in everything. . . . Pantheism is the doctrine that God is the substance [Spinoza] or essence of all things, not the meaningless assertion that God is the totality of all things.[2]

Elsewhere Tillich describes the false concept of "the God of pantheism" with these words: "Wherever the concept of the world is complete without God [i.e., where no transcendent supernatural mind exists above the universe], God has become an empty name that one utters for the sake of religion, but which can be dispensed with completely, since it is all the same whether the universe is called 'matter' or 'spirit.'"[3] Again: "It must be emphasized that pantheism does not say that God is everything. It says that God is the [metaphysical] substance of everything."[4]

Tillich's "God has become an empty name" (when it means the physical universe) remark invites elaboration. If I timidly tell acquaintances that I believe God is nature or the universe, I am probably equivocating. I can assume, or at least hope, that they will misinterpret what I am saying. Although unfamiliar with the term pan*en*theism, they are apt to think I mean God exists as a transcendent supernatural mind—that's presumably why I said "God"—but that God is immanent, within everything, as well as transcendent. But if I use a different atheistic definition of God, "God is coffee" or "God is honesty," my listeners will immediately recognize that I don't *believe* in God. They will see through my dissembling. They will know that I don't *believe* God is coffee but am simply *defining* God as coffee, and that I am doing this for no other reason than to pretend to believe in God. They will understand that I have made the word "God" superfluous: the phrase "this coffee tastes delicious" does the job much better than "this God tastes delicious." By the same token, "birds are a part of nature" is much clearer than "birds are a part of God."

The coffee and honesty examples are not as far-fetched as they might sound. Both Tillich and John A. T. Robinson, Bishop of Woolwich, pretended to believe in God although they were really just redefining God as something nonsupernatural. Tillich redefined God as humanity. He did this using obscurantist language that was easily as foggy as Hegel's. His ambiguities and his use of standard Christian terms, given hidden new definitions, misled almost everyone into believing he was either a theist, a deist, a panentheist, a pantheist, or a mystic. His Hegelian phrasing was so convincing, and misleading, that most readers paid no attention to the facts that he (*a*) explicitly disavowed just about every Christian doctrine,[5] (*b*) said atheism is the correct response to the God of theism,[6] (*c*) denied that his "God above the God of theism"—also called "the ground of being," "being," "being-itself," and "he"—was pantheistic or mystical in character,[7] and (*d*) referred to "something . . . that is fundamental to *all* my thinking—the anti-supernaturalistic attitude."[8] Bishop Robinson, heavily influenced by Tillich (whom he did not fully understand) and by Dietrich Bonhoeffer, was somewhat more open, though still evasive, in declaring his atheism. He redefined God as Love, which he capitalized.[9] We see that *defining* God as X is not the same as *believing* God is X. This axiom applies regardless of whether God is defined as coffee, honesty, humanity, Love, nature, or the universe.

Some interpreters, including eleven whose views I will examine in chapter 6, graft onto pantheism the concept of a transcendent, rational, self-conscious, theistic God akin to the God of Christianity, Judaism, and Islam. The God of pantheism thus acquires an independent mind and a presumed interest in and an inclination to interfere in human affairs. This blending of pantheism and theism—an immanent God (within everything) and a transcendent God (apart from everything)—is called pan*en*theism, spelled with that *en* in the middle.

Hegel's Spirit is neither pantheistic nor panentheistic. Certainly the best evidence of this is the nonsupernatural structure of Hegel's Spirit, but that structure will have to wait until we get some other matters out of the way. Another fault of the pantheism-panentheism interpretation is the effete state into which metaphysics had declined by the time Hegel wrote *Phenomenology*: science and reason had reduced supernaturalistic speculation about "being" to a state of low repute. Beiser, in an outstanding background essay on Hegel's thought—outstanding except for its nonsupernatural concept of "metaphysics," used in reference to Hegel's thought—provides context. He writes, "The term 'metaphysics' had fallen into disrepute by the early 1800s, as Hegel himself noted, so reviving it would have been impossible without invoking negative connotations."[10] Beiser elaborates: "Schelling and Hegel . . . insist that their metaphysics has nothing to do with the supernatural [in which case Beiser shouldn't call it metaphysics]. Their conception of metaphysics is indeed profoundly naturalistic. They banish all occult forces and the supernatural from the universe, explaining everything in terms of natural laws."[11]

A related point is that Hegel, though indoctrinated in the Lutheran religion as a child, rejected it in his college years and became vehemently antireligious. His antireligious attitude is seen in, among other places, his early religious writings and *Phenomenology*'s sections dealing with Unhappy Consciousness and "The Revealed Religion." I will examine the *Phenomenology* material later in this chapter when I describe the Trinitarian symbolism in Hegel's macrodialectic. For now, a superficial summary of "The Revealed Religion" will have to do. Hegel treats the death of Jesus, theology's incarnate God, as the death of God. Not just God on earth but God in heaven too. Whereas Christian theology says Jesus was resurrected and that he returned to heaven, Hegel treats the resurrection differently. Hegel transmogrifies (as a Christian might view this development) the Holy Spirit, which supposedly repossessed the resurrected Jesus and thereby united him with God in the Trinity, into just plain Spirit, a radically different concept. And instead of possessing God-Jesus, who is dead and stays dead, Spirit possesses all human beings. All humans become part of Spirit. Man becomes God. This is atheism, pure and simple.

Hegel's unqualified atheism has been recognized by the more perceptive interpreters: Beiser (quoted above), Tucker, McCarney, Solomon, Hyppolite, Findlay, Kaufmann, Pinkard, and Westphal. McCarney seems to accept the idea that Hegel is a metaphysical pantheist, but he nevertheless understands that Hegel's "God" is in no sense Christianity's God. The views of these interpreters provide considerable insight into Hegel's antitheistic, antipanentheistic concept of Spirit.

Tucker writes: "Hegelianism . . . is a religion of self-worship whose fundamental theme is given in Hegel's image of the man who aspires to be God himself, who demands 'something more, namely, infinity.' The whole system is spun out of the formula concerning man's self-elevation from finite to infinite life. The finite mind [man's] is seen as aggrandizing itself to infinity, becoming universal [God's] mind."[12] Hegel thus "gives us a picture of a self-glorifying humanity striving compulsively, and at the end successfully, to rise to divinity."[13] This is atheism: "From the standpoint of the Hebraic-Christian theology, which places God above and beyond nature and history, this would of course have to be qualified as 'atheism.'"[14]

McCarney firmly refutes the view that Hegel's references to "God" are affirmations of the God of Christianity. Hegel "conspicuously fails to endorse what is surely the simple essence of the matter for ordinary Christians, the unique status of Jesus as the incarnate second person of the Trinity. His [Jesus's] role for Hegel is that of making manifest a universal truth [the truth that *all* men are incarnations of "God"] rather than of personally embodying a singular one [Jesus alone as God incarnate]. Jesus is the emblem [symbol] of and witness to the unity of the divine and the human, not its sole exemplar and meeting point. It follows that, however outstanding he [Jesus] may be in that role, he does not partake essentially of the divine nature in any qualitatively different sense from any other member of the human race."[15]

Solomon uses Hegel's treatment of the Unhappy Consciousness to emphasize Hegel's antagonism toward Christianity's God: "What is . . . obvious but not so often recognized is the extremely sarcastic tone in which the entire section [on Unhappy Consciousness] is cast. Hegel despises traditional Christianity just as much in 1806 as he did in 1793 [in his early writings on Christianity], and his treatment of Catholicism is particularly vicious."[16]

Turning to Hegel's discussion of "The Revealed Religion" (Christianity), Solomon points out how Hegel demolishes the divine God and the uniquely divine Christ, at the same time transforming the Holy Spirit into Hegel's Spirit. "He [Hegel] even pokes fun at the very idea of a 'Trinity' (Why not a Quaternity, or even a five-in-one? he asks (776 [Miller's translation]). In Hegel's search for Spirit, however, it is the Father and the Son who are sacrificed to the third term; God is reduced to pure thought ['picture-thinking'] and the Son becomes no one in particular [just another incarnation of the divine]. . . . God is nothing but the Holy Spirit, and the Holy Spirit is only in us."[17] Solomon concludes that Hegel does not "believe anything that a thorough-going atheistic humanist cannot believe. . . . Does he believe in any sense in a God other than ourselves, in the Divinity of Christ in the only sense that can be called 'Christian,' in the literal or at least symbolic truth or much (if not all) of the Scriptures? The answer seems to be in every case 'no.'"[18] In subsequent comments, Solomon again labels Hegel an atheist: "What then does Hegel's conception of God admit which any atheist would not? To say that God exists is no more than to say that humanity exists. That is atheism."[19]

Like Solomon, Hyppolite turns to Hegel's "Revealed Religion" discussion to confirm Hegel's atheism. Hegel wrote that "the death of the divine Man [Jesus] . . . ends only in *natural* universality."[20] Hegel's italicizing of "natural" emphasizes the distinction between supernatural and natural. The God of Christianity's "revealed religion" is supernatural and universal; Hegel is saying that God—Spirit—has become natural and universal. "Natural" refers to man, who is natural rather than supernatural. The idea of a supernatural God incarnated in just one man is replaced by the idea of a natural God, "the Spirit who dwells in His community, dies in it every day, and is daily resurrected."[21] God has become mankind, which experiences daily deaths and births (resurrections). Hyppolite has no trouble understanding what Hegel is saying: "The death of Christ is not only the death of the God-man [God on earth, the second person of the Trinity], but also the death of the abstract God [God in heaven, the first person of the Trinity] whose transcendence radically separated human existence from his divine essence."[22]

Findlay characterizes Hegel as anti-metaphysical, an enemy of supernaturalism, and thus a disbeliever in God. He writes: "Hegel's philosophy is one of the most anti-metaphysical of philosophical systems, one that *remains* most within the pale of ordinary experience, and which accords no place to entities or properties lying beyond that experience, or to facts undiscoverable by ordinary methods of investigation. Hegel often speaks the language of a metaphysical theology, but such language, it is plain, is a mere concession to the pictorial mode of religious expression. As a philosopher, Hegel believes in no God and no Absolute except the one that is revealed and known in certain experiences of individual human beings."[23] Findlay also remarks that, "despite his later verging towards reaction, he remains the philosopher . . . of liberal Humanism."[24]

Kaufmann comes down hard on the notion that Spirit is transcendent. Hegel's description of Spirit "should have caused no misunderstanding, had it not been for Hegel's occasional references to God."[25] Hegel did not believe in God, and his

"God" was not the God of theism: "The *Phenomenology of the Spirit* ends with the death of God, with Golgotha [Calvary hill]. . . . To put it in our own words: there is no supreme being beyond."[26] Later, Kaufmann says this: "[Hegel's] God comes into being only when man 'knows' him. Findlay has therefore called Hegel 'the philosopher . . . of liberal Humanism.' One may cavil at 'liberal': the temperament of the mature Hegel was conservative rather than liberal. But his religious position may be safely characterized as a form of humanism."[27]

Pinkard and M. Westphal recognize Hegel's unqualified antisupernaturalism by presenting totally nonsupernaturalistic interpretations of Spirit. Both interpreters hold that Spirit is society or certain aspects of society. Although these interpretations are wrong in their specifics—Spirit is not society or facets thereof—they are right in affirming that Spirit is nonsupernatural. In chapter 6, I will discuss these two interpretations in more detail. For now, we merely need recognize that Pinkard and Westphal view Hegel as an atheist. His "God" is a figurative God.

The Tillich Analogy. Both Tillich's nonsupernatural God, humanity, and Hegel's nonsupernatural God, Spirit, have the same structure. This is not at all surprising: Tillich used Hegel's Spirit, along with Hegel's dialectics, as the model he copied. Tillich's deceptively labeled "God" and Hegel's Spirit, also called "God" in many places, both have these two characteristics: (1) they have a physical side and a mental side and (2) both sides are subdivided into (*a*) a general or "universal" characteristic and (*b*) a particularistic characteristic. In outline form, and in the abstract, both Gods look like this:

1. Physical Side (tangible)

   a. General (universal)
   b. Particular

2.
   Mental Side (intangible)
   a. General (universal)
   b. Particular

Moving from the abstract to the concrete, we find that Tillich's "God above the God of theism" has the following structure:

1. Physical Side: humanity (tangible)
   a. General: humanity itself, the "universe" of human beings
      (the infinite)
                  b. Particular: individual human beings (the finite)
2. Mental Side: ultimate concern (intangible)
                  a. General: A humanist's ultimate concern for humanity
               b. Particular: "Preliminary" concerns that are "transparent to"
   humanity

The physical side of Tillich's God shouldn't create any comprehension problems. But the mental side will be unfamiliar to most Hegel scholars and are a source of confusion to Tillich's would-be interpreters. (The confusion results from Tillich's ambiguous use of "ultimate concern," which sometimes refers to the general and sometimes to the particular.) An ultimate concern is whatever is the highest or supreme concern, that which is "absolute," for a particular person. It can be anything. It can be one's country, one's religious community, power, money, or fame. Any concern that is "transparent to" less than all of humanity is "demonic" or "idolatrous" (both words mean the same thing). One's country and one's religious community are therefore idolatrous. Power, money, and fame are among the worst concerns: they are transparent to just one individual. Humanity is Tillich's ultimate concern, and he thinks it should be everyone's. Tillich identifies humanity as the ultimate concern of humanists: "For humanism the divine is manifest in the human; the ultimate concern of man is man."[28]

A preliminary concern is a particular concern that reflects (is "transparent to" in Tillich's metaphor) the general concern. If a religious fanatic detonates a car bomb intended to kill members of a different religion or different religious sect, the preliminary concern is killing people and the truly ultimate concern is the fanatic's religion, or perhaps its god. If a woman dives into a lake to save a drowning child, her preliminary concern is saving the child. Her ultimate concern is humanity, of which the child is a part.

The four-part, two-level Tillichian God undergoes a dialectical "divine life." This is the life of Yes-No-Yes described in chapter 1. The second Yes is "the negation of the negation," the negation of the No. In the divine life man progresses from theism to atheism to humanism. The divine life goes like this:

- The initial Yes, theism, finds man potentially united with God. The union is only potential because man worships the wrong God, the God of theism. This stage is the dialectic's thesis: Yes to God + Yes to supernaturalism (also: potential + union).

- The No, the antithesis of Yes, is atheism: man rejects the God of theism. Man is now actually separated from God: he has gone from *potential* union to *actual* separation. He is now in a state of self-estrangement. He sees other humans, but he is unaware that they are himself, God—because all humans are God. The human (finite) is estranged from humanity (infinite). This stage is the antithesis: No to God + No to supernaturalism (also: actual + separation).

- Finally, man sees the light, the second Yes of Yes-No-Yes. He realizes that he himself is God: humanity is God, and he is a particular representative of humanity. The other humans he sees are himself, because he and they are both humanity. This stage is the synthesis: Yes to God + No to supernaturalism (also: actual + union).

Note once again that in both versions of the dialectic—Hegel's and Tillich's—the synthesis borrows one part from the two-part thesis and one from the two-part antithesis.

Hegel's Spirit Identified. In the Tillichian divine life (theism-atheism-humanism), humanity is metaphorically conceived as a living organism. Hegel's Spirit is conceived the same way: it is metaphorically (figuratively, not literally) a living organism. And it has its own divine life, which Hegel calls "the life of the Spirit."[29] Beiser, without recognizing the concrete meaning of his abstract description, provides informative background material on the divine life of Hegel's Spirit:

> What Schelling meant by describing the absolute as "subject-object identity" is *apparently* Spinozistic: the mental and the physical, the subjective and objective, are only different attributes of a single infinite substance. . . . Schelling saw substance as a living force . . . [found in] all of nature.

. . . Schelling thought he had good reason to conceive of the absolute in organic . . . terms. . . . Hegel inherited this organic conception of the absolute from Schelling in the early 1800s, the period of their collaboration on the *Critical Journal of Philosophy* (1802–04). Hegel accepted the broad outlines of Schelling's conception of the absolute. . . .

Nevertheless, even during their collaboration, Hegel began to have serious doubts about some of Schelling's formulations of the nature of the absolute. . . . Schelling sometimes spoke of the absolute as if it were nothing more than "subject-object identity.". . . Hegel felt that it was necessary to correct Schelling's restricted formulation of the absolute. . . . [But] all his life Hegel adhered to Schelling's organic [the figuratively living organism] concept of the absolute.[30]

Hegel's revised absolute became Spirit. In "subject-object," subject is the mental aspect of Spirit—the mind, which produces thought, opinion, perception, and interpretation. Or, as *The American Heritage College Dictionary* explains, subjective means "proceeding from or taking place within a person's mind such as to be unaffected by the external world." Object is the physical aspect of Spirit—the external world, the world of matter. Tillich's four-part God, we saw, has a definite separation of the physical and mental sides of God. Hegel, like Tillich (or more correctly Tillich, like Hegel), conceives the absolute as, figuratively, a living organism. Spirit has the following form:

1. Physical side: the universe—both natural and artificial objects (objective, tangible)
    a. General: the universe conceived of as *one* entity
    b. Particular: the *many* particular "objects" that constitute the universe

2. Mental side: the human mind (subjective, intangible)
    a. General: Mind, the collective Mind of humans (Spirit's Mind)
    b. Particular: minds (the minds and thoughts of individual humans)

The natural-and-artificial aspect of the physical side of Spirit requires amplification. In several places, Hegel identifies Spirit as encompassing "all reality."[31] All reality includes man-made or artificial objects. Hegel emphasizes this by constructing both a natural-artificial microdialectic (chapter 4) and a natural-artificial history dialectic (chapter 5). Both go from natural (thesis) to artificial (antithesis) to natural *and* artificial (synthesis). Spirit thus includes not only the stars, comets, the moon, clouds, mountains, lakes, pebbles, trees, dandelions, moss, bears, birds, worms, and humans but also houses, shoes, bread, boats, paintings, saucers, wine, fences, axes, and doorknobs. The inclusion of artificial objects in the concept of Spirit is further supported by the "Actuality and Faith" dialectic, described in chapter 4. I emphasize the inclusion of artificial objects in the concept of Spirit because this feature (in addition to other considerations) refutes three interpretations of Spirit that I review in chapter 6. Two of these interpretations come from Pinkard and Westphal. Both of them argue that Spirit is society or certain of its characteristics. The third interpretation is one of three presented by Solomon: Spirit is "us, nothing more," meaning humanity. Neither society nor humanity is partly artificial.

The natural-artificial dichotomy also helped Hegel defend himself against charges of pantheism, a form of atheism. McCarney describes the problem succinctly: "One needs to invoke the fact . . . of the difficulty, indeed pre-cariousness, of Hegel's personal situation in the final period in Berlin. This showed itself in, for instance, his vulnerability to the charge of pantheism, a charge virtually indistinguishable from atheism in the eyes of his enemies at Court."[32] Hegel was in the same precarious situation in his earlier position at the University of Jena, where he wrote *Phenomenology*.[33] Were his atheism to become known, Hegel would be out of a job. Technically speaking, Hegel's God was not a God of pantheism. Hegel's version of the universe had no metaphysical substance, and Spirit's status as God was a matter of definition rather than belief. But Spirit was close enough to being a pantheistic god that these distinctions didn't matter. By including artificial things in his concept of Spirit, Hegel could privately distinguish Spirit from Spinoza's "substance," which was present only in nature. Two other distinctions also helped: Spirit had that *dialectical* "life," and Spirit placed heavy emphasis on the mental aspect of the god, Spirit's Mind. With these three distinctions in place, Hegel could deny charges of pantheism by privately meaning that his God lacked the attributes of Spinoza's pantheistic God—and had attributes that Spinoza's "substance" lacked. In particular, his God was not Spinoza's, the invisible essence of nature alone, artificial objects excluded.

Turning to the mental side of Spirit, we encounter a remarkable feature. Spirit's Mind, the collective minds of humans, is extremely active. It produces that parade or "succession" (Hegel's word) of human thoughts or "spirits" (lowercase) that Kaufmann referred to in this earlier quotation: "The infinite spirit has to be found in the comprehension of this world, in the study of the spirits summoned in the *Phenomenology*." Those thoughts or spirits are the product of the human mind. The human mind is Spirit's Mind, its only Mind. This fact makes you wonder whether *Phenomenology of Mind*, the title Baillie's translation gives to Hegel's book, isn't superior to Miller's title, *Phenomenology of Spirit*. Solomon informs us that "phenomenology (the word Hegel borrowed from Herder and Kant, among others) is 'the study of phenomena,' the systematic description of experience, trying to make sense of it and showing it to have a certain 'necessity.'"[34] Because Hegel's *Phenomenology* indeed does study the experience of thought, which emanates from Spirit's Mind, Hegel's book does describe the phenomenology of Mind. *Phenomenology* is about the experiences—or more precisely, the *products*—of Mind as it marches through history. The products are customs, moral beliefs, laws, religions, philosophies, literature, theories, superstitions, and other things that emanate from the human mind.

Mind's march through history ties in with the problem of subject-object identity, viewed in the context of Schelling's organic concept of the absolute. Subject-object identity is part of this organic concept of the absolute. Hegel's view of subject-object identity is considerably different from Schelling's. True, both Schelling's absolute and Hegel's renamed Spirit include both the subjective (mental) and the objective (physical) side of reality. In Schelling's thought man, whose mind provides subjectivity, was certainly present in nature, the absolute. Man was even a focal point. Schelling had written that "God must become man, in order that man comes again to God."[35] Here we see that Schelling was every bit as concerned as Hegel was about deifying man. But Schelling certainly didn't emphasize man's *mind* the way Hegel did. With Hegel, Mind's travels are what *Phenomenology* is about. And this is where the difference between Schelling's and Hegel's subject-object identity materializes. In Hegel's thought, subject

(Spirit's Mind, consciousness) and object (things perceived by consciousness) are *nonidentical* until the very end of *Phenomenology*. Subject mistakenly thinks the objects it perceives, objects that are essentially itself (Spirit), are "alien," things other than itself. Only at the end of the book, where Hegel comes along and, acting as Spirit's Mind, recognizes that subject (mind, itself) and object (nature, including man) are identical—that both are Spirit—do subject and object become identical. Only then does subject recognize object as *itself*. Only then does Spirit achieve Absolute Knowledge and thereby become Absolute Spirit. Only then does the "absolute" become a reality.

Kroner treats Hegel's philosophy as, in part, an effort to achieve what Schelling tried to achieve—a reconciliation of nature and mind. Kroner writes, "Schelling, at least in these years of companionship with Hegel [at the University of Jena], was convinced that ultimately the unity of nature and mind had to be conceived in terms of a universal philosophy of nature and not in those of a universal philosophy of mind."[36] Schelling's endeavor was unsuccessful; it was "a leap into intuition . . . which violated the intellect without reconciling it with intuition."[37] Hegel took up Schelling's abortive effort by devising the concept of Spirit, which Kroner unfortunately does not understand. (Kroner thinks Hegel believes in God and that Spirit is a panentheistic entity.) Spirit has those two sides, the physical side (predominantly nature) and the mental side (human minds). Part of the difference between Schelling's philosophy and Hegel's is that Hegel augments nature by adding artificial (non-natural, man-made) objects to the physical dimension. That dimension is all reality, or the physical universe. Nevertheless, the physical side of Spirit consists primarily of nature. And the mental side is mind, the human mind, which of course derives from nature: man is a part of nature. Hegel's four-faceted Spirit thus achieves what Schelling failed to achieve, "the unity of nature and mind." I should add that Hegel differentiates his philosophy from Schelling's not only by (*a*) augmenting nature with artificial objects but by (*b*) substituting for Schelling's philosophy of nature a philosophy of "all reality," a philosophy that makes mind (subject) far more important than nature or matter (objects).

You might wonder how the four-faceted Spirit, which has a clearly visible outer physical side, can be the hidden "inner" essence of objects. Here we must distinguish between (*a*) Spirit as a mental concept or idea and (*b*) Spirit as "all reality." Hegel uses the word Spirit in both senses—the concept and all reality. It is the *concept* of Spirit that is the "inner" essence of every object in the universe. You might also wonder how Spirit can be partly mental when most of the objects perceived by subject are nonhuman and thus have no mental side. That problem is easily disposed of. Hegel treats Spirit as a living organism with a divine life. It is analogous to living human beings. Just as humans have many parts—the head, neck, chest, abdomen, arms, legs, hands, and feet—but have mentality only in the head, Spirit has many parts (the many perceived objects) but has mentality only in the human parts.

We saw that Tillich treats God metaphorically as a living organism with a dialectical divine life. Since Tillich's God is based on Hegel's, we should expect that Hegel's God—Spirit—is similar. Our expectations are realized. Hegel too conceives Spirit metaphorically as a living organism; it has a divine life, which is both (a) the macrodialectic, the divine life's general aspects, and (*b*) *Phenomenology*'s long parade of "spirits," the divine life's details. The long parade is the antithesis stage, or conscious + separation, of the macrodialectic. Hegel calls this life "the life of the Spirit," a life whose goal is to achieve "the awareness of what it really is in itself."[38] Spirit's divine life is where the Schelling-Hegel "organic concept of the absolute," described by Beiser, comes into play. At the highest level of abstraction, no difference exists between Tillich's and Hegel's versions of the divine life:

- Tillich: (1) *thesis*: potential union, (2) *antithesis*: actual separation, (3) *synthesis*: actual union
- Hegel: (1) *thesis*: potential union, (2) *antithesis*: actual separation, (3) *synthesis*: actual union

It is when we get into the divine life's details that the Tillich and Hegel versions differ. In the Tillichian divine life, man progresses from theism to atheism to humanism. In the Hegelian divine life, Spirit progresses from unconsciousness to consciousness to self-consciousness.

A final point about Spirit: Hegel did not actually *believe* in Spirit. He no more believed in Spirit than Bishop Robinson believed God is Love, a human emotion. Spirit is not an eccentric concept of a supernatural God that differs from the God of customary belief. No, Spirit is just a *definition*—an arbitrary definition not based on customary usage. It is a definition used for philosophical purposes. As such, it represents neither truth nor falsehood. Like Tillich's humanity, Spirit is just a figurative God, an ersatz God.

SEPARATION AND RETURN

To understand Hegel's thesis-antithesis-synthesis dialectics you must first understand that they are analogically based on Christian theology. Tillich has written, "Obviously—and it was so intended by Hegel—his dialectics are the religious symbols of estrangement and reconciliation conceptualized and reduced to empirical descriptions."[39] In another passage, Tillich identifies estrangement and reconciliation with separation and return and with the divine: "The doctrine of the Trinity [Tillich's version] does not affirm the logical nonsense that three is one and one is three; it describes in dialectical terms the inner movement of the divine life as an eternal separation from itself and return to itself."[40] Correspondingly, Hegel wrote that the Spirit "becomes estranged and then *returns* [reconciliation] to itself from estrangement, and is only then presented in its actuality and truth and becomes the property of [recognized by] consciousness" (my italics).[41] (Note, incidentally, the references to "actuality" and "truth" as characteristics of Spirit's self-realization.) Hegel also wrote that "the third stage [of his macrodialectic] is the *return* of the self [Spirit] thus alienated [separated from itself, antithesis stage] . . . into its first [thesis stage] primal simplicity" (my italics).[42]

Hegel's primary separation-and-return theme, the macrodialectic, depicts a purely conceptual Spirit—an idea—that (1) begins as an unconscious union ("one") of constituent parts (everything in the universe), then (2) becomes conscious and consciously separates into a multitude of observed "objects" ("many"), and ultimately (3) returns—consciously this time—to its original state of union. The reunion or "return" takes place when Spirit consciously recognizes that the many constitute the one ("one composed of many," "one = many"). Other dialectical formulations depict "consciousness"—the human mind advancing through history—as separating from and returning to a wide variety of things: divinity, freedom, monarchy, essence, truth, predation, one, subject, nature, and so on—whatever the dialectic's thesis concept happens to be.

Hegelian separation and return actually has two antecedents in Christian theology. The first features Adam and Eve. They represent mankind. Adam and Eve are (1) initially united—*union*—with God (i.e., on good terms with God) in the Garden of Eden. Tillich confirms that Adam-God unity is the initial state to which he alludes in his "religious symbols of estrangement and reconciliation" quotation in my earlier paragraph: "Mythologically speaking, Adam before the fall was in an essential, though untested and undecided, unity with God."[43] Note that "essential" is equivalent to the concept of "essence." "Untested" means potential, so we have a state of "potential essence." Then (2) Adam and Eve sin by eating the forbidden fruit. God punishes them by casting them out of Eden. They are now estranged or separated—*separation*—from God. In Christian doctrine, this act of separating from God is "the Fall." Tillich writes that "in Hegel's system. . . . the Fall is reduced to the difference between ideality [Eden] and reality [outside of Eden]."[44] The ideal is not the real. The Fall is "the transition from essence to existence."[45] "Existence," then, is to be understood as the state in which Spirit, hence man, is estranged from himself through failure to recognize himself as Spirit, or God. Finally, (3) Jesus redeems mankind through his sacrificial death on the cross. The crucifixion vicariously punishes mankind for the "original sin" of Adam and Eve. Mankind, including Adam and Eve, can now go to heaven. They can be reunited—*reunion*—with God. Union, separation, reunion.

In theology's second separation-and-return drama, God separates from and returns to himself in heaven. John 1:14 portrays Jesus as God incarnate: "the Logos became flesh and dwelt among us." (John is proselytizing a Hellenistic—culturally Greek—audience by identifying God with the Greek Logos, misleadingly translated as "Word" in the New Testament. To oversimplify, the Logos was an impersonal metaphysical force that supposedly influenced developments in history and society.) God (1) is initially *one* being, dwelling in heaven. Then (2) God *separates* from himself, becoming *two* beings—the Father in heaven and the Son (God incarnate) on earth. God actually prays to himself: "Our Father, who art in heaven, . . ." God has become self-estranged, self-alienated.

Now the Johannine story gets a little complicated: there are two versions of how God in heaven and God on earth are reunited. In one version, God incarnate is crucified and (3a) *returns* to himself—he becomes reunited with himself—in heaven. There (according to the Apostles' Creed) the Son "sitteth at the right hand of God the Father Almighty." In the second version of reunion, Jesus (God incarnate) is baptized by John the Baptist.[46] As soon as Jesus gets out of the water, the heavens open and (3b) the Holy Spirit descends on him like a dove. Spirit possession thus reunites God incarnate, dwelling on earth, with God in heaven, even though they remain spatially separated. When Jesus, the Son, finally does get to heaven, he remains bound to the Father by the Holy Spirit, which binds the three together in the Trinity.

The Holy Spirit version of the incarnation-of-God story is what Hegel primarily uses for his separation-and-return symbolism. But the Adam and Eve myth provides a better fit for the antithesis stage, since the two sinners become morally as well as spatially *estranged* from God. (The spatial estrangement results when Adam and Eve are kicked out of Eden, where God is present.) The reason Hegel emphasizes the Johannine tale in its Holy Spirit version is that it allows him to base his dialectics on not just one but two Christian theology antecedents. The first is the one just described: God's separation from and return to himself. The second antecedent is the Trinity: Father, Son, and Holy Spirit.

Here is how Hegel uses Christianity's Trinity:

1. **Father:** Before the arrival on earth of the Son, the Father is the only God. There is just *one* God, united with himself—not separated into Father and Son, or God and God incarnate. So "Father" symbolizes two alternative thesis concepts: (*a*) one and (*b*) union. For the moment, the union is only potential, for the union that really counts is a higher form of union, that of God and man.

2. **Son:** The Son (Jesus, God incarnate) eventually materializes. God separates from himself, coming to earth while remaining in heaven. On earth, God assumes the form of humanity, which represents the concept of many (many humans constitute humanity). So "Son"

symbolizes two alternative antithesis concepts: (*a*) many (the antithesis of one) and (*b*) separation (the antithesis of union).

3. **Holy Spirit:** The Son grows up and is baptized. Immediately thereafter the Holy Spirit possesses him. Through this act of spirit possession, God incarnate on earth is reunited with himself, God in heaven. So the Holy Spirit symbolizes two alternative synthesis concepts: (*a*) one composed of many (or one = many), with Jesus still representing the many humans, and (*b*) union—this time the *actual* union of God and man, the man being Jesus.

In *Phenomenology*, the Holy Spirit metamorphoses into Hegel's Spirit. Spirit is "all reality," everything in the universe. As such, it includes man. Man, indeed, is Spirit's most vital constituent, the only constituent that really counts. For one thing, man provides Spirit with a mind, and therefore with consciousness. Using man's mind, Spirit can now advance from consciousness to self-consciousness or self-realization: Spirit can ultimately become aware that it embraces all reality. Just as important, man's being Spirit's most vital component allows Hegel to express his hidden (but not too well hidden) message: man is God, man is the divine (though only part of the divine).

Hegel grounds his philosophy on separation and return—union, separation, reunion. The Spirit separates from and returns to union, going from potential (unconscious) union to actual estrangement to actual (conscious) union. Lest there be doubt that the state of separation is a dialectical antithesis and that reunion is the synthesis, we can again consult Tillich, one of only three people (the other two were Marx and Engels) who understood Hegel's dialectics. Tillich asserts that "the blood that courses through his [Hegel's] whole system" is "his 'estrangement and reconciliation,' or the more formalized 'antithesis' and 'synthesis.'"[47] There you have it from the man who understood Hegel best: estrangement is the antithesis, and reconciliation (reunion) is the synthesis. And preceding the antithesis, there must be a thesis stage that, by implication, is the union to which Spirit "returns" in the synthesis. (In Tillich's own dialectics, man separates from and returns to union with God: he begins in a state of union with the God of theism, becomes separated—becomes an atheist—and then returns to "the God above the God of theism," humanity.)

THE TRINITY AS "REVEALED RELIGION"

Before examining in detail Hegel's basic Yes-No-Yes dialectic with its antithetical concepts of unconsciousness and consciousness, we need to view more closely the Trinitarian aspect of Hegel's plot. Hegel develops his thoughts about the Trinity in his discussion of "The Revealed Religion" (*Phenomenology* heading VII-C). The "Revealed Religion" is a redefined Christianity with (1) a radically redesigned Father, all material reality plus the human mind, (2) a radically redesigned Son who does not get resurrected but is instead just a representative human, (3) a radically redesigned Holy Spirit who possesses everyone, not just the Son, (4) a radically revised tale of separation and return, and (5) a theology totally stripped of supernaturalism.

Describing Christian belief, Hegel retells the "picture-thinking" (imaginary) story of the Christ. In doing so, he sometimes uses his own concept, "Spirit," to refer to all three members of the Trinity—Father, Son, and Holy Spirit. At other times, he relates the picture-thinking version. His underlying purpose is to show that the picture-thinking separation-and-return story told by Christianity anticipates Spirit's self-realization. Christianity becomes a springboard from which Spirit analogically leaps from (*a*) a picture-thinking union of God and man—man is symbolized by Jesus—to (*b*) Spirit's self-realization, wherein genuine union of God and man occurs. God becomes Spirit, and Jesus is replaced by all mankind.

Near the beginning of his "Revealed Religion" discussion, Hegel says that the "absolute Spirit has given itself *implicitly* the shape of self-consciousness [the shape of a self-conscious human, Jesus]." This shape "now appears as the *belief of the world* that Spirit [used here as a synonym for God incarnate] is *immediately present* as a self-conscious Being, i.e., as an *actual man*."[48] (Important: the incarnation is just a "belief," not a reality.) "*This individual* self-consciousness" (Jesus) is "an antithesis to the universal self-consciousness" (God).[49] Hegel has now implicitly identified the Trinity's Father as the thesis ("universal") and has explicitly identified the Son as the "antithesis" in a dialectic. But there is a problem: "Spirit [the picture-thinking God of Christianity in this context] as an individual Self [as the Son, Jesus] is not yet equally the universal Self, the Self of everyone [the Hegelian, non-picture-thinking 'God,' humanity]."[50] In other words, in this picture-thinking of Christian believers, the God incarnate is just one human, Jesus. He is "not yet" the whole of mankind. We see that Hegel is leading up to an assertion that the true incarnate God, Spirit, is incarnated in *all* humanity, not just in Jesus.

Hegel creeps closer to his point in the next paragraph. There he says that "a consciousness [a conscious human] that sensuously sees and hears Him [Jesus] . . . knows this objective individual [Jesus, perceived by other humans as an 'object'], but not itself, as Spirit [God]."[51] This statement means that a typical Christian believer ("consciousness") recognizes the Son, Jesus, as God incarnate but remains unaware that "itself," the believer, is also God incarnate—because all humans are incarnations of Spirit, the true non-picture-thinking God.

Then Jesus dies: "his *'being'* passes over into *'having been.'*" But despite "the vanishing of the immediate existence known to be absolute being [despite the death of God]. . . . Spirit remains . . . as the *universal self-consciousness* of the [religious] community."[52] God has died in the person of Jesus, but "God" (Spirit) lives on in the living believers, who are *all* incarnations of Spirit. The believers, however, don't realize this. They still use picture-thinking. They imagine God lives in heaven instead of on earth. "This *form of picture-thinking* . . . is not yet Spirit's self-consciousness . . . [because] the mediation [the unifying of God and man] is still incomplete. . . . Before the true content [Spirit as the inner "truth" of all humans] can also receive its true form [man's *awareness* that he is Spirit, the divine], a higher formative development of consciousness is necessary."[53] Hegel, a new conscious mind, must arrive and realize that he and everyone else are incarnations of God.

Spirit, after "descending into existence [contrasted with essence] or into individuality [particularity]"—after moving from thesis to antithesis—must move on to the dialectical synthesis, the third stage or "third moment" of the dialectic. "The third moment is the return [a word from 'separation and *return*'] from picture-thinking [thought, contrasted with the physical 'sub-

stance' of humanity] and otherness [subject's perception of objects as things
other than itself]."[54] This third stage is also "self-consciousness as such,"[55]
which occurs when subject realizes that the perceived object is itself. To
reach the third stage, the synthesis, Spirit must depart from the antithesis
stage, wherein "the object is revealed to it [to consciousness] by [as] something alien [Jesus], and it does not recognize itself [as the same Spirit that
is embodied in the observing subject]."[56] In this movement from antithesis
to synthesis, "Spirit passes over from the second element [the antithesis] . . .
i.e., from picture-thinking [thinking that Jesus alone is God incarnate], into
the third element [the synthesis], self-consciousness [Spirit's recognition of
all humanity—itself—as Spirit]."[57] Notice in these quotations that, despite
Kaufmann's and Pinkard's arguing that Hegel seldom says "antithesis" and
"synthesis," Hegel has other ways of referring to the stages of a dialectic: "
third moment," "second element," "third element," "existence," "negation of
the negation," and so on. And in one place in the quoted lines (three paragraphs back), he actually does say "antithesis" in reference to the second stage
of the dialectic.

The synthesis is the union of God (thesis) and man (antithesis). Man,
represented by Jesus in the antithesis, becomes all humanity in the synthesis.
When this synthesis materializes, "Spirit is . . . posited [made actual] in the
third element [synthesis], in *universal self-consciousness* [not the *particular* self-
consciousness of the Son]; it [Spirit] is its *community*."[58] That is, in the dialectical synthesis God ceases to be a particular self-conscious human, Jesus,
and becomes the "community" of self-conscious humans. Now every human
is God. And, since "God" is Spirit, Christianity's one incarnate God has been
replaced by a "universe" of incarnate gods. Because every human is the incarnation of God, Jesus is no longer unique. And God incarnate is no longer
just a "particular" human being. (At this point, as we shall see in chapter
6, Pinkard and Westphal go astray by assuming that the "community" of
humans is all there is to Spirit. Actually, the human community is merely
what Hegel is emphasizing. Spirit is all reality, everything in the universe.)

Hegel then tells us that, after God dies on the cross, he is resurrected not
as Jesus "ascending unto heaven" (as per the Apostles' Creed) but as an entirely
new and different God who "dwells" on earth in the "community" that is

humanity: "The *death* of the divine Man [the God-man of Christianity] . . . becomes transfigured [redefined] from its immediate meaning, viz., the non-being of this *particular* individual [God], into the *universality* [contrasted with *particularity*] of the Spirit who dwells in His community, dies in it every day, and is daily resurrected."[59]

Two details merit elaboration. First, Hegel's capitalization of "His" underscores his point that the Christian Holy Spirit, which unites God and the *particular* man Jesus, has become the Hegelian Spirit who is the union of the divine and the entire *universe* or community of humans. Whereas the biblical Holy Spirit descended on and possessed Jesus alone (after the baptism), the Hegelian Holy Spirit possesses *every* human being. Second, the reference to daily death and resurrection of the Spirit means that every day some humans die and every day new humans are born. These daily deaths and resurrections remove all doubt that, when Hegel speaks of "the Spirit who dwells in His community," the Spirit is the human race. The transfigured Holy Spirit, the third member of the Trinity, thus symbolizes humanity (plus everything else in the universe).

Is it conceivable that Hegel really does think Jesus was literally resurrected and now dwells in heaven as part of the Trinity? Could the Holy Spirit still unite the Father and the Son? Absolutely not. Hegel pokes fun at the very idea of a Trinity. He scoffs at the counting system used by theologians to get a Trinity. "A multiplicity of other shapes," by implication the angels, saints, and saved souls, exists in heaven. "If these are to be counted"—collectively counted as one—the Trinity might "be more exactly expressed as a quaternity." Moreover, since the angels include two groups—the "good" angels (in heaven) and the "evil" angels (Satan's fallen angels, or demons, from Milton's *Paradise Lost*)—the Trinity "might even be expressed as a five-in-one."[60] You can rest assured that Hegel does not believe Jesus was resurrected and ascended unto heaven to become part of a newly formed Trinity.

Hegel provides still more detail: "This self-consciousness [God in the abstract] therefore does not actually *die*, . . . but its particularity [its status of being just one individual, Jesus] dies away in its [new status as] universality." Is Hegel really saying, "God is dead"? That is exactly what he is saying: "The death of the Mediator [Christianity's God incarnate, Jesus, who reconciles

God and man through his redeeming death on the cross] is the death . . . of the *abstraction* of the divine Being."[61] The abstract God is not Jesus; Jesus is concrete, material. The abstract God is the God of picture-thinking who dwells in heaven. God the Father is dead. He has been replaced by a concrete God, humanity, who lives on earth. "In this way, therefore, Spirit is *self-knowing* Spirit; it knows *itself*."[62] Which is to say, Spirit has achieved self-realization or Absolute Knowledge by becoming aware, through the mind of man (hence through its own Mind), that every man who observes (subject) and every man or thing observed (object) is Spirit. Subject recognizes that object is itself. We have "subject-object identity."

Unfortunately, "the community is not yet perfected in this its self consciousness; in general its content [still] exists for it in the form of *picture-thinking*."[63] "In general" is the key phrase here. The community in general—Hegel is the only exception—does not realize that the true mediation (reconciliation, or synthesis) of God and man has the form of man's realization that he is God, or Spirit. Humans in general remain stuck on picture-thinking. They continue to think that Jesus's death mediated the split between God and man (the split that began with the "original sin" of Adam and Eve) by vicariously punishing man. The humans think Jesus has borne their punishment, thereby qualifying them to be reunited with God *in heaven* (not on earth) after the death of their mortal bodies (but not of their immortal souls). Therefore, true self-realization of Spirit must await the final pages of *Phenomenology*. This true self-realization "is a reconciliation that lies in the beyond." Picture-thought provides implicit self-realization, "but this merely *implicit* [potential] unity is not [yet] realized [actual]."[64]

Notice the words "for it," equivalent to "for itself," buried in the quotation in the first sentence of the preceding paragraph. I pointed out in chapter 2 that "for itself" (from the duo "in itself" and "for itself") is one of Hegel's ways of referring to an antithesis. The community still thinks God is the imaginary or "picture-thinking" God. He is the God in heaven, the God who is pictured as a separate being—separate from the human observers. In saying "for it," Hegel is saying that the humans are still in the antithesis stage of separation—separation from the true God, Spirit. This antithesis is the middle stage of union-separation-reunion (thesis-antithesis-synthesis). Notice also that the words "for it" could be removed from the sentence without altering the sentence's meaning. Then why are the words there? They are there to remind people who understand Hegelese that the stage of picture-thinking is the dialectic's antithesis.

Hegel smuggles another dialectic, the last of the long series of microdialectics, into his analysis of "The Revealed Religion." (A microdialectic is a dialectic that covers relatively few pages—in contrast to the macrodialectic, which covers the entire book.) This microdialectic features the antithesis between the opposing concepts of *thought* and *substance*. "Pure thought," or picture-thinking, is the thesis. Actual "substance," or physical reality, is the antithesis. This physical substance should not be confused with anything resembling the metaphysical "substance" of Spinoza's pantheism. The "substance" is now nonmetaphysical; it is something material, tangible; it is *humanity*—sometimes just one human, Jesus, and sometimes all human beings.

This dialectic moves from (1) pure thought, an imaginative mental picture of a divine God, to (2) substance, the actual physical reality of a human being, Jesus, to (3) an unrecognized synthesis of thought (the heavenly Father) and substance (the human Son). In the synthesis, the thought of a divine God becomes the reality of a divine humanity. This movement is, in effect, a movement from (1) Father, the picture-thinking God of pure *thought*, to (2) Son, the human Jesus who was a real person and thus had real physical *substance*, to (3) Holy Spirit, which unites Father and Son, thought and substance. But in the synthesis, (*a*) the Holy Spirit becomes the Hegelian Spirit, (*b*) Father becomes the concept "divine," and (*c*) Son becomes the concept "human." Spirit unites the divine and the human; they become one. God is man. Man is God.

Hegel describes this thought-substance dialectic. "The element of pure thought [first dialectical stage] . . . passes over into [changes into] the element [second dialectical stage] . . . in which the moments of the pure Notion [stages of the overall dialectic] obtain a *substantial* existence."[65] "Obtain a substantial existence" means "becomes material substance—matter—rather than thought." In the antithesis stage of the dialectic, the believer's mere picture-thought of God residing in heaven becomes the actual physical substance of a real human being, Jesus, residing on earth. God becomes flesh. Heaven (the God of thought) has moved to earth (Jesus, physical substance).

Meanwhile, the word "existence" illuminates another opposition, that between essence and existence. The heavenly God created by pure thought represents essence; the earth-bound God incarnate who is Jesus represents actual existence, the "substantial existence" Hegel refers to. In moving from pure thought to substance, the dialectic has also moved from essence to existence. "Thus the merely eternal or abstract Spirit becomes an 'other' to itself, or enters into existence."⁶⁶ "Becomes an 'other' to itself" means that God incarnate on earth becomes another being from the heavenly perspective of the God in heaven who looks down on earth. God in heaven sees *himself*, something "other," on earth.

The picture-thinking synthesis occurs when "this divine Being in human shape [God incarnate] sacrifices his immediate existence [dies on the cross] again and *returns* to the divine Being [in the sky]." In the process, God and man are reconciled: "In this picture-thought [of God returning to himself] there is depicted the reconciliation of the divine Being with its 'other' in general"— the "in general" being humanity in general rather than just the one human, Jesus.⁶⁷ Here Hegel has a double meaning. The theological meaning is that the divine God and the human God incarnate are again just one God, united by the Holy Spirit in the Trinity. Thought (God in heaven) and substance (God on earth) are now combined in a dialectical synthesis. The Hegelian meaning, expressed in the words "in general" (humanity in general), is that the divine becomes united with *all* humans, not just Jesus. Man becomes the divine. *All* men become God.

The result of this three-stage-progression is a triple dialectic:

- One dialectic moves from (1) thought to (2) substance to (3) thought = substance.

- A second dialectic moves from (1) essence to (2) existence to (3) essence = existence.

- A third dialectic moves from (1) Father to (2) Son to (3) Holy Spirit.

In the third dialectic, Father symbolizes both thought (something nonsubstantive, the divine) and essence; Son symbolizes both substance (something material, tangible, the human) and existence (visible presence on earth); and the Holy Spirit symbolizes both (*a*) thought = substance and (*b*) essence = existence. Thought = substance is, in turn, equivalent to divine = human, or God = man.

Thus does separation and return emerge as a triple dialectic. In Hegel's macrodialectic, coming up, the uniting of the divine and the human is the *return* of the previously *separated* Spirit ("God") to its primordial (prehuman) state of unity. The above three "Revealed Religion" microdialectics anticipate the macrodialectic, preparing the way for the latter.

HEGEL'S MACRODIALECTIC: THE UNCONSCIOUS STAGE (THESIS)

Hegel makes separation and return the basis of his philosophy. In his main dialectic, the macrodialectic ensconced in *Phenomenology*, the Spirit separates from and returns to union. This journey of separation and return is the divine life of the figuratively "organic" Spirit. In terms of the abstract movement from Yes (affirmation) to No (negation) to a higher Yes (negation of the negation), Spirit moves from (1) Yes to an *unconscious* form of union to (2) No, a conscious No, to union—this No means separation—to (3) Yes to a higher form of union, *conscious* union. Unconsciousness and consciousness drive the dialectic forward.

And there begins the interpretation problem. A crucial weakness with all but one of the interpretations of Hegel to date is their failure to recognize the fundamental role *unconsciousness* plays in his dialectical system. The one exception is Tucker, who writes: "God [Spirit] passes from primal unconsciousness in the form of nature [thesis] to ultimate self-consciousness in the person of historical man [synthesis]."[68] As I pointed out in chapter 1, Tucker does not explicitly identify unconsciousness with a thesis; he is not yet discussing dialectics. And when, in his following chapter, he does describe the thesis of what he thinks is Hegel's basic dialectic, that thesis says nothing about unconsciousness. Instead, it seems to imply consciousness: "The given world-form or creative self-objectification of spirit is the 'thesis.'"[69] How can a self, presumably a person, objectify (interpret as an object) itself if the self that objectifies is not conscious? Perhaps, and perhaps not, Tucker's earlier reference to "unconsciousness" simply means unawareness, the unawareness of consciousness that it is Spirit. Later, as I showed in chapter 1, Tucker actually does use "unconscious" to mean "unaware."

Whatever Tucker meant, every other analyst has assumed that the road to self-consciousness (a particular form of consciousness) begins with consciousness, albeit non-*self*-conscious consciousness. That is understandable. Consciousness is where Hegel starts his discussion in *Phenomenology*. *Phenomenology*'s first chapter has the title "Consciousness." Interpreters have naturally assumed that consciousness is where everything begins. For example, we saw in chapter 1 that Findlay makes the absurd claim that Hegel's "main" dialectical triad moves from consciousness to self-consciousness to reason. Likewise, Pippin, in summarizing his conclusions in an essay on transition problems in *Phenomenology*, has nothing to say about unconsciousness or a transition from unconsciousness to consciousness. His first conclusion: "First and most obviously, even those most skeptical about the work [*Phenomenology*] have to try to take into account the fact that Hegel intended a transition from 'Consciousness' to 'Self-Consciousness.'"[70] True enough. But what should be "first" is the fact that Hegel intended an earlier transition from unconsciousness to consciousness. This earlier transition is part of a broader transition from unconscious union via conscious separation to conscious union, or self-consciousness.

The error is not just Findlay's and Pippin's. One interpreter after another has made consciousness the supposed context in which the entire evolution of Spirit progresses. But that's not the real state of affairs. *Phenomenology*'s overarching dialectic begins with unconsciousness, part of the thesis. The dialectic includes both unconsciousness and consciousness. It begins with unconsciousness.

Here's how things work. The thesis of Hegel's basic thesis-antithesis-synthesis dialectic has two parts: "unconscious" and "union," where union means "universality." Union or universality is the state of being one, as opposed to being many, separated into particulars. Unconscious means the same thing as potential, the opposite of actual, so "unconscious union" can also be called "potential union."[71] Hegel's dialectic follows the first of the three patterns illustrated in chapter 1 with Tillich's dialectics. The thesis, the antithesis, and the synthesis have two parts, two concepts. The synthesis borrows the best part from the thesis and the best from the antithesis. This dialectic results:

> Thesis: Unconscious + Union (i.e., potential union, or latent universality)
>
> Antithesis: Conscious + Separation (i.e., actual separation, or self-estrangement)
>
> Synthesis: Conscious + Union (i.e., actual union, or self-realization, self-awareness)

The reason interpreters have overlooked the first stage of Hegel's basic dialectic is that Hegel doesn't discuss it in *Phenomenology*; he merely hints that it is there. But eight considerations permit no doubt that a preconscious thesis stage, "unconscious union," *is* there.

1. Hegel says, in a previously quoted statement, that the Spirit "becomes estranged and then returns to itself from estrangement."[72] Here Hegel alludes to his basing his dialectic on Christian theology's separation-and-return doctrine. Whatever Spirit returns to must be what Spirit began with, before becoming estranged. And it must be a return from separation, from self-estrangement. *A return from separation has to mean a return to separation's opposite*, which is union or universality, the state of being one, unseparated. We can thus *deduce* that the Spirit starts from a preliminary form of union (Yes to union), separates (No to union), and then returns to a higher form of union (a higher Yes). The preliminary form of union, the initial Yes, happens to be *unconscious* union, potential union. And the higher Yes is *conscious* union, actual union.

2. Hegel explicitly says that, in the beginning, Spirit is not separated into particulars: Spirit "is only, *to begin with*, the universal [all reality,

viewed as *one* entity]."[73] The reason it isn't separated into particulars is that separation requires human perception of separate, *external* objects. Without a human mind with which to perceive "otherness," Spirit in its primal state is incapable of being aware that external particulars exist. No human minds exist in the beginning, in the primordial state of nature, before the arrival of humans.

3, The separation stage of Spirit's journey entails *conscious* separation. To repeat, Hegel's *Phenomenology* begins with Chapter A, "Consciousness," and retains consciousness as the context in which all the rest of the book progresses. We cannot doubt that Spirit's estrangement or separation is conscious separation. Spirit's mind, which is the mind of man, is consciously aware of separate "objects"—separate from the person or "subject" (sometimes called "consciousness") who perceives the external objects. In essence, those perceived objects are the "subject" (observer), because both subject and objects are Spirit. But subject doesn't know this. Hence subject is *consciously* estranged, separated, from itself. That is what *self*-estrangement means.

4. If you seriously look for thesis-antithesis-synthesis dialectics, and if you then recognize that "conscious separation" must be either the thesis or the antithesis of the dialectic (self-realization obviously being the synthesis), then you must grant that both "conscious" and "separation" have opposites. And who can fail to recognize that "unconscious" is the opposite of "conscious"? The question is: Does "unconscious" belong to the thesis or to the antithesis? The answer is clear. Given that the synthesis, self-consciousness, is a "return" from separation, separation must be the stage that immediately precedes the synthesis. So "conscious separation" is the antithesis. "Unconscious" must therefore relate to the starting point, the thesis. We can now see that the dialectic moves from (1) unconsciousness to (2) faulty consciousness to (3) perfected consciousness.

5. In *The Philosophy of History*, Hegel plainly states that the separation stage, faulty consciousness, is the second stage, not the first: "But

what is Spirit? It is the one immutably homogeneous Infinite—pure Identity—which in its *second phase* separates itself from itself" (my italics).[74] If conscious separation is the second phase or second stage, it must be preceded by a first stage. That stage, which involves "pure identity," is one in which Spirit is not separated; its parts are identical, "homogeneous"—all are Spirit— because no human mind is present to misperceive the many "objects" in the universe as separate things.

6. If consciousness requires a mind (this is beyond dispute), and if Spirit's only mind is the mind of man, then unconsciousness must belong to an earlier stage, a primitive stage of nature, that exists before man arrives on the planet—before human minds arrive. True, in the everyday context of *human* life, unconsciousness requires humans; but in the Hegelian context of *Spirit's* life, all that unconsciousness requires is Spirit. And Spirit, because it is "all reality," does exist in nature, including stars, the earth, oceans, geological structures, plant life, and lower forms of animal life, before man arrives.

7. Hegel actually says—here I use Kaufmann's translation of Hegel's Preface—that "knowledge in its initial form . . . *lacks* . . . the *consciousness* of the senses" (awareness of one's surroundings).[75] Miller's translation uses "first phase" in place of "initial form";[76] Baillie says "primitive stage."[77] "Initial form," "first phase," and "primitive stage" all tell us we are dealing with a thesis, the first stage of a dialectic, and "lacks . . . consciousness" tells us that this thesis stage is characterized by unconsciousness. Since man's mind is the only mind Spirit has, hence is the source of Spirit's consciousness, the "primitive stage" of unconsciousness must be nature as it exists *before* man appears. In this stage, Spirit is the analog of God in his Johannine not-yet-separated state (and of Adam and Eve before they indulge in the "original sin" and, consequently, become separated from God). Spirit is not yet separated into subject (any human observer) and the many "alien" objects perceived by subject—that is, perceived by any human mind.

8. Other statements by Hegel confirm that this "primitive stage" is prehuman and unconscious. Example: "The first stage [thesis] is the immersion of Spirit in natural life, the second [antithesis] its stepping out into . . . consciousness."[78] Consciousness means *human* consciousness. Hegel knew that mankind had not always been present on the planet.[79] In his lectures on the philosophy of history, he declared, "After the creation of nature appears man."[80] But in the earlier "stage" of prehuman nature, "the first organism . . . does not exist as a *living creature*,"[81] because that "first organism," Hegel says, is the earth, a prehuman manifestation of Spirit. At first, therefore, although Spirit does exist as everything *physical* in the universe, it does not yet exist in its *mental* aspect. Spirit has no human mind with which to perceive external objects and to think; it lacks consciousness. Hegel describes this stage as one where "the Earth-spirit . . . has not yet reached the stage of opposition."[82] The "stage of opposition" is the antithesis, which opposes the thesis. This first stage is like "the movement and dreaming of one asleep, until it awakes and receives its consciousness in Man."[83] Conclusion: the thesis is "unconscious union."

This conclusion receives additional support from Tillich, whose dialectical theology of humanism closely imitates Hegel's dialectical philosophy of Spirit. Recall from chapter 1 that Tillich calls his thought "dialectical realism" and describes this as "thinking" that "moves through 'yes' [affirmation] and 'no' [negation] and 'yes' again [negation of the negation]."[84] Here man moves from theism to atheism to humanism. Also recall from earlier in this chapter that the thesis is Yes to God + Yes to supernaturalism, the antithesis is No to God + No to supernaturalism, and the synthesis is Yes to God (from the thesis) + No to supernaturalism (from the antithesis).

Tillich frequently calls his thesis stage (Yes to God + Yes to supernaturalism) "dreaming innocence."[85] Referring to theists whose belief is too strong to be challenged, Tillich says, "As long as the pupil lives in a dreaming innocence of critical questions, he should not be awakened."[86] Describing "dreaming innocence," Tillich writes: "Both words point to something that precedes actual existence. It has potentiality, not actuality."[87] We know that (*a*) what precedes existence is essence, which is the thesis stage of a dialectic, and (*b*) what precedes actuality (in "actual existence") is potentiality (in "potential essence"), which again is the thesis stage. "Dreaming innocence," it becomes clear, is Tillichian shorthand for his philosophy's thesis stage of theism. Dreaming, meanwhile, is a state of unconsciousness. We can see that Tillich recognizes and is basing his own thesis terminology, "dreaming," on the Hegelian thesis concept, unconsciousness. Tillich might in fact have directly lifted the word "dreaming" from Hegel's phrase "the movement and dreaming of one asleep," quoted in the penultimate sentence of point 8 above. This Hegel-Tillich parallelism corroborates my inference that the Hegelian thesis concept indeed *is* unconsciousness. (And it is one of the reasons why I said in chapter 1 that Tillich is one of only three authors—Marx and Engels are the other two—who understand Hegel's dialectics.)

Hegel became thoroughly acquainted with the unconscious-conscious theme from his friend and colleague, Schelling. Tillich, whose dissertation topic for his 1912 Licentiate of Theology degree was Schelling's thought, enlightens us:

> His [Schelling's] whole philosophy of nature was an attempt to show the indwelling of the potential spirit in all natural objects and how it comes to its fulfillment in man. . . . In this construction the process of nature proceeds from the lowest to the highest forms of nature, and finally to man in terms of a contrast between two principles. He called one principle the *unconscious* and the other the *conscious*. He tried to show how slowly in all different forms of nature consciousness develops until it comes to man where it becomes self-consciousness.[88]

The conclusion that the macrodialectic's thesis stage entails unconsciousness also gets unintended support from Pinkard. He observes that Hegel is aware that humans have not always been present on earth. In the beginning, "God, as spirit, is already metaphorically asleep [unconscious] in nature, and the divine principle of 'spirit' comes to fruition only as humans appear on the planet and create religions." When this happens—when humans arrive and create religions—"spirit, as it were, wakes up from its natural slumber and becomes conscious of itself."[89] Pinkard is not intentionally implying that an unconscious *thesis* stage precedes consciousness—he specifically denies that Hegel uses dialectics—but he definitely is acknowledging an unconscious stage that precedes consciousness. And since (1) this unconscious stage is explicitly followed by (2) a "conscious" stage of estrangement and then (3) a final stage of self-consciousness, or self-realization, Pinkard has unwittingly set before us the three pieces of Hegel's macrodialectic. (Note, by the way, how "slumber" is complementary to Tillich's thesis concept of "dreaming" and how "wakes up" is complementary to Tillich's "awakened." It is almost as though Pinkard were paraphrasing Tillich.)

HEGEL'S MACRODIALECTIC: THE FULL DIALECTIC

We are now in a position to analyze Hegel's main dialectic—the macrodialectic—in more detail. In this dialectic, the Spirit, all reality, journeys dialectically from

- a thesis stage, the primitive state of nature in which Spirit is *unconsciously* a unified whole, *one* universal entity, through

- an antithesis stage, where man arrives and Spirit becomes *consciously* self-estranged, separated into *many* "subjects" and "objects"—many particulars—because human minds (Spirit's Mind) recognize as Spirit neither their bearers (the humans) nor the external "objects" the humans see, to

- a synthesis stage, where Spirit becomes self-conscious when man, in the person of Hegel, finally recognizes *consciously* that both he and everything he sees are essentially Spirit, *one* universal entity *composed of many* particulars. In this synthesis of one and many, Spirit becomes Absolute Spirit—philosophy's absolute. Absolute Spirit is Spirit in its ultimate state of self-awareness: Spirit (Hegel) finally becomes aware that it constitutes all reality, the entire material universe, plus the nonmaterial minds and thoughts of humans.

The thesis stage has been explained under my preceding heading. In the *antithesis* stage of Spirit's "divine life," Spirit is consciously "self-estranged" or "self-alienated," separated from itself. It lacks self-awareness, awareness that the external world is itself, Spirit. It thinks itself—say, a rose it sees—is a separate, "alien" object. In Hegel's words, "The object is revealed [to the subject, a person, who is also Spirit]," but Spirit "does not recognize itself."[90] So Spirit thinks, mistakenly, that the universal entity it sees, the entity that is essentially *one* ("universal"), is actually a particular object (the rose) among *many* external objects. Spirit has separated from itself, just as God, the analogical prototype of Spirit, did in John 1:14, when God came to earth incarnated as a man, separating from his self in heaven.

The clash between Spirit's *essential* universality and its *existential* (apparent, perceived) particularity—between thesis and antithesis—is what Hegel calls "the antithesis [opposition] between the universal and the individual [particular]."[91] Alternatively phrased, the clash is "this antithesis of its [Spirit's] appearance [many] and its truth [one]."[92] Or, in Tillich's words, it is "the problem of the one and the many," a problem whose "answer is that there must be an *original unity* of the one and the many" (my italics).[93] That original unity comes from the thesis, "unconscious union." (Tillich again displays his solid grasp of Hegelian dialectics.) Elsewhere, Tillich emphasizes that the state of estrangement—"man's [existential] predicament"—is that existential man is not what he essentially is: "Man as he exists is not what he essentially is and ought to be. He is estranged from his true being."[94] This description applies to both Hegel's philosophy and Tillich's.

Spirit has now moved from unconscious union (two parts: unconscious + union) to conscious separation (two parts: conscious + separation); it has become "self-estranged" or "self-alienated."[95] To reach its goal of self-awareness—to become Absolute Spirit—Spirit must return *consciously* to the previously unconscious state of union, to the state of "oneness"[96] or to "the identity of itself [subject] with itself [objects seen by subject]."[97] The two-part goal: conscious + union ("conscious" from the antithesis, "union" from the thesis), or "conscious union."

This goal, the *synthesis*, is reached, and Spirit becomes Absolute Spirit, when the greatest of all human minds, Hegel's, finally realizes that subject (now Hegel) and object (every object Hegel sees) are identical—that everything that exists is essentially Spirit, essentially *one*, one entity. That one entity is our universe, including everything in it, both natural and artificial. Hegel's mind is a crucial part of Spirit's mind: Hegel, like you, is Spirit. So, with Hegel's (man's) recognition that he is Spirit, Spirit achieves self-consciousness. Spirit has separated from itself and returned to itself: "Hence the third stage [the synthesis] is the return of self [Spirit] thus alienated . . . into its first primal [thesis stage] simplicity [unity]."[98] Finally, "the *goal*, Absolute Knowing, or Spirit that knows itself as Spirit" has been achieved;[99] Spirit has become "Absolute Spirit."[100] Spirit has moved from (1) *one* (universal) to (2) *many* (particular subjects and objects) to (3) the synthesis of *one and many*, or one universal Spirit composed of many particulars. Spirit has separated from and returned to *one*, union, or universality.

Spirit's self-realization (*a*) begins with the death of God, (*b*) achieves a first climax when the Holy Spirit is transfigured into the Hegelian Spirit and "possesses" (that's what spirits do) not the one dead Jesus but the entire *living* "community" of humans, uniting them with the divine and thereby deifying them, and (*c*) reaches a second climax when Hegel arrives on the scene and realizes what has happened. Hegel affirms that Jesus's crucifixion symbolizes not just the death of Jesus but the death of God (the supernatural God): "The death of the Mediator [Jesus] is the death also of the *abstraction* of the divine Being [God]. . . . That death is the painful feeling of the Unhappy Consciousness that *God Himself is dead*."[101] God's death leads to a very different resurrection than the one taught by theologians. Not one man but all men are "resurrected" as God: "The *death* of the divine Man . . . becomes transfigured from its immediate [original] meaning, viz., the non-being of this *particular* individual, into the universality [encompassing *all* individuals] of the Spirit [the divine, "God"]."[102] Solomon does a commendable job of contrasting the New Testament's Calvary with Hegel's version: "Where the New Testament Calvary murders a man, returning Him to God, Hegel's Calvary murders God and returns him to man."[103] Man at first does not comprehend what has happened. The second climax arrives in the last paragraph of *Phenomenology*, where Hegel—Spirit's mind—undergoes self-realization, becoming aware that he is Spirit, the divine, "God." This self-realization constitutes the acquisition of "Absolute Knowledge," which elevates Spirit to the status of "truth" and "actuality," or Absolute Spirit.

Lest someone doubt that Hegel implicitly credits himself with being the mind that brings Spirit to conscious maturity, remarks by Tucker and Tillich are worth considering. Tucker writes: "Hegel . . . conceived himself as the particular man in whom God [Spirit]—the absolute self—finally achieves full actualization."[104] Hegel's act, according to Tucker, is nothing less than "man's self-recognition as the divine being."[105] In a lecture alluding to Spirit's role in history, Tillich accused Hegel of "arrogance" (arrogating unto himself the role of Spirit) for "sitting on the throne of God [Spirit] as Hegel implied he was doing when he construed world history as coming to an end in principle in his philosophy."[106] ("In principle" means that *dialectical* history comes to an end but ordinary history continues.)

Those remarks by Tucker and Tillich, along with my own remark about Hegel's "recognition" that he is Spirit, require qualification. Hegel does not really experience a flash of insight or otherwise literally come to a "realization" or recognition that he and everything else are Spirit. That just happens to be the way he treats Spirit's self-realization—treats it as a long deferred realization by a human mind that all reality is Spirit. But Hegel has really known all along that Spirit is nothing but his own philosophical creation, something he has painstakingly designed for philosophical purposes and has *defined* as the universe or "all reality." You could even say that Hegel's invention of Spirit is an act of one-upmanship intended to supersede the absolute of Hegel's erstwhile friend Schelling, not to mention the absolutes of Spinoza and other earlier philosophers. Spirit is not in any sense a belief, comparable to a belief in God.

The concept of union and the antithetical concept of separation can be conceptualized eight different ways: (1) union and separation, (2) one and many, (3) universal and particular, (4) inner and outer, (5) essence and existence, (6) divine and human, (7) infinite and finite, and (8) identity and non-identity:

1. Union and separation is the basic dichotomy from which the others flow.

2. Union is practically a synonym for one. The *uni* in union means one, as in unicorn (one horn), unicycle (one wheel), and uniform (one mode of dress or other form). Many is the opposite of one.

3. A universe is a single realm or entity; hence, Hegel can speak of "the task" as being "to give actuality [conscious recognition] to the universal."[107] Particular is the opposite of universal (general).

4. Inside each thing in the universe is its inner hidden essence, the mental concept of Spirit. Everything is the same inside. But everything differs in outer appearance. On the outside, what we see is a multitude of diverse particulars.

5. Spirit's state of being unified is essence, Spirit's essential state. Hegel can therefore say that, "in pressing forward to its true existence [Absolute Spirit], consciousness will arrive at a point . . . where appearance [existence, the antithesis] becomes identical with essence [the thesis]."[108] He relates essence to universal when he says that "the universal is meant to express the essence of the actual."[109] Existence, which has a negative connotation, is the condition that exists when essence is unrealized (but it also exists when essence is finally realized as *actual* essence, that is, when essence *comes into existence*).

6. In both the *Phenomenology* context and the Judeo-Christian context, if not in other contexts, divine is another way of saying one, universal, and essence. There is one Spirit and one God; God rules the universe, not just certain tribes as the Hebrew Yahweh did; Hegel's Spirit is the essence of the universe. Human is the opposite of divine.

7. That which is spatially infinite is unlimited not in the mathematical sense of infinity but in the sense that it includes everything. The infinite is not limited to certain particulars, or even to most particulars. Spirit, the physical universe, includes everything. No one familiar with Hegel can fail to see that his references to the infinite are either to the one

universal Spirit or, when he is describing Christianity, to the one universal God. What is finite or limited is individual (particular) humans or other objects; they are limited to one person or one thing. Hegel's emphasis is on the finite humans.

8. All pieces of the universe are identical before humans arrive on earth and start seeing objects, including other humans, all around them,. They are identical in the sense that nobody is around to perceive them as non-identical. When the humans arrive, all these pieces or "objects" become non-identical, because that is how the humans perceive them. Hegel calls this dichotomy "identity and non-identity."[110]

To go with these eight ways of saying union and separation we have two ways of saying unconscious and conscious. Unconscious union is *potential* union; conscious union is *actual* union. Because there are so many equivalent concepts, Hegel's macrodialectic can be expressed $8 \times 2 = 16$ different two-concepts-per-stage ways. (There are additional one-concept-per-stage ways plus two late-arriving two-concepts-per-stage ways of saying union and separation.) In each variation, the synthesis describes the result of a human mind's (consciousness's) conscious realization that it and everything else in the universe are Spirit. Here are the sixteen two-concepts-per-stage variations of the macrodialectic:

1. Thesis: unconscious + union
   Antithesis: conscious + separation
   Synthesis: conscious + union

2. Thesis: potential + union
   Antithesis: actual + separation
   Synthesis: actual + union

3. Thesis: unconscious + one
   Antithesis: conscious + many
   Synthesis: conscious + one

4. Thesis: potential + one
   Antithesis: actual + many
   Synthesis: actual + one

5. Thesis: unconscious + universal
   Antithesis: conscious + particular
   Synthesis: conscious + universal

6. Thesis: potential + universal
   Antithesis: actual + particular
   Synthesis: actual + universal

7. Thesis: unconscious + inner universality
   Antithesis: conscious + outer separateness
   Synthesis: conscious + inner universality

8. Thesis: potential + inner universality
   Antithesis: actual + outer separateness
   Synthesis: actual + inner universality

9. Thesis: unconscious + essence
   Antithesis: conscious + existence
   Synthesis: conscious + essence

10. Thesis: potential + essence
    Antithesis: actual + existence
    Synthesis: actual + essence

11. Thesis: unconscious + divine
    Antithesis: conscious + human
    Synthesis: conscious + divine

12. Thesis: potential + divine
    Antithesis: actual + human
    Synthesis: actual + divine

13. Thesis: unconscious + infinite
    Antithesis: conscious + finite
    Synthesis: conscious + infinite

14. Thesis: potential + infinite
    Antithesis: actual + finite
    Synthesis: actual + infinite

15. Thesis: unconscious + identity
    Antithesis: conscious + non-identity
    Synthesis: conscious + identity

16. Thesis: potential + identity
    Antithesis: actual + non-identity
    Synthesis: actual + identity

The journey from union to separation to reunion can also be described by the two principal formats that use one concept per stage. (Refer to the Tillich examples in chapter 1.) The first additional format is (1) thesis: A, (2) antithesis: B, and (3) synthesis: A = B. In each case A refers to the prehuman period of unity, B to the self-estrangement period, and C to self-realization, where man (hence Spirit) realizes the antithesis is really the thesis in disguise. This format has five versions, differing only in the words used to express union and separation. The five versions bring the total to twenty-one:

17. Thesis: one (one Spirit)
    Antithesis: many (many particulars or objects that constitute Spirit)
    Synthesis: one = many (the one Spirit *is* the many particulars)

18. Thesis: universal
    Antithesis: particular
    Synthesis: universal = particulars

19. Thesis: inner (unseen identity)
    Antithesis: outer (observable differences)
    Synthesis: inner = outer (realized identity of inner and outer)

20. Thesis: essence (divinity, unperceived)
    Antithesis: existence (humans and other "objects," perceived and
        misinterpreted)
    Synthesis: essence = existence (divinity is now perceived, hence
        realized)

21. Thesis: infinite (the universal Spirit)
    Antithesis: finite (individual humans and other finite objects that
        constitute Spirit)
    Synthesis: infinite = finite

The third dialectical format is (1) thesis: A, general, (2) antithesis:
B, particular, and (3) synthesis: A composed of B, or general composed of
particulars. This last format simply substitutes "one composed of many" for
"one = many" in the first one-concept-per-stage version above, substitutes
"universe composed of particulars" for "universe = particulars" in the second
version, and "infinite composed of finite" for "infinite = finite" in the fifth
version. The inner-outer and essence-existence versions don't readily convert
to this format. Here are the macrodialectic's next three variants:

22. Thesis: one
    Antithesis: many
    Synthesis: one composed of many

23. Thesis: universal
    Antithesis: particular
    Synthesis: universe composed of particulars

24. Thesis: infinite (universal)
    Antithesis: finite (particular)
    Synthesis: infinite composed of finite particulars

Next, we the Hegelese-jargon way of presenting the macrodialectic:

25. Thesis: in itself (Spirit turned inward, no external objects perceived; Spirit is one)
    Antithesis: for itself (Spirit looking outward, external objects "for itself to see")
    Synthesis: in and for itself (external objects recognized as inner Spirit)

FREEDOM AND BONDAGE

In a highly significant development, Hegel in the last four pages of *Phenomenology* characterizes self-realization, the multifaceted synthesis of the macrodialectic, as freedom. Through the act of self-realization, Spirit escapes from the bondage of self-estrangement (the macrodialectic's antithesis) and thereby becomes free. This meaning of freedom appears in the fifth, fourth, and third from last paragraphs of *Phenomenology*. There Hegel describes "Spirit . . . which is both *in itself* [thesis] and *for itself* [antithesis]," where "in and for itself" is Hegel's standard reference to any dialectical synthesis—the macrodialectic's synthesis in this case. The synthesis is "knowledge" (Baillie translation)—Absolute Knowledge, the last chapter's title. Knowledge arrives when what was previously "differentiated" (separated into a multitude of objects, perceived as alien, in the antithesis stage) "returns into its unity"—that is, when the dialectical movement of separation from and return to unity is completed.[111] Continuing: "In this knowledge, . . . Spirit has concluded the movement [of separation and return] in which it has shaped itself," and "the self-alienating Self [Spirit]" has achieved the "unity of self-knowledge [Absolute Knowledge]."[112] This self-knowledge constitutes "the *freedom* of its being."[113] Hegel restates this point in his next paragraph: "This release of itself from the [self-alienated] form of its Self [from the bondage of self-alienation] is the supreme *freedom*."[114]

It becomes clear that Hegel's concept of freedom springs from and depends on the closely related concept of bondage. Although Hegel does not explicitly mention bondage in the final pages of *Phenomenology*, he does treat bondage as the antithesis of freedom in his famous master-and-slave parable, where the slave is held in bondage. That parable falls under the heading "Lordship and Bondage." In the parable the Lord "holds the bondsman in bondage."[115] I shall show in a moment that the parable is really the macrodialectic in miniature and that it contains a dialectic that proceeds from an antithesis of bondage to a synthesis of freedom. "Bondage" is again the antithesis of freedom in two of Hegel's history dialectics (chapter 5). In one the bondage is Greco-Roman slavery; in the other medieval Catholic religious "superstition" is a "slavish" condition under which Spirit (represented by the human mind) "has lost its Freedom, and is held in adamantine bondage to what is alien to itself."[116] The object that is "alien to itself" is the supernatural God that Spirit, using man's collective mind, has imagined into existence.

But what is it in Spirit's antithesis stage of self-estrangement that constitutes bondage? Self-estranged Spirit, thinking with man's mind, does not yet know that it is God. Man (Spirit), using picture-thinking, has created the imaginary supernatural God in heaven. Around this God, man has created whole systems of superstitions. These systems constitute man's religions. Religion and religious superstition hold man in bondage; man is a slave to religion. Spirit escapes from the bondage of religious superstition when it undergoes self-realization. Spirit then realizes that it, the conscious "subject," and the "objects" it formerly mistook as "alien" are both itself, Spirit, and that Spirit—man included—is God. Spirit, thinking with its human mind—its only mind—finally realizes that there is no *supernatural* God. This realization, man's realization that *he* is God, is what releases man from bondage to religious superstition. The release from bondage is what Hegel calls freedom.

The idea that self-realization constitutes freedom is repeated many years later in Hegel's *Lectures on the Philosophy of Religion*. There Hegel says that "the third stage"—clearly the synthesis—or "the return . . . to itself [to unity] out of the particularity [antithesis stage of separation] in which it is unequal to itself [in which 'subject' and 'object' are not identical or 'equal']" produces a situation where Spirit "has attained its *freedom*."[117]

This concept of freedom is highly unconventional, purely metaphorical, and arbitrary; it is not what freedom ordinarily means. But that's beside the point. What matters is that Hegel is implicitly characterizing the macrodialectic's antithesis stage as bondage, psychological bondage to the distress of religious superstition and of alienation from the true God. And he is explicitly characterizing the synthesis stage, self-realization, as freedom. Spirit's "return" to unity is thus also a return to freedom. And that implies that the thesis concept to which Spirit is returning is also a state of freedom, *unconscious* or *potential* freedom. Spirit's original freedom is only potential because freedom, to be actual, must belong to humans. Humans do not yet exist in the thesis stage, the primordial state of nature; Spirit is not yet actually conscious of its freedom.

We now see that the macrodialectic has two more variants:

26. Thesis: unconscious + freedom
    Antithesis: conscious + bondage
    Synthesis: conscious + freedom

27. Thesis: potential + freedom
    Antithesis: actual + bondage
    Synthesis: actual + freedom

These two dialectics embody the basic message of *Phenomenology*: self-realization is an escape from the bondage of religion. The macrodialectic is essentially an extended parable (you could also call it an allegory), a story conveying a religious lesson and having characters, events, and things that symbolize other things. A classic illustration of a parable is Jesus's parable of the prodigal son (Lk. 15:11–32). The wayward son requests his inheritance in advance from his father, receives it, squanders it on "loose living," and is forced to become a swineherd. Realizing his sinfulness, the prodigal son repents, returns humbly to his father, and is greeted with open arms. The father slays the fatted calf and holds a feast celebrating the son's return. Here the prodigal son symbolizes a sinner, the father symbolizes God, the son's repenting symbolizes a sinner's repenting his sins, and the feast is heaven. The parable's moral is that if you are a sinner but repent, God will forgive you and admit you to heaven.

In Hegel's macrodialectic parable, Spirit symbolizes man. (That's pretty close to what Spirit actually is in Hegel's philosophy, but we're now talking about the symbolism, not Hegel's surface story, the macrodialectic.) Man has the potential to be free from bondage to religious superstition. Spirit's primal state of universality, in which the unconscious Spirit can neither create nor submit to an alien deity, symbolizes this potential freedom from bondage. At this thesis stage, freedom is only potential because, to repeat, actual human freedom requires the presence of humans. Another reason this freedom is only potential is that bondage requires the presence of a second person, someone who might enslave the humans or otherwise hold them in bondage. That second person is the supernatural God, who has not yet been imagined into existence.

Hegel's famous master-and-slave microdialectic, coming up in chapter 4, is another parable. In that parable this second person (the enslaver) is the master. The master symbolizes God. After God materializes (after man's imagination creates God) in the master-and-slave parable, God holds mankind—the slave—in bondage; man becomes a slave of God, of religion, and of religious superstition. When Hegel writes that "their reflection into a unity has not yet been achieved,"[118] he is saying that the master (God) and the slave (man) are *essentially* one ("a unity"): God is man. But because man doesn't yet know this—because man thinks God is a separate being in heaven—the unity or identity of man and God "has not yet been achieved" (recognized). Describing the antithesis stage ("middle term") of servitude, Hegel says that "servitude in its consummation [in the synthesis] will really turn into the opposite."[119] The opposite of servitude is mastery, or Godhood: Hegel is saying in his customary obscurantist language that when the macrodialectic's synthesis replaces the antithesis, man will become God. "Through work . . . the bondsman becomes conscious of what he truly is":[120] through mental effort, by gradually learning the "Science" of dialectics, man becomes conscious that *he* and not a supernatural being in heaven is the true God. The master ultimately becomes dependent on the slave, who (says Hegel) thereby achieves "freedom." The meaning of this development is that when the existence of God—the true God, self-realized Spirit—becomes dependent on the existence of man, through whose mind self-realization occurs, man is released from bondage to the supernatural God and to religion. In the dialectical synthesis, the slave "destroys this alien negative moment" (man destroys the God of supernaturalism, perceived as an "alien" object) and "posits *himself* as a negative."[121] Here "a negative" alludes to Hegel's abstract label for any dialectical synthesis, "negation of the negation." Hegel is saying that when man realizes that *he* is the true God, he becomes the "negative" or negation that negates the original negation. The original negation is belief in the supernatural God, who negates man's freedom. As a "negation of the negation," the new negation—freedom—is a dialectical synthesis.

Back to Hegel's macrodialectic parable: When man arrives on earth, he uses "picture-thinking" to create an imaginary, man-made God in heaven—the master of the master-and-slave dialectic. For thousands of years, the picture-thinking God holds man in bondage. Both physical suffering and psychological suffering result. The physical suffering includes the early Jewish genocidal slaughter of entire populations of numerous non-Jewish towns (Josh. 6, 8, 10, 11), Moses's slaughter of three thousand golden-calf worshippers (Ex. 32:15–28), the feeding of Christians to the lions in ancient Rome, the bloody early Muslim conquests, the possibly bloodier subsequent Christian crusades against Jews and Muslims, the torture and deaths associated with the inquisitions, the persecution and extermination of European Jewish communities, human sacrifice in both the early Americas and the Old World, the 1572 St. Bartholomew's Day massacre of nearly seventy thousand French Huguenots, witch burnings, and the Thirty Years War between Catholic and Protestant forces in northern Europe (mainly in Germany); these examples omit post-Hegel developments. The psychological suffering is associated with the persecution of religious minorities everywhere—Christians, Jews, Muslims, Protestants, Catholics, Huguenots, Puritans, and atheists—and with heresy hunts, witchcraft accusations, the gnawing fear of burning in hell for such petty offenses as premarital sex and out-of-wedlock pregnancy, the embarrassment of confessing to priests details of one's personal life, certain forms of penance, and Mennonite shunning. This physical and psychological suffering is the slave's bondage.

The "subject" of Hegel's surface story, the macrodialectic, perceives external "objects" as "alien" objects, things other than itself, whereas the objects are really itself, Spirit. This false interpretation of the objects as things other than the subject symbolizes man's false interpretation of God as an alien (separate) entity other than man's self; the objects collectively symbolize the false God. (I'm not saying the objects *are* the God of theism; I'm saying they *symbolize* God, a nonexistent person believed to exist in heaven, separate from man.) The Unhappy Consciousness microdialectic (chapter 4) describes the suffering humanity experiences because of its bondage to religious superstition. This hidden story of bondage and freedom, symbolically told by the macrodialectic, is the real message of *Phenomenology*. *Phenomenology* is the story of man's idealized release from bondage to religious superstition. Hegelian freedom can thus be defined as follows: *Freedom is the state of having escaped from bondage to God and religious superstition by becoming an atheist.*

Hegel concludes *Phenomenology* with two poetic lines adapted from Schiller's *Die Freundschaft*. Hegel introduces these lines with his own word, "only," a word that gives the lines their meaning. "Only

> from the chalice of *this* realm of spirits
> foams forth for Him his own infinitude."[122]

This realm of spirits is our world, earth, contrasted with the supernatural God's world, heaven. Hegel lowercases "spirits" to show that he is referring to the finite spirits, humans, who collectively constitute the true God, Spirit, who is the infinite. "Him" is uppercased to make it clear that the pronoun refers to God, but the God referred to is us rather than the traditional God. "His own infinitude" means his (God's) *divinity*; infinitude = divinity. Hegel is saying that God's divinity, and therefore God, is to be found only in our material world, the world of the humans who are the essence and the Mind of the true God, Spirit. He is saying in esoteric poetry that theology's God is dead and that the true God is man. The death of God is what releases man from bondage and gives him freedom.

Kaufmann, from whom I have borrowed in my analysis of the Schiller poetry, has brilliantly interpreted those concluding lines: "To be sure, the tone of the ending seems affirmative; but we should not overlook a crucial word that Hegel has placed before the concluding quotation—a word that, being foreign to Schiller's text, carries immense weight: *nur* (only). In Schiller's last stanza the presumption is that the infinity of the supreme being is mirrored by the whole realm of souls: though no single one equals the master's infinity, all the souls together do mirror it. For Hegel, the infinite God is dead."[123] Furthermore, this time "the death of God . . . is not followed by any resurrection," because "the spirit [God] is not to be found in another world."[124]

With this concluding Schiller epitaph, the message of *Phenomenology* becomes clear. *Phenomenology* is the dialectically told story of man's quest for freedom—freedom from subjugation to God, to religion, and to religious superstition. Freedom belatedly arrives when the slave becomes the master; freedom arrives when man becomes God—by realizing (self-realization) that finite man, not an imaginary supernatural being in heaven, is "the infinite." Freedom is thus a dialectical synthesis: infinite (thesis) = finite (antithesis), or God = man.

Hegelian "freedom" has no visible application to anyone but Hegel. Hegel treated himself as the person through whom Spirit achieves self-realization. Though others had forsaken religion before and during Hegel's time, none of the others is known to have regarded his conversion to atheism as self-deification or as the dialectical self-realization of a philosophically defined Spirit. Hegel, whose mind was the most important of the roughly one billion cells of Spirit's Mind (as of 1807),[125] was apparently the only person who, in forsaking religion, achieved what Hegel calls freedom. From this perspective, the freedom Hegel speaks of in *Phenomenology* is seen as an egocentric concept spawned by a philosopher who assumed the role of God.

Barely any room for doubt exists that *Phenomenology*'s concept of freedom— freedom from bondage to God, religion, and religious superstition—is the same as that found in *The Philosophy of History*. In the latter work Hegel says, "Historical development . . . is . . . the production of an end . . . [that] is . . . the concept of freedom."[126] And in one of Hegel's two main history dialectics, "actual freedom" is the synthesis. The second dialectic identifies Prussia, recognizable as a monarchy comprising many territories, as the Germanic nation where freedom materializes.

The reasons for thinking *Phenomenology*'s freedom is the same concept as *History*'s freedom are compelling. Hegel does not say that the end of history is freedom per se; he says that the end of history is the *concept* of freedom. Why this subtle distinction? Political and religious freedom remained heavily circumscribed in Hegelian history's Germanic world, which boils down to

Hegel's Prussia. (More about this in a moment.) Hegel could not possibly be saying that Prussia is where a historical goal of sociopolitical freedom was finally realized. But Hegel's Germanic world is when and where Hegel lived and shed the religious beliefs of his childhood. In shedding those beliefs, he freed himself from bondage to God. And he alone applied an unorthodox definition of "freedom" to that release from bondage. The Germanic world thus became the place where the uniquely Hegelian *concept* of freedom came into being. And the Germanic freedom Hegel so proudly applauds is nothing more than Hegel's conversion to atheism.

Many interpreters, including ten who have written specifically about Hegel's concept of freedom,[127] have tried to interpret Hegel's history-related concept of freedom as it relates to Hegel's Germanic world. The debate, such as it is, has been informed largely by what Hegel says in *The Philosophy of Right* about the proper role of the state. All interpreters have given freedom a more or less conventional interpretation. Freedom is said to be a relative concept having to do with the extent to which individuals can act without running into social and political barriers, particularly barriers imposed by the state. In line with this view, McCarney writes: "The core of its [freedom's] meaning does not . . . seem hard to formulate. Speaking somewhat roughly and provisionally, it is that to be free is to be independent of outside control."[128] McCarney alludes primarily here to "outside control" by social mores and legal strictures of the state, not by God and religious strictures. Knowles emphasizes that Hegel's concept of the state incorporates family life and civil society, and that these institutions in turn incorporate further complications: ethical life and morality.[129] Freedom, in other words, becomes a matter of the rights of the individual vis-à-vis the rights of the state. The freedom debate has revolved around the issue of how much political control the state should be allowed to exercise as reasonable and necessary restrictions on the individual's right to act as he pleases. This summarization hides disagreement about details. Patten argues that "Hegel denies that the state should be considered a limitation on freedom and instead claims that a kind of freedom is realized in the state that, by its very nature, could not be enjoyed outside the state."[130] Wallace takes an in-between position leaning toward Patten: "The role of the state is to promote this [ethical] freedom consciously and intentionally in the civil society and the families that make it up, but which . . . can't themselves promote it systematically." According to Wallace, Hegel's position is that promoting freedom requires state-imposed restrictions: "The laws by which the state does this [promotes freedom] represent limitations (*Schranken*) for the individual, but they are also the goal and 'work' of the whole, produced by the functioning of the estates and individuals, and freely willed by them."[131]

The point I wish to emphasize is that all previous discussions of Hegel's concept of freedom have centered on personal freedom and its relationship to social and, particularly, political restrictions. Religion has been almost totally out of the picture, except insofar as social mores may be said to incorporate religious laws. Hegelian freedom, in other words, has been treated as a sociopolitical concept, not as a freedom-from-religious-bondage concept.

Hegel certainly does have opinions on how much freedom individuals should have as citizens of the state. But this sort of freedom, sociopolitical freedom, cannot be what he refers to in *Phenomenology*, the freedom that arrives with self-realization. Neither can it be the freedom he refers to when he says (1) the concept of freedom is the goal of history and (2) this goal has finally been achieved for the first time in Prussia. Did historical freedom in the sense of reasonably limited restrictions on the right of the state to constrain the rights of citizens to act independently arrive first in Prussia? That idea is ludicrous. The plain truth is that both Britain and the United States achieved meaningful sociopolitical freedom long before Prussia did. Arguably, Prussia never did achieve such freedom before it evolved into the German empire forty years after Hegel's death.

When Hegel published *Phenomenology* in 1807, and when he later delivered his history lectures in Berlin, Britain and the United States had four basic freedoms, among others, that Hegel's Prussia lacked. First, citizens—the men anyhow—had the freedom to vote for persons to represent them in Parliament or Congress. Second, citizens had the right to trial by jury. Third, citizens had freedom of the press and other forms of freedom from censorship by the state. Fourth, citizens had freedom to determine, indirectly (via Parliament and Congress), the laws that limited personal freedom, laws that in Prussia were determined autocratically by the monarch (who, for example, ordained censorship).

Moreover, the British and American freedoms antedated and exceeded the limited freedom Prussians had during Hegel's lifetime. Specifically, in Britain the 1215 Magna Carta restricted the powers of the monarch and prohibited extralegal punishment; a 1641 act of Parliament reiterated an earlier right to trial by jury; the 1679 Habeas Corpus Act provided protection against unlawful detention; and the 1689 Bill of Rights provided for elections to Parliament. In the United States the Constitution, ratified in 1788, provided for the election of members of Congress and the right to a writ of habeas corpus; and the Constitution's first ten amendments, called the Bill of Rights and ratified in 1791, guaranteed freedom of religion, freedom of speech, freedom of the press, freedom of assembly, the right to bear arms, protection against unreasonable searches and seizures, the right to a speedy trial by jury, and protection against cruel and unusual punishment.

Hegel was aware of these British and American freedoms. He certainly could not have believed that freedom from excessive interference by the state with self-determined actions of individuals was something first achieved in Prussia. Freedom in the conventional sense of the word cannot be what Hegel meant when he said the concept of freedom is the goal of history and that Prussia is where this goal has been realized. Hegel instead was referring to his own private, idiosyncratic concept of freedom—freedom from bondage to the God of supernaturalism, to the supernatural master who enslaves the superstitious slave. That *concept* of freedom was first realized in Prussia, where Hegel invented the release-from-bondage concept.

Counting the macrodialectic and the three dialectics identified in chapter 2—the Preface's dialectic, the Introduction's microdialectic, and the lengthy "Consciousness" chapter dialectic—we now have four dialectics; these exclude the many variants of the macrodialectic. But we are barely started. Chapter 4 will add twenty-four more dialectics from *Phenomenology*, and chapter 5 will add another ten from *The Philosophy of History*.

Chapter 4

THE INTERMEDIATE DIALECTICS AND MICRODIALECTICS

Besides the *Phenomenology* dialectics already discussed, there are three additional intermediate-level dialectics (in addition to the "Consciousness" dialectic discussed in chapter 2) and twenty-one more microdialectics (in addition to the previously explained one at the end of the Introduction). The three new intermediate-level dialectics span either three Roman-numeral-level headings in Hegel's table-of-contents outline (specifically VI, VII, and VIII) or three next-level headings (A, B, and C under both VI and VII). They also arch over several bottom-level microdialectics covering relatively short stretches of text. The new Roman-numeral dialectic bridges eleven microdialectics; the first A-B-C dialectic bridges eight of these microdialectics, and the second A-B-C dialectic bridges three microdialectics. Another characteristic of the three new intermediate dialectics is that their theses, antitheses, and syntheses are closely related to the headings themselves; you don't have to do much digging in the text to spot the dialectics. In contrast, the microdialectics are well hidden in the text. But the microdialectic theses, antitheses, and syntheses still relate to particular section or subsection headings—two headings combined in a few instances.

THE INTERMEDIATE DIALECTICS

The three intermediate dialectics other than the "Consciousness" dialectic, already described, use the following outline:

VI. Spirit (Reason, human, many)

    A. The true Spirit: The Ethical Order (potential + union)

    B. Self-Alienated Spirit: Culture (actual + separation)

    C. Spirit that is certain of itself: Morality (actual + union)

VII. Religion (Revelation, divine, one)

    A. Natural Religion (Natural, alluding to human)

    B. Religion in the Form of Art (Artificial, alluding to the man-made divine)

    C. The Revealed Religion (Natural = Artificial, alluding to human = divine)

VIII. Absolute Knowing (human = divine, or many humans = one God)

I will discuss the VI-VII-VIII dialectic first and then the two A-B-C dialectics.

The Spirit-Religion Dialectic. The first sentence of the text under heading VI, "Spirit," reads, "Reason is Spirit when its certainty of being all reality has been raised to truth."[1] This sentence identifies reason with self-realization, whereby Spirit becomes Absolute Spirit. Spirit, when it advances to the stage of Absolute Spirit, becomes Reason. And reason is "all reality," Spirit. As Sidney Hook states, "In Hegel's system, 'reason' (*Vernunft*) was identified with 'reality' (*Wirklichkeit*),"[2] But that is not precisely my point in quoting Hook. My point, rather, is that Hegel is telling us that his nominal topic, Spirit, is being equated with reason. Part VI is about reason, not religion. That statement may sound questionable, because part V used the heading "Reason." Part V (Hegel's third chapter) evidently was originally intended to be the last section of *Phenomenology*.[3] But by the time he finished part V, Hegel realized he had a lot more to say. And much of it, including Part VI, Spirit, was still about reason. Part VI is a survey of human thought, which is reason. By beginning part VI with a statement identifying Spirit with reason, Hegel is launching his reason-religion or reason-revelation (VI-VII) dialectic.

Reason stands in opposition to revelation, the subject of the next chapter, which bears the title "Religion." Revelation is the antithesis of reason; so already we have a thesis, reason, and an antithesis, revelation. Reason, in turn, is the tool of philosophers. And revelation is the tool of theologians. We thus have a second thesis-antithesis combination: philosophy and theology. That's just the start of things. Philosophy is the word of man; theology is supposedly the word of God. This gives us man and God as a thesis-antithesis pair. Man is human; God is divine. That gives us a fourth thesis-antithesis pair: human and divine. The humans are many; God is one. We now have a fifth pair: many and one. This last pair is found in variations 3, 4, 15, and 20 of Hegel's chapter 3 macrodialectic. In the Spirit-Religion dialectic, Hegel has barely disguised what he is doing by transposing one and many. Many (derived from reason) is now the thesis; one (derived from revelation) is the antithesis.

We are ready to complete the five versions of the Spirit-Religion dialectic. Reason and revelation form the first thesis-antithesis pair. Their synthesis is "Absolute Knowing." Here reason produces knowledge of Spirit, the Hegelian God's other name. Knowledge of God comes from revelation. Hence reason has become revelation. The complete dialectic:

> Thesis: reason (the product of man)
> Antithesis: revelation (the product of God)
> Synthesis: revelation = reason (when man is God)

Heading VIII is "Absolute Knowing" in Miller's translation and "Absolute Knowledge" in Baillie's superior translation. ("Knowledge" is the word we use in English when the context calls for a noun rather than a participle, a verbal adjective; Miller should have known better than to use "knowing" in this context.) This chapter might better be labeled "Philosophical Theology." It amounts to a synthesis of philosophy and theology. Hegel's *Phenomenology* is theology in the sense that it is writing about "God," Hegel's alternative name for Spirit. But *Phenomenology* is also, indeed primarily, philosophy. Its subject matter is mainly that of philosophy, and its concept of God is nontheistic. What Hegel is doing is taking theological language—the words God, Father, Son, and Holy Spirit—and giving the words new meanings expressing philosophical concepts based on philosophical atheism. We thus have a dialectic that moves from philosophy ("Spirit") to theology ("The Revealed Religion") to philosophical theology ("Absolute Knowledge"). Summary:

> Thesis: philosophy (the wisdom of man)
> Antithesis: theology (the wisdom of God)
> Synthesis: philosophical theology (the wisdom of the God who is
>   mankind, Spirit's Mind)

The third thesis-antithesis pair is the one that really counts: man and God. Absolute Knowledge—knowledge of philosophy's "absolute"—arrives when Hegel discovers that man (plus everything else in the universe) is God. The dialectic:

> Thesis: man (the source of reason)
> Antithesis: God (the source of revelation)
> Synthesis: man = God

The fourth thesis-antithesis pair is human (man, the source of reason) and divine (God, the source of revelation). Their synthesis is obvious. The dialectic:

> Thesis: human (man)
> Antithesis: divine (God)
> Synthesis: human = divine

The fifth thesis-antithesis pair is many (man) and one (God). Adding the again-obvious synthesis, we get this dialectic:

> Thesis: many (man)
> Antithesis: one (God)
> Synthesis: many = one (alternatively, one composed of many)

The man = God version of the dialectic can be formulated still another way. This is the way Tillich handles it in his own philosophical theology.

Tillich reverses the order of the first two stages, going from theology (God) to philosophy (man). He does this to conform to the order of his basic Yes-No-Yes dialectic. It moves from theism to atheism to humanism. The result is this dialectic:

> Thesis: God (theism's Yes to God)
> Antithesis: man (atheism's No to God)
> Synthesis: God = man (humanism's Yes to "the God above God," humanity)

This Tillichian dialectic is only an approximate fit for Hegel's theology of Spirit. Hegel's God is man insofar as man is part of Spirit. Man is, in fact, the most important part—the source of Spirit's Mind. In his material on "The Revealed Religion," Hegel places almost total emphasis on the idea that, after the death of God, God is resurrected not as just one man (Jesus) but as all human beings in the worldwide community of humans. Still, unlike Tillich's God, humanity, Spirit is not exclusively man; everything else in the universe is also part of Spirit. Therefore, as I shall explain in more detail in chapter 6, Pinkard and M. Westphal are wrong when they conclude that Spirit is society.

The True Spirit and Self-alienated Spirit Dialectic. The next intermediate dialectic consists of headings A, B, and C under VII, Spirit. The headings bear the labels (A) "The *true* Spirit," (B) "Self-alienated Spirit," and (C) "Spirit that is certain of itself." Now the dialectic is easy to spot, because the second heading ("Self-alienated Spirit") uses standard Hegelian terminology. The other two headings are easily interpreted when placed before and after self-alienation.

Let's start with the antithesis, self-alienated Spirit. It is not begging the question to refer to self-alienated Spirit as the antithesis. We already know from the macrodialectic that Spirit progresses separation-and-return style from (1) union to (2) self-alienation, or separation, to (3) reunion. In stage one, union, Spirit is only unconsciously (potentially) united because it has no mind with which to recognize its essential unity. In stage two, self-alienated (also called self-estranged) man appears on earth, giving Spirit its Mind. Spirit's Mind, working through man's mind, perceives external objects that it fails to recognize as itself, as being unified by an internal essence that is Spirit. Spirit thereby becomes alienated from itself. In stage three, Spirit becomes reunited with itself when Hegel's brilliant mind finally recognizes that he and every-thing else in the universe are essentially Spirit, one entity.

Both the words "self-alienated" and the placement of those words in second position, B, within the A-B-C triad identify "Self-alienated" Spirit as an antithesis. Self-alienated Spirit, Spirit's *existential* state (existence), is an untrue concept of Spirit, for it treats Spirit as many entities. Spirit in its *essen-tial* state (essence) is the true Spirit. The true Spirit is what Spirit essentially is, one entity; the truth is that Spirit is a union of all of the particulars in the universe. We can see, therefore, that heading A, "The *true* Spirit," should be interpreted as the thesis.

Once headings A and B are identified as the dialectic's thesis and antith-esis, there is no room for doubt that (C) "Spirit that is certain of itself," is the synthesis. Confirmation comes from the wording of the heading itself. Spirit becomes reunited with itself when it realizes ("self-realization") that "subject" (a human observer) and "object" (anything observed) are both Spirit, hence that they are one. When this happens, Spirit is certain of itself—certain of what it really is. Here "certain" is a variant of the word "certainty," which is part of the description of self-realization in the penultimate sentence of *Phenomenology*. There Hegel says that history and science (Hegel's dialectical concept of science) form "the actuality, truth, and *certainty* of his [Absolute Spirit's] throne" (my italics).[4]

The words "truth" and "actuality" in the quoted sentence have their own dia-lectical implications. "Truth" alludes to the contrast between true Spirit, which is just one entity, and self-alienated Spirit, which perceives itself as many entities ("objects"). Here we have confirmation that "The *true* Spirit" refers to Spirit in its thesis stage, where it is one rather than many; as such it is potentially (but not yet realized as) true. "Actuality" refers to the potential-actual dichotomy. Spirit moves from (1) the thesis of *potential* union to (2) the antithesis of *actual* separa-tion, or self-alienation, to (3) the synthesis of *actual* union. True Spirit becomes actuality—Absolute Spirit—when Spirit becomes "certain of itself."

We see that the A-B-C dialectic under the "Spirit" heading is nothing but a disguised form of variant 2 of the macrodialectic from chapter 3:

Thesis: potential + union ("The true Spirit")
Antithesis: actual + separation ("Self-alienated Spirit")
Synthesis: actual + union ("Spirit that is certain of itself")

Since true Spirit is one and self-alienated Spirit is many, this dialectic can also be conceptualized the same way as two variants of the VI-VII-VIII dialectic, but with one and many transposed:

Thesis: one   Thesis: one
Antithesis: many   Antithesis: many
Synthesis: one = many   Synthesis: one composed of many

The Natural-Artificial Dialectic. The last intermediate dialectic consists of the three subheadings under heading VII, Religion. Those subheadings are (A) "Natural Religion," (B) "Religion in the Form of Art," and (C) "The Revealed Religion." Although the thesis-antithesis concepts are new, this dialectic is the easiest of all to recognize. The reason is that the concepts are the least disguised among those of the three intermediate dialectics discussed here. The thesis concept is "natural." No disguise at all here. Hegel actually uses the word "natural": "*Natural* Religion." The antithesis concept is disguised, but barely so. Hegel now uses the word "art": "Religion in the Form of Art." Art is man-made. Anything man-made is artificial rather than natural. And *artificial* just happens to be the opposite or antithesis of the first concept, *natural*. Once "art" is recognized as a disguised phrasing of "artificial," the first two stages of a dialectic are plainly visible. Natural is the thesis; artificial is the antithesis.

The synthesis of natural and artificial is obviously going to be "natural = artificial." But the synthesis heading we are working with is (C) "The Revealed Religion." How do we get from (a) revealed religion to (b) natural = artificial? Hegel provides two routes. The first route treats what Hegel calls "revealed religion" as a synthesis of Christianity and philosophy. Christianity provides the labels—Father, Son, and Holy Spirit—and Hegelian philosophy provides new substance for those labels. All three members of the Trinity become Spirit.

Where this particular dialectic is concerned, the label that really matters is Son. Son refers to Jesus of Nazareth, believed by Christians to be the Christ (messiah). According to Johannine theology, Jesus was God incarnate. And according to the Council of Chalcedon (451 CE), Jesus was "fully God and fully man." Viewed as man, Jesus, the real historical person, was a *natural* being. Viewed as God incarnate, Jesus is an *artificial* being, because gods are artificial creations that emanate from the human mind. (Whatever you may believe, this was certainly the belief of Hegel, an atheist.) So the Johannine Jesus is a synthesis of natural and artificial, both a natural being (the historical Jesus) and a man-made artifact (God incarnate), created by what Hegel calls "picture-thinking." Jesus, Christianity's Son, can therefore symbolize the Hegelian notion that man is God, or Spirit, given that Hegel sometimes calls Spirit "God." And if man is "God," we have an indirect repetition of the man = God synthesis of the first intermediate dialectic. The new synthesis: natural (man, Jesus) = artificial (God).

The second route to synthesis, which will be repeated in the last micro-dialectic, is Hegel's Trinity dialectic. God, the thesis, is artificial, the product of human thought. The Son, Jesus, is natural, a human being, *not* an imaginary being created by human thought. The third member of the Trinity, the Holy Spirit (the anthropomorphic God's inner self or soul), unites Father and Son when it descends on and possesses Jesus after he is baptized by John the Baptist. This event, spirit possession, creates a synthesis of God and man, the artificial being and the natural being.

The full dialectic is

> Thesis: natural
> Antithesis: artificial
> Synthesis: natural (Jesus, *man*) = artificial (*God*)

This dialectic can be reconceptualized as a man-God dialectic:

> Thesis: man (natural)
> Antithesis: God (artificial)
> Synthesis: man = God

THE MICRODIALECTICS

The Spirit progresses toward Absolute Spirit via a series of twenty-two microdialectics. All of these display separation from and return to something in the thesis. The microdialectics—short dialectics covering relatively few pages—can be likened to the play of children. Play develops a child's muscles and physical coordination. Spirit in its juvenile state is exercising its mind. It is going through lots of practice dialectics—little thoughts—that bring it to maturity, to the Big Thought of self-realization.

Using a different metaphor, education, Hegel describes this long series of dialectics as a process through which consciousness becomes *educated* in the ways of dialectics so that, in the end, it can recognize and comprehend the macrodialectic and its synthesis. You will recall from chapter 2 that Hegel, in *Phenomenology*'s Preface, announces that dialectics ("the triadic form") is the new "Science" he will use to arrive at "truth." A long road, twenty-two micro-dialectics long as it happens, must be traversed to reach Absolute Knowledge, or truth. Each microdialectic, or perhaps each thesis, antithesis, and synthesis, is one of the "stations on the way."[5] And "the series of configurations [dia-lectics] which consciousness goes through along this road is, in reality, the detailed history of the *education* of consciousness itself to the standpoint of Science [dialectics]."[6] The overall journey is a process of "Becoming," and "this Becoming presents a slow-moving succession of [human] Spirits" in which "their goal is the revelation of the depth of Spirit."[7]

1. The Introduction's Dialectic. The first microdialectic is in *Phenomenology*'s Introduction. It was described in some detail in chapter 2 under the "Introduction" heading. A bare-bones summary of it will therefore suffice. The dialectic has two forms:

Thesis: potential + essence   Thesis: in itself
Antithesis: actual + existence   Antithesis: for itself
Synthesis: actual + essence   Synthesis: in and for itself

The second version (in itself, for itself) is particularly significant. This version is more easily recognized than the essence-existence version as restatement of,

or the analog of, the macrodialectic. In the macrodialectic's thesis state, Spirit
is unconscious (human minds have not yet arrived on earth). Spirit thus cannot
yet perceive anything external, so everything is "inner." The microdialectic's
"in itself" stage represents this "inner" stage of Spirit. In the macrodialectic's
antithesis stage, Spirit becomes conscious: man has arrived with his mind. Now,
using man's mind, Spirit can perceive external "objects." It interprets these
objects as alien. And because the objects all differ in their "outer" appearance,
they are perceived as many. The macrodialectic's "for itself" stage now has
perceived objects with "outer" features "for itself to display." These features are
misinterpreted as alien during the "outer" stage of Spirit—the antithesis stage.
In the microdialectic's synthesis stage, consciousness—Hegel's consciousness
on this occasion—recognizes that the hidden inner universality of everything
unites all the many external objects into one universe. The microdialectic's "in
and for itself" stage (inner + outer) depicts Spirit's self-realization.

2. **Master and Slave.** The microdialectics under Hegel's Roman numeral
headings begin in Part IV with the "master-and-slave" parable. ("Master and
slave" is sometimes translated as "master and servant" or "lord and bondsman.")
This parable provides (*a*) three variations of a basic two-concepts-per-stage
dialectic and (*b*) two more dialectics having one concept per stage. These five
dialectics are notable because they imitate the macrodialectic, which at this
point we—Hegel's readers—are not supposed to have yet figured out. (We are
still at a very early stage of our education in dialectics.) The first two-concepts-
per-stage dialectic is hard to miss if you are looking for a dialectic, because
its theme of independence is repeated over and over in the master-and-slave
discussion: Hegel injects the words "independent" and "independence" eleven
times in nineteen paragraphs.[8]

The basic master-and-slave dialectic's *thesis* is potential + independence.
The slave-to-be is, in his natural state, potentially independent. But he is
not yet actually independent, because he has not yet encountered another
human vis-à-vis whom he has established genuine independence: independence requires a relationship. The slave-to-be's status before meeting another
person, an external object, is equivalent to—and symbolizes—Spirit's status
in the macrodialectic before acquiring a human mind and perceiving external
objects.

The parable's *antithesis* is actual + dependence. The slave-to-be encounters, fights, and submits to the person who becomes the master. The encounter symbolizes Spirit's acquiring a mind and perceiving alien external objects. The *synthesis* is actual + independence. The master becomes dependent on the slave and thereby involuntarily bestows a sort of independence—de facto dominance—on the slave; the slave returns to independence. The master's dependence symbolizes Absolute Spirit's dependence on man's realization that *he* is Spirit. Summary:

> Thesis: potential + independence
> Antithesis: actual + dependence
> Synthesis: actual + independence

A second potential-actual variant more precisely anticipates Hegel's macrodialectic as well as one of Hegel's two main history dialectics, the freedom dialectic that I discuss in chapter 5. History's goal, according to the history dialectic, is freedom. Variant 27 of the macrodialectic and history's freedom dialectic are both identical to the master-and-slave freedom dialectic, presented below. Freedom, in addition to being the goal of a history dialectic is also one of the goals of self-realization in the macrodialectic. There Hegel treats self-realization as freedom in the sense of being an escape from the bondage of religion. Solomon aptly summarizes the importance of freedom in the master-and-slave dialectic: "The discussion of 'freedom' in the *Phenomenology* begins with Hegel's famous discussion of the 'Master-Slave' relationship, which would seem like a parable of freedom except for one thing: that discussion turns on a paradox according to which it is the slave, not the master, who comes to realize his freedom."[9]

In Hegel's vernacular, independence is a synonym for freedom. The concept of freedom, in turn, brings us back to the freedom that arrives when Spirit undergoes self-realization, becoming Absolute Spirit. This freedom, previously discussed in chapter 3's last section, is release from bondage to God, to religion, and to religious superstition. When man (Spirit's mind) realizes that *he* rather than the imaginary supernatural being in heaven is "the divine," or God, man no longer endures the psychological—and sometimes physical and economic—pain caused by religion. Because this release-from-bondage form of freedom equates with independence, the independence dialectic converts to the freedom dialectic:

Thesis: potential + freedom
Antithesis: actual + bondage
Synthesis: actual + freedom

This dialectic is what underlies Hegel's famous master-and-slave tale. I pointed out in chapter 3 that the tale is a parable, a story in which people, things, and events have hidden meanings. In Hegel's parable, the master symbolizes God and the slave symbolizes man. The slave-to-be is *potentially* free in his natural state. But freedom cannot be actual unless there exists an external power that might place the subject (man) in bondage.

The thesis of potential freedom becomes the antithesis of actual bondage when man meets and surrenders to another person, an external entity. That person, the master (God), overpowers and enslaves the subject. Potential freedom becomes actual bondage. This development symbolizes early man's use of his imagination ("picture-thinking") to create gods and associated religions. Since Hegel is primarily concerned with Christianity, the development more specifically symbolizes the work of the ancient Jews, who imagined Yahweh into existence and created a Yahweh-based religion. Yahweh evolved into Christianity's God, and an originally Jewish sect centered on Jesus worship evolved into Christianity when the Jesus-oriented sect spread into the Hellenistic (culturally Greek) world and incorporated various non-Jewish ideas. Christianity placed, or at least kept, man in bondage by imposing the suffering (e.g., "fastings and mortifications"[10]) detailed in (*a*) Hegel's discussions of "the Unhappy Consciousness," (*b*) "The Revealed Religion," and (*c*) the Rome-to-Germanic-World subdialectic of *The Philosophy of History* (see chapter 5).

When the master later becomes dependent on the slave, and both parties recognize this, the slave in effect becomes the master. The slave "receives back its own self," a self that is essentially free; the master, recognizing his own dependence, "lets the other again go free."[11] This role reversal symbolizes man's (the slave's) becoming God (the master). Man becomes God when self-realization occurs—when man, thinking with Hegel's mind, realizes that there is no supernatural God and that *man* (plus everything else in the universe) is the true God. God's dependence on man allows two interpretations. First, the false God's existence depends on man's false belief that supernaturalism's God exists. Second, the existence of the true God, Absolute Spirit (no longer just plain Spirit), depends on man's realization that he is Spirit and that Spirit is "God," the divine. In the parable, the master (God) recognizes his dependence on the slave (man) because God is man: man's recognition = God's recognition. When man becomes God and the enslaver God vanishes, the dialectic's synthesis of actual freedom materializes.

The potential-actual microdialectic can also be construed a third way: as potentially *united*, actually separated, and then actually united, a unified pair of interdependent persons. Before the master and slave meet, their ultimate relationship is only potential; it hasn't yet been established. But there is no perceived separation, because neither is aware of the other's existence. Then they meet and fight. Now, as they fight, they are actually separated; they view each other as separate beings, opponents; each is "alien" to the other. Here Hegel is symbolizing subject's failure to recognize that the objects it sees and misconstrues as "alien" are really itself, because both subject and object share an invisible inner reality, Spirit (just a concept). Finally, the weaker combatant submits and becomes the stronger man's slave. The stronger man becomes the master. But only temporarily, because the master soon becomes dependent on the slave. In this new relationship each person is dependent in some sense on the other. Master and slave thus constitute an interdependent whole, a union; they represent actual unity. Summary:

> Thesis: potential + union
> Antithesis: actual + separation
> Synthesis: actual + union

We can easily see that this third version of the microdialectic mimics the macrodialectic's three stages—specifically, variant 2 of the macrodialectic. The master-and-slave dialectic is variant 2 of the macrodialectic in disguise. Hegel has devised this piece of fiction to analogically illustrate what is happening in the macrodialectic. The microdialectic's thesis stage, where the slave has never encountered another human, is analogous to the macrodialectic's thesis stage, where Spirit has never perceived an external object (because Spirit is in its unconscious, prehuman stage). The microdialectic's antithesis stage, where the slave sees another human and treats him as alien, is analogous to Spirit's antithesis stage of separation. This is the stage where Spirit acquires a Mind (man, with his mind, has evolved) and perceives external objects. Spirit, in the guise of "consciousness," construes the objects it sees as alien, things other than itself. The microdialectic's synthesis stage, in which master and slave merge into *one* entity, is analogous to Spirit's synthesis stage, where the one and the many merge into "one composed of many." (The "many" are really just two in the parable, but the analogy remains reasonably intact.)

A fourth variant of the master-and-slave microdialectic again uses the parable's symbolism, wherein the slave symbolizes man and the master symbolizes God. This variant abandons the two-part-stages format in favor of the equality format. In this format, the synthesis reveals that the antithesis is the thesis in disguise: thesis = antithesis. *Thesis*: The parable first introduces the man symbol, the slave. *Antithesis*: The God symbol, the master, appears next. The slave's submitting to the master symbolizes man's using his imagination to create God, to whom man submits, thereby entering the stage of bondage. *Synthesis*: The slave ultimately realizes (self-realization) that the master depends on him, and that he (the slave) has become the master. The slave's becoming the master symbolizes man's becoming God when Spirit, thinking with Hegel's mind, finally realizes that it is all reality or "the divine," God. It follows that *man* is God: man embodies Spirit's mind and is thus the most important part of reality. Summary:

> Thesis: man (the slave)
> Antithesis: God (the master)
> Synthesis: man = God (slave = master)

One other feature of the macrodialectic's state of self-realization that the master-and-slave dialectic foreshadows is subject-object identity. In Hegel's system, "subject" is a human mind, also called "consciousness." "Object" is anything whatsoever, sometimes another human, that subject perceives through its senses, typically sight. Subject and object are both essentially Spirit; Spirit is the hidden *inner* essence of both. Subject and object are therefore identical. But, in its pre-self-realization state of self-estrangement, subject doesn't know this. Subject (Spirit) thinks object (also Spirit) is what object's visible *outer* appearance suggests: something apart from itself, or "alien." When Spirit finally undergoes self-realization, becoming Absolute Spirit, it realizes that the object—and every object it perceives—is itself. At that point the potential identity of subject and object becomes their actual identity, or "subject-object identity." Subject-object identity is also the identity of mind (subject, consciousness) and matter (object, the physical universe)—the physical side and the mental side of the four-faceted Spirit.

Hegel narrates the master-and-slave dialectic from the perspective of the slave, whose original name is "self-consciousness." Self-consciousness (the slave-to-be) sees another self-consciousness (the master-to-be). The first self-consciousness is therefore the observer or, in Hegel's subject-object parlance, the subject. The second self-consciousness is the object. Hegel even calls the master "the object" and "that object."[12] He adds: "What is 'other' for it [the slave-to-be] is an unessential, negatively characterized object."[13] In the synthesis, where the master becomes dependent on the slave, each character is both a master and a slave. That makes them identical, if only for philosophical purposes. What happens in the macrodialectic is analogous: in the synthesis, subject realizes that object is identical to itself. The parable thus provides another preview of the macrodialectic. The result is this additional master-and-slave dialectic:

> Thesis: subject
> Antithesis: object
> Synthesis: subject = object (subject-object identity)

These parallels show that other interpreters have completely missed the point in the extensive literature analyzing the master-and-slave fable. The interpreters have variously, and imaginatively, claimed the fable conveys commentaries on slavery, Greek society, clashes between and conquests by nations, the Adam and Eve myth, Kant's or Fichte's or Rousseau's philosophy,

Hegelian ideas about morality, the social nature of knowledge, and the nature of and requirements for self-consciousness. The microdialectic does not allude to these things. Its referent is instead the macrodialectic. The master-and-slave dialectic is the macrodialectic in miniature. Hegel is educating us, and Spirit, in dialectics. This step in our joint education is designed to acquaint us with five aspects of Spirit's self-realization:

1. The potential-actual (thesis-antithesis) conceptual pair. In the master-and-slave dialectic, we encounter three examples of syntheses that turn an initially potential state (thesis state) into an actual state: (1) actual independence, (2) actual freedom, and (3) actual union.

2. The union-separation (thesis-antithesis) conceptual pair. The third of the above variants of the master-and-slave dialectic introduces us to union, separation, and reunion, also called separation and return. Every dialectic separates from and returns to something in the thesis.

3. Spirit's dual goal of freedom. Freedom is both (*a*) another way of expressing Spirit's goal of self-realization in *Phenomenology* and (*b*) one of history's two primary goals—the other is Prussian style monarchy—in *The Philosophy of History*. I elaborate below.

4. The subject-object identity theme. In Spirit's self-realization, Spirit in the guise of subject (the observer or "consciousness"), finally—after twenty-two microdialectics of "education" in dialectics—recognizes its identity with object, whoever or whatever subject observes, something originally perceived as separate from itself or "alien."

5. Spirit's realizing that man (slave) and everything else in the universe is "God" (master), the divine. Spirit recognizes that subject (itself) and object (also itself) are one and that the one, a universe composed of particulars, is the true divine, or God—a figurative God, not a literal supernatural God. This recognition (self-recognition, self-realization) is the recognition that God (Spirit) is man (the most important part of Spirit, its Mind).

Regarding point 5 above, self-realization equates with freedom—for two reasons. First, self-realization frees man from bondage to religious superstition, as symbolized by self-estrangement. When man receives the Absolute Knowledge that he, not an imaginary supernatural being in heaven, is the divine, man no longer subjects himself to the torment of subjugation to God and to the outrageous demands (worship, tithing, celibacy, flagellation, and so on) God imposes on humans. Second, self-realization gives Spirit "complete freedom" from the bondage of self-estrangement, which amounts to the same thing as the bondage of religion.[14]

3. Stoicism. The master-and-slave dialectic encapsulates the big picture, the macrodialectic, in a small parable that has elements of realism but is ultimately unreal, a work of fiction that symbolically delivers a message about freedom. From this fictional beginning Hegel moves on to the real world, where real people are striving to become free. Now, instead of describing the travails of a person in physical bondage (the slave), Hegel describes the plight of "self-consciousness in a new shape, . . . a being which thinks."[15] Here Hegel is contrasting the physical enslavement of the parable's slave with the mental enslavement found in the real people of Greek and Roman society. The real people are the stoic, the skeptic, and the religious person. They wish to escape from the despair of their personal situations (sometimes literal slavery). The first two—the stoic and the skeptic—seek freedom through philosophy, the last through religion. Hegel subsumes these real people under the heading "Freedom of Self-Consciousness"; Solomon substitutes a more apt heading, "Freedom through Fantasy."[16]

Man is free to think, but his thoughts arise in the material world of existence. In the stoic's case, and the skeptic's too, man's thinking returns abstractly to the freedom variant of the master-and-slave parable. "Self-conscious" man is potentially free, because his being is defined by thinking, which cannot be bound by chains. But he is not actually free, because the historical period in question was "a time of universal fear and bondage," fetters on the enjoyment of life.[17] Hegel elaborates: "Freedom in thought has only *pure thought* as its truth, a truth lacking the fullness of life. Hence freedom in thought . . . is only the Notion [concept] of freedom, not the living reality of freedom itself."[18] Man escapes from this plight by becoming a stoic. He becomes indifferent to his material world situation and thereby becomes actually free. What we have here is a repetition of the freedom variant of the master-and-slave dialectic:

Thesis: potential + freedom
Antithesis: actual + bondage
Synthesis: actual + freedom (interpreted as indifference to bondage)

Like the master-and-slave dialectic, the stoicism dialectic is (*a*) a miniature version of variant 27 of the macrodialectic. And it will be repeated in (*b*) the skepticism dialectic, coming up next, (*c*) an overarching history dialectic, and (*d*) two shorter history dialectics describing subperiods of history. All told, the freedom dialectic appears seven times. Why so much repetition? Because this dialectic conveys Hegel's most basic message: the goal of Spirit (in *Phenomenology*) and the goal of history (in *The Philosophy of History*) are the same: freedom. In the context of Spirit's divine life, this goal is achieved when Spirit achieves self-realization, the realization that the true God is not supernatural but natural: man, who constitutes Spirit's Mind. In the context of history, the goal is achieved when the Prussian monarchy arrives and with it a philosopher named Hegel, who comes to the realization that he is God.

4. Skepticism. The stoic's solution to human despair over the conditions of life proves unworkable. If you don't understand Hegelian dialectics, you won't understand why. This is because stoicism's being unworkable results from its failure to completely fulfill the requirements of a dialectical synthesis. A Hegelian dialectical synthesis is a "negation of the negation." It must negate an earlier negation. The earlier negation is the dialectic's second stage, the antithesis, which negates the first stage, the thesis or affirmation. The stoic's dialectical synthesis (mere indifference to the plight of existence) results in "the *incomplete* negation of otherness" (my italics), where "otherness" is the oppressive nonmental side of existence.[19] In other words, the stoic recognizes—affirms—the oppression rather than denying that it exists. The stoic's synthesis therefore "has not . . . achieved its consummation as absolute negation."[20] Partial negation—mere indifference or apathy—is not complete or "absolute" negation.

The skeptic solves this problem. He does so by using "thinking which annihilates [fully negates] the being of the world." Now "the negativity of free self-consciousness comes to know itself in the many and varied forms of life as *real* negativity" (my italics). The result is "a negative attitude towards otherness, to desire and work."[21] Skepticism thus "exhibits the *dialectical movement* which Sense-Certainty, Perception, and the Understanding each is" (Hegel's italics).[22] This last quotation not only verifies that, in referring to "negativity," Hegel is talking dialectical talk; it also verifies the correctness of my chapter 2 interpretation of Hegel's discussion of consciousness. In that interpretation I said that (1) "Sense Certainty," (2) "Perception," and (3) "Force and the Understanding" are, respectively, the thesis, antithesis, and synthesis of a dialectic. Both "Force and the Understanding" and the skeptic's negation of the pain of existence negate earlier negations. Both bear the label "negation of the negation." Skepticism uses exactly the same microdialectic that stoicism uses. But the synthesis, actual + freedom, comes from a different philosophical premise. The skeptic goes beyond indifference by denying that bondage exists. The bondage is both figurative and literal. Many citizens had to endure harsh conditions in Greek and Roman society (figurative bondage); many others, the slaves, were literally in bondage. The most important thing to be understood about Hegel's discussion of skepticism is this: the point of the discussion is not what just about every other interpreter thinks it is. Hegel is not particularly concerned with appraising the philosophy of skepticism. He is simply constructing another dialectic. He is educating us in his "Science" of dialectics. In the process, he is padding his discussion with irrelevant details of skepticism and its history so as to disguise what he is doing and also to add bulk to his discussion. At the same time he is restating his call for freedom from bondage to religious superstition. Summary:

> Thesis: potential + freedom
> Antithesis: actual + bondage
> Synthesis: actual + freedom (interpreted as denial of bondage)

Hegel does throw in a nondialectical criticism of skepticism, but he does so mainly to effect a transition from philosophy to religion, not because of any genuine need to refute the tenets of skepticism. His criticism—a remarkable outburst of clarity—is this: "Its talk is like the squabbling of self-willed children, one of whom says *A* if the other says *B*, and in turn says *B* if the other says *A*, and who by contradicting *themselves* buy for themselves the pleasure of continually contradicting *one another*."[23] Skepticism, in short, is "internally contradictory."[24]

5. Unhappy Consciousness. Both of the two featured schools of Greek and Roman philosophy have now proven themselves inadequate to overcome the plight of human existence. So "consciousness"—the human mind doing double duty as Spirit's Mind—turns to religion in its search for fulfillment . . . and becomes the Unhappy Consciousness.

The Unhappy Consciousness moves a step closer to Absolute Knowledge by seeking fulfillment in a relationship not with another human (analogous to the master) but with a supernatural entity. That entity is a rational, self-conscious deity (the wrong entity, God, but the right general idea, the more abstract "divine"). The Unhappy Consciousness microdialectic has stages identical to those of the macrodialectic: (1) potential + union, (2) actual + separation, and (3) actual + union (union with God). Conscious first tries devotion, "pure consciousness" of the divine—a blend of such worshipful practices as "the chaotic jingling of bells" and "a mist of warm incense."[25] This union is merely potential, because the communication—acts intended to please the deity—is unidirectional, human to divine.

Unsatisfied, man turns away from the external deity and, moving closer to the truth, treats *himself* as an "incarnate" form of the divine: he tries to please *himself* by seeking fulfillment in desire and work. When something nice happens, he dutifully thanks the divine, but otherwise he largely ignores the divine. This low degree of reverence—the replacement of religiosity with secularism—passes for alienation from the divine. Hegel surely alludes here to Greek religion. If we overlook the Greek mystery cults, the Greek citizenry's relationship with the Greek gods can definitely be characterized as the antithesis of religious fervor—the antithesis of bells and incense. Hegel can therefore say that stage two is "the antithesis of [contrast between] the universal [divinity] and the individual [humans]."[26] This quotation gives us the dialectic's antithesis: actual + separation.

The synthesis, actual + union, arrives with medieval Christianity. Now a Catholic priest overcomes the unidirectional communication of the thesis by serving as a mediator in two-way communications between man and God. (In *The Philosophy of History*, Hegel makes this "mediator" role even more explicit in describing the Catholicism of the Middle Ages: "The clergy are the medium between man on the one hand and God and Christ on the other hand."[27]) Consciousness *returns* to God by confessing to God, via the priest, the "petty actions" that have "defiled" it.[28] The priest, in turn, reconciles the alienated consciousness with the deity by acting as God's agent and discharging consciousness's sins (confession and absolution). Hegel's animosity toward Catholicism and its practice of confession is revealed in this passage, which also provides another reason ("the terrors of Hell") why consciousness is unhappy: "The terrors of Hell are exhibited to man in the most terrible colors, to induce him to escape from them, not by moral amendment, but in virtue of something external—the 'means of grace.'. . . The 'Confessor' [priest] must furnish him with them."[29] The priest also "ministers by giving advice [relaying God's word] on what is right," namely, giving away to the Church "part of what it [consciousness] has acquired through work," enduring "fastings and mortifications," surrendering "its right to decide for itself," and "practising what it does not understand" (Latin services).[30] The upshot is the aforementioned two-way communication, which is what the thesis stage lacked. Now man speaks to God via the mediator-priest, and *God speaks to man* via the priest. God and man are finally united through two-way communication.

This microdialectic emphasizes the separation-and-return theme of Hegel's dialectics by (1) using a unified, nonincarnate deity (God is entirely in heaven, not present on earth) to symbolize the Trinity's unified, pre-incarnation God, (2) using the incarnate-God status of man (who is now treating himself as God) in the antithesis to symbolize the Son, separated from God, and (3) using the priest of the synthesis to symbolize the Holy Spirit, the intermediary between and reuniter (spirit possession) of God and man. The second stage really has double symbolism, because it alludes to the multiple gods of Greek religion: the divine is *separated* into many gods. In summary, the dialectic is

Thesis: potential + union (one-way communication)

Antithesis: actual + separation (indifference to the divine, rare thanks)

Synthesis: actual + union (two-way communication, the priest as
mediator)

Hegel's treatment of the Unhappy Consciousness has been widely
misinterpreted as referring almost exclusively to Christianity. Baillie relates
Unhappy Consciousness to "the religious life of the Middle Ages and the
mental attitude assumed under the domination of the Roman Catholic Church
and the Feudal Hierarchy."[31] Findlay believes "this Unhappy Consciousness
is for Hegel the two-world consciousness of medieval Christendom."[32]
Kaufmann thinks "Hegel becomes absorbed in allusions to the specific
features of the medieval Christian mentality that, as he sees it, exemplified the
unhappy consciousness."[33] Norman thinks the Unhappy Consciousness relates
exclusively to "the doctrines and practices of Christianity";[34] he relates it to
no other religions. Solomon states, "There can be no doubt that 'Unhappy
Consciousness' is orthodox Christianity."[35] He specifically associates the
earliest stage of unhappiness—"the chaotic jingling of bells, a mist of warm
incense"—with "traditional Catholicism."[36] Pinkard likewise associates this
early bells-and-incense stage with "the early Christian church."[37] Forster says
Unhappy Consciousness has a touch of Neoplatonism but refers "mainly to
Christianity from its emergence in the Roman Empire down to medieval
Europe."[38] Stern also identifies Unhappy Consciousness, including the bells
and incense, with Christianity.[39]

Although some of the above scholars mention that Hegel's jibes are aimed
partly at religion in general, the only analysts I have found who think Hegel
has significant targets other than Christianity are Burbidge, M. Taylor, and
S. Rosen. Burbidge cites both Buddhism and the oriental religions that came
to Rome in the second and third centuries, Mithraism in particular.[40] Taylor
devotes a paragraph to "the unhappy consciousness of the Jewish religion."[41]
Rosen says that "the unhappy consciousness surely has pagan, Jewish and
Christian forms" and that "in its Jewish manifestation, the unhappy consciousness renders man the slave of God."[42]

My own view is that all of these authors are overlooking a historical chronology reflected in the Unhappy Conscious dialectic. The middle stage, which displays relative indifference to divinity and a consequent *absence of unhappiness*, resembles Greek religion, not Christianity. I refer to Greek polytheism, not to the Greek mystery cults and Gnostic cults. The Greek polytheists didn't take their gods too seriously: that perfunctory "thank you" to the gods when something went right surely has the sound of Greek religion. It can hardly be Christianity. Another reason for thinking that the middle stage refers to Greek religion is that the Greeks recognized *many* gods. Using Greek polytheism as the antithesis (middle stage) gives Hegel a dialectic that moves from a thesis of *one* (Jewish religion, coming up next) to *many* (Greek religion) to *one and many* (the mediated union of the *one* God of Christianity with the *many* Christian worshippers).

Now, if the antithesis does allude to Greek religion, the thesis stage or "first mode,"[43] with its jingling bells and incense, should refer to something still earlier. Moreover, "first mode" is a dead giveaway. By now it should be obvious to everyone that Hegel is using thesis-antithesis-synthesis dialectics and that "first mode" refers to the first stage, the thesis. Greek religion and early Hebrew religion overlapped chronologically. But Greek religion didn't begin until around 1500 BCE, whereas Judaism with its Yahweh worship began much earlier. And whereas early Christianity may have incorporated bells and incense, so did Old Testament Judaism, which is where the idea originated. We find references to jingling bells in Exodus 28:33–35 and 39:25–26 and in Zechariah 14:20. Incense is mentioned in Exodus 30:7, 25–27, and 35–37 and in Jeremiah 44:20–21. In Matthew's tale of the three wise men and the Christ child, the wise men bring gifts of frankincense and myrrh (Mt. 2:10–11), ingredients of incense. This was a pre-Christian event: Mary and Joseph were Jews, and the gifts implicitly recognized Jewish, not Christian, religious practices. Christianity didn't yet exist.

These observations suggest that only the synthesis stage of the dialectic, the stage with mediating Catholic priests, alludes to early (maybe, maybe not) and medieval (preponderantly if not exclusively medieval) Christianity. The synthesis stage and only the synthesis stage is the object of Hegel's scarifying criticisms of Christianity.

Hyppolite, without identifying Unhappy Consciousness's three stages with specific religions, has a relevant observation: "Hegel . . . envisaged the Greeks as the happy people of history and the Jews as the unhappy people. He also viewed Christianity as one of the great forms of unhappy consciousness."[44] This observation supports my inference that three stages of the Unhappy Consciousness dialectic chronologically represent early Judaism, Greek religion, and Christianity. Hegel definitely associates unhappiness with the first stage, with its jingling bells and incense. Referring to the thesis stage or "first mode," he says, "Consciousness, therefore, can only find as a present reality the grave of its life."[45]

The second stage, where man becomes more or less alienated from the divine, is characterized by "work and enjoyment." Consciousness finds itself "enjoying . . . existence in the form of independent things"—independence from divine harassment.[46] Surely we can all interpret enjoyment as happiness. This enjoyment corresponds to the happiness of the Greeks, as described by Hyppolite. Hegel can thus refer to "the free, joyful Spirit of Greece."[47]

In the third stage, man returns to religion ("separation and return" again) and experiences particularly severe unhappiness. This is the stage where the allusions to specifically Christian things apply. And, whereas Forster sees these allusions as applying to both early and medieval Christianity, Hegel's attack seems directed almost exclusively at medieval Christianity. The bells and incense, which I take as the basis for Forster's conclusion that early Christianity is also under attack, relate to early Judaism, not to early Christianity. The Unhappy Consciousness's separation from God (Greek religion) and return to God (medieval Christianity) alludes, of course, to Spirit's separation from and return to unity in the macrodialectic.

It is undeniable, however, that all three stages of the dialectic also allude to the members of the Trinity—Father, Son, and Holy Spirit:

- **Father:** In the thesis stage, unity of God and man is only potential because communication runs in only one direction: man to God (prayer and ritual). The allusion is to the Trinitarian Father stage, potential unity; we shall encounter this allusion again in Hegel's "Revealed Religion" microdialectic. (The separation-and-return formula, you will recall from chapter 3, uses Trinitarian symbolism.)

- **Son:** In the antithesis stage, the Unhappy Consciousness's indifference to the divine represents separation. This separation alludes to the Son who separates from God and comes to earth as a man, God incarnate. In the process, God separates from himself.

- **Holy Spirit:** In the synthesis stage of the Unhappy Consciousness microdialectic, the reunion of God and man (through mediated two-way communication) symbolizes the work of the Holy Spirit, which unites God and man through spirit possession. The Holy Spirit mediates, unites. When it descended on Jesus at the baptism, it united Jesus and God. Catholicism's mediating priest represents the unifying Holy Spirit.

Hegel, I should mention, is quite fond of Father-Son-Holy Spirit symbolism. When we get to his history dialectics (chapter 5) and to the Rome-to-Germanic-World subdialectic, we will find him explicitly calling the dialectic's three periods the Father, the Son, and the Holy Spirit.

Yet, despite these Trinitarian allusions, the Judaism-Greece-Christianity set of allusions is also apparent. I don't think the Trinitarian and the historical allusions conflict. Hegel intended both. The three stages of the dialectic allude both to the three historical periods (early Judaism, Greece, and medieval Christianity) and to the three members of the Trinity (Father, Son, and Holy Spirit).

6. Observation of Nature. The section on Unhappy Consciousness concludes the material on self-consciousness. Hegel moves on to the next main heading, "Reason," and to heading V, "The Certainty and Truth of Reason." Naturally, the religious solution leaves consciousness unhappy—abused financially, physically, and emotionally and denied freedom of thought. So consciousness drifts away from religion and seeks solace in reason.

The first microdialectic under Hegel's "Reason" heading involves "Observation of Nature." But this microdialectic really reaches back to the preceding heading, IV-B, "Stoicism, Scepticism, and the Unhappy Consciousness." The three dialectical stages of the new microdialectic are (1) potential + truth, (2) actual + falsehood, and (3) actual + truth. Scepticism and the Unhappy Consciousness respectively represent philosophy and religion. Both are potential sources of truth. Philosophy yields truth because Hegel's philosophy will at the end of the book become the source of truth. Religion yields truth because the Christian religion rightly proclaims the unity of man and the divine, albeit (*a*) the wrong concept of man (Jesus alone instead of all mankind) and (*b*) the wrong "divine" (God instead of Spirit). That is to say, Christianity is "true," but only in the abstract.

When we advance from the abstract concepts of philosophy and religion to their concrete teachings, however, we encounter actual falsehoods, the antithesis of potential truth. The skeptic's assertion that real situations are unreal is false. The Church's assertion that all sorts of supernatural things are factual is also false. We now have a two-concept antithesis, actual + falsehood, both of whose concepts are antithetical to the two concepts of the thesis, potential + truth.

Finished with the thesis and the antithesis, Hegel moves from heading IV to heading V. Here he describes a particular form of "reason" that produces genuine truth, or actual + truth. This truth is not the Absolute Knowledge consciousness is seeking but is nevertheless a preliminary form of truth. Hegel's observational reason (V-A, "Observing Reason") is certainly rational, but it might better be labeled empiricism or science. Focusing on biology and physics, Hegel lauds the virtue of observing relationships in large numbers of cases and then using inductive reasoning (particular to general) to formulate universal laws. Reason "puts the law to the test of experiment" and eventually arrives at "pure law"—truth.[48] The result is actual truth, or actual + truth.

Although the truths of science are not the truth consciousness is seeking, scientific truth does abstractly represent Absolute Knowledge, truth in another sense. In fact, the laws of science are closely analogous to the truth of Hegelian Absolute Knowledge: the law is general or "universal," and the many observations that support the law are particulars. So in the laws of science we have syntheses of universal and particular, the very thing we find in Absolute Knowledge. Summary:

> Thesis: potential + truth (of stoicism, skepticism, and medieval
>   Christianity)
> Antithesis: actual + falsehood (of stoicism, skepticism, and medieval
>   Christianity)
> Synthesis: actual + truth (of the natural sciences)

Once again allusions to the macrodialectic's separation and return are apparent. Truth has its referent in Spirit's essential unity, the state from which Spirit separates. We previously encountered truth in the first intermediate dialectic's thesis. Falsehood has its referent in the falseness of Spirit's perception of external objects as alien in its antithetical stage of separation. The synthesis of truth (unity) and falsehood (separation) has as its referent the macrodialectic's synthesis, wherein the many external objects, previously perceived as alien, are recognized as parts of a unified whole. Is this macrodialectic synthesis really "truth"? It is. Let's hear it from Hegel once more: "Reason [Absolute Knowledge] is Spirit when its certainty of being all reality has been raised to truth."[49]

7. **Observing Reason.** At this point Hegel begins a microdialectic that overlaps both the preceding one and the next one. This dialectic spans sub-headings a, b, and c of heading V-A, "Observing Reason." The three sub-headings deal with (a) observation of nature, or natural laws, (b) observation of self-consciousness, or psychological laws, and (c) physiognomy and phrenology, sources of what might be called pseudoscientific psychophysical laws. (The "psycho" refers to the mental inner character of a person, the "physical" to a person's outer physical characteristics.)

Observation of nature leads to the discovery of laws about the material world, the "outer" or visible world. The word "outer" provides the dialectic's thesis. Observation of self-consciousness, otherwise described as the study of psychology, leads to the discovery of behavioral laws that operate within human beings. These laws concern an "inner" or invisible world, the world of the mind. And so we arrive at the antithesis of "outer," which is "inner." The outer-before-inner order of presentation is, by the way, contrary to the usual order in which Hegel presents these concepts. Recall that the macrodialectic goes from inner to outer. The potential unity of the macrodialectic's thesis describes the inner essence, universality. The actual separation of the macrodialectic's antithesis describes the outer or external world, which subject perceives as a multitude of separate or alien objects with visible outer characteristics.

The synthesis of outer and inner is outer = inner. This synthesis is found in the pseudosciences of physiognomy and phrenology. These are the theories that a person's character is revealed by the shapes of faces (physiognomy) and the shapes of skulls (phrenology). The two pseudosciences, long since disproven, deal with the relationship between inner and outer. Persons are assumed to have inner behavioral tendencies or determinants; their actions are guided by inner (nonobservable) personality traits and tendencies—perhaps a tendency to murder—that are hidden. These inner tendencies are supposedly revealed by facial features and skull configurations, or outer (observable) traits. The inner and the outer come together when a person's actions or behavior (the inner tendency) conform to the person's physical features (the outer predictor): a person with (*a*) an inner tendency to murder and (*b*) facial characteristics that reveal that tendency actually (*c*) murders somebody. Physiognomy and phrenology thus provide a synthesis of inner and outer. The synthesis: outer = inner. The dialectic's three stages can be given the labels (not to be confused with the concepts the labels represent) nature (outer, visible), psychology (inner, the mind, invisible), and pseudoscience (outer = inner). Summary:

> Thesis: outer (natural laws, or physical laws)
> Antithesis: inner (psychological laws, or behavioral laws)
> Synthesis: outer = inner (psychophysical laws)

8. Physiognomy and Phrenology. Having used the two pseudosciences for one dialectic's synthesis, Hegel discovers that he can construct another microdialectic lying entirely within the physiognomy-phrenology sphere. In the abstract, this dialectic is like one of the variants of Hegel's macrodialectic: potential + essence, actual + existence, actual + essence, where "essence" is union and "existence" is separation. As already mentioned, the two pseudosciences hold that people have an inner character, say, that of a murderer or a philanthropist. This inner character is analogous to the macrodialectic's unconscious (potential) stage, wherein Spirit is divorced from externalities (outer things). The dialectic's thesis becomes inner, which refers to a person's essential (inner) character. Alternatively, the thesis can be called essence, because a person's essence is what that person essentially is, say, a murderer.

The antithesis of a person's inner character is his or her outer or external appearance—the face or the skull. Facial characteristics or bumps on the skull supposedly are the outward evidence of someone's inner character. These visible features can supposedly be used to predict behavior. This stage is closely analogous to the macrodialectic's "actual existence" stage (a variant of "actual separation"), wherein a human "subject" perceives external objects: we are now considering externality or outerness. Externality is the tangible reality we can actually see; it contrasts with a person's hidden, intangible character. The microdialectic's antithesis thus becomes outer (actual, seen). It can also be expressed as existence, or that which is seen to exist. Remember, existence refers to appearance, to what things appear to be (see chapter 2).

Thesis and antithesis merge into a synthesis when the person acts in a certain way—perhaps kills someone (internal character = murderer) or establishes and endows a new charitable institution (internal character = philanthropist) or writes a remarkable poem (internal character = poet). The person's outer actions are seen (but only by physiognomists and phrenologists, not by Hegel and modern science) to conform to both his inner character and his outer appearance. The actions prove that the inner character matches the outer character, as represented by face-skull features. (This assumes for dialectical purposes that physiognomy and phrenology are valid sciences.) The synthesis is inner = outer. The alternative synthesis is essence = existence (appearance). Summary:

Thesis: inner   Thesis: essence
Antithesis: outer   Antithesis: existence
Synthesis: inner = outer Synthesis: essence = existence

The proclivity of the microdialectics to imitate the macrodialectic becomes increasingly clear. The inner character of a person, as hypothesized by the two pseudosciences, is analogous to Spirit's innerness in its unconscious stage: Spirit is cut off from perception of externality. When the inner-outer microdialectic shifts its focus to a person's outer appearance, the result is analogous to Spirit's becoming conscious of external objects in its antithesis stage. The objects are judged by their outer appearance. They differ in appearance, so they are judged to be many different particulars. And when, in the microdialectic, inner and outer are merged in something a person does that shows agreement between his inner character and his outer appearance, we have the analog of Spirit's union of its inner essence (Spirit) and its outer appearance (the "alien" external objects).

By now just about all doubt should be gone about what Hegel is doing. He seldom has much if any concern about what he pretends is the substance of his analyses. His real concern is dialectics. He is constructing a long series of dialectics—the microdialectics—that imitate or describe parts of the macrodialectic or that otherwise describe Spirit. In a few cases, the microdialectics look forward to the history dialectics—to freedom and monarchy. I smile when I see an entire chapter in a book of essays about *Phenomenology* devoted to Hegel's musings about "Faces and Skulls."[50] That is taking the overt substance of Hegel's physiognomy-phrenology material much too seriously. It is probably true that Hegel wanted to get a few things off his chest where stupid theories are concerned, but refuting those theories is hardly the main purpose or even an important purpose of Hegel's commentary. Physiognomy is a scientific issue, not an issue of philosophical concern to Hegel. The real purpose of section V-A-c is to construct a dialectic that leads to a synthesis of inner and outer, the one essence (inner) and the many particular appearances (outer) that the essence unites.

Hegel is fascinated with dialectics. It is what he calls his Science, spelled by him with a capital S. He is pretending that the only way consciousness can reach the synthesis of his macrodialectic is to go through a lot of exercises that gradually give consciousness an awareness that it needs to think dialectically. Consciousness is maturing. Sooner or later—and it will definitely be later, much later—consciousness will catch on to the techniques of dialectical thinking. Or perhaps it will merely become conscious that it has been subconsciously thinking dialectically all along. It will then be able to extract "conscious" from "conscious + separation" and "union" from "unconscious + union," put the two extracts together, and achieve the glorious final synthesis: conscious + union.

Solomon has the right idea when he devotes just two sentences of his 646-page book, *In the Spirit of Hegel*, to physiognomy and phrenology. What Solomon says is all that needs to be said about the substance of Hegel's material: "Finally, in what is universally recognized to be the oddest single section of the entire book, Hegel considers the relationship between mind and body, 'inner activity' and 'outer expression,' a perennial philosophical question which Hegel hides quaintly and misleadingly behind the two notable pseudo-sciences of his day, *physiognomy* (the theory that one can tell a person's character from his facial features and body shape) and *phrenology* (Franz Joseph Gall's theory that character is reflected by the various bumps and shapes of the skull)."[51] I must add to these words the observation that the section does not seem nearly as odd when we recognize that there is dialectical method in Hegel's seeming madness.

9. **Faust.** Hegel turns next to moral perspectives, starting with hedonism, the pursuit of pleasure. In section V-B-a, "Pleasure and Necessity," Hegel alludes to an early version of Goethe's *Faust* that was available when Hegel wrote *Phenomenology*. Faust enters into a pact with Mephistopheles (the devil), who empowers Faust to obtain the pleasure he seeks. Faust then seduces Gretchen. But, in doing so, he indirectly causes the deaths of Gretchen's mother, her brother, and ultimately Gretchen herself. Regretting what he has done, Faust realizes that he, like Gretchen, her mother, and her brother, has become a victim—of Mephistopheles. Consciousness, now manifested in Faust, recognizes that it is one of the victims of its hedonism and that the "universality" of victimhood is "its own essence."[52] Gretchen has been seduced by Faust; Faust has been seduced by the devil.

The *Faust* tale generates several microdialectics. In the first, the thesis is predator (Faust), the antithesis is prey or "victim" (Gretchen), and the synthesis is predator = victim (Faust). Predator and victim are united in Faust, who is both. He is the synthesis. The dialectic:

> Thesis: predator (Faust)
> Antithesis: victim (Gretchen)
> Synthesis: predator = victim (Faust is now both)

This first *Faust* dialectic is actually a subtle restatement of the master-and-slave dialectic, which itself is subtle. Recall that the master symbolizes God, the slave symbolizes man, and the master = slave synthesis is a coded message: God = man. In the *Faust* dialectic, the predator is a reincarnation of the master and therefore an indirect symbol of God. The victim is a reincarnation of the slave and therefore an indirect symbol of man. And the predator = victim synthesis restates the earlier master = slave synthesis. Since the master-and-slave dialectic is a parable, you might say the *Faust* dialectic is a parable that retells or illustrates an earlier parable. This parable-of-a-parable formula elevates what has heretofore seemed like a pointless retelling of the *Faust* story to the status of second-most-important microdialectic. The most important microdialectic is, of course, the master-and-slave microdialectic, a more nearly direct statement of Hegel's message: there is no supernatural God, because the true God is, in essence, man.

A variation of this microdialectic comes from Hegel's line "uncomprehended power of universality, on which individuality is smashed to pieces."[53] This alludes to the universality of victimhood. When Faust makes his pact with Mephistopheles, he becomes a potential victim. He is not yet an actual victim, because he has not yet suffered his fate. Faust then becomes an actual predator, seducing Gretchen. When things go terribly wrong, Faust becomes an actual victim, as does everyone else. Everyone in the story (except Mephistopheles)— Faust, Gretchen, Gretchen's mother, and Gretchen's brother—becomes a victim; this explains Hegel's use of the word "universality." The new synthesis combines "victim" from the thesis with "actual" from the antithesis. This microdialectic results:

> Thesis: potential victim
> Antithesis: actual predator
> Synthesis: actual victim

The plot also has a self-alienation (separation from one's essential self) twist. The inner essence of both Faust and Gretchen is "victim." Faust and Gretchen are thus essentially one: both are victims and, as such, both are Hegel's "universal," victimhood. So Faust begins in a state of potential union with victimhood. But, just as "subject" does not recognize "object" as itself in Hegel's macrodialectic, Faust (subject) at first does not recognize Gretchen (object) as himself, a victim. Faust therefore becomes separated from his essential self, a victim, through his perception of Gretchen as a separate or "alien" object. It is only when Gretchen, her mother, and her brother die that Faust realizes that the object of his attention, Gretchen, is essentially himself, a victim. In essence, both are victims. The dialectic:

> Thesis: potential + union (with victimhood)
> Antithesis: actual + separation (Gretchen perceived as an "other" object)
> Synthesis: actual + union (with victimhood)

The *Faust* dialectic is much more than just another step in the education of Spirit in the ways of dialectics, more than a practice dialectic helping to develop Spirit's dialectical muscles. Like the master-and-slave dialectic, the *Faust* dialectic is a symbolized solution to the subject-object identity problem.

In the *Faust* dialectic, Faust symbolizes the Hegelian subject, the observer. Faust is filled with "desire." Gretchen is "its object," or "the object of [his] desire."[54] There you have it: Faust is the subject, Gretchen the object. Subject and object are potentially identical, but Faust doesn't recognize this. Then Faust too becomes a victim. He and Gretchen are now identical: both are victims. And Faust now realizes the *truth*. (Remember, Absolute Knowing is "truth"; and in the final two sentences of *Phenomenology* Spirit, by realizing that all objects are itself, realizes "the actuality, *truth*, and certainty" of its "infinitude," its being the divine.[55]) That truth is that Faust (subject) and Gretchen (object) are both victims. Subject and object are identical. And so we have this subject-object identity dialectic:

> Thesis: subject (Faust)
> Antithesis: object (Gretchen)
> Synthesis: subject = object (Faust and Gretchen are both victims)

10. The Law of the Heart. Hedonism gives way to sentimentalism, or what Hegel calls "the law of the heart."[56] This law is the idea that what is morally right should be determined by sentiments generated *within* a person. The objects of sentiment—deer or antiques, for example—can be anything a particular person happens to get emotional about. We can see that the law of the heart is a person's *inner* self. As such, it is also a person's essence, or essential self. The dialectic thus has two theses: inner and essence.

The law of the heart lacks universal appeal: different people get sentimental about different things (and possibly some don't get sentimental about anything). By establishing a law that says, in effect, that an individual's sentiments rule, the individual has placed himself in conflict with the differing sentiments of *other* individuals whose sentiments are alien to his own: "Others . . . turn against the reality *he* set up, just as he turned against theirs."[57] These "others" convert what the first individual intended as a universal "inner" law into an "outer" morass of particularity. This conflict of sentiments is the state of actual existence that the law of the heart creates. And so we have a double antithesis: outer and existence.

Eventually consciousness recognizes, begrudgingly, that an externally imposed "law of every heart," which is "the established living order" (customs and standards that everyone upholds), is as much a part of "its *own essential being*" as its internally imposed law of the heart.[58] The resulting microdialectic has a synthesis that combines the internal (the law of the heart) and the external (the variety of sentimental concerns) into "the law of every heart," which includes the heart of "consciousness," the observing person. When the "outer" particularity is rephrased as "existence" (conflicting laws of the heart), the dialectic becomes essence (one law of the heart), existence (many laws of the heart), and essence = existence. This, of course, is one of the variants of the macrodialectic toward which consciousness is creeping. The dialectic:

Thesis: inner   Thesis: essence
Antithesis: outer   Antithesis: existence
Synthesis: inner = outer   Synthesis: essence = existence

In the "law of the heart" dialectic, we once more see parallelism with the macrodialectic's movement from (1) a "universal" thesis stage where world's particulars go unperceived to (2) a "particular" antithesis stage of awareness of the outer world and its many particulars to (3) a reconciliation of the universal and the particular, the law of every heart. This is also a movement from one to many to their synthesis, the law of every heart. Two more microdialectics result:

Thesis: universal	Thesis: one
Antithesis: particular	Antithesis: many
Synthesis: universe	Synthesis: one
composed of particulars	composed of many

11. Virtue. The third and last moral viewpoint Hegel examines is virtue. Hegel calls virtue the "antithesis" of hedonism (Faust) and sentimentalism (the law of the heart). Hedonism and sentimentalism jointly constitute "individuality."[59] The two egoistic viewpoints assume that what is best or, in a sense, "right" for the individual is whatever that individual wants, be it pleasure (Faust) or upholding a sentimental value (the law of the heart). Under this self-centered approach, *one* (thesis) person determines what is right.

Virtue is the antithesis of individuality. Virtue assumes the existence of natural impulses or values that, because they are natural, are widely shared. *Many* (antithesis) persons supposedly determine what is right. We have arrived at a familiar Hegelian dichotomy: one and many.

Leaping wildly from ethics to the laissez-faire economic doctrines of Adam Smith, Hegel argues that individually determined actions taken in self-interest actually have the effect of maximizing the welfare of the many (society). He thus presents a synthesis in which what is best or right for the one is also best or right for the many. This Adam Smith synthesis isn't exactly the macrodialectic's synthesis of "one composed of many," but it amounts to much the same thing. The microdialectic can be phrased as follows:

Thesis: best for one (individuality: hedonism and law of the heart)
Antithesis: best for many (virtue: universal concepts of what is right)
Synthesis: best for one = best for many (laissez-faire economics)

12. The Matter in Hand. Individualism gets a new twist when Hegel begins discussing personal actions having practical rather than moral implications. He begins with activity in "the spiritual animal kingdom." This is the spiritual jungle where people behave like selfish animals. Consciousness first seeks what we today call self-esteem by finding worth in its own works. But it soon becomes apparent that the approval of others is necessary if those works are to boost the ego. To get this approval, consciousness does—or at least pretends to do—work related to some popular cause or recognized problem. Hegel calls this problem a "matter in hand."[60]

Unfortunately, everyone else has the same idea: doing something that others are sure to approve of. All the "animals" rush to the "matter in hand." The collective insincerity becomes apparent to all. This makes it impossible for consciousness to gain the recognition it seeks. Everyone's consciousness then recognizes the truth. "The matter in hand" is everyone's property; work on this "matter" serves both "universal and individual" ends; and "consciousness of it is the *ethical* consciousness" (contrasted with self-gratification).[61]

The microdialectic's thesis, then, is *internal* approval (individuality), analogous to the inward-directed orientation of the macrodialectic's potential union. The antithesis is *external* approval (universality), the approval consciousness seeks from external beings who participate in "testing laws." This testing by external persons is like subject's perception of *external* objects in the macrodialectic. The synthesis is *internal and external* approval—approval by both consciousness (the individual) and the community (universe) it participates in. The dialectic:

> Thesis: internal approval
> Antithesis: external approval
> Synthesis: internal *and* external approval

The "Matter in Hand" microdialectic is a transformation of variant 10 of the macrodialectic (chapter 3). The macrodialectic begins with inner essence: Spirit as yet has no Mind with which to perceive externality. This state is potential essence. Then the human mind arrives. Spirit becomes aware of external objects, which it interprets as alien—things other than itself. The result is actual existence. Finally, Spirit recognizes that the internal and external are both Spirit. We get a synthesis of internal and external. This is actual essence.

13. Morality. Hegel is now finished with heading V, "Reason." He moves on to heading VI, "Spirit" and to its first subheading, A, "The *True* Spirit." In this context, "true" means true to moral principles. By becoming ethically conscious, consciousness has advanced to the realm of morality. Consciousness begins moralizing by trying to validate as rational such moral laws as "everyone ought to speak the truth." This approach—the attempt to use reason as the basis of moral law—is that of *theory*. The ethical theorist soon finds, however, that society's "given" moral laws are too ambiguous. They must be interpreted and qualified in ways that render them meaningless. The laws are potentially valid but not yet actually valid: reason has failed to validate them. We now have the microdialectic's thesis: potential + validity.

Still trying to validate the laws, consciousness turns from theory to a new criterion: *practice*, the antithesis of theory. The laws are tested. This approach seems to render the moral laws invalid: a law that says "private property is good" proves to have no more validity than a law that says the opposite, "communally owned property is good." The test of practice results in the dialectic's antithesis: actual + invalidity.

Hegel concludes that the universally accepted mores of a given society are valid simply because "they *are*." That is, the mores are valid because everyone accepts them as valid: "Thus Sophocles' *Antigone* acknowledges them as the unwritten and infallible law of the gods. 'They are not of yesterday or today, but everlasting. Though where they came from, none of us can tell.'"[62] And with this conclusion we have the dialectic's synthesis: actual (from the antithesis) + validity (from the thesis). Summary:

> Thesis: potential + validity
> Antithesis: actual + invalidity
> Synthesis: actual + validity

This microdialectic is not closely parallel to any variant of the macrodialectic. But it does repeat the basic separation-and-return pattern of dialectics, in this instance separating from and returning to validity. It also repeats the potential-actual pattern of the macrodialectic.

14. Antigone. Greece had those universally accepted mores. Why, then, Hegel asks, did the supposedly happy ethical society of Greece fail? But that question is just a cover story. Hegel isn't really pondering Greek society or its failure. Neither is he displaying disorganized thought by returning to a topic,

Greek thought (stoicism and skepticism), that he has already discussed. And neither is he taking sides in the story of Antigone. Instead, his real purpose is to show Spirit dialectically moving closer to the realization that the human (man) and the divine (Spirit) are one and the same.

The *Antigone* discussion revolves around the conflicting perspectives of women and men. Women represent both divinity (they obey the laws of the gods) and the family; men represent both humanity (they subscribe to the human laws) and the state. Hegel uses Sophocles's tragedy *Antigone* to illustrate the conflict between the divine and the human—and between family and state. Antigone, a woman of the city-state of Thebes, learns that her brother, Polynices, has died while fighting for the wrong side in a war against his own city-state, Thebes. Creon, king of Thebes, ordains that anyone who buries this traitor shall be killed. Antigone, out of loyalty to her brother, part of her *family*, upholds her perceived duty to her family. From a woman's perspective, the family ranks above the state. She defies Creon by burying Polynices. In doing so she also upholds divine law, the law of the gods, the law that is right because everyone accepts it as right. We now have three theses: woman (Antigone), family, and divine law.

Creon, upholding his own duty to the state, orders that Antigone be buried alive in a sealed tomb (a slow, agonizing death) for violating the state's human law, of which he is the author. Creon's wife, Eurydice, and his son, Haemon (who is also Antigone's fiancé), beg Creon to relent. Creon refuses, insisting that human law—his responsibility—be upheld. Haemon departs, angrily. Hegel has given us three antitheses: man (Creon), state, and human law.

Warned by a blind prophet that bad things will happen if Creon defies the gods by having Antigone killed, Creon relents. But it is too late. Haemon commits suicide. So does Eurydice when she learns of her son's death. And so does Antigone. Creon then makes it a foursome: he too takes his own life. Let us now search for syntheses.

It is apparent that Hegel is treating this story and the Greek culture it represents as another microdialectic. This dialectic's synthesis presages the macrodialectic's synthesis, in which a union of the divine and the human occurs. Hegel first presents the *Antigone* dialectic's thesis and antithesis in the subtitle of section V-A-a: "Human and Divine Law: Man and Woman." The primary thesis is divine law, the law of the gods, to which women subscribe. The primary antithesis is human law, the law of the state, to which men subscribe. In the thesis, "woman" (Antigone) represents the family, which is governed by the law of the Greek gods. In the antithesis, "man" (Creon) represents the state, which is governed by human law. The woman seeks the welfare of her family and follows divine guidance. This is why Antigone flouts Creon's human law and buries her brother Polynices, a member of her family: her highest loyalty is to her family. The man seeks the welfare of society and follows human guidance. Man's concern for the welfare of society is, in turn, the reason Creon orders Antigone's death.

The dialectic's synthesis is the union of woman and man, or woman + man. Baillie's translation does a better job than Miller's of capturing the synthesis, so I will quote Baillie: "The union [synthesis] of man with woman constitutes the operative mediating [bringing together] agency for the whole, and constitutes the element [synthesis] which, while separated into [containing] the extremes of divine and human law, is, at the same time, their immediate union [synthesis]."[63] Continuing: "This union . . . turns both those . . . mediate connexions [divine law and human law] (*Schlusse*) into . . . the same synthesis."[64] "Union" can be interpreted to mean sexual union, marriage (Creon and Eurydice), a betrothed couple (Haemon and Antigone), or brother and sister (Polynices and Antigone); Hegel probably gives it all four meanings. What matters is that man and woman are united, at least in Hegel's eyes.

In the synthesis, both divine and human law are right, depending on whether you go by the male perspective or the female perspective. Pinkard does an excellent job of making this point: "Both sides were in the right: Creon as the ruler of the city had the absolute obligation to protect it from attack by traitors (and he considered Polyneices [alternate spelling] to be a traitor), whereas Antigone had the absolute duty to perform the proper burial rites on her brother . . . Antigone sees Creon as directly defying the divine law, and Creon sees Antigone as someone willfully and stubbornly violating the conditions under which the community can exist and flourish."[65]

The synthesis holds that both divine law and human law are right. We could say that "right" is the inner essence that unites human and divine in this context—and that "right" is also what unites man and woman. Both are right.

And this joint rightness produces three dialectics:

1. Thesis: woman
   Antithesis: man
   Synthesis: "union of man with woman"

2. Thesis: family perspective is right
   Antithesis: state perspective is right
   Synthesis: both perspectives are right

3. Thesis: divine law (woman's law) is right
   Antithesis: human law (man's law) is right
   Synthesis: both divine law and human law are right
   (human law = divine law)

The synthesis of divine law and human law in the last of the microdialectic's three forms points to a deeper synthesis, still hidden from consciousness. The deeper synthesis: the real divine law *is* the human law, because humans are Spirit and thus divine. Humans, the source of human law, are divine. Man is God. With this deeper synthesis, still hidden, consciousness (Spirit) moves a step closer to self-realization.

That Hegel is far more concerned with dialectics than with substance in the topics he discusses is shown by his even-handed treatment of the two sides in the Antigone tragedy. Stern discerningly articulates Hegel's nonjudgmental position: "It is less clear exactly how Hegel wants us to understand the play, and thus exactly what lesson he wants us to draw from it." Hegel viewed Antigone "sympathetically," but "it seems wrong to infer from this that Hegel therefore thought Antigone was 'right.'. . . In fact, Hegel simply took Antigone to be representing her social sphere." Stern characterizes as a "mistake" the tendency of some analysts "to look for evidence that Hegel wanted to 'take sides.'"[66]

But why didn't Hegel take sides? The specific topic of *Antigone* is subsumed under the general topic of morality: Hegel is supposedly pontificating on morality. But if Hegel were at all concerned with defining morality, he would pulverize Creon for inhumane behavior. Almost any human being with a modicum of decency (Hegel belongs in this category), men as much as women, would side with Antigone. Human law must be upheld, yes. Violators of human law should be punished, yes. Personally, I would go so far as to say that divine law, such as that of the Old Testament and that of religious conservatives who decree that abortion and gambling and even patronizing physicians (Christian Science) are sinful, should be ignored. But almost everyone would agree that the punishment for violating human law should fit the crime. Humane rulers don't execute poverty-stricken people for stealing loaves of bread. Neither do they execute sisters for burying their dead brothers—or for burying anyone else. For that matter, humane rulers don't promulgate laws forbidding families to bury their dead. Such laws don't serve to protect the state; they don't deter treason; they are purely vindictive. Even where death is considered the appropriate penalty for a certain crime, that doesn't mean death by physical and psychological torture is an acceptable means of execution. Just as burning someone at the stake is death by torture, so is entombing someone alive.

So why doesn't Hegel say what needs to be said: that both sides are partly right but Antigone's virtue or morality in this matter far outweighs Creon's? Having himself raised the topic of morality, why does he have nothing significant to say? And if he has nothing significant to say, why did he choose to discuss *Antigone*? The reason Hegel displays such a high level of impartiality is that his only serious concern here is to construct a dialectic, not to define what is or isn't moral behavior. Actually, he does have one other concern: he wants to once more hint at the basic message of *Phenomenology*, the message that the human *is* the divine. This hint is visible in the implied conclusion that both human law and divine law are right. They are both right because *they are the same*. The true divine law *is* the human law, because the humans are collectively the divine.

My conclusion—the conclusion that Hegel isn't concerned with the overt substance of his topic—supports the similar one I reached at the end of the physiognomy-phrenology topic. Hegel wasn't seriously concerned about the two pseudosciences. He wasn't out to refute them. His real concern was covert. His purpose was to construct another microdialectic, one that imitates the macrodialectic. Much the same thing could be said about the *Faust* dialectic and the others. The microdialectics all presage either the *Phenomenology* macrodialectic or, in one instance, history's freedom macrodialectic. Hegel is educating us in dialectics so as to enable us to apprehend the macrodialectic. It's time to repeat an earlier quotation from Hegel: "The series of configurations [dialectics] which consciousness goes through along this road [the progression of dialectics] is, in reality, the detailed history of the *education* of consciousness itself to the standpoint of Science [dialectics]" (Hegel's italics).[67]

15. Lord and Master. Finished with Greece, Hegel and consciousness move ahead to Rome (VI-A-c, "Legal Status"). Consciousness is still formulating conscious thoughts while subconsciously—that is, unconsciously—formulating dialectics that struggle to rise to the surface. With Rome, consciousness once more formulates the macrodialectic's variant that moves from the thesis "one" to the antithesis "many" to the synthesis "one composed of many."

Rome consists of one emperor and its many citizens, who might better be called subjects. The emperor, whom Hegel calls "the lord and master of the world," is "the solitary person [one] who stands over against all the rest [many]."[68] "The rest," the emperor's subjects, are a fragmented society, "a sheer multiplicity of personal atoms," to whom the emperor is "alien" because of "the destructive power he exercises against . . . his subjects."[69] Those atomistic (fragmented, particularized) subjects, unlike the citizens of Greece, have only the most tenuous sense of unity. Whereas the Greek citizens, especially the men, had a strong sense of loyalty to their city-states, the Romans feel alienated from the person who represents the state, the emperor. Their only allegiance to the emperor comes from appreciation of the property rights accorded them by Roman law. Nevertheless, both the *one* emperor (thesis) and his *many* subjects (antithesis) constitute the state, "one composed of many" (synthesis). Summary:

> Thesis: one (the emperor)
> Antithesis: many (the subjects)
> Synthesis: one composed of many (the state)

This dialectic reproduces the same concepts—one and many—found in the Virtue dialectic. Both microdialectics imitate several variants of the macrodialectic. Consciousness is really beginning to get the hang of things. It won't be long now until it has matured enough to grasp the macrodialectic. That will happen on the last pages of *Phenomenology*.

16. **Actuality and Faith.** The next microdialectic differs from the preceding ones in that it bridges several subheadings and sub-subheadings. But, unlike the intermediate dialectics, it does require the reader's immersion in the text if the dialectic is to be perceived. For this reason, and because the microdialectic is far down in Hegel's outline, I view it as a microdialectic, not as an intermediate dialectic. The general heading is "The World of Self-Alienated Spirit." The relevant subdivisions are (Ia) "Culture in its realm of actuality," (Ib) "Faith and pure insight," and (II) "The Enlightenment."

The self-alienated Spirit's world has two parts: the world of reality ("actuality") and the world of Faith (spelled with a capital F), which is an imaginary world. Hegel's discussion of the first world is incredibly complicated, verbose, and discursive. Conscious wanders through all sorts of tribulations.[70] But the essential development is that, after the failure of many serious and sincere endeavors, "nobles" ignobly turn to flattery. They create a monarch and give him both (*a*) a title, by which he "is absolutely separated off from everyone else," and (*b*) an ornamental throne around which the nobles gather and hypocritically "praise" the monarch.[71] But the nobles are inwardly alienated from the monarch, who (unknown to them) happens to symbolize (in Hegel's eyes) Spirit, the true "absolute." This alienation, in turn, symbolizes man's alienation from Spirit—subject's perception of external "objects" as "alien" entities rather than as itself—in the macrodialectic. But that's really an aside. Hegel has taken a long time to get to the point, but the point is simply this: in the actual world of reality, a monarch rules. The dialectic's thesis has two facets: (1) the actual material world and (2) human rule.

In the microdialectic's antithesis, the monarch's subjects express their alienation by turning to a second world, the world of Faith. Although Faith refers to religion, Hegel distinguishes religion in the context of Faith from the religion of the Unhappy Consciousness: "Here [in the Faith context], however, religion . . . is . . . merely a *belief*,"[72] whereas the Unhappy Consciousness was concerned with religious *practices*—burning incense, ringing bells, giving thanks to the deity, confessing sins, doing penance, fasting, listening to uncomprehended Latin services, tithing, buying indulgences, and the like. This distinction between beliefs and practices is a distinction between spiritual (the world of Faith) and material (the world of reality). Belief—the spiritual element—relates to intangible, spiritual things like God, the Holy Spirit, Mary, Satan, heaven, hell's fire, angels, demons, and divine law. Practice relates to earthly, material things like incense, bells, candles, churches, priests, churches, and money. We are now talking about the world of belief or Faith, the spiritual world, not the material world of practices.

Where the world of belief is concerned, the relevant belief is belief in the one supernatural God of Christianity, contrasted with the many gods of the Greeks. Just as the monarch is the real world's absolute, God is the absolute of the unreal world of Faith. God is thus the antithesis of the real world's monarch. The monarch is real; God is imaginary, a creation of Faith. Superficially, man seems to be united with God: man sincerely believes. But God is a false god. The true God, the one Hegel sometimes hypocritically calls "God," is Spirit. By uniting himself with the wrong God, man has alienated himself from the true God, Spirit, whose Mind is the mind of man. To overcome this alienation, man must become God so that reason can rule. The dialectic's antithesis, like the thesis, has two facets: (1) the imaginary spiritual world and (2) divine (supernatural) rule.

Faith with its divine ruler is one alternative to the real world of alienation from the human monarch; the Enlightenment is another. And it is the one that provides the synthesis for the microdialectic. The Enlightenment was an eighteenth-century philosophical movement that (*a*) criticized both political and religious authoritarianism, that is, both monarchic authority and divine authority, (*b*) advocated principles friendly to the common man—principles such as republican governance (a republic has no monarch), freedom of thought, and liberty—and (*c*) generally upheld reason and science as the bases for authority. Hegel weighs the pros and cons of Enlightenment thought as it relates to Faith. He finds both error and truth in Enlightenment thought. Although Hegel deliberately fogs his argument, his chief point is that Faith in God is good when man becomes God (Spirit) and rules with reason—the reason of the Enlightenment. The rule of reason is the essence of the Enlightenment.

The "truth" of the Enlightenment is that it recognizes a material world, a world of "matter" that stands in contrast to Faith's imagined world of thought.

The world of matter displays man-made objects (these are, of course, Spirit) that have utility and can promote human happiness, which is what God supposedly does. But whereas "*faith* lacks . . . actuality," "useful" artificial objects actually exist and (though Hegel can't say this) are "God," because all material reality is "God," Spirit. *Important*: Here Hegel is smuggling in a minor point of his two natural-artificial dialectics. That point is that Spirit includes artificial things in addition to natural things. In the Enlightenment, "The two worlds [Faith's world of thought and the real world of material things] are reconciled and heaven is transplanted to earth below."[73] Hegel means that, in Enlightenment thought, the divine God of Faith and thought is transplanted into man, a material being, who produces reason. The result is a ruler who is neither the earthly monarch nor the celestial God. The ruler is man. His law is the law of reason.

Now we have the dialectical synthesis: material world = spiritual world. What Hegel won't say clearly is how this happens to be so. But we know the answer. It is so because Hegel has redefined the spiritual world by redefining the divine. The divine is now man, a nonspiritual material being who rules by reason. The Enlightenment made *reason* instead of the monarch or God the source of authority. Reason is the product of humans, who are Spirit and therefore are also "God." Spirit, which is "God," rules in the real world when reason rules. Summary:

> Thesis: the material world (the monarch is the absolute)
> Antithesis: the spiritual world (God is the absolute)
> Synthesis: material world = spiritual world (when reason is the absolute)

The synthesis can also be viewed a second way. Since all humans are Spirit, the monarch is Spirit, and Spirit is "God." The monarch (reality) and God (spirituality) are therefore identical: Monarch = God, if only when the monarch of reality becomes human reason. Summary:

> Thesis: human rule (man, the earthly monarch)
> Antithesis: divine rule (God, the celestial monarch)
> Synthesis: human rule = divine rule (when man = God)

The Actuality and Faith (or material and spiritual) microdialectic is among those that are only loosely related to the macrodialectic. As with the Antigone dialectic, the thesis and antithesis must be transposed for the macrodialectic connection to be seen. The macrodialectic moves from the divine (one) to the human (many) to the synthesis of divine and human: one divine entity (Spirit) composed of many separate particulars.

17. The Reign of Terror. The French Revolution and its attendant Reign of Terror arose as a sort of climax to the Enlightenment. In this development Hegel finds his next microdialectic. Its thesis is what Hegel, borrowing from Rousseau, calls a "general will."[74] Representing the concept of universality, the general will amounts to unanimous agreement (one opinion) by all citizens on political matters. "Its purpose is the general purpose, its language universal law, its work the universal work."[75] Don't forget, universality is a thesis concept. In the macrodialectic, the potential union of the thesis is the same thing as potential universality. And in the Consciousness dialectic explored in chapter 2, the thesis, developed under the heading "Sense Certainty," is universality: Hegel very specifically states that "the universal . . . is the true [content] of sense certainty." The Reign of Terror microdialectic's thesis is universality.

Even the universal, however, needs government to accomplish the objectives of the general will. And government requires a specific will, an individual will. That will turns out to be the will of "the *victorious* faction."[76] As it happened, the victorious faction was the twelve-man Committee of Public Safety, dominated by Robespierre. We now have Hegel's antithesis: individuality. This individual (particular) entity, the Committee, representing only twelve Frenchmen, produced the Reign of Terror. Almost thirteen hundred persons were beheaded with the guillotine in less than seven weeks.

The dialectical escape from this terror (though not the historical escape, the beheading of Robespierre) occurs when Spirit leaves the real world and passes over into the world of thought, specifically, moral thought. For no good reason other than that moral thought comes from humans, who are essentially Spirit, and as such are both universal and particular, Hegel implies that his synthesis is both universal *and* particular (individual). This synthesis, though formally correct, is surely a bit of a stretch. Morality is a theoretical answer to terror, but not a realistic one: the terrorists aren't suddenly going to change and behave morally. Still, this latest dialectical exercise is subconsciously familiarizing consciousness with the workings of dialectics. When consciousness ultimately grasps the technique of thinking dialectically, it will be able to perceive the macrodialectic and its all-important synthesis. The Reign of Terror dialectic:

> Thesis: the general will (shared by everyone)
> Antithesis: a particular will (that of the Committee of Public Safety)
> Synthesis: general will = particular will (moral thought, which is of divine origin, is both general and particular when the God [one, universal] is man [many, particular])

Although this microdialectic resembles the macrodialectic's one-and-many variants, there is a difference. In this microdialectic, just one particular (the Committee) stands in opposition to the thesis. The concept "particular" is present, but its corollary, "many," is not.

18. Morality, Human Nature, and Conscience. In bringing the Reign of Terror dialectic to its conclusion, Hegel leaves the world of "Culture" (heading VI-B) and enters the world of "Morality" (heading VI-C). This seems strange, because he has already discussed morality in several contexts. But this time morality becomes German ideas of morality, as expressed primarily in the philosophies of Kant and Fichte. Like the preceding microdialectic, the "Morality" microdialectic bridges more than one section—two in this instance—of Hegel's outline: (VI-C-a) "The moral view of the world" and (VI-C-b) "Dissemblance or duplicity."

Predictably, German morality has a problem. The problem relates to the familiar dichotomies of universality and particularity, one and many, divine and human, and internal and external. Kantian morality revolved around a conflict between two human impulses that operate independently and therefore sometimes conflict. These impulses are (1) morality per se, which involves *externally* imposed—universally recognized—"divine" moral laws that consciousness has a duty to obey, and (2) nature, man's *internally* imposed behavioral laws based on personal wants and preferences. The former impulse or personality Kant called *homo noumenon*, man's godlike self. Noumenal man idealizes himself as virtuous. Because noumenal man thinks in terms of universally shared moral ideas, he represents not only the divine but the concept of universality. The other self, *homo phenomenon*, is man's human self. This self is guided by natural impulses. These impulses vary from person to person. Phenomenal man thus represents the concepts of human and particularity. Man, in short, has a schizophrenic personality—part godlike, part human. The resulting conflict concerns "the relation between the absoluteness of morality and the absoluteness of Nature." This relation "is based, on the one hand, on the complete *indifference* and independence of Nature towards moral purposes and activity, and, on the other hand, on the consciousness of duty alone as the essential fact."[77] The dialectic's thesis becomes moral law, man's godlike or divine impulse. The antithesis is natural behavior, the human impulse.

In the section on "dissemblance or duplicity," Hegel wanders through various reasons why the thesis-antithesis conflict can't be resolved within a Kantian framework. Hegel summarizes: "The moral world-view is, . . . to employ here a Kantian expression where it is most appropriate, a 'whole nest' of thoughtless contractions."[78] Hegel's non-Kantian solution is the Jiminy Cricket solution: always let your conscience be your guide. In Hegel's own words, consciousness becomes "the simple Spirit that, certain of itself, acts conscientiously regardless of such [contradictory] ideas, and in this immediacy possesses its truth."[79] Hegel doesn't explain how conscience constitutes a synthesis. He doesn't even explain how conscience differs from man's godlike self, *homo noumenon*. But the word "Spirit" is all we need to figure out the answers. Conscience resides in a human being. All humans are Spirit, because Spirit embraces all reality. Spirit is the true divine, the true God. So all humans are divine. Conscience, which is ostensibly of human origin, is therefore also of divine origin. Conscience thus represents both the divine or universal, *homo noumenon*, and the human or particular, *homo phenomenon*. In this way, conscience combines—is a synthesis of—moral law and human nature. Summary:

> Thesis: moral law (divine, externally imposed)
> Antithesis: natural impulses (human, internally imposed)
> Synthesis: conscience (divinely *and* humanly imposed when divine = human)

An alternative formulation is the following:

> Thesis: divine (moral law has God as its source)
> Antithesis: human (natural impulses have man as their source)
> Synthesis: divine = human (man is God, so conscience is both divine and human)

19. Duality. Man's conscience, successful in the context of the preceding dialectic, becomes unsuccessful for purposes of the next dialectic. This new microdialectic is one in which universality and particularity (individuality) again clash. The new thesis is "Conscience"—a unique case upholding the old belief that each Hegelian synthesis becomes the thesis of a new dialectic. Conscience, as now described by Hegel, seems to be little more than moral intuition, a moral judgment that comes from within, as opposed to (*a*) obedience to the externally imposed (universal) moral law of morality and (*b*) the internally generated (individual, personal) impulses of nature. Its salient feature is freedom from the agonizing conflicts between morality and nature that leave the moralist frustrated, unable to decide, unable to act. Conscience instinctively knows what is right and acts accordingly. The action it takes falls under the rubric "particular": no universal moral law comes into play. Conscience is the judgment of a particular individual. Different persons display different judgments—different particulars. This gives us the dialectic's thesis, a familiar one: particular. (Particular is usually the antithesis, but in this case Hegel transposes "universal" and "particular," making particular the thesis.)

At this point Hegel gets sidetracked onto a dialectically irrelevant but philosophically popular concept of his era, the Beautiful Soul. One theory, espoused by Solomon, is that Hegel's Beautiful Soul is Jesus. I discuss this theory—it is untenable—in chapter 7. But we can ignore the Beautiful Soul where the Duality dialectic is concerned.

Because externally imposed moral law has been snubbed (when the act of conscience conflicts with moral law), the moralist—another person—steps in and criticizes the person who acts according to conscience: "The antithesis of individuality to other individuals, and to the universal, inevitably comes on the scene."[80] (Who says Hegel never uses the word "antithesis" when referring to the second stage of a dialectic?) The antithesis of conscience thus becomes morality, which represents the concept of universality. The antithesis is again familiar: universal. (Universality is usually the thesis, but we still have the opposition of universal and particular.)

Conscience and morality clash: "Each of these two self-certain Spirits has no other purpose than [establishing the legitimacy of] its own pure self."[81] After some delay, both conscience and morality recognize the other's point of view and apologize for their parochialism. Hegel calls this synthesis, this act of reconciliation, "duality." The particular (conscience) and the universal (morality) are now one, a duo. This synthesis, duality, is similar to the Antigone synthesis. Both sides are right. It all depends on a person's perspective. Summary:

> Thesis: conscience (the *many* particular opinions of conscience are
>   right)
> Antithesis: morality (the *one* universal opinion of morality is right)
> Synthesis: conscience + morality (both conscience and morality are
>   right)

Hidden from view in this synthesis is the now-familiar concept of man as God. When man is God, the many particular opinions of man are also opinions of God. Hence both the many particular opinions and the one universal opinion come from "God," who is Spirit. Since God is always right, both the particular and the universal are right.

20. Natural Religion. Having finished his table-of-contents outline's general heading VI, "Spirit" (Philosophy), Hegel turns to heading VII, "Religion." What Hegel calls religion goes way beyond conventional concepts. The longest subsection, "Religion in the Form of Art," treats Greek art as religion. This art is broadly conceived to include not only (*a*) sculpture but (*b*) the mystery cults—these aren't art by any stretch of the imagination—and (*c*) the literary arts. Hegel seems to rationalize his calling Greek art "religion" by noticing that the statues include statues of gods and that the literary tales—epics, tragedies, comedies—have gods (often offstage) among their characters. A far less visible reason for using the "Religion" heading is that Hegel is setting up one of the intermediate-level dialectics discussed earlier, the dialectic that uses philosophy (man) and religion (God) as thesis and antithesis. That dialectic needs religion for its antithesis. If Hegel were serious about analyzing and criticizing Greek religion, he would base his discussion heavily on Zeus and the rest of the Greek pantheon. Instead, all we get is a seemingly arbitrary selection of the Dionysus cult plus a fleeting reference to the protogod Titans, who are mentioned only as the antecedents of some statues.

Why does Hegel *pretend* his discussion of Greek art is about Greek religion? The answer is simple: he needs "art" to represent the concept "artificial," which is the antithesis in the natural-artificial intermediate dialectic described earlier in this chapter.

"Religion" has three subsections: (A) "Natural Religion," (B) "Religion in the Form of Art," and (C) "The Revealed Religion." The last is overtly Christianity but covertly Hegelian new-wine-into-old-wineskins philosophy. The chief old wineskins are God, Father, Son, Holy Spirit, and divine. A, B, and C are the thesis, antithesis, and synthesis of that earlier intermediate dialectic that went from (1) natural to (2) artificial to (3) natural = artificial (Jesus of Nazareth = God incarnate). Subsections A and B each have lowercase-lettered (a-b-c) sub-subsections that constitute microdialectics; subsection C has no lettered sub-subsections but nevertheless has a Father-Son-Spirit microdialectic. We begin with (A) "Natural Religion."

The "Natural Religion" subsection has (*a*) "God as Light" as its thesis, (*b*) "Plant and Animal" religions as its antithesis, and (*c*) "The Artificer"—the builder of pyramids, the sphinx, and such—as its synthesis. Hegel scholars generally agree that the god of light is the god of Zoroastrianism, the ancient Persian religion. Zoroastrianism featured conflict between light and darkness, specifically, between Ahura Mazdah, the god of light, and Angra Mainyu (also called Ahriman), the lord of darkness, an early prototype of Satan. Although chronology suggests otherwise, it is possible that Hegel secondarily had in mind Gnosticism. Gnosticism featured a remote god of light from whom human souls, sparks of light, were separated. Hegel could even be alluding to the quasi-Gnostic theology of the Gospel of John.[82] The concept light represents is "abstract" (the opposite of "concrete"), which is essentially the same thing as "one." Something abstract is extremely general, vaguely defined, either actually shapeless (in abstract sculpture) or metaphorically shapeless, lacking in identifying detail. Light is shapeless. Hegel even says it has "the 'shape' of 'shapelessness.'"[83] The dialectic's thesis, we can see, has two forms: (1) "abstract," as exemplified by light, and (2) "divine," as exemplified by Ahura Mazdah, the god of light.

Natural religion's antithesis is "plant and animal." Hegel seems to have in mind some gods of ancient India and Egypt, which took the form of various plants and animals. He might also be thinking of earlier forms of primitive animism, which assumed that spirits were present in plants and animals and, for that matter, even in inanimate objects such as boulders. Plant and animal religions represent the abstract's opposite: "concrete" (specific rather than vague, identifiable rather than uncertain, a particular member of a general category, furnished with detail). Indirectly, via the concept "many," these plant and animal religions also represent the concept "human." Hegel uses "many" to represent humanity in quite a few contexts, including the macrodialectic. Hegel's associating the concept "many" with plant and animal religion can be seen in several phrases: "the numberless multiplicity of weaker and stronger, richer and poorer Spirits," "animal religions" (plural), "multiplicity of passive plant forms," and "a host of separate, antagonistic national Spirits who . . . become conscious of specific forms of animals as their essence."[84] The dialectic's antithesis, like the thesis, has two forms: (1) "concrete" (particular), the opposite of abstract (general), and (2) "human" (many), the opposite of divine (one).

For his synthesis, Hegel focuses on Egypt. There he finds "the artificer," a craftsman who creates objects. The artificer's earliest creations are pyramids and obelisks, bigger "objects" than you would expect from someone called an artificer. These early objects are abstract geometric forms—abstract in the sense that they are highly simplified, lacking detail. Such abstractions can represent anything.[85] Abstractness, the thesis, is thus represented. Abstractness can also be conceptualized as divinity: abstractness signifies *one* multifarious entity, analogous to the one God (divinity) of Judaism and Christianity. As time passes the artificer experiments with plant and animal forms. Best known among these is the half-man, half-animal sphinx. It represents a godlike mythological creature. These later creations—full of detail, recognizable, and varied, hence concrete—

represent concreteness. Concreteness, in turn, describes the *many* concrete forms something abstract might signify. And *many* describes humanity. The artificer's creations, viewed collectively, are thus a synthesis of abstraction (pyramids and obelisks) and concreteness (plant and animal forms, such as the sphinx), or one (abstract) and many (particular). One and many symbolize the divine (one) and the human (many). The dialectic thus takes two forms:

Thesis: abstract (universal, one)   Thesis: divine (abstract, one)
Antithesis: concrete   Antithesis: human (concrete,
   (particular, many)   many)
Synthesis: abstract and   Synthesis: divine and human
   concrete (artificer)

Once more we see the macrodialectic being imitated. Since abstract and concrete are alternate ways of saying universal and particular, or one and many, several variants of the macrodialectic are covered. And since abstract also describes divinity while concrete describes specific human beings, we also have the macrodialectic's divine-human dichotomy.

21. Religion in the Form of Art. After "Natural Religion" comes heading VII-B, "Religion in the Form of Art." This section is mostly about Greek art, with just a smattering of attention to genuine Greek religion. (The religion that does get attention—the mystery cults—is arbitrarily classified as "art" for the sole reason that Hegel needed something Greek for an antithesis.) The three subsections offer (*a*) a thesis called "The Abstract Work of Art," (*b*) an antithesis called "The Living Work of Art," and (*c*) a synthesis called "The Spiritual Work of Art."

The word "abstract" in the first subsection's heading tips us off to what's coming up: a repetition of the abstract-concrete dichotomy from "Natural Religion." The "abstract" work of art, the microdialectic's thesis, is Greek statues, statues that take "the form of the gods," particularly the Titans.[86] Hegel really has to strain to interpret the statues as abstractions. He does so by saying they are "shapes which only dimly [abstractly] recall those Titans" and by also saying that they represent "nations."[87] I must admit that using statues with human shapes (vaguely human shapes?) to represent nations does qualify as abstraction. We'll just have to take Hegel's word about just how abstract the sculptures are and about the sculptor's intent.

For concreteness, the antithesis of abstraction, Hegel turns to "The Living Work of Art." This isn't art in any recognizable sense but, rather, the Greek mystery cults, particularly the cult of Dionysus, also called Bacchus. Dionysus was a wine god, and some of the cult's activity involved drunken revelry. Like Christianity's Christ, Dionysus had a virgin birth, died, and was resurrected. Also like the Christ, he inspired his devotees to eat his flesh and drink his blood in bread-and-wine (flesh and blood) ceremonies, ceremonies (also found in Roman Mithraism) later incorporated into Christianity. The bread and wine, and the drunken revelers, are where concreteness enters the picture. In the bread and wine, the god ceased to be an abstraction and became concrete reality. Dionysus "at first enters into the objective [concrete] existence of the fruit [wine grapes], and then, . . . in it [in the wine, made from the grapes] attains to *genuine reality*—and now roams about as a crowd of frenzied females, the untamed revelry of Nature [concreteness] in self-conscious [human] form" (my italics).[88] Hegel reinforces the antithesis by alluding to a second god, Helios, the Greek sun god. Helios can be recognized as the "Light of the risen Sun."[89] Just as Dionysus morphs from a spiritual entity to a material (concrete) entity when he becomes wine, Helios does likewise when his sunshine helps produce the grapes from which the wine is made. (Although Hegel doesn't say so, I presume Helios also materializes in the grain from which the bread, representing the flesh of Dionysus, is made. As in Christianity, the bread and wine are the flesh and blood of the God, historically consumed by the devotee in order to acquire desired traits of the god.)

Revving up his dialectical engine, Hegel roars into the dialectic's synthesis with something unprecedented: a triple synthesis. The synthesis's subheading is "The Spiritual Work of Art." More than anything else, "spiritual" alludes to the role of Christianity's Holy Spirit as a uniter (synthesizer) of God and man—the abstract and the concrete—through spirit possession: "spiritual" in this context means unifying, mediating, or synthesizing, words that describe what the Holy Spirit supposedly does when it possesses a human and thereby unites the human with God. The "Spiritual Work" subsection centers on Greek literature—epic poems, tragedies, and comedies. Each of these three literary forms displays, in Hegel's dialectical eyes anyhow, a synthesis. The third synthesis is the only one that isn't somewhat forced, but it is truly brilliant. Here are the three syntheses:

1. The Greek epic poems, such as Homer's *The Odyssey*, featured a minstrel (the poet-narrator) and story characters. The minstrel is *one* (the abstract), the "actual spirit . . . by whom [the story world] is borne."[90] In turn, the story characters are *many* (the concrete), the humans in the divine-human synthesis, the story. The story reveals "the relation of the divine to the human."[91] The *story* is thus the synthesis.

2. In tragedy, "the hero is himself the speaker," counterpart of the epic's symbolically divine minstrel.[92] Hegel's equating the tragedy's hero with the epic's minstrel tips us off that the epic's synthesis is being repeated. The hero-speaker (divine) and the other characters (human) are united by the tragedy—the *story*—itself. Tragedy also provides a second abstract-concrete (one-many) synthesis. In the tragedy *Antigone*, the subject of an earlier microdialectic, the masculine (the state, one, abstract) and feminine (the family, many, concrete) antagonists are combined on the Greek stage.

3. Comedy is the third Greek literary form. In Greek theater, both tragedy and comedy, the actors traditionally wore masks that identified characters and emotions. In the comedies, a masked actor, representing an external (divine) point of view, mocks everyone and everything in society. Then the actor "drops the mask" and "plays with the mask" to reveal himself as the human who is being ridiculed.[93] Thus are the abstract and the concrete—the divine and the human—united in one actor. He alternates between divine (masked) and human (unmasked). The *actor* is the synthesis.

The result of these syntheses—the third is the one that really counts—is a dialectic that has the same two forms that the preceding microdialectic ("Natural Religion") has:

Thesis: abstract   Thesis: divine
Antithesis: concrete   Antithesis: human
Synthesis: abstract *and* concrete   Synthesis: divine *and*
                                                   human

The divine-human pair of concepts again can be found in variants of the macrodialectic.

22. The Revealed Religion. The twenty-second and last microdialectic arrives under heading VII-C, "The Revealed Religion." This dialectic brings man close to Absolute Knowledge, for it adumbrates Spirit's macrodialectic of (1) unconscious (potential) + union, (2) conscious (actual) + separation, (3) conscious (actual) + union. The analogous Revealed Religion microdialectic, identical to variant 16 of the macrodialectic, runs from (1) potential + identity (of man and God) to (2) actual + nonidentity (separation of God and man) to (3) actual + identity. The difference is that, in the Revealed Religion microdialectic, the God who achieves self-realization is the God of Christianity, not Spirit. "The world [the community of man] is indeed *implicitly* reconciled with the divine Being; . . . but . . . this immediate presence [Jesus, God incarnate] still has not the shape of Spirit."[94] Nonetheless, this last dialectic prepares man for the redefinition of God that will transform Spirit into Absolute Spirit.

I have already analyzed the Revealed Religion dialectic in considerable detail in chapter 3 under the "The Trinity as 'Revealed Religion'" heading. Therefore, and although this is easily the most important microdialectic other than master and slave, I will omit much of the detail.

The Revealed Religion microdialectic uses the Trinity—Father, Son, and Holy Spirit—to represent thesis, antithesis, and synthesis. Father (the thesis) stands for the potential identity of man and God that exists in the pre-Christian era, before the Christ is created. In this era, God is still in his pre-incarnation, unseparated state. This state is analogous to Spirit's unconscious, *prehuman*, unseparated state in the macrodialectic. I have italicized "prehuman" to call attention to an important analogy. This analogy relates (*a*) God in his prehuman (pre-Son) thesis status as Father to (*b*) Spirit in the macrodialectic's prehuman thesis stage of unconscious unity, wherein Spirit is not yet separated into particulars because humans ("subjects") and their minds are not yet present to perceive and misinterpret "objects" as things other than themselves (Spirit). In the microdialectic's Father stage, the identity of man and God is merely potential because theology's God is not the real God, Spirit. In addition to using the Trinity symbolism, Hegel conceptualizes God as "thought" (intangible, nonmaterial), the opposite of "substance" (tangible, material). Hegel also uses a third concept: essence. Essence refers to what God essentially is, a nonmaterial spirit, as opposed to what he existentially becomes when he is incarnated as Jesus, a material being. Spirit is likewise essentially a nonmaterial entity, but it ultimately becomes existentially "incarnated" in all material reality, including humanity.

Son (the antithesis)—the separation of God into two beings—stands for the separateness of man and God that results when God is incarnated as a man, the event that leads to Christianity. Man's misperception of God in heaven and God incarnate (Jesus) as two separate beings is analogous to (*a*) subject's misperception of objects as entities separate from itself in the macrodialectic's antithesis and (*b*) the Christian's misperception of God (divine) and humans (also divine) as separate entities. Hegel's second antithesis concept is substance, the opposite of thought. The Son has real physical substance; he is just like every other human in this respect. The third antithesis concept is existence, which describes the nonspiritual (material) form in which God incarnate exists on earth. Jesus is a flesh-and-blood human, not a noncorporeal spirit.

In the Bible's three synoptic gospels (Matthew, Mark, and Luke), the Holy Spirit (the synthesis) reunites Father and Son through Spirit possession after the baptism of Jesus. In an alternative version—or, we could say, an extended version—of the reuniting, the Holy Spirit unites Father and Son in the Trinity after the Son is crucified and resurrected. Either way, the reunion is analogous to Spirit's self-realization in the macrodialectic. In the Trinitarian reuniting, thought (the Father) becomes identical with substance (the Son). Similarly, essence (God) becomes identical with existence (Jesus). Three dialectics result:

Thesis: Father	Thesis: thought (Father)	Thesis: essence (Father)
Antithesis: Son	Antithesis: substance (Son)	Antithesis: existence son
Synthesis:	Synthesis: thought	Sythesis: essence
Holy Spirit	= substance	= existence

The "Revealed Religion" microdialectic is the platform from which Spirit leaps to self-realization under heading VIII, "Absolute Knowledge." All it takes is a little reinterpreting of theology. Hegel prepares the way by saying, "The death of the Mediator [Son] is the death . . . also of the *abstraction* of the divine Being"—that is, the death of theology's God![95] The old abstract (imaginary) God must be replaced by a concrete God, a God that includes all humanity instead of just *one* unique human, Jesus, the Christ. *All* men must be incarnated as God.

This preliminary reinterpretation leads to the main one. Christianity's Holy Spirit, the often-out-of-body-and-off-to-earth-to-possess-someone soul or spirit of early Christianity's highly anthropomorphic God,[96] is replaced by *Hegel's* Spirit. Hegel's Spirit is now the unifier of "God" and man. Whereas theology's Holy Spirit descended on Jesus alone (when Jesus was baptized by John the Baptist), Hegel's Spirit "possesses" the whole community of humans. Man and God are still united. But, as in Tillich's Yes-No-Yes dialectic, the "God" man's thought identifies with in the synthesis is not the God he worshipped in the thesis; it is Hegel's Spirit, whom Hegel often calls God in order to conceal his atheism. This reinterpretation of Holy Spirit brings Spirit to maturity and to Hegel's climactic, atheistic insight: he and everything else in the universe—especially the humans—are Spirit. *Man* is God. The old God is dead. In the Yes-No-Yes dialectical format, the original Yes is replaced by a higher Yes, the negation of the negation. That is, the Yes to the imaginary God created by human thought is replaced by the Yes to the true God, which is man, the most important component of Spirit, or all reality.

In short, the three Revealed Religion dialectics summarized above all lead to syntheses describing the actual identity of God and man. I said at the beginning of this Revealed Religion analysis that a microdialectic analogous to the basic macrodialectic and identical to variant 16 was coming up. Those two chapter 3 dialectics, the second of which is another variant of the Revealed Religion microdialectic, are these:

1. Thesis: unconscious + unity
   Antithesis: conscious + separation
   Synthesis: conscious + union

16. Thesis: potential + identity (of God and man)
    Antithesis: actual + nonidentity (of God and man)
    Synthesis: actual + identity (of God and man)

In chapter 6, I discuss the interpretations of other authors who have written about *Phenomenology*. One of these authors is Stanley Rosen. He speaks of Hegel's concept of "the identity of identity and non-identity," but he has no idea what this means.[97] Forster also displays confusion about the meaning of this phrase.[98] The confusion is understandable. None of Hegel's interpreters is aware that Hegel is using thesis-antithesis-synthesis dialectics. Absent such awareness and a concomitant understanding of the identity dialectic, accurate interpretation of "the identity of identity and non-identity" is impossible. But the above dialectic, variant 16 of the macrodialectic, reveals what Hegel means. We start with the basic macrodialectic, then substitute (*a*) "potential" for "unconscious," (*b*) "actual" for "conscious," (*c*) "identity" for "union," and (*d*) "nonidentity" for "separation" to get variant 16. The two-part synthesis, actual + identity, borrows "identity" from the two-part thesis and "actual" from the two-part antithesis. In the phrase "the identity of identity and non-identity," Hegel uses "identity" as shorthand for the thesis, "non-identity" as shorthand for the antithesis, and a second "identity" as shorthand for the synthesis. The result should be understood as "the *actual* identity [synthesis] of *potential* identity [thesis] and *actual* nonidentity [antithesis]." In other words, identity in the "actual" sense is identical to, meaning a synthesis of, (1) identity in the "potential" sense, the thesis, and (2) actual nonidentity, the antithesis.

THE MESSAGE OF OUR EDUCATION IN DIALECTICS

Throughout *Phenomenology*, Hegel has been educating Spirit—that's us—in his "Science" of dialectics. Recall once more what he said in his Introduction he was going to do: "The series of configurations [dialectics] which consciousness goes through along this road [the road to self-realization] is, in reality, the detailed history of the *education* of consciousness itself [us again] to the standpoint of Science [dialectics]."[99] In presenting the last of his microdialectics, Hegel completes this task of educating us in his "Science" of dialectics.

Most of the microdialectics are disguised—sometimes not even disguised—permutations and combinations of the macrodialectic. During our education, Hegel has exposed us to numerous dialectics, both intermediate and micro, many of them closely analogous to the macrodialectic. If we count multiple dialectics ensconced in particular dialectically structured narratives, we have observed twelve intermediate dialectics and forty-two microdialectics, or a total of fifty-four dialectics. Some, such as the third master-and-slave microdialectic, the Unhappy Consciousness microdialectic, and the third *Faust* microdialectic, are identical to variants of the macrodialectic. The structure of dialectics and the divinity of humans have been subtly but repeatedly implanted in our psyches. We are now ready for the major challenge: apprehending the macrodialectic and deducing its structure.

We have the tools. We now understand that a Hegelian dialectic indeed does have three stages, not just the two claimed by so many reinterpreters. We also understand that the second stage is the opposite of the first, not just something different. And we understand that the third stage returns to (incorporates) the first stage or to something in the first stage—a fact those authors who have tried unsuccessfully to provide examples of three-stage dialectics haven't understood. (Consider, for example, Singer's false example of a history dialectic, wherein the falsely identified thesis is the "customary morality" of ancient Greece but the synthesis is Prussia, "the German society of Hegel's time," where customary morality has been replaced by codified law.[100] That supposed synthesis is not a return to customary morality.) We have seen in many examples that, where the return is not to the entire first stage but to just one part of a two-part first stage, the synthesis borrows one part from the thesis and one from the antithesis. Just as important, we have learned that dialectics often lead to, or at least imply, the identity of the divine (universal, one) and the human (particular, many).

These insights give us the knowledge we need to recognize the existence of a macrodialectic and to figure out its structure: we, the humans whose minds constitute Spirit's Mind, are ready to undergo self-realization, wherein Spirit comes to know that it is Spirit or "God." Knowing, as we now do, that self-realization is a dialectical synthesis and is also a return from separation, we can infer that separation is the second stage or antithesis of a dialectic, the stage that immediately precedes the synthesis. Also knowing, as we have always known, that the separation is *conscious* separation, we can likewise infer that the first stage or thesis is the opposite—the double opposite—of conscious + separation. Ergo: what else can the macrodialectic's thesis be but *unconscious* + union, where unconscious is the opposite of conscious and union is the opposite of separation? These two inferences tell us that the synthesis includes either (*a*) the first part of the thesis and the second part of the antithesis or (*b*) the second part of the thesis and the first part of the antithesis. So what is the synthesis—(*a*) unconscious + separation or (*b*) conscious + union? That queston is what the younger generation calls a no-brainer. A return *from* separation can't be a return *to* separation, and self-realization can't be unconscious; so the correct answer is obviously (*b*) conscious + union. We have now deduced that Hegel has a macrodialectic that advances from a thesis of unconscious + union to an antithesis of conscious + separation to a synthesis of conscious + union.

The microdialectics have also taught us that union refers to universality, the state of being one, and that separation refers to particularity, the state of being many. Because the macrodialectic's synthesis returns Spirit to the state of universality, we can further deduce that self-realized Spirit is a universal category, which means it is *one*. The microdialectics have further taught us that "one composed of many" is a form many syntheses take. Other syntheses have an equivalent form, such as universal (one) composed of particulars (many) or the will or moral viewpoint of the individual (one person) = the will or moral viewpoint of society (many persons). So if Spirit is a universal, it must in its self-realized state be a universe composed of particulars, or one composed of many. Meanwhile, Hegel has told us in several places that self-realization is "truth" and that this truth is Spirit's "certainty of being all reality."[101] So we can deduce yet another fact: Hegel's universal is literally the universe—all reality, including artificial objects (as we learned in microdialectic 16 and intermediate dialectic VII A-B-C). Finally, we have learned from all three of this chapter's intermediate dialectics and from microdialectics 14, 16, 18, 19, 20, 21, and 22 that "all reality" is the divine (abstracted from theology's one God and metaphysical monism's one absolute) and that Spirit is a synthesis of the divine (artificial, created by man) and the human (natural). Conclusion: in the macrodialectic's synthesis, the state of self-realization, we (Spirit's mind) realize that we humans are—or at least are part of—the divine or "God." We humans, not the supernatural being of picture-thinking, not the Almighty who sits on a throne in the sky, are God.

This conclusion yields one more insight. Contrary to what others have sometimes implied, *Phenomenology* is not a disjointed, randomly arranged series of commentaries on such diverse topics as literal slavery, Greek philosophy, inductive reasoning, phrenology, *Faust*, *Antigone*, Romanticism, Kantian philosophy, and Egyptian religion. What Hegel *seems* to be saying about those topics is just window dressing. Look closely and you will see that Hegel's comments on these subjects—phrenology and *Antigone*, for example—often express no opinion; the comments are purely descriptive. Where Hegel does offer an opinion, as with skepticism, it usually amounts to two or three sentences, sometimes worded in cryptic language ("has not . . . achieved it's consummation as absolute negation") that only dialectically trained insiders can interpret. The reason Hegel's comments are largely descriptive, lacking in detailed critical analysis, is that Hegel has nothing significant to say. Each topic is a facade that hides a dialectic, or sometimes just one stage of a dialectic developed in consecutive topics. The dialectic, not the ostensible topic under discussion, is the whole point of Hegel's discussion. Hegel is educating "consciousness," Spirit's mind, in the technique of thinking dialectically. He is preparing conscious to undergo self-realization. We readers are consciousness. We will undergo self-realization if and when we humans realize that we are God.

Chapter 5

THE DIALECTICS OF HISTORY: HEGEL VS. MARX

Hegel claims he has discovered a pattern in history that guides it to two goals, freedom and monarchy; the monarchy goal is intertwined with the idea that the monarch must govern a multiplicity of territories (descriptive of Prussia). This discovery of history's pattern is "an inference from the history of the World"—an inference that, he says, "happens to be known to *me*, because I have traversed the entire field [of history]."[1] Hegel's inference is that history's "development has been a rational process; that the history in question has constituted the rational necessary course of the World-Spirit—that Spirit . . . which unfolds this its one nature in the phenomena of the World's existence."[2] The "rational process" is dialectics. It is rational because it operates through human minds. Humans do things and make decisions that cause history to develop in a certain way. It all sounds quite metaphysical—a metaphysical force seems to direct history—but Hegel's dialectical history is really nothing more than a pick-and-choose interpretation of history. The picking and choosing is calculated to make history go where Hegel wants it to go. Marx too sees history as unfolding dialectically. His history dialectics, however, are entirely different and imply metaphysical causation. In this chapter I first discuss Hegel's history dialectics. Marx's history dialectics follow. The Marxian dialectics use the Hegelian pattern and prove that Marx (and Engels) understood Hegel's thesis-antithesis-synthesis dialectics, which is more than I can say about anyone else except Tillich.

207

HEGEL'S HISTORY DIALECTICS

Hegel has ten history dialectics. These cover a three-level hierarchy of time periods, as follows:

- Two overall-period dialectics—overarching dialectics—cover the full range of history from (1) Oriental despotism, the thesis period, through (2) Greco-Roman society, the antithesis period, to (3) Hegel's Germanic world (the Protestant nations of northern Europe), the synthesis period.

- Two subperiod dialectics split the overall period in half. One subperiod runs from Oriental despotism to Rome; the other runs from Rome to the Germanic world. Each subperiod has three stages, clearly identified by Hegel.

- Six sub-subperiod dialectics split each stage of both subperiods into a thesis, an antithesis, and a synthesis. Each stage has its own dialectic (three substages). The result is 2 subperiods × 3 sub-subperiods each = 6 dialectics.

One of the overall-period dialectics and one of the subperiod dialectics lead to freedom. The other two first-level and second-level dialectics lead to monarchy, specifically, multi-unit states governed by one monarch—one monarchy comprising many territories. (This is a reprise for the macrodialectic's "one composed of many" synthesis.) Freedom and monarchy—Prussian style multistate monarchy—are thus, according to Hegel, the two goals of history.

LEVEL ONE:
HEGEL'S TWO OVERALL-PERIOD DIALECTICS

Kaufmann expresses a view that epitomizes the widespread misunderstanding of the structure of Hegel's theory of history:

The basic structure of Hegel's philosophy of history furnishes another striking corroboration of our reinterpretation: nobody could possibly construe it in terms of thesis, antithesis, and synthesis, although there are, as usual, three stages. At first, in the ancient Orient, only *one*, the ruler, is free. The second stage is reached in classical antiquity [the Greek and Roman worlds] where *some* are free, but not yet the slaves. The third stage is reached in the modern world with the recognition that *all* men are free, or—as Hegel also puts it, and we have these ideas not only in students' lecture notes but also in his own manuscript—"man as man is free."[3]

Here Kaufmann is dreadfully wrong in his poorly contemplated "nobody could possibly construe it" remark. The movement from (1) Oriental despotism to (2) Greco-Roman slavery to (3) Germanic monarchy is definitely dialectical. And Hegel's three-stage progression of history does culminate in universal freedom. But the three dialectical concepts are not "one is free," "some are free," and "all are free." (One-all-some—the second and third concepts transposed—*would* be a dialectic: some is a synthesis of, a sort of compromise between, one and all.) Also, the story is much more complicated than that of a three-stage advance to freedom.

The Overall-Period Freedom Dialectic. Hegel says, "The History of the world is none other than the progress of the consciousness of Freedom."[4] Friedrich comments that this "vision that was Hegel's" was "most extraordinary." He elaborates: "History is seen as the march of freedom through the world. This march of freedom is interpreted as what the World Spirit wants, as it seeks to realize itself. And in its effort to realize itself, it employs peoples, world-historical peoples to do its work."[5] Spirit does this by imposing a dialectical pattern on history. Hegel recognizes "the *dialectical* nature of the Idea [of freedom] in general, viz., that it is self-determined—that it assumes successive forms which it successively transcends; and by this very process of transcending its earlier stages, gains an affirmative . . . shape."[6] The "affirmative" shape alludes to the terminal higher Yes in the basic Yes-No-Yes pattern of dialectics (affirmation, negation, negation of the negation).

Tillich affirms that "actual freedom" is the goal of Hegel's overarching history dialectic—and thereby hints that "potential freedom" is the thesis. He writes that Hegel "made freedom the aim of the universal process of existence." When the "nonbeing [of freedom] has been conquered . . . history has come to its end; freedom has become *actual*" (my italics).[7] In saying "history has come to its end," Tillich does not mean Hegel fails to foresee further developments in history; he means that the *dialectical* pattern of history is complete, that no further *dialectical* unfolding will occur.

These references surely give us good reason for expecting to find a history dialectic with freedom in its synthesis. Moreover, knowing that a dialectic has a separation-and-return structure, we can anticipate a dialectic that begins with freedom, separates to freedom's antithesis, bondage (slavery in this case), and then returns to freedom. And that is what we do find. The overall-period dialectic that separates from and returns to freedom has the following structure:

> Thesis: potential + freedom (Oriental despotism)
> Antithesis: actual + bondage (Greco-Roman slavery)
> Synthesis: actual + freedom (Germanic monarchy)

This dialectic is identical to variant 27 of the macrodialectic (chapter 3) and to the second of the four master-and-slave dialectics (chapter 4). It is also identical to the stoicism and skepticism microdialectics. As in those and many of the other *Phenomenology* dialectics, the synthesis borrows one concept from the two-concept thesis and one from the two-concept antithesis. Also as in many of the earlier dialectics, the movement is from a potentially ideal situation to an actually ideal situation, from potential to actual essence.

How do we get the two-part concept "potential freedom" from Oriental despotism? Despotism certainly doesn't sound like freedom. But Hegel has a solution, three solutions in fact. Hegel's third derivation of freedom is the most important, but let's begin with the first two. The first derivation of potential freedom begins with the idea that, under Oriental despotism, *one* is free: "The Orientals have not attained the knowledge that Spirit—man *as such*—is free; and because they do not know this, they are not free. They only know that *one is free*."[8] The one is, of course, the despot or monarch. Only he is free. But his freedom can potentially spread to all his subjects. The problem here is that the same could be said of the Greco-Roman world with its slavery:

the freedom of *some*, like the freedom of *one*, could spread to all. Yet Hegel does not conceptualize Greco-Roman slavery as expressing potential freedom.

Hegel's second derivation of potential freedom is better but rests on the ridiculous idea that the Oriental people lacked conscience. Hegel draws a distinction between "rational freedom" and "subjective freedom."[9] Rational freedom is that of the despot, who imposes rational laws, laws based on the despot's sense of morality. The people must obey these laws without necessarily agreeing with them. Subjective freedom is "realized only in the Individual," the monarch's subjects.[10] Subjective freedom is the freedom of citizens to act according to the dictates of conscience. Stated otherwise, subjective freedom is freedom of the monarch's subjects to obey their own moral commands. Both rational freedom and subjective freedom must be present for true freedom to exist: "The idea of freedom necessarily implies law *and* morality"—both rational freedom and subjective freedom.[11]

Hegel claims, unconvincingly, that rational freedom is "realized" in the East "without advancing to *subjective* freedom."[12] The alleged reason for the Orient's lack of subjective freedom is that the oriental people lack that ingrained sense of morality. In the West, this sense of morality supposedly comes from the commands of a heavenly god or gods. But "what we call God has not yet in the East been realized in [personal] consciousness, for our idea of God involves an elevation of the soul to the supersensual [the supernatural]."[13] In contrast, the Chinese monarch is a sort of patriarch who substitutes for the Western gods. And the Mongolian monarch, the lama, "is honored as God."[14] But the laws of these oriental monarchs, though enforced, are not viewed by the people as self-imposed moral laws, akin to conscience. "There is no want of a will to command moral actions, but there is lacking the kind of will to perform them which would result from their being commanded from within."[15] Oriental despotism provides no freedom of "conscience," no "formal Freedom."[16] The upshot is that, although subjective freedom does not exist in the Orient, rational freedom (the monarch's laws and edicts) does. This rational freedom represents the potentiality for true freedom's required combination of rational freedom and subjective freedom. That combination will ultimately be realized in Germanic monarchy.

The third, and more persuasive, derivation of the idea that Oriental despotism represents potential freedom relates to slavery. This derivation draws a contrast between the Oriental world and the Greco-Roman world. The Oriental world may lack "subjective freedom," but none of the citizens is enslaved. This freedom from enslavement establishes the potentiality for true freedom. We can infer that this third derivation is the primary one by remembering that a thesis is the opposite of its antithesis. The antithesis, coming up, is slavery—"actual bondage." The thesis must therefore at least imply the absence of slavery. The Orient's lack of slavery constitutes "potential freedom," the dialectic's thesis.

The freedom dialectic's antithesis, slavery or bondage, carries the Greco-Roman label. This antithesis emerges in "the Greek and Roman world," where "some are free."[17] "Some are free" alludes to slavery. Elsewhere, allusion becomes specific reference: "The Greeks . . . had slaves."[18] Hegel later goes into detail:

> Another circumstance [of Greek society] that demands special attention here, is the element of *Slavery*. This was a necessary condition of an aesthetic democracy, where it was the right and duty of every citizen to deliver or to listen to orations respecting the management of the State in the place of public assembly, to take part in the exercise of the Gymnasia, and to join in the celebration of festivals. It was a necessary condition of such occupations, that the citizens should be freed from handicraft occupations; consequently, that what among us is performed by free citizens—the work of daily life— should be done by slaves.[19]

The Romans likewise had slavery. Slavery is, in fact, a basic reason why Hegel links the Roman world with the Greek world: "Elegance—Culture— was foreign to the Romans *per se*; they sought to obtain it from the Greeks, and for this purpose a vast number of Greek slaves were brought to Rome. Delos was the centre of this slave trade, and it is said that sometimes on a single day, ten thousand slaves were purchased there. To the Romans, Greek slaves were their poets, their authors, the superintendents of their manufactories, the instructors of their children."[20] And so we have the dialectic's antithesis: actual bondage.

We move on to the freedom dialectic's synthesis. It strides under the banner "Germanic world." Hegel's Germanic world is more than Hegel's Prussia; it is the Protestant nations of northern Europe, including Prussia, most of Switzerland, parts of France, the Netherlands, the United Kingdom, Denmark, and Sweden (which then included Norway). General agreement among Hegel's interpreters exists on this point. For example, McCarney, author of a leading work on Hegel's philosophy of history, asserts that "the Germanic peoples . . . are above all the peoples of Protestant Northern Europe, the peoples of the Reformation."[21] Hegel thus claims, "The German nations, under the influence of Christianity, were the first to attain the consciousness that man, as man, is free."[22]

Man's Germanic freedom arises in two realms, religion and government. Consciousness that man is free arose first, according to Hegel, in religion. His opinion is hardly surprising. Both *Phenomenology of Spirit* and *The Philosophy of History* are, more than anything else, subtle—and sometimes not so subtle—attacks on religion and religious superstition. Religion is the realm where the Protestant Reformation occurred. And it was in the Germanic nations that Protestantism replaced Catholicism. Hegel believed Catholicism represented religion at its worst. As McCarney puts it, "the Catholic middle ages were, for Hegel, a dark night of the spirit from which humanity was rescued by the Reformation."[23]

How did the Reformation produce freedom? The medieval Catholic Church not only embraced corruption (e.g., the sale of indulgences) but, more important, repressed free thought. The inquisitions, the persecution of heretics, the witch burnings (the Bible, Exodus 22:18, says "Thou shalt not suffer a witch to live"), the pre-burning torture that elicited witch confessions, the Church's denying men the right to interpret the Bible—all this constituted denial of free thought. This lack of freedom is perhaps best represented by Galileo's being imprisoned, threatened with permanent imprisonment and possible torture, and then brought (at the age of seventy) on his knees before Pope Urban VIII to recant his heresy. That heresy was Galileo's endorsing the heliocentric theory of Copernicus, who held that the earth revolved around the sun. The Church knew better: the sun revolves around the earth.

Northern Europe was rescued from this oppression of free thought (though not to the degree claimed by Hegel) when Martin Luther launched the Reformation. He began by attacking Church corruption. But he soon was attacking the very authority of the Church. Hegel elucidates: "Luther repudiated that authority, and set up in its stead the *Bible* and the testimony [biblical interpretation] of the Human Spirit [individual men]. . . . [H]enceforth each individual enjoys the right of deriving instruction for himself from it, and of directing his conscience in accordance with it."[24] These words describe what became a Protestant slogan: "every man a priest." Luther went on to facilitate freedom of interpretation by translating the Bible into German. (Luther's translation was published in 1534.)

Hegel, though privately a nonbeliever, maintained his Lutheran facade by extolling the virtue of Luther's work.[25] The newfound religious freedom of the Germanic (Protestant) nations became the chief basis for Hegel's claim that, in the Germanic nations, man's freedom was finally realized. *All* were now free.[26] (Ironically, this Germanic freedom failed to relieve Hegel of the need to conceal his atheism behind obfuscatory verbiage in order to safeguard his professorship. Neither did it stop the execution of witches, sometimes by fire, in lands that had become Protestant. Nor did it prevent the establishment of Calvin's theocracy in Geneva.)

The second realm in which Germanic freedom arose was that of government. Well in advance of reaching favorable conclusions about the Prussian monarchy, Hegel explored the requirements of freedom in relation to political institutions. The goal was to achieve a balance between personal freedom and the needs of government. If personal freedom has no restrictions, he observed, there can be no government, no constitution. Yet people generally recognize the need for government and leadership. "This necessitates the selection and separation from the rest of those who have to take the helm in political affairs, to decide concerning them, and to give orders to other citizens, with a view to the execution of their plans." But too much government, too many orders, and too much planning and direction can unduly restrict personal freedom. How is the right balance achieved? "It is, however, urged," says Hegel, "that . . . the constitution should be at least so framed, that the citizens may obey as little as possible, and the smallest modicum of free volition be left to the commands of the superiors."[27] The evasive words "it is urged"—passive voice—fail to establish that it is Hegel who is urging this point of view. Yet the opinion seems to be Hegel's, or at least shared by Hegel; it is consonant with Hegel's undeniable belief that governmental rights must be weighed against human rights.

Hegel was born in 1770 and died in 1831; he began his teaching career in 1801, at the University of Jena. The Prussian monarchy that took shape in the roughly half century preceding Hegel's academic career brought Prussia to fruition. But even before this the foundations of Germanic monarchy had been laid. First, feudalism had largely disappeared (certain feudal property rights and titles remained); a weak central government replaced the feudal institutions. Second, the state, which had been subordinated to the Catholic Church, had regained its supremacy: "The State no longer occupies a position of real inferiority to the Church, and is no longer subordinate to it."[28] Frederick the Great, king of Prussia from 1740 to 1786, then arrived on the scene. He expanded and consolidated the Prussian realm, strengthened the monarchy, and instituted work on a Prussian code of laws, essentially a constitution. He also established a policy of religious tolerance, an important advance for freedom.

In 1794, under Friedrich Wilhelm II (successor to Frederick the Great, his uncle), Prussia completed and adopted the new, modern, liberal code of laws. The right balance of personal freedom and governmental authority seemed to have been achieved. Hegel described the reforms with these words: "Feudal obligations are abolished, for freedom of property and of person have been recognized as fundamental principles. Offices of State are open to every citizen, talent and adaptation being of course the necessary conditions. . . . [Although] the personal decision of the monarch constitutes its [government's] apex . . . firmly established laws, and a settled organization of the State, [mean that] what is left to the sole arbitrament of the monarch is, in point of substance, no great matter."[29] Thus did Spirit realize the dialectical goal of history, *actual* freedom—actual + freedom—in the secular as well as the sectarian realm.

An important qualification must now be added. I pointed out in chapter 3 that Hegel could not have believed Prussia was the first state to place reasonable restrictions on the right of the state to control the rights of persons to act independently. Britain and the United States were far ahead of Prussia in this respect, and Hegel knew it. Hegel used the limited personal freedom found in Prussia to formulate his dialectical description of history. But he privately held that the freedom that arrived with Germanic monarchy was not that of a proper balance between the rights of individuals and the rights of the state. The freedom that was historically realized in Prussia was instead the *concept* of freedom, contrasted with freedom per se. That concept was *Phenomenology*'s concept of freedom, which treats freedom as release from bondage to God, religion, and religious superstition. For Hegel, this release from bondage occurred in the 1780s, when he was a teenager. The release-from-bondage concept became philosophically "official" in 1807. That is when Hegel, acting as Spirit's Mind, interpreted his own release from bondage as Spirit's self-realization. In effect, Hegel declared himself God. Freedom's triumph in history can thus be seen as a highly egocentric interpretation of history.

The Overall-Period Monarchy Dialectic: Preliminary Matters. Although Hegel saw the *concept* of freedom as the primary goal of history, attaining this freedom *under monarchy* was an important secondary goal. Disagreement exists among Hegel's interpreters concerning whether Hegel's espousal of monarchy was a ploy used by Hegel to ingratiate himself with his sponsors in the Prussian monarchy. Popper is the leading twentieth-century exponent of the ingratiation thesis. He contends that Hegel wrote "with a singleness of purpose, . . . to . . . serve his employer, Frederick William of Prussia." The monarch had made Hegel the official philosopher of the monarchy. Popper continues: "My assertion that Hegel's philosophy was inspired by ulterior motives, namely, by his interest in the restoration of the [pre-Napoleonic-wars] Prussian government of Frederick William III [Prussia's king from 1797 to 1840] . . . is not new. The story was well known to all who knew the political situation, and was freely told by the few who were independent enough to do so. The best witness is Schopenhauer." Schopenhauer, referring to Hegel, wrote that philosophy had "become a tool of interests; of state interests from above, of personal interests [Hegel's] from below."[30] Popper also quotes Schwegler, whom he identifies as "an admiring disciple" of Hegel's. Schwegler says Hegel "acquired, from his connections with the Prussian bureaucracy, political influence for himself as well as the recognition of his system as the official philosophy; not always to the advantage of the inner freedom of his philosophy, or of its moral worth."[31]

Popper further supports his position with a telling point. He observes that

Hegel divides the third period of the German World into three more subdivisions. The last is "the Modern Times, dating from the end of the last century."[32] Modern Times, according to Popper, is therefore 1800–30, with 1830 being the last year in which Hegel lectured on history before his death in 1831. This is the period in which Spirit, with Hegel's help (in 1807), achieved self-realization and in which the dialectical history of freedom supposedly reached its climax. (To repeat, history's reaching its climax doesn't mean history comes to an end; it means the goals of history have been achieved and that *dialectical* change has come to an end.) Those facts suggest that *Prussia's* monarchy is the culmination of history. Popper comments: "I ask whether I was not justified when I said that Hegel presents us with an apology . . . for Prussia . . . and whether it is not clear that the state which Hegel commands us to worship as the Divine Idea on earth is not simply Frederick William's Prussia from 1800 to 1830."[33]

(Two minor corrections of Popper's argument are in order, but they are not much more than quibbles. The first is semantic. Popper has confused "Modern Times," which begin with the Protestant Reformation (1517),[34] with "our own time," which includes the French Revolution. The year 1517 is when Martin Luther posted his ninety-five theses on the church door in Wittenberg, launching the Reformation. So, if we allow some "getting started" years, "Modern Times" seems to begin around 1530; it has no precise starting date. The storming of the Bastille—the beginning of the French Revolution—took place in 1789. "Our own time" therefore might be said to begin around 1785, when Hegel turned fifteen.[35])

For the most part, recent authors of books about Hegel have avoided the ingratiating-himself-with-the-king issue. Those who have commented generally express doubts that Hegel's defense of monarchy was designed to curry the monarch's favor. The most detailed comments come from Charles Taylor. He describes Hegel as a defender of monarchy and an opponent of democracy, but also an opponent of restoring lost rights to the old feudal aristocracy. Taylor bases his analysis not on Hegel's *Philosophy of History* but on his *Philosophy of Right*. Hegel's "disenchantment with the contemporary aristocracy" convinced him that Germany needed a strong monarch.[36] Not only that, legislative power should not entail direct election of representatives: "Hegel

thus turns his face against what has become an absolutely fundamental principle of the modern democratic state, universal direct suffrage."[37] Legislative
power would instead be vested in two "estates," or social classes. An upper
house, somewhat analogous to Britain's House of Lords, would represent the
landed class; membership would be by birth. A lower house, loosely—very
loosely—resembling Britain's House of Commons, would represent economic
and social groups; these groups would appoint their members. Whether this
proposal is designed to impress Frederick William III, Taylor doesn't say. But
he seems to imply that a sincere distrust of democracy is guiding Hegel's
thoughts. Or is it the monarch's dislike of democracy that is guiding Hegel?

Singer has the most balanced—but not necessarily the most accurate—
appraisal. He sees both merit and flaws in Popper's attack. On the one hand,
Hegel opposed suffrage, accepted the monarch's right to censor newspapers,
and opposed freedom to slander or verbally abuse the government and its officials. On the other hand, he advocated greater freedom of speech than Prussia
then allowed, and he also advocated trial by jury, which Prussia didn't have.
Singer concludes that Hegel's criticisms of existing restrictions on freedom
"are sufficient to acquit Hegel of the charge of having drawn up his philosophy *entirely* in order to please the Prussian monarchy" (my italics). He
adds that "Popper's case is not as strong as it seems." Still, Hegel pulled the
punches he threw at monarchical restrictions on freedom: "The most likely
explanation is that Hegel was too conservative, or else too cautious, to advo-
cate a radical departure from the political system under which he lived and
taught. To say that Hegel's 'one aim was to please the King of Prussia' is
clearly wrong; but it may be fair to say that in order to avoid the wrath of the
King of Prussia . . . Hegel muted the radical thrust of his underlying philosophical theory."[38]

The consensus of other recent interpreters leans toward the opinion
that Hegel did not tailor his philosophy to personal considerations. Avineri
displays the strongest opinion: "On no account can Hegel's theory be so
construed as to refer to any existing state; it is the *idea* of the state with
which Hegel is dealing and any existing state cannot be anything but a mere
approximation to the idea."[39] I think, though, that these words are more
applicable to *The Philosophy of Right* than to Hegel's history dialectics. The

dialectics, viewed in relation to Popper's focus on 1800–1830, do seem to emphasize Prussia.

Solomon says, "Hegel was not primarily a political philosopher, and to view him as a political theorist and a philosopher of the State is to look at him through a strained perspective which he would not, at any point in his career, have recognized."[40] Solomon's words, of course, do not deny that Hegel was *secondarily* a political philosopher (witness both Taylor's and Avineri's analyses) and an apologist for the Prussian state. Hegel was definitely a political theorist. George Sabine's political theory textbook, *A History of Political Theory*, affirms this by devoting an entire forty-nine-page chapter to Hegel. Without adopting any sort of "strained perspective," Sabine writes that Hegel believed "that the extinguishing of feudalism and the rise of a national state could be achieved only through monarchy."[41] The only national state Hegel was concerned about was Prussia.

Fox offers a slightly stronger defense of Hegel: "Hegel was no mere idolator of the state in general, or of the repressive, militaristic Prussian state in particular. He makes this even more evident when he tells us, 'The state is not a work of art; it exists in the world, and hence in the sphere of arbitrariness, contingency, and error, and bad behavior may disfigure it in many respects.'"[42] But that quotation from Hegel refers to the state in general, not to Prussia in particular. And saying that the state isn't perfect is a far cry from not defending it: conceding that something "isn't perfect" or "is not a work of art" is always an anemic defense.

Pinkard, in another recent opinion, labels "false" the belief that Hegel "glorified the Prussian state, claiming that it was God's work, was perfect, and was the culmination of all human history."[43] Yet what Pinkard denies exaggerates ("glorified," "was perfect") the negative things that have been said about Hegel. The quotation in my preceding paragraph finds Hegel saying, in substance, that no state is perfect. A gentler and more accurate claim is that Hegel defended not only monarchy in general (contrasted with democracy) but the Prussian monarchy in particular.[44] Hegel may not have made the absurd statement that Prussia's monarchy was "perfect"—neither Popper nor anyone else accused him of saying that—but Hegel indeed did praise monarchy and emphasize the Prussian monarchy. He portrayed monarchy as both the highest form of government and the acme of freedom. I must add that Pinkard, in the sentence preceding the one quoted, denies what is manifestly true: that Hegel claimed history "developed according to the process of thesis/antithesis/synthesis." As it happens, Hegel not only had ten history dialectics but used the one we are about to examine to describe monarchy as a second goal (along with freedom) of history. My point: Pinkard isn't reliable. Without doubt, Hegel defended monarchy as the highest form of political development. At the very least, this conclusion applied to Prussia, even if it applied to a few other monarchies too.

It seems clear to me that Hegel intended to emphasize the *Prussian* monarchy as one of the two goals of history. Hegel delivered his lectures on the philosophy of history during his 1818–31 tenure at the University of Berlin. The period Hegel focuses on really begins with the Second Treaty of Paris, signed in 1815 following the final defeat of Napoleon; the treaty restructured the political geography of Europe. The period effectively ends on December 30, 1830, when Belgium declared its independence from the Netherlands. During the 1815–30 period, there existed six northern European monarchies: Britain, France, Prussia, the Netherlands, Denmark, and Sweden. (Belgium was a part of the Netherlands, Norway a part of Sweden, Finland a part of Russia, and Poland—Catholic—also a part of Russia.) Hegel was certainly not praising the monarchies of Britain and France. Britain had become a democratic monarchy. The French king, like most Frenchmen, was Catholic. Scratch those two monarchies. The question becomes: Did Hegel consider the Protestant monarchies of the Netherlands, Denmark, and Sweden coequal with Prussia as bearers of the standard of freedom?

Hegel could not have perceived a Prussian advantage where religion was concerned: Prussia and the other three countries were all Lutheran countries with Lutheran monarchs. A Prussian advantage might also arise from Prussia's having a superior balance of liberalism and conservatism in its laws and in the monarch's rulings. But which country, if any, had the best balance is not something that any historian could answer objectively. Who was "best" depends on Hegel's personal prejudices. The real issue is whether Hegel's praise of monarchy was *intended* to impress Frederick William III, king of Prussia from 1797 to 1840. Here I think Hegel sincerely believed in monarchy but, at the same time, was trying to ingratiate himself with the Prussian king. The best evidence that Hegel was buttering up the court is the synthesis of his overarching monarchy dialectic (coming up next): one ruler + many territories. Of the four non-Catholic, nondemocratic monarchies of northern Europe, only Prussia could boast "many territories." The inclusion of Belgium in the Netherlands monarchy and the inclusion of Norway in the Swedish monarchy hardly justifies a claim that those monarchies included *many* territories. Only Prussia qualifies. What reason other than to impress Frederick William III could Hegel have had for making "many territories" part of the synthesis? Surely Hegel's "one ruler + many territories" refers to Prussia alone.

The Overall-Period Monarchy Dialectic: The Dialectic Itself. The monarchy dialectic uses the familiar one-composed-of-many format:

> Thesis: One ruler + one territory (Oriental despotism)
> Antithesis: Many rulers + many territories (Greco-Roman democracy and ristocracy)
> Synthesis: One ruler + many territories (Germanic monarchy)

As is customary when Hegel uses two-part stages, the synthesis borrows one part from the thesis and one from the antithesis.

The thesis derives its two concepts—one ruler and one territory—from the first of Hegel's three broad historical stages, Oriental despotism. Hegel identifies four realms of Oriental despotism. These follow an east-to-west classification scheme: China, India, Persia, and Egypt. (Egypt is not Oriental at all but is used by Hegel as a final transition stage—one of three—leading to Greece). Hegel's justification for this scheme is this: "The History of the World travels from East to West, for Europe is absolutely the end of history, Asia the beginning."[45] China is the purest form of Oriental despotism and is where "history begins."[46] The other three realms, particularly Egypt, are transitional steps that lead to the Greek world. Note that Hegel is equating an east-to-west spatial progression with a China-to-Germany chronological progression.

Strictly speaking, China according to Hegel consists of two subrealms: China and the Mongols. They are similar. Hegel calls both theocracies, because no clear separation of the secular kingdom and the religious kingdom exists. What is essential for the monarchy dialectic is that both China and the Mongols have one ruler and one territory.

The Greco-Roman world is the opposite. It has many rulers and many territories. The many rulers are the citizens of the Greek city-states and the aristocrats of Rome: "Democracy was the fundamental condition of political life in Greece, as despotism was in the East. In Rome, it is the aristocracy, rigid and opposed to the people."[47] Hegel later adds this remark: "The Roman principle admits of *aristocracy* alone as the constitution proper to it."[48] Hegel is referring here to the early years of Rome, before Roman emperors (beginning with Julius Caesar) took control. Both democracy and aristocracy were systems with *many* rulers. In Greece all the citizens ruled; in Rome the aristocrats, called patricians, ruled. The patricians exercised their power through the Roman senate.

Greece and Rome differ in how they represent the concept of many territories. In Greece, the many governed territories are the many city-states. Each city-state is independent; Greece has no central government. Correspondingly, the citizens have no sense of Greek national unity. Although city-states might join forces against an external enemy, war between one city-state and another belied the idea of unity. In Rome, the many governed territories are Rome itself plus the conquered territories of the Roman Empire.

Germanic monarchy was the dialectical synthesis: one monarch + many territories. Although Hegel normally used "Germanic" as an ethnic rather than a political term, in this synthesis the monarchy with many territories had to be Prussia: no other Germanic monarchy had "many territories." The one ruler was the monarch, Frederick William III, king of Prussia. Hegel's justification of monarchy as the goal of "rational" history is feeble. The primary justification is the somewhat arbitrary assertion that "monarchy is the source of real freedom."[49] But why can't democracy do the job just as well? Part of the answer is that democracy, Hegel thinks, is practical only in small states. Hegel remarks that democracy was possible in Greece because "democratic constitutions are possible only in small states—states which do not much exceed the compass of cities."[50]

That may be true of participatory democracy, but it does not hold for representative forms of government. Why was monarchy better than the system then prevailing in England and America, where people elected legislators to speak and vote for them? The closest thing to an answer from

Hegel concerns England. There, he says, "the Parliament governs." But this leads to "corruption" in the form of vote buying, or "bribery." Yet Hegel concedes that the parliamentary system has "one advantage": "It introduces a majority of men into parliament who are statesmen, who from their very youth have devoted themselves to political business and have worked and lived in it." He leaves open the question of whether "reform in Parliament" is possible.[51] Hegel's conclusion that monarchy is history's rational choice as the best form of government thus becomes arbitrary. Well, not really arbitrary: it is what a dialectical synthesis should be. It is the negation of the negation. The negation (antithesis) that monarchy negates is democracy, part of the dialectic's antithesis. Dialectical necessity becomes Hegel's real justification for monarchy.

The many territories—the second half of the synthesis—were the array of principalities, duchies, free cities, and other mostly small political units that Prussia comprised. These gave Prussia the familiar Hegelian one-composed-of-many flavor. In the monarchy dialectic, this "many" element in the synthesis comes from Greco-Roman democracy and aristocracy. The "one" element, the monarch, comes from Oriental despotism. The monarch reprises separation and return: Germanic monarchy was the end of a long voyage of *separation and return*, separation from and return to one monarch. The dialectical synthesis, once again, is: one ruler + many territories. Summary:

> Thesis: one ruler + one territory (Oriental despotism)
> Antithesis: many rulers + many territories (Greece and Rome)
> Synthesis: one ruler + many territories (Prussia)

LEVEL TWO: HEGEL'S TWO SUBPERIOD DIALECTICS

Hegel divides the overall period into two subperiods: (1) Oriental despotism to Rome and (2) Rome to the Germanic world. Bear in mind that Rome is not the synthesis of the first subperiod or the thesis of the second; it is the *label* used for those two stages. The actual synthesis and thesis are *concepts*. So these two dialectics are not an example of a synthesis's becoming the thesis of a follow-on dialectic.

The Oriental-Despotism-to-Rome Subdialectic. In the Oriental-despotism-to-Rome subdialectic, the overall period's Greco-Roman middle stage is broken into two substages: Greece and Rome. Rome becomes the third stage of the subdialectic. The new dialectic has these three stages: (1) Oriental despotism, (2) Greek democracy, and (3) Roman despotism (no longer aristocracy). The dialectic thus created is identical to the overall period's monarchy dialectic:

> Thesis: One ruler + one territory (Oriental despotism)
>
> Antithesis: Many rulers + many territories (Greek democracy)
>
> Synthesis: One ruler + many territories (Roman despotism)

The first two stages have already been explained in connection with the monarchy dialectic. In China, where history begins, the one ruler is the despot. He governs one territory. The second stage reduces Greco-Roman democracy and aristocracy to Greek democracy alone. The many rulers are again the citizens. The many territories are, as before, the Greek city-states.

The third stage, Rome, embodies what is new. Hegel reconceptualizes Rome from aristocratic government to emperor government. He does this by dividing the "Roman World" into three sub-subperiods. These become the basis for a third-level sub-subdialectic that does not immediately concern us. The three sub-subperiods are (1) "Rome to the time of the Second Punic War," (2) "Rome from the Second Punic War to the Emperors," and (3) "Rome under the Emperors."[52] The Punic Wars were fought between Rome and Carthage, a city in what is now Tunisia; the Punics were an ethnic group that lived in Carthage. The first Punic War was 264–241 BCE; the second was 218–201 BCE; a third Punic War, which ended with the destruction of Carthage, was 149–146 BCE.

In the overall-period monarchy dialectic, the first two Roman subperiods are the source of the concept of aristocratic rule—the "many rulers" of Rome. The aristocrats were called patricians. Below them were the common people, the plebeians. Hegel describes their relationship during the first period: "The struggle between patricians and plebeians begins; and after this has been set at rest by the concession of the plebeian demands, there ensues a state of contentment in the internal affairs of Rome."[53] In 244 BCE, three years before the end of the first Punic War, some early Roman kings were banished; the Roman Republic, governed by patricians, began. Aristocratic rule continued through the second period.

But in the third period, Roman emperors took control; aristocratic rule came to an end. The decisive change occurred when Julius Caesar crossed the Rubicon River and occupied the city of Rome. Caesar then became the first of a long line of Roman emperors. Emphasizing that Caesar's rule launched a one-ruler period, Hegel says Caesar "became the sole ruler of the state."[54] Eventually, the Roman Empire separated into the western Roman Empire and the eastern Roman Empire. The western Roman Empire fell to the Visigoths in 476 CE. The eastern Roman Empire lasted until 1453 CE, when Constantinople fell to the Ottoman Turks. Hegel describes this one-ruler period as a period of despotism: "The Roman Empire . . . closes with Despotism, which marks the *third period*."[55] We see that the dialectic begins and ends with "despotism," going from Oriental despotism to Greek democracy to Roman despotism—another instance of separation and return. But whereas Oriental despotism had one territory, the Roman despotism included the many territories of the Roman Empire. The dialectic's third stage is thus a synthesis of one ruler (from the thesis, Oriental despotism) and many territories (from the antithesis, the Greek city-states). Summary:

> Thesis: one ruler + one territory (Oriental despotism)
> Antithesis: many rulers + many territories (Greece: city-states)
> Synthesis: one ruler + many territories (Rome under the emperors)

The Rome-to-Germanic-World Subdialectic. Hegel's second subperiod is the "German World" (Sibree translation) or "Germanic world" (Friedrich translation).[56] This subperiod overlaps the preceding one. It begins with the arrival in Rome of Christianity during the time of the Roman emperors. (Christianity became the official religion of Rome in 380 CE.) The dialectic has three historical stages: (1) the early Christian German world, extending through Charlemagne's reign as king of the Franks (771–814 CE), (2) the

Middle Ages and Catholic theocracy, ending with the early stages of the Protestant Reformation, which began with Luther's posting of his ninety-five theses on the church door in Wittenberg, Germany, in 1517, and (3) the Protestant Reformation and its culmination in Germanic monarchy. Although Hegel uses the adjective "Germanic," this period seems more Roman than Germanic in its first two stages.

Having repeated the overall period's monarchy dialectic with his first subdialectic, Hegel repeats the overall period's freedom dialectic with his second subdialectic. The format, first used in variant 27 of the macrodialectic (chapter 3), then in the master-and-slave microdialectic (chapter 4), and again in the first overarching history dialectic, is familiar:

>Thesis: potential + freedom (early Christianity)
>Antithesis: actual + bondage (Catholic theocracy)
>Synthesis: actual + freedom (the Reformation)

Hegel says the three periods can be compared to the realms of the Father, the Son, and the Holy Spirit. During the first period, the church and state are so closely linked that they are essentially *one*. This state of union is the state of the Johannine Father before he separates from himself and becomes two. In the second period, the Middle Ages, the church breaks apart from the state and gains superior status. This condition is like that of God when he separates from himself and becomes two: the Father in heaven and the Son (God incarnate) on earth. The Son represents separation. In the third period, the Reformation, church and state become reunified, with the state firmly in control. This state relates to the Holy Spirit, which unites Father and Son.

During the thesis stage, "the Spiritual [church] and the secular [state] form only different aspects" of "one mass."[57] But the one mass does not yet project freedom. The rulers are cruel and repressive: "We behold the terrible spectacle of the most fearful extravagance of passion in all the royal houses of that period. Clovis, the founder of the Frankish Monarchy, is stained with the blackest of crimes. Harshness and cruelty characterize all the succeeding Merovingians; the same spectacle is repeated in the Thuringian and other royal houses."[58] Freedom is thus only potential: "The will [of the state], *poten-*

tially truthful, mistakes itself and separates itself from the true and proper end [freedom] by particular, limited ends" (my italics).⁵⁹ Another reason freedom is merely potential is that the prevailing religion is Catholicism. Catholicism, with its dogma and related opposition to free thinking, is not equipped to carry the torch of freedom: "The Church has to ordain and the laity have simply to believe. Obedience is their duty, the obedience of faith, without insight on their part."⁶⁰ Protestantism can do the job; it *is* equipped to carry the torch of freedom.

The dialectic's antithesis stage, the Middle Ages, sees the two sides— the spiritual and the secular, church and state—drift apart. We now have "independence and opposition, with the Church by itself as a theocracy, and the state by itself as a feudal monarchy."⁶¹ But the western Roman Empire has collapsed, civil authority is weak, and the church is firmly in command. Theocracy now prevails. And we now learn why Solomon says that "[Hegel's] treatment of Catholicism is particularly vicious."⁶² The Church's harsh reign, Hegel says, is characterized by "utter derangement" (e.g., the inquisitions, the witch burnings), "corruption" (e.g., the sale of indulgences), and "immoral excess" (e.g., Galileo on his knees before the pope).⁶³ This means that "a condition of absolute un-freedom is injected into the very principle of freedom."⁶⁴ Hegel goes into detail:

> And thus absolute un-freedom became the established law through the perversion of the principle of freedom. . . . The individual has to confess, is bound to expose all the particulars of his life and conduct to the view of the confessor, and is then informed what to do. . . . Thus the Church took the place of *conscience*: it put men into apron strings like children and told them that man could not be freed from the torments which his sins had merited by any self-improvement, but only by outward actions; actions not of his own good will, but performed by command of the ministers of the Church. They consisted of hearing Mass, doing penance, going through a certain number of prayers, and undertaking pilgrimages, for example, actions which are unspiritual, stupefy the soul, and . . . are not only mere external ceremonies, but are such as can be even in one's stead performed by others. One could even buy some of the extra good works ascribed to the saints and thus secure salvation earned by them.⁶⁵

The result is "bondage," the opposite of freedom.[66] The dialectic's antithesis: actual + bondage.

The dialectic's third stage "extends from the Reformation to our own times."[67] Church theocracy vanishes in northern Europe as the "rational principles" of Protestantism replace Catholic dogma. In explaining the synthesis of the overall period's freedom dialectic, I described how Hegel saw freedom emerge in two sectors—religion and government. The fundamental change in the religion sector was the replacement of Catholic dogma—the prohibition of freedom of belief—with the "every man a priest" doctrine of Luther. In the government sector, the main developments were the reestablishment of monarchy and Prussia's adoption of a "rational" code of laws. Hegel, we saw, considered monarchy to be more predisposed to minimize restrictions on freedom than was the papacy. And the supposedly rational laws of Prussia provided what Hegel thought was the proper balance between necessary powers of government and personal freedom (despite the allowing of censorship and the disallowing of suffrage). In Hegel's eyes, "our own time" is the time when "the principle of freedom has realized itself."[68] The thesis and the antithesis have merged into a synthesis: actual (from the antithesis) + freedom (from the thesis).

LEVEL THREE: HEGEL'S SIX SUB-SUBPERIOD DIALECTICS

Both of the subperiod dialectics, like all dialectics, have three stages: thesis, antithesis, and synthesis. That gives us six stages ($2 \times 3 = 6$) for the two subperiods combined. Each of the six stages is divided into three still-lower-level stages. Six third-level dialectics result: (1) Oriental despotism, (2) Greece, (3) Rome, (4) the early German world, (5) the Middle Ages, and (6) the Germanic world.

Oriental Despotism. Hegel's east-to-west breakdown of Oriental despotism moves from (*a*) China, the thesis, to (*b*) India, the antithesis, to (*c*) Persia, the synthesis. This dialectic is another example of the one-and-many format. The format is the same as that used with the overall period's monarchy dialectic and the Orient-to-Rome subdialectic:

> Thesis: one ruler + one territory (Oriental despotism)
> Antithesis: many rulers + many territories (India)
> Synthesis: one-ruler + many territories (Persia)

We have seen the two Oriental despotism concepts twice already in the history context; no further explanation is required. Moving on to India, we find Hegel saying this: "When the Europeans became acquainted with India, they found a multitude of petty Kingdoms, at whose head were Mahometan [Mohammedan, Islamic] and Indian princes."[69] It is immediately apparent that Hegel is establishing his "many" antithesis, the opposite of his "one" thesis. But the concept of many rulers now differs from that used with Greek democracy and Roman aristocracy. In Greece the many rulers were the citizens of each city-state; in Rome the many rulers were the aristocrats of the Roman senate. In India the multiplicity of rulers depends on the multiplicity of states, since there is only one ruler per state.

Persia offers a third arrangement: a multi-unit empire headed by one king. Hegel describes Persia: "The Persian Empire is an Empire in the *modern* sense—like that which existed in Germany, and the great imperial realm under the sway of Napoleon; for we find it consisting of a number of states, which are indeed dependent, but which have retained their own individuality, their manners, and laws."[70] In short, Persia is a prototype of Prussia. It is one composed of many, a *synthesis* of one and many—one ruler and many states.

Greece. The Greece dialectic is easily the most unusual history dialectic. Instead of resurrecting familiar forms from the first-level and second-level history dialectics, it reaches back to one of the intermediate dialectics discussed in chapter 4. I refer to the religion dialectic, based on the opposition between natural and artificial. That dialectic took this form:

> Thesis: natural (natural religion, found in Persia and Egypt)
> Antithesis: artificial (religion in the form of art, found in Greece)
> Synthesis: natural = artificial (the Revealed Religion: the Son
>   [natural] = God [artificial])

The present dialectic is similar but reaches its natural = artificial synthesis by a different route:

> Thesis: natural (Egypt)
> Antithesis: artificial (Greece)
> Synthesis: natural = artificial (Egypt, after its conquest by Alexander, or Greece)

In chapter 4's intermediate dialectic, the natural religion was found in Persia (Ahura Mazdah, the God of light) and Egypt (plant and animal gods). The artificial religion came from Greece. So in the present dialectic we should not be surprised to find the concept of "natural" once more coming from Persia and Egypt and that of "artificial" again coming from Greece.

But isn't this dialectic about Greece? What is this talk about Persia and Egypt? Hegel treats Egypt as quasi-Greek in the sense that it represents a transition from Persia to Greece. Persia was part of that transition, because Persia conquered Egypt and incorporated it into the Persian Empire. Hegel puts it this way: "If Persia forms the external transition to Greek life, the internal transition is mediated by Egypt."[71] Hegel first notes that the Persians displayed "the adoration of Light [Ahura Mazdah]—regarded as the Essence of universal Nature [natural]."[72] This concept was carried over into the Egyptian god Osiris, god of the sun and agriculture. The general concept of nature also accompanied Isis. She was the wife of Osiris and, among other things, goddess of the Nile. The Nile's banks overflowed each year because of the tears Isis shed over the death of Osiris. Hegel recognizes these things: "We have spoken of the Nile, of the Sun, and of the vegetation depending on them. . . . The Nile and the Sun constitute the divinities, conceived under human forms [Isis and Osiris]."[73] Hegel goes on to discuss animal gods, also natural: "But among the Egyptians this worship of beasts was carried to excess under the forms of a most stupid and non-human superstition . . . each district had a brute deity of its own—a cat, an ibis, a crocodile, etc."[74] Further discussion of animal gods leads to this observation: "We thus see Egypt intellectually confined by a narrow, involved, close view of Nature."[75] Conclusion: Egypt symbolizes the concept of nature. That which reflects nature—Egypt's religion in this case—is natural. "Natural" becomes the dialectic's thesis.

Completing his transition from Egypt to Greece, Hegel discusses Greek art. This art falls under three chapter headings: "I. The Subjective Work of Art"; "II. The Objective Work of Art"; and "III. The Political Work of Art."[76] The detailed content of these chapters is not relevant to the dialectic. What is relevant is that Hegel says art is the essence of the Greek Spirit: "The first period [of Greek history] saw the Greek Spirit attain its aesthetic development and reach maturity—realize its *essential being*" (my italics).[77] As in chapter 4's natural-artificial dialectic, art is artificial, man-made. This gives us the chapter 5 dialectic's antithesis: "artificial."

"The Second Period of Greek history" is, according to Hegel, a long period of warfare. Since Egypt, the "natural" period, is the first period of the dialectic and the first Greek subperiod is the dialectic's second period, this second subperiod period of Greek history is really the third period of the dialectic. Most of the third period's fighting doesn't concern us. What does concern us is the conquests of Alexander the Great, who first united Greece and then proceeded to subdue many foreign territories. Among those territories was Egypt. In conquering Egypt and founding the city of Alexandria in the process, Alexander created a union of Egypt (natural) and Greece (artificial), hence a union of natural and artificial. That union, natural = artificial (alternatively, natural + artificial), is the Greece dialectic's synthesis.

Hegel identifies a "third [sub]period in the history of the Hellenic World," but it "interests us less."[78] Indeed it does interest us less: the chapter titled "The Fall of the Greek Spirit" takes up only three pages—these describe the decline of Greece—and is not part of the dialectic. The "crushing Destiny" of Greece is "Roman power";[79] this destiny is really part of the rise of Rome.

This particular history dialectic has a special point. In making that point, Hegel retreats from *The Philosophy of History* to *Phenomenology*. The point: Spirit is a blend of natural and artificial, or man (natural) and the divine (artificial, invented by man). "God" is man—that is, man and everything else in the universe.

Rome. Rome is the third stage of the first subperiod's dialectic. There can be little doubt that Hegel has created a third-level dialectic for Rome.

Not only has a clear pattern of dialectics on three levels emerged, Hegel has also provided three precisely defined periods within the Roman era. Even the concepts represented by these three Roman periods can be discerned. What is not clear is whether the thesis concept of potential despotism is represented by Romulus or by later kings. The dialectic is this:

> Thesis: potential + despotism (Romulus and other early Roman
>   kings)
> Antithesis: actual + aristocracy (era of Roman aristocracy)
> Synthesis: actual + despotism (Caesar and later emperors)

Rome's first period, the thesis period, extends from Rome's beginnings through the First Punic War (264–241 BCE). According to Roman mythology, Rome was founded by Romulus, who became its first king. Romulus and Remus were twins, fathered by the god Mars, born of a virgin, and nursed by a wolf. Romulus killed Remus and made himself king. The possibility that Hegel views Romulus as the model for potential despotism arises because Hegel mentions Romulus three times in discussing Roman history.[80] In the third instance, Hegel says, "Romulus is said to have appointed 100 *patres.*" The patres were Rome's patricians, the aristocrats. They held the king's authority in check, preventing him from acting like a despot. So the mythical Romulus was merely a potential despot, held in check by aristocrats.

The other possible representative of potential despotism is the early kings. According to Hegel, "the kings were banished in the year 244," or three years before the end of the First Punic War.[81] They were banished by the patricians, whose power had already limited the authority of the kings, preventing the kings from becoming more than *potential* despots.

The dialectic's antithesis is aristocracy: actual + aristocracy. The aristocrats, acting through the Roman senate, were in power during part of the first Roman period and all of the second.

The dialectic's synthesis returns to despotism—separation and return. Caesar crossed the Rubicon, took control, and proclaimed himself emperor. Many other emperors followed. Hegel calls their rule despotism, giving us the synthesis: actual + despotism.

The Early Christian Germanic World. The first of the second subperiod's three stages is the early Germanic world. It has three stages of its own: (1) the Barbarian Migrations, (2) Islam, which Hegel calls Mohametanism, and (3) the Empire of Charlemagne. These produce another universal-and-particular dialect. But it is a dialectic with a difference: universal (normally the thesis) and particular (normally the antithesis) are transposed.

The first period begins with the arrival in the Roman Empire of Germanic people. These belong to many groups—Hegel calls them nations—and they gradually spread themselves across the empire. Although they ultimately convert to Christianity, they are slow to do so. This slowness Hegel attributes to "an idiosyncrasy which we may call *Heart* [Gemüth]."[82] The basic characteristic of *Heart* is that the Germanic individual becomes devoted to nothing in particular but becomes superficially attached to a wide variety of objects. In two different senses, particularity becomes the theme of the first period. First, the many Germanic nations migrating into Germany are not yet united into an empire; they are particulars, particular Germanic "nations" (more aptly described as tribes or groups). Second, *Heart* slows the process of Christianization, preserving for the moment *many* Germanic religions and also preserving the *Heart*-based attachment to *many* objects. Many particulars means particularity. "We behold them [the Germanic migrants] beginning their work by bringing all social relations under the form of *particularity*."[83] Particularity is Hegel's thesis, expressly stated.

In the East, the opposite sort of development occurs, and occurs rapidly. Islam takes over. The Islamic *"Revolution of the East"* that took place "destroyed all particularity . . . making the abstract One [Allah] the absolute object of attention and devotion."[84] Note the word "abstract"; it is the opposite—the antithesis—of "concrete," which is another way of saying "particular." "One" is, of course, another way of saying "universal"—that which encompasses all the particulars. Hegel has now presented us with the dialectic's antithesis: universality.

The dialectic's third stage, the synthesis, is the Empire of Charlemagne, king of the Franks. Clovis was the founder of the Frankish Empire, which more or less replaced the western Roman Empire. After Clovis's death, the empire went through various tribulations until Charlemagne emerged. The pope, who was now a powerful figure, crowned Charlemagne emperor of the Holy Roman Empire in 800 CE. This act marked the founding of the Holy Roman Empire, although Charlemagne's reign actually extended from 771 CE until 814 CE. (The Holy Roman Empire excluded the eastern Roman Empire, which collapsed much later, in 1453.) The Holy Roman Empire's founding is the first of two developments that create the synthesis of universality and particularity. The empire unites the *many* German nations into *one* empire. The second development is the completion of the conversion of the Germanic people to Christianity. Now, like the Muslims, the particularistic Germanic people have brought their focus onto the One, in this case God. This too is a synthesis of universality and particularity: the universal, God, absorbs and thereby replaces the many particular objects toyed with by *Heart*. Here is the dialectic that results:

> Thesis: particularity (many Germanic "nations," many non-Christian religions)
> Antithesis: universality (Islam, one religion, one God)
> Synthesis: universe (one empire, one religion) composed of particulars (many Germanic "nations")

The Middle Ages. The middle stage of the Rome-to-Germanic-World subperiod dialectic is the Middle Ages. As usual, Hegel divides the period into three stages. In this instance the stages are (1) the breaking up of the Frankish Empire and the concurrent rise of both feudalism and the Roman Catholic Church, (2) the Crusades, and (3) the transition from feudalism to monarchy. Hegel seems to read *two* familiar dialectics into this trio of stages. The first dialectic has inner and outer as its thesis and antithesis; the second uses one and many.

We begin with the inner-outer dialectic. These two concepts form a pair that appeared in a variant of *Phenomenology*'s macrodialectic and in four microdialectics: (1) Observing Reason, (2) Phrenology, (3) Law of the Heart, and (4) Matter in Hand. In the macrodialectic, "inner" refers to the inner essence of an object, which is Spirit; "outer" is the outside of "objects" an observer ("subject") sees and misinterprets as something other than himself. These concepts are closely related to "one" and "many." The internal essence, Spirit, is the same for every object; everything in the universe is Spirit. So there is just *one* internal entity. But, judged by their outer appearance, the external or alien objects seem to be *many*, many particulars.

The clue that brings our attention to the internal-external dialectic is something Hegel says about the antithesis stage, the Crusades. Christianity exhibited a "craving" to recover the Muslim-controlled Holy Land, particularly Jerusalem. This craving "drove it [Christianity] out of itself."[85] "Out of itself" is recognizable as an alternate phrasing of the second member of Hegel's intended-to-be-recondite "in itself" and "for itself" dichotomy. That which is "in itself" (inside itself as an inner essence) is the internal; that which is "for itself" is "out of itself," or on the outside. "In itself" always refers to a thesis, "for itself" always to an antithesis. Now we get the point of Hegel's depicting the Crusades as a separate stage of the Middle Ages. The Crusades send Christian militants into the *outside* world, the Middle East, to slaughter the Muslims. ("Still dripping with the blood of the slaughtered inhabitants of Jerusalem, the Christians fell down on their faces at the tomb of the Redeemer, and directed their fervent supplications to him."[86])

With "outer" (i.e., "out of itself") thus established as the antithesis, it is easy to see how "inner" can be read into the thesis stage. Everything discussed in connection with the first stage of the dialectic relates to *internal* developments in the Holy Roman Empire. First, following Charlemagne's death, the Frankish Empire breaks up into many smaller sovereign units. The Holy Roman Emperor retains his throne, but his authority greatly diminishes. Second, the weakening of central authority leads to the development of feudal institutions. Third, the Church replaces the state as the de facto governing authority: "The Church gained the victory in the struggle . . . and in this way secured as decided a supremacy in Germany, as she did in the other states of Europe."[87] Lest doubt remain about whether Hegel really conceptualizes these developments as "internal," Hegel explicitly delivers the message. This message appears in the introductory paragraph of his section on "The Middle Ages." There he says that "the culminating point of this period is the Crusades; for with them arises a universal instability, but one through which the states of Christendom first attain *internal* and *external* independence" (my italics).[88] These words do not mean that the internal independence comes from the Crusades; they mean that the Crusades add "external independence" to the "internal independence" already achieved by internal states of the Frankish kingdom.

You probably wonder: How is Hegel going to produce his synthesis of "inner" (internal) and "outer" (external)? I wondered the same thing. The third stage's heading, "The Transition from Feudalism to Monarchy," does not sound promising. On its face, it offers nothing external. But in the penultimate paragraph of nineteen paragraphs—extremely long paragraphs for the most part—we find the answer:

> As a *third* leading feature demanding our notice in determining the character of the period, [it] might be mentioned that urging of Spirit *outwards*— that desire on the part of man to become acquainted with *his* world. The chivalrous spirit of the maritime heroes of Portugal and Spain opened a new way to the East Indies and discovered America. . . . The aim of Columbus was by no means a merely secular one; it presented a distinctly religious aspect; the treasures of those rich Indian lands which awaited his discovery and were destined in his intention to be expended in a new Crusade . . . [in which] the heathen inhabitants of the countries themselves were to be converted to Christianity.[89]

Note that Hegel italicizes the word *outwards* and that he also characterizes the maritime explorations as a "crusade," a word used earlier to describe the external crusades of the middle period.

The complementary internal developments need not be summarized here. Suffice it to say that they take place within the Holy Roman Empire and the Germanic world, the realm of Western (non-Orthodox) Christianity. And so we have a synthesis: internal + external. The dialectic:

> Thesis: inner
> Antithesis: outer
> Synthesis: inner + outer

The second dialectic of the Middle Ages can be summarized quickly. The Western Christian world is *one*. The Crusades are *many*. Christianity is a synthesis of the one and the many: one Christianity with many Crusades. The dialectic:

> Thesis: one
> Antithesis: many
> Synthesis: one composed of many

The Modern Time. The sixth and last third-level dialectic—also the last stage of the second subperiod's dialectics—is "The Modern Time" (not to be confused with "our own time," the very last substage, roughly Hegel's "own" 1785–1830 era, beginning with pre-revolution developments in France). We have long since confirmed what Hegel is doing, so it is no surprise that there are again three chapters, one for each stage of the new dialectic. The chapters (and dialectical stages) are (1) "The Reformation, (2) "Influence of the Reformation on Political Development," and—here I use Friedrich's translation—(3) "The Enlightenment and the [French] Revolution." (Sibree unwisely substitutes Hegel's "Eclaircissement" for "Enlightenment," a terrible burden for those of us who don't understand French.)

This dialectic ends at the same historical time (1815–30) and place (Prussia) two earlier dialectics end. The overall period's freedom dialectic leads to a synthesis of "actual freedom." So does the second subperiod's Rome-to-Germanic-World dialectic. You would expect, then, that the third-level Modern Time dialectic would have the same familiar form: (1) a thesis of "potential freedom," (2) an antithesis of "actual bondage," and (3) a synthesis of "actual freedom." But this expectation turns out to be wrong.

The Modern Time dialectic *seems* to begin with "potential freedom" as its thesis. The first stage is labeled "The Reformation." In this stage, Protestantism has evolved and is now the agent of potential freedom. Man is free to think his own thoughts and to interpret the Bible for himself; the Church no longer tells him what to think. But this freedom is still only potential, incomplete. Two problems prevent its becoming actual. One is that freedom requires not only Protestantism but Prussian style monarchy. Not just monarchy in general—the Reformation era already has that—but Prussian style monarchy: "We have, as yet, no reconstruction of the State, the system of jurisprudence, etc., for thought must first discover the essential principle of Right."[90] (We need not digress here to discuss the complicated and ambiguous concept of Right; we need merely recognize that Hegel thinks something is missing in earlier Protestantism.)

The second problem preventing the immediate realization of freedom under the Reformation is "the belief in *Evil*."[91] Unfortunate women were thought to be witches, persons who had made pacts with the Devil and thereby exercised the Evil One's powers. These women were tortured into confessing, then executed, sometimes by burning. Protestants as well as Catholics shared the madness: "This delusion raged among the nations in the sixteenth century with the fury of a pestilence," and "even as late as the year 1780 a witch was publicly burned at Galarus in Switzerland."[92] Freedom, then, was still only potential.

But if the Modern Time dialectic's thesis were "potential freedom," its antithesis would have to be "actual bondage." Yet nothing Hegel says about the second stage describes bondage. He might have made "the belief in Evil" his second stage. He could then have used the witch trials to represent bondage— bondage to superstition. But he didn't: the witch trials are discussed under the Reformation heading (the thesis heading). Hegel might also have used France's Reign of Terror—the mass guillotining of innocent citizens—to represent bondage. But his discussion of the Reign of Terror, quite brief, comes under the synthesis heading, "The Enlightenment and the Revolution." Nothing Hegel says under the antithesis heading, "The Influence of the Reformation on Political Development," qualifies as bondage. It becomes apparent that this last dialectic does not begin with "potential freedom" and progress to "actual bondage." A different dialectic must be found.

This different dialectic isn't hard to find. Like chapter 4's natural-artificial intermediate dialectic, history's last dialectic is hidden in plain sight—in the labels of the first two stages. The first stage, the Reformation, points to religion. The second stage's words "Political Development" point to government. These two concepts—religion and government, or church and state— are familiar. They are two opposing sources of rule. They were discussed in connection with earlier dialectics. In particular, the two primary dialectics— the overall period's freedom and monarchy dialectics—are based on the two concepts. In the freedom dialectic, Protestantism (church) and Germanic monarchy (state) are the two pillars on which freedom rests. The monarchy dialectic emphasizes the importance of the second pillar (monarchy). The new church-state dialectic is the following:

> Thesis: church (Protestantism)
> Antithesis: state (Germanic monarchy)
> Synthesis: freedom—the joint product of church (free thought)
>   and state (judicious rule)

The historical opposition, or antithesis, between church and state requires little elaboration. The Church and the state (the state was first the Roman Empire, then the Holy Roman Empire) vied with each other for power. At first the state had the upper hand. The Roman state initially fed Christians to the lions or had them crucified, then reversed course and made Christianity the official religion of the state while exercising considerable control over the church. Later, in the Middle Ages, the church gained the upper hand. It assumed powers that rightly belonged to government. Even today, in the United States, fundamentalist Protestant churches—assisted and even led by the Catholic Church on the abortion, birth control, and parochial school aid issues—seek to gain control of government so as to advance their religious agenda (authorizing school prayer and Bible reading the public schools, suppressing the teaching of evolution, providing taxpayer-financed tuition vouchers for parochial school students, outlawing abortion, displaying the Ten Commandments and crosses in public buildings and on public property, authorizing pharmacy employees to refuse to fill birth control prescriptions, outlawing stem cell research, and so on). Although church and state have sometimes cooperated for their mutual benefit, they are inherently opponents: the church becomes the master-and-slave enemy of the state when the church seeks control of the state—and vice versa, as in the former Communist USSR. In that sense, the state is the antithesis of the church.

The synthesis of church and state arises in the concept of freedom. Freedom's first prerequisite is Protestantism, the essence of the Reformation. Until Protestantism arrived, Catholicism suppressed free thought. Under threat of being tried for heresy, not to mention the threat of burning in hell, people had to accept as true whatever the Church taught. They could not question the "facts" that the sun revolved around the earth, the earth was flat, God is shaped like a human and sits on a throne in a place in the sky called heaven, the first humans were Adam and Eve, all humans ever born except Mary were infected with original sin, Jesus was born of a virgin, Jesus returned to life after dying on the cross, Mary's physical body (not just her soul) floated up to heaven, stars would fall from the sky during a future apocalypse, demons caused insanity, witches really exist and cause all sorts of trouble, divine laws the violation of which constitutes sin also exist, sexual intercourse undertaken purely for pleasure (even between husband and wife) is sinful, unredeemed sinners go to hell where they are eternally tortured with fire, sins can be expiated by such means as manipulating the beads on a rosary while reciting Hail Marys, children who die in infancy go to limbo, and so on. Even worse, the Church suppressed personal liberty and brought death to thousands of human beings through such means as the inquisitions, the crusades, heresy trials, and the persecution of witches. Protestantism introduced a reformed set of religious values. The value most highly lauded by Hegel was the right of each person to interpret the Bible for himself, instead of being told by the Church what the Bible means and what dogmatic beliefs to accept.

The second prerequisite for freedom is monarchy, the purest form of government. Hegel distrusted both democratic rule by citizens and aristocratic rule by feudal nobles. Referring to British democracy, Hegel said that "of institutions characterized by real freedom there are nowhere fewer than in England."[93] Monarchy is necessary because, where policy must be decided, "the personal decision of the monarch . . . is . . . absolutely necessary."[94] But monarchy is not in itself sufficient to produce freedom. It must be accompanied by a proper constitution, one based on judiciously formulated laws that strike the right balance between personal freedom and the administrative requirements of the state. "Reason embodied in Laws" is essential.[95] McCarney underscores the importance of this point: "It is plain that Hegel is wholly committed to the view that freedom must be embodied as an objective structure of law and justice."[96] In addition, the monarch must be Protestant, committed to the Protestant principle of free thought.

Monarchy could not guarantee freedom in France, because the monarch and a majority of his subjects were Catholic.[97]

By uniting church (Protestantism) and state (monarchy), Hegelian-style freedom provides a dialectical synthesis of church and state.

PICKING AND CHOOSING

Hegel might have thought he had really discovered a dialectical pattern in history. Or he might have known that he was picking and choosing the bits of history—and the associated concepts—he used to build his history dialectics. The latter alternative is surely the case. Hegel was not a metaphysician. Both his strong antagonism toward religion and the nonsupernatural character of Spirit leave no doubt on this point. Hegel could not have been unaware that he was distorting history when he created his dialectics. The distortion and the picking and choosing are too obvious. By defining periods and regions differently, or by emphasizing different concepts for the regions chosen by Hegel, we can just as easily create history triads that wreck Hegel's dialectics by disabling one of the three stages. We can also create new dialectics with different "goals" and outcomes. Here are some substitute choices, no more arbitrary than Hegel's, that smash the history dialectics:

- Substitute ancient Judaism for Oriental despotism as the first stage of history. The Jews had slaves (Exodus 21:2–11, 20; Leviticus 25:39–46; Numbers 31:15–18; Deuteronomy 15:12–18, 20:10–14; Joshua 9:22–27). So the thesis is now "actual + bondage" instead of "potential + freedom." The new thesis is identical to Hegel's Greco-Roman slavery antithesis. Hegel's antithesis is no longer antithetical. The dialectic lies in ruins.

- Substitute sixteenth-century England, featuring the reigns of Henry VIII (1509–47) and Elizabeth I (1558–1603), for Greece and Rome as the freedom dialectic's antithesis. England had no slavery, so actual + freedom is the antithesis. Now there is no "actual + bondage" antithesis to oppose the "potential + freedom" thesis. The antithesis and the synthesis are identical. The dialectic again has crumbled.

- Substitute early nineteenth-century United States for early nineteenth-century northern European monarchies as the synthesis stage. (The United States, being the latest historical development as of Hegel's Berlin tenure, is surely a more rational choice.) Now the monarchy dialectic becomes (1) thesis: one ruler + one territory, (2) antithesis: many rulers + many territories, (3) synthesis: many rulers (the voters) + many territories (the states). The synthesis is now the same as the antithesis. Another dialectic destroyed.

- Create an entirely new set of three periods with Athens (just the one city-state) as the thesis period, the Rome of Caesar and the post-Caesar emperors as the antithesis, and the United States as the synthesis. The three conceptual stages become (1) democracy + one territory, (2) despotism + many territories, and (3) democracy (from the thesis) + many territories (from the antithesis). We now have a genuine synthesis that borrows one concept from the thesis and one from the antithesis. But democracy has replaced monarchy as the goal of history. And the United States has replaced Prussia.

- Substitute for Hegel's geographically oriented periods three abstract, nongeographical historical periods: primitive society, medieval society, and the "modern" nineteenth-century society of Hegel's Berlin period. Make weaponry the conceptual scheme. For the three stages of weaponry we get (1) bow and arrow + spear, (2) broadsword + catapult, and (3) rifle + cannon. The middle stage is no longer antithetical to the first stage, and the third stage is no longer a synthesis of the first two.

- Keep all three of Hegel's time periods but substitute Catholic southern Europe for Protestant northern Europe. Change the concepts used for each period to religious concepts. Hegel says the Mongolian despot, the lama, was revered as God, the only God. But he was not actually a God—he was a human—so he was only potentially the God of Catholicism, who represses freedom of thought. Thesis: potential + one anti-free-thought God. Greece and Rome had gods who didn't suppress freedom of thought but they were the wrong gods. Antithesis: actual + many free-thought gods. Southern Europe had the one anti-free-thought God of Catholicism. Synthesis: actual (from the antithesis) + one anti-free-thought God. Now Hegel's goal of freedom (derived from Protestantism) has become a goal of bondage, submission to a repressive, anti-free-thought God.

I'm not arguing that Hegel was wrong about history's having dialectical goals. His being wrong is so obvious that the subject is beyond argumentation. My point is, rather, that Hegel, as a highly intelligent man, knew exactly what he was doing. He was inventing history and its supposed goals. He could not have failed to understand that he and not dialectics was responsible for the way his version of history unfolded. Sabine understands exactly what Hegel was doing: "In Hegel's hands it [dialectics, vaguely conceived by Sabine] worked out to conclusions that he had reached without it and the dialectic contributed nothing to their proof."[98]

I must admit that not everyone agrees that Hegel knew what he was doing. Bertrand Russell, who regards Hegel as a metaphysician, thinks Hegel was just plain naive. Russell describes Hegel's interpretation of history with these words: "Like other historical theories, it required, if it was to be made plausible, some distortion of facts and considerable ignorance. Hegel, like Marx and Spengler after him, possessed both these qualifications. It is odd that a process which is represented as cosmic should all have taken place on our planet and most of it near the Mediterranean."[99] Russell is wrong about the metaphysics, but he is right about the distortion (I would say "selectivity") of facts and about the consequently implausible nature of the outcome.

MARX'S HISTORY DIALECTICS

I stated in chapter 1 that Karl Marx, Frederick Engels, and Paul Tillich are the only people whose writing reveals a firm understanding of Hegel's thesis-antithesis-synthesis dialectics. (I'm not entirely sure about Engels.)

My assertion stems from the facts that (*a*) both Marx (in collaboration with his colleague, Engels) and Tillich based their own dialectical systems on the Hegelian prototype, (*b*) nobody else has either used similar dialectical formulations or provided specific examples of thesis-antithesis-synthesis triads taken from either *Phenomenology* or *The Philosophy of History*, and (*c*) the thirteen interpreters quoted in chapter 1, after failing in their own literature surveys and in their own analyses of Hegel's works to find any evidence of thesis-antithesis-synthesis dialectics, have forcefully asserted that the long-held belief that Hegel used such formulations is just a legend. I have already provided examples of Tillich's dialectics and have shown that these adopt the formats used by Hegel, including the separation-and-return characteristic. Now we need to examine Marx's dialectics.

Although this book is about Hegel, five considerations justify devoting part of a chapter to Marx:

1. I need to substantiate my assertion in chapter 1 that Marx and his colleague understood Hegel's dialectics, whereas nobody else except Tillich had this understanding.

2. The presence of thesis-antithesis-synthesis dialectics in Marx's writing, dialectics that Marx acknowledges are based on Hegel's, is powerful additional evidence that Hegel actually used thesis-antithesis-synthesis dialectics. Marx could not possibly have come up with dialectical triads using two-concept theses, antitheses, and syntheses if Hegel hadn't provided his two-concepts-per-stage prototype. I refer to the format wherein the synthesis borrows one concept from the thesis and one from the antithesis. Marx's dialectics even employ a separation-and-return theme and a related self-alienation theme analogous to Hegel's themes. All these similarities can't be a coincidence.

3. Marx's dialectics, every bit as unrecognized and misunderstood as Hegel's, need to be introduced to the world of scholarship. In particular, the authors of survey textbooks on philosophy, political theory, and the history of economic thought need a much better grasp of Marxian

dialectics if they are to replace their incomprehensibly abstract, and typically downright erroneous, descriptions of Marx's dialectics with concrete descriptions, complete with examples. What does "turns Hegel's dialectics right-side up" mean to the student if the textbook's author can't compare examples of "upside down" dialectics taken from Hegel and "right-side up" dialectics from Marx?

4. Bringing Hegel's and Marx's historical dialectics together in one place should facilitate the work of future scholars doing comparative studies of Hegel and Marx or studies describing Hegel's influence on Marx.

5. Marx's thought can't be adequately explained without referring in detail to Hegel's prototype thesis-antithesis-synthesis dialectics. What better place to explain Marx's dialectics than a study that first explains Hegel's dialectics?

MARX'S DIALECTICAL FRAMEWORK

Marx openly declares that he is using Hegelian dialectics, albeit in purified form. In the preface to *Capital* he writes that he has "openly avowed myself the pupil of that mighty thinker [Hegel]." But he then attacks "the mystification which dialectic suffers in Hegel's hands." Hegel's dialectics is "standing on its head." Dialectics "must be turned right side up again, if you would discover the rational kernel within the mystical shell." By this Marx means Hegel falsely assumed that dialectical activity takes place in the world of ideas—the world of the mind—and is "the life-process of the human brain, *i.e.*, the process of thinking." On the contrary, says Marx, dialectical activity really takes place in the "material world," the tangible physical world where production and other economic activity takes place.[100] His philosophy, which has been dubbed "dialectical materialism," seeks to show how this dialectical activity operates in the material world. Marx never used the phrase "dialectical materialism," but the phrase was later coined by the Marxist philosopher G. V. Plekhanov.[101] His intent was to connect the two salient features of Marx's method—Hegelian dialectics and "the materialistic basis of my [Marx's] method."[102]

That materialistic basis of Marx's dialectical method consists largely of the goods people produce, the inputs used in producing these goods, the tools by which the goods are produced, and the human beings who produce the goods. All these things are matter, contrasted with mind; matter is "material." To combine this material emphasis with dialectics, Marx and Engels divide history into five periods. All except the last (final communism, which lies in the future) they view as deeply flawed. Yet each period except the first (primitive communism) is better than the preceding one. In this regard, A. J. P. Taylor observes: "Nearly all nineteenth-century historians believed in Progress. They saw man's story as a record of almost uninterrupted improvement and were convinced that the Higher triumphed at each stage."[103] The steady improvement, according to Marx, results from improved methods of production and resultant higher output—greater wealth. The five periods are based on the predominant mode of production. The periods are these:

1. **Primitive Communism, or Gens:** The earliest societies were primitive societies that featured communal ownership of property, contrasted with private property. Marx gave these societies the label "gens." Such societies began as hunter-gatherer-fisher societies and later progressed to agriculture. Marx thus can say that primitive communism "corresponds to the undeveloped stage of production, at which a people lives by hunting and fishing, by the rearing of beast or, in the highest stage, agriculture."[104] Whatever was collectively gathered or produced was divided among the people. In more advanced stages of gens, crafts such as pottery making and weaving were introduced. Engels used America's Iroquois Indians as an example of gens. Despite being a form of communism—the goal of Marxian history—gens was the worst of the five periods. Primitive methods resulted in so little production that extreme poverty prevailed.[105]

2. **Slavery:** Primitive communism gradually gave way to slavery. Improved methods of production and gradual accumulation of private

property, including family-owned plots of land, paved the way. Family cultivation of private plots created situations where additional labor from outside the family could enhance the family's well-being. Labor now acquired value. "But," Engels explains, "within the community . . . there were no superfluous labour forces available. On the other hand, such forces were provided by war. . . . Up to that time they had not known what to do with prisoners of war, and had therefore simply killed them. But at the stage of the 'economic order' which had now been attained the prisoners of war acquired a value; their captors therefore let them live and made use of their labour. . . . *Slavery* was invented."[106] Slavery became the new form of production in Greece and Rome and to a degree elsewhere. (The ancient Jews and Egyptians had slaves.) With slavery came social classes—Greek citizens, Roman aristocrats, Roman plebeians, and Greek and Roman slaves. What had been a classless society became the first of three sequential class societies. Generically speaking, each society had two broad classes: the exploiters and the exploited. The exploiters included subclasses, such as slave owners, merchants, artisans, fishermen, and soldiers. Oppressive as slavery may seem, it was better than primitive communism. Prisoners were no longer put to death. Some slaves performed tasks that were not oppressive. Moreover, the use of slaves to produce food and other goods gave citizens time to produce the art, philosophy, and science of ancient Greece.

3. **Feudalism:** With the collapse of the Roman Empire, slavery gradually faded and was replaced by feudalism. Its basic characteristics were "the hierarchical structure of land ownership," "the enserfed small peasantry," and, where handicraft production took place, cottage industry and guilds.[107] Feudal institutions took many forms. In general, the king at the top provided land to a baron in exchange for knights needed for protection. The baron might subdivide his land among lesser nobles, who might or might not proceed with further subdivision among still lesser nobles. At the bottom of the hierarchy, the land was parceled out to serfs, who worked the land and also engaged in handicraft labor.

The serfs, essentially tenants, paid for the use of their plots of land by giving their nobles shares of their crops and, sometimes, shares of their handicrafts. As commerce expanded and money came into use, the serf might pay cash instead of crops and handmade articles for use of the land. The cash was acquired through the sale of surplus production. Although better off than the slave, who kept none of his production, the serf was still exploited: much of the serf's production went to the exploiting class, the nobles, who did no work.

4. **Capitalism:** According to Marx and Engels, many factors helped turn feudalism into capitalism. These factors included (*a*) the increased demand for marketable goods that resulted from expansion of trade with distant markets, (*b*) the hiring of labor by merchants and artisans seeking to accommodate increasing demand for their goods, and—especially—(*c*) the displacement of peasants from their land by nobles desiring to convert the land to new uses. The displaced peasants, desperate for work, became the new proletarian class. Marx did not think the inefficiency of cottage industry, economies of large-scale production, or the invention of the steam engine contributed significantly to the beginning of capitalism: "With regard to the mode of production itself, manufacture . . . is hardly to be distinguished, in its earliest stages, from the handicraft trades of the guilds, otherwise than by the greater number of workmen simultaneously employed by one and the same individual capital[ist]."[108] Soon, however, task specialization, or "division of labour," created economies that gave impetus to the new economic system.[109] But capitalism was in place for two centuries before the Industrial Revolution introduced modern mechanical production techniques based on the waterwheel and the steam engine. These techniques brought the factory system and capitalism into full bloom.

5. **Final Communism:** Marx believed capitalism could not long endure. The oppressed working class—the proletariat—would rise up against the bourgeoisie class, its exploiter,[110] and take over the

means of production. Marx happily anticipated what was going to happen: "The monopoly of capital becomes a fetter upon the mode of production. . . . The knell of capitalist private property sounds. The expropriators are expropriated. . . . It is the negation of negation." (Note the words "negation of [the] negation." They come from Hegel and refer to a dialectical synthesis.) Thus will the oppressed workers (*a*) regain ownership of the tools and the output that were taken from them and (*b*) convert the factories to communal ownership. Production will be socialized and a dictatorship of the proletariat established. Then the state will wither away.

These five stages of history provide the raw material for Marx's dialectics. Where, or what, are these dialectics? The answer requires that a distinction be made between two different types of Marxian dialectics. The first might be called base-superstructure dialectics; the second is Hegelian thesis-antithesis-synthesis dialectics. Marx's expositors and critics always discuss Marx's base-superstructure dialectics; the Hegelian dialectics have been overlooked, except in two fairly superficial treatments that identify stages but fail to identify the thesis and antithesis *concepts* and to show how they are combined in syntheses. We are, of course, concerned only with Marx's Hegelian dialectics. But to justify my statement that the Hegelian dialectics have been overlooked, I must first clarify in more detail what has *not* been overlooked.

Marx's base-superstructure dialectics begin with the idea that in every period or society production is organized into an economic base. Under Greek slavery, the slaves largely took over the tasks of producing food and goods, although citizen artisans still produced some of the handicrafts. Marx and Engels don't say who did the fishing, but it seems unlikely that slaves were entrusted to man fishing boats, means of flight. A small merchant class also began to develop; the merchants produced nothing but lived off the work of the slaves. The slave owners, merchants, free artisans, and other free citizens formed the privileged classes. These classes, or at least the first two, were the exploiters.

Marx believed that the economic base of every society generates a noneconomic superstructure of government, laws, religion, philosophy, and other aspects of thought and culture. This superstructure has to be tuned to the economic base; the economic base of every period and society requires a unique superstructure. But the economic base keeps changing, slowly evolving. "Contradictions" then develop between the economic base and the superstructure of thoughts, ideas, and political institutions. These contradictions are analogous to but not the same as the opposition between a thesis and its antithesis. (Some of Marx's expositors seem to regard the base and the superstructure as thesis and antithesis.) When the contradictions become strong enough, the social and political institutions adapt and reorganize themselves into a new superstructure. A new system of social classes arises, as with feudalism's nobles, artisans, and serfs, who replaced the slave owners and slaves of slavery.

The new base-superstructure combination is analogous to but not the same as a dialectical synthesis. Yet some of Marx's expositors seem to imply that the new combination *is* a synthesis. If that were so, the thesis would have to be the original base and superstructure combined—two parts. The antithesis would then be the new base combined with the old superstructure, because the thesis and antithesis must follow the same pattern—two parts. The synthesis would be the new base combined with the new superstructure. The following pseudodialectic results:

Thesis: base 1 + superstructure 1
Pseudoantithesis: base 2 + superstructure 1
Pseudosynthesis: base 2 + superstructure 2

You can immediately see five problems exhibited by the base-superstructure interpretation of dialectics:

1. We have a two-part thesis and a two-part antithesis. In this format, both parts of the antithesis should be the opposite of their thesis counterparts. For example, in the thesis-antithesis pair (*a*) potential union and (*b*) actual separation, actual (in the antithesis) is the opposite of potential *and* separation is the opposite of union. But in the base-superstructure misconception of dialectics, only the base of the antithesis differs from that of the thesis. The old and new superstructures are the same; both are superstructure 1.

2. Whereas the contradiction should be *between* the thesis and the antithesis, it has become a contradiction *within* the antithesis. The contradiction is between base 2 and superstructure 1. That is not where the contradiction occurs in genuine thesis-antithesis-synthesis dialectics.

3. Although the antithesis base (base 2) differs from the thesis base (base 1), the two bases are not opposites; they are not antithetical to one another. They are just *different*. And that characteristic does not meet the requirements of a Hegelian antithesis. A Hegelian antithesis is the *opposite* of the thesis.

4. When the thesis and the antithesis both have two parts, the synthesis must borrow one part from the two-part thesis and one part from the two-part antithesis; otherwise there is no synthesis. The base-superstructure synthesis therefore should be either (*a*) base 1 + superstructure 2 or (*b*) base 2 + superstructure 1. Instead it is (*c*) base 2 + superstructure 2. Superstructure 2, far from being something from either the thesis or the antithesis, is from neither: it is brand-new. And the ostensible synthesis contains nothing from the thesis; it contains neither base 1 nor superstructure 1.

5. Hegelian dialectics employ the theme of separation and return, derived from Christianity. The dialectic separates from and returns to something in the thesis. But in base-superstructure dialectics, there is no return to a thesis concept. The dialectic does not separate from and return to base 1; it stays separated.

My point is that the base-superstructure type of "dialectics" is not thesis-antithesis-synthesis dialectics. It is not the dialectics that has gone unrecognized in Marx's thought. Base-superstructure "dialectics" has been recognized all over the place. What has not been recognized is the Hegelian dialectics, the dialectics of thesis, antithesis, and synthesis. To this topic we now turn. Marx's dialectics, like Hegel's, take place at more than one level of an outline of history. Hegel had three levels; Marx has two. The outline is different, but the dialectical process is the same.

LEVEL ONE: MARX'S OVERALL-PERIOD DIALECTICS

Like Hegel, Marx has more than one dialectic for the overall historical period, though now the additional dialectics are variations on a basic theme. Also like Hegel, Marx divides the overall period into two subperiods, each with its own subdialectic. And once more like Hegel, Marx uses the concept of separation and return: the thesis concept from which the antithesis separates is returned to in the synthesis. But differences are also present. Unlike Hegel, Marx extends history into the future: he includes final communism, a future stage of history, in the overall period. Also unlike Hegel, Marx employs the concept of alienation in his history dialectic. (Hegel uses it only in *Phenomenology*'s macrodialectic.) In doing so, Marx creates overall-period history dialectics that combine features of Hegel's macrodialectic of self-alienated Spirit with features of Hegel's history dialectics. A sort of hybrid dialectic results.

Approximations to Marxian Dialectics. Easily the two best studies of Marx's philosophy are Robert Tucker's *Philosophy and Myth in Karl Marx* and M. M. Bober's *Karl Marx's Interpretation of History*.[111] Both authors, without actually describing Marx's thesis-antithesis-synthesis concepts, have provided important clues pointing to the concepts. Tucker shows that Marx reworked Hegel's theory of self-alienated Spirit into a concept of self-alienated man.[112] This reworking is how Marx turned Hegel's supposedly upside down dialectics into what Marx regarded as right-side up dialectics. That is, instead of placing the dialectical movement in the nonmaterial (mental) world of thought or ideas, Marx put the movement in the material (physical) world of man and the goods man produces. Marx did this by positing that man, like Spirit, undergoes three stages of existence:

1. Man begins in his essential state, wherein he is united with himself in the sense that, under primitive communism, a classless society, he is united with the products of his labor. Those who produce collectively

share the product; there are no exploiters, no exploiting and exploited classes. But this state of "essence" is merely *potential*, for there is hardly any output to share. Poverty and want cannot be man's *actual* essential state.

2. Class societies develop. In these, man becomes separated or alienated from his essential self. Exploiting classes—for example, the slave owners and merchants in slave societies—separate man from the fruits of his labor by taking most of the output and leaving the laborer with barely enough for subsistence. Just as Hegel's Spirit becomes separated from its essential (unified) self, Marx's man becomes separated from his essential self—from the man who remains united with what he produces.

3. Under final communism, man returns to a higher form of his original essential state: he keeps what he produces, all of it. Classes disappear. The exploiting classes that formerly took most of what the exploited workers produced vanish. Man is again unified, united with his labor. But what he returns to is better than what he originally separated from. New methods of production mean that the collectively produced and owned output is now far greater than it was under primitive communism. The poverty is gone.

Bober, although writing well in advance of Tucker, in effect picks up where Tucker leaves off. He does this by answering the question on everyone's mind: how do you get three dialectical stages out of five stages of history? Bober's answer is that you combine the three middle stages—slavery, feudalism, and capitalism—into one. The three middle stages are characterized by (*a*) class societies, consisting of exploiting and exploited classes, (*b*) separation of man from what he produces, and (*c*) private property, which replaces communal property. By combining the three middle periods of history, Bober is able to explicitly identify the basic Marxian dialectic's three stages: "Primitive communism represents the thesis; the private property of slavery, feudalism, and capitalism is the antithesis; and the communism of the future will reestablish the communal property of the archaic days, but as a synthesis of a higher dimension."[113] Note the words "higher dimension." They refer to the higher Yes, the negation of the negation (synthesis) in the Yes-No-Yes dialectal format. The Marxian *higher* Yes is comparable to the Tillichian higher Yes, Yes to "the God *above* the God of theism."

What Bober offers, however, is only labels, not substantive concepts. The labels identify the three dialectical stages without identifying the underlying dialectical concepts. In fact, Bober criticizes the idea that dialectical transformation really takes place. His criticism confuses base-superstructure dialectics with thesis-antithesis-synthesis dialectics. "The idea of the unity of opposites," he says, "may not always apply." Why not? "Many facts . . . embody a union of several attributes, but the attributes are not opposites." Moreover, the idea "that the negation of the negation yields a synthesis of a higher order is not always valid." Note that "negation of the negation" refers to thesis-antithesis-synthesis dialectics whereas Bober, definitely confused here, is describing base-superstructure dialectics.

Bober reveals his base-superstructure perspective by alluding to a multiplicity of dialectics, whereas the three historical stages he identifies do not constitute multiplicity; they constitute just one dialectic. Describing multiple dialectics, Bober writes: "The dialectic may be regarded as a game of classifying and putting into pigeonholes aspects of phenomena after the event. . . . *Often* enough there is no dialectic at all, and *frequently* an aspect of the dialectic triad is missing" (my italics).[114] It is evident that, in saying "often" and "frequently," Bober is not thinking of the three historical stages he identifies. The words "after the event" also betray his base-superstructure perspective. The event of final communism hasn't arrived. So Bober can't be describing the one big dialectic that goes from primitive communism to private property to final communism. Bober is speaking abstractly. He is thinking of base-superstructure dialectics. He is envisioning a whole series of base-superstructure dialectics, one for every economic base, and apparently for more than five economic bases. In doing so, he is failing to recognize that, in the overall history dialectic that advances from primitive communism to final communism, nothing is "missing" from "the dialectic triad": no "aspect of the dialectical triad" is "missing."

The Overall Dialectics in Non-Hegelian Language. The insights of Tucker and Bober provide labels for the dialectical stages but stop short of identifying the thesis and antithesis *concepts* and showing how they merge in a synthesis. To this task we now turn. Marx's first dialectic describes separation from and return to communal ownership of property. This dialectic can be expressed in both non-Hegelian language and Hegelian language. In non-Hegelian language, the dialectic goes like this:

> Thesis: communal ownership + poverty (primitive communism)
> Antithesis: private ownership + wealth (slavery, feudalism, and capitalism)
> Synthesis: communal ownership (from the thesis) + wealth (from the antithesis)

Marx admired communism (communal ownership) but despised the poverty that accompanied it in primitive societies. As society moved ever deeper into the three class societies, improved methods of production brought increasing wealth: society now produced more than enough for bare subsistence. What was wrong was that the surplus production—production beyond what the worker needed to subsist (i.e., wealth)—went into the hands of the owners of private property. The private property included slaves, land, mercantile establishments, ships, factories, money in the hands of usurers, and of course the surplus goods. In the future synthesis, final communism, private ownership would be abolished and communal ownership reestablished. At the same time, and in sharp contrast to primitive communism, the machinery-based factory system would continue to produce abundant output—wealth—that the communal owners of the factories would keep and enjoy.

In the above dialectic, communal ownership is equivalent to a classless society; private ownership is equivalent to a class-structured society. So by replacing the original concepts with their equivalents, we get this revised dialectic:

> Thesis: classless society + poverty
> Antithesis: class society + wealth
> Synthesis: classless society + wealth

In the three historical periods marked by social classes, the classes changed with the period. Under slavery, the slaves were the exploited class. Slave owners, land owners, self-employed artisans, merchants, and traders were the exploiting classes. Under feudalism, the serfs and handicraft workers were the exploited class. The nobles of various grades, the merchants, the ship owners, and the usurers were the exploiting classes. Under capitalism, the workers, now called the proletariat, constituted the exploited class. The factory owners, land owners, merchants, traders, and bankers—all of them capitalists—were the exploiters, now called the bourgeoisie. The classes disappear under final communism. This gives us the above second Marxian version of separation and return: separation from and return to a classless society.

A third version of the poverty-and-wealth dialectic replaces the concept of classes with the concept of freedom:

> Thesis: freedom + poverty
> Antithesis: bondage + wealth
> Synthesis: freedom + wealth

Under primitive communism man was free. With the advent of slavery, freedom became bondage. Bondage continued under feudalism, though in limited form. The serf had to give part of his output to the feudal lord, and he was also required to provide military service if the need arose. Under capitalism the bondage was more metaphorical than literal, yet the factory conditions Marx observed were so oppressive—long hours and unspeakably cruel child labor were features—that metaphor came close to literalism. In *The Communist Manifesto*, Marx actually called factory workers slaves: "Not only are they slaves of the bourgeois class, and of the bourgeois State; they are daily and hourly enslaved by the machine, by the overlooker [foreman], and, above all, by the individual bourgeois manufacturer himself."[115] Final communism would restore man's freedom.

Marx's overarching dialectic has one more non-Hegelian version. Strictly speaking, the capitalist is the exploiter in only one of the three private property systems, the capitalist system. But in this dialectic, "capitalist"—the exploiter Marx was most concerned about—epitomizes the generic exploiter and represents all three middle economic systems of Marx's five stages of history. The new dialectic focuses on the person who is the recipient of the economic system's production. This dialectic separates from and returns to the worker:

> Thesis: worker (primitive communism: the worker keeps what he produces)
>
> Antithesis: capitalist (private property systems: the capitalist gets the production)
>
> Synthesis: worker = capitalist (final communism: the worker *is* the capitalist)

In the synthesis, the worker becomes the capitalist when the expropriators are expropriated, and this leads to "the possession in common of the land and of the means of production."[116]

The Overall Dialectics in Hegelian Language. Marx rarely uses such Hegelian terminology as potential and actual, union and separation, and essence and existence. The overall-period historical dialectic can nonetheless be described more abstractly as variants of Hegel's macrodialectic (chapter 3). If anyone doubts that Marx was consciously imitating Hegel's dialectics, that person should observe that Marx has even borrowed from Hegel the potential-actual version of the freedom-and-bondage theme. The freedom of primitive communism is only potential: true freedom entails freedom to enjoy wealth or surplus production, surplus that does not exist in the first period. True, or actual, freedom materializes only under final communism, where freedom from slavery (literal or metaphorical) includes freedom to enjoy the wealth produced under the advanced technological structure of the former capitalism. The revised freedom dialectic:

> Thesis: potential + freedom
>
> Antithesis: actual + bondage
>
> Synthesis: actual + freedom

This dialectic has now appeared in four places: (1) variant 27 of Hegel's macrodialectic, (2) Hegel's master-and-slave dialectic, (3)

Hegel's first-level freedom-and-bondage history dialectic, and (4) Marx's first-level history dialectic. Marx's copying of (*a*) Hegel's freedom-and-bondage theme, (*b*) Hegel's use of two-part theses and antitheses to get two-part syntheses, and (*c*) Hegel's separation-and-return format leaves no doubt that Marx understood Hegel's dialectics.

If that isn't evidence enough, we can also recognize that Marx even copied Hegel's self-estrangement, or self-alienation, theme. Marxian man becomes alienated from his essential self during history's three middle stages when he becomes separated from (estranged from) the fruits of his labor. Alienation is overcome under final communism.

> Thesis: potential + union (of man and his surplus output, or wealth)
> Antithesis: actual + separation (of man and his surplus output, or wealth)
> Synthesis: actual + union (of man and his surplus output, or wealth)

During the thesis stage, primitive communism, the union of man and the fruits of his labor is only potential because there are hardly any fruits. There is no surplus output. The means of production, particularly in hunter-gatherer societies, are so primitive that no meaningful union exists; the union of man and his output formally exists but has no legitimating substance. Engels remarks that "it was only where these [ancient communes] . . . dissolved that the peoples made progress of themselves, and their first economic advance consisted in the increase and development of production by means of slave labour."[117] During the three antithesis periods, the exploiting classes separate the working man from most of the goods he produces, hence from his essential wealthy self. Final communism, the synthesis, will make the union of man and his labor actual, no longer just potential: the surplus output man unites with will be abundant.

Union is equivalent to essence, and separation is equivalent to existence; so the preceding dialectic easily converts to variant 10 of Hegel's macrodialectic:

> Thesis: potential + essence
> Antithesis: actual + existence
> Synthesis: actual + essence

Here you will recall that, in Hegel's terminology, essence is the way things ought to be. More specifically, Spirit ought to be united with itself. Or, in the Marxian world, man ought to be united with the fruits of his labor *and* those fruits ought to be abundant. Existence, for its part, is the way things actually are. The Spirit of Hegel's world of ideas is actually separated from itself through man's failure to recognize external objects as himself, Spirit. Man of Marx's material world is actually separated from himself because man's labor, represented by his surplus output, has been taken away from him. When man regains what he produces, essence will become actual: the way things ought to be (essence) will become the way they actually are (existence).

A variant of the above dialectic takes the form of chapter 3's variant 18 of Hegel's macrodialectic:

> Thesis: essence (potential unity of man and his surplus output)
> Antithesis: existence (actual separation of man and his surplus output)
> Synthesis: essence = existence (actual union of man and his surplus output)

LEVEL TWO: MARX'S SUBPERIOD DIALECTICS

Bober observes that the last three of Marx's five historical periods provide a less encompassing dialectic: "In *Capital* Marx depicts a dialectic formula on a reduced scale. The thesis is embodied in the latter [*sic*] Middle Ages, when the means of production were the private possession of the direct producers, the peasant who owned the land and the artisan who owned the tools. The negation of this thesis is . . . capitalism, which separated both peasant and laborer from the means [tools] of production. The negation of this negation will emerge when communism restores the productive property [tools] to the cooperative association of the workers."[118] The presence of this feudalism-capitalism-communism subdialectic, which definitely *is* present, suggests the further presence of a preceding gens-slavery-feudalism dialectic. This preceding dialectic isn't hard to find, although Bober doesn't notice it. To keep things in their proper historical order, I will begin with the first subperiod.

The First Subperiod. The first of Marx's five periods of history is primitive communism, also called gens. Two of this period's characteristics enter into the first subperiod's dialectic. First, the workers owned the tools of production—the spear, the bow and arrow, the fish net, the basket used for gathering fruit, nuts, berries, root vegetables, and other edibles. Second, the worker kept the fruits of his labor. Society was classless. No exploiter appropriated those fruits.

In the second of the five periods, slavery, both of these characteristics disappeared. The slave owner rather than the slave (worker) owned the tools. And the worker kept none of the fruits of his labor beyond a small share of food and clothing. Society was now divided into social classes—the exploiters and the workers. Now the fruits of the worker's labor went to the exploiter, the slave owner.

In the third period, feudalism, the worker largely regained ownership of the tools of production. The tools, of course, were sometimes different: the plow, the horse, the hoe, the milking pail, the loom, the potter's wheel, and to some extent the land. (I'll elaborate on the land ownership question in discussing the second subperiod.) But society remained divided into social classes. The feudal lord, the new exploiter, assumed ownership of the worker's surplus production. This latest arrangement provided the synthesis of the following dialectic:

> Thesis: classless society + worker ownership of tools
> Antithesis: class society + exploiter ownership of tools
> Synthesis: class society + worker ownership of tools

In this dialectic the worker separates from and returns to ownership of the tools of production. Once again we see that Marx understood that Hegelian dialectics is based on Christianity's theme of separation and return. (Review: In the New Testament's Gospel of John, God separates from himself in heaven, becoming God incarnate on earth, then returns to himself in heaven after being resurrected from the dead. In a second biblical separation-and-return myth, this time based partly on the Old Testament's book of Genesis, man and woman are initially united with God in the Garden of Eden, then sin—they eat the forbidden fruit—and become separated from God, and finally return to God—this time in heaven—after Jesus sacrifices himself on the cross in order to bear man's punishment for Adam's and Eve's "original sin.") No other author except Tillich, who called my attention to this theme, understood that a Hegelian dialectic must incorporate separation and return. No other author except Tillich also understood that, in Hegel's main (but not sole) dialectical format, each of the dialectic's three stages embodies two concepts, and that the synthesis stage borrows one concept from each of the first two stages. We can be sure that Marx understood Hegel.

A classless society is equivalent to nonexploited workers. And a class society is equivalent to exploited workers. The above dialectic can therefore be expressed in this alternative manner:

> Thesis: nonexploited workers + worker ownership of tools
> Antithesis: exploited workers + exploiter ownership of tools
> Synthesis: exploited workers + worker ownership of tools

The Second Subperiod. Bober, we saw, recognizes feudalism-capitalism-communism as a thesis-antithesis-synthesis subperiod. But he provides only labels, not concepts. The labels do not display the two basic characteristics of Marx's Hegelian dialectics: (1) separation and return and (2) two-concept stages, with the third stage borrowing one concept from each of the two preceding stages. Separation and return? Are we to believe that final communism is a return to feudalism, from which capitalism separated? And if communism is a synthesis of—a combining of or compromise between—feudalism and capitalism, just what is it that communism incorporates from each of the two preceding periods? Bober has no answers, because his base-superstructure interpretation of dialectics doesn't raise the questions.

Before answering the questions, we need to verify that the three periods identified by Bober really contain a dialectic. Recall Marx's famous words, quoted earlier: "The knell of *capitalist* private property sounds. . . . It is the negation of negation" (my italics).[119] Note the adjective "capitalist." Were it not there, Marx could easily be referring to the private property of all three middle periods, viewed collectively. But the adjective tells us he is referring narrowly to capitalism alone. And when he goes on to say "negation of nega-

tion," capitalism becomes the original negation that is negated: "The capitalist mode of appropriation . . . is the *first* negation" (my italics).[120] Any
negation that is negated by a dialectical synthesis is an antithesis, the middle
term of Yes-No-Yes. (The final Yes, as a double negative, is an affirmative.)
This means that the dialectic's thesis is whatever precedes capitalism. And
what precedes capitalism in Marx's five periods of history is feudalism.

Marx leaves no room for doubt that feudalism is what capitalism replaces.
He first describes feudalism or "serfdom." Then he says it is "annihilated"
by capitalism. His description of what is annihilated confirms that it is feudalism. Serfdom is a "petty mode of production . . . where the labourer is the
private owner of his own means of labour set in action by himself: the peasant
of the land which he cultivates, the artizan of the tool which he handles as a
virtuoso."[121] (Clarification: Under many forms of feudalism the peasant owned
his tools but not the land. Under other forms, as in England, the peasant had
practical ownership of the land, although technically all land belonged to a
noble and ultimately to the king. Describing "feudalism," Bober provides
additional detail: "In the country, the serf possesses the land by hereditary
right or by some other understanding, although absolute ownership is vested
in the lord. In addition to farming, the peasant and his family are engaged in
domestic industry in order to provide for the other needs."[122]) Back to Marx:
"This mode of production [feudalism] pre-supposes parceling of the soil, and
scattering of the other means of production [the handicraft work]. As [because]
it excludes the concentration of these means of production, so also it excludes
cooperation, division of labour within each separate process of production,
the control over, and the productive application of the forces of Nature by
society."[123] Notice that the mode of production being described has the attributes of feudalism (e.g., parceling of land); the things this mode "excludes"
are attributes of capitalism (e.g., division of labor). Marx is describing feudalism, "serfdom."

What happens to feudalism? "It is annihilated. Its annihilation, the
transformation of the individualized and scattered means of production into
socially concentrated ones, of the pigmy property of the many into the huge
property of the few, the expropriation of the great mass of the people from the
soil . . . forms the prelude to the history of capital."[124] Capitalism arrives: "The

labourers are turned into proletarians."[125] Conclusion: feudalism is the thesis whose antithesis or "negation" is capitalism. And the "negation of the negation" (the negation of capitalism) is final communism.

The dialectic that goes from feudalism to capitalism to final communism extracts four concepts from the Marx commentary quoted above. Feudalism is marked by (1) small-scale or "pigmy" production on small parcels of land or in cottages and (2) worker ownership of the tools of production—the plow, the hoe, the loom, the potter's wheel, the land, the cottage where cottage industry (handicraft manufacture) takes place. Capitalism is marked by (3) large-scale or "huge" production on large agricultural tracts or in factories and (4) capitalist ownership of the tools of production—the horses, the plows, the looms and other factory machines, the factory. These four concepts give us the following dialectic:

> Thesis: domestic or "pigmy" production + worker ownership of tools and place
>
> Antithesis: factory or "huge" production + capitalist ownership of tools and place
>
> Synthesis: factory or "huge" production + worker ownership of tools and place

This dialectic can be reconstructed by replacing the scale of production (pigmy vs. huge, cottage industry vs. factory) by the scale of output. Doing so shifts the emphasis from technology to the amount of output or wealth that is created. By emphasizing wealth, the new dialectic (*a*) spotlights one of the supposed strengths of final communism and (*b*) reintroduces one of the concepts, wealth, used in the overall-period dialectics. The result:

> Thesis: low output (low wealth) + worker ownership of tools and place
>
> Antithesis: high output (high wealth) + capitalist ownership of tools and place
>
> Synthesis: high output (high wealth) + worker ownership of tools and place

264   HEGEL'S UNDISCOVERED THESIS-ANTITHESIS-SYNTHESIS DIALECTICS

At the risk of belaboring a point presented many times previously, I again call attention to the format of the feudalism-capitalism-communism dialectic. Both the thesis and the antithesis have two parts. The synthesis borrows one part from the thesis and one from the antithesis. And the format displays separation and return: the dialectic separates from and returns to worker ownership of tools and place.

METAPHYSICS

I do not think Marx regarded himself as a metaphysician. His atheism certainly suggests that he regarded himself as an opponent of supernaturalism, of which metaphysics is a subcategory. Marx's historical determinism seems to have been viewed by him as some sort of scientific law.[126] I suspect he viewed dialectics as something like gravity or supply and demand, a natural force belonging to the realm of science, social science in this case. Yet Marx clearly *was* a metaphysician. He viewed dialectics as a deterministic force that structured history, controlled its path, and would necessarily lead to final communism. Metaphysics aside, he differed from Hegel only in claiming that the dialectical force operated through inevitable developments in the material world rather than through the mental world—that is, rather than through human thoughts, ideas, and their influence on human behavior.

You might wonder how I can interpret Marx's history dialectics as metaphysical yet interpret Hegel's history dialectics as nonmetaphysical. Shouldn't we say that what's sauce for the goose (nonsupernaturalism in this instance) is sauce for the gander? Certainly it is true that both men were atheists. But metaphysics is not a form of theism, and theism isn't metaphysics; a metaphysician can be an atheist. Theism posits the existence of a rational, self-conscious being (God in the case of Christianity) with the capacity to observe, remember, organize facts, reason, plan, make decisions, harbor likes and dislikes, experience emotions such as love and anger, possibly listen to prayer, and intervene in human affairs. Metaphysical entities, being impersonal, lack these characteristics, except that they can mindlessly intervene in human affairs, just as a tornado can. They are more like computers: intelligently performing, applying certain built-in rules, but mindless. So the atheism shared by Hegel and Marx is irrelevant.

What is relevant is that Hegel made no predictions about the future. His dialectics ended with the arrival of Germanic monarchy and its concomitant freedom. His dialectics were designed to reach a conclusion pleasing to the Prussian monarchy. In contrast, Marx's history dialectics hadn't reached their conclusion in his day. The climactic synthesis, final communism, lay in the future. Marx was absolutely convinced that final communism was inevitable. History was moving ineluctably through a series of stages that would end in a final stage of communism. And if final communism was inevitable, that inevitability could only be the work of a metaphysical force. Marx identified this force as dialectics. Hegel also interpreted history in dialectical terms, but his dialectics was more a matter of after-the-fact picking and choosing of times and places. Although Marx also picked and chose, he did so to a lesser degree. And where final communism was concerned, he couldn't pick and choose. Moreover, Marx wasn't trying to please any sponsors by crafting conclusions friendly to the sponsors. Marx's conclusions were actually unfriendly to the rulers of both England (where Marx lived most of his life) and Germany (where he was born and educated). More important, the after-the-fact element is missing where final communism is concerned.

I am not alone in regarding Marx as a metaphysician. Tucker argues that Marx "regards the victory of the proletariat to be historically preordained."[127] He considers Marx a "mythic thinker" who believes in "the active promotion of the inevitable" because he "sees his paramount practical task as that of making the good forces more fully conscious of the nature, conditions and prospects of the conflict, more clearly aware of the total evilness of the evil forces against which they are pitted, more cognizant of the utter hopelessness of any compromise solution in terms of justice, which would imply a delimitation of mutual claims and a cessation of hostilities."[128] Popper explicitly describes Marxian dialectics as metaphysical by referring to "Marx's metaphysical theory of an economic reality."[129] Sabine writes, "The dialectic was a method, and is quite clear that he [Marx] meant to retain the main outline of Hegelian methodology," which was "metaphysical." (Sabine is wrong about Hegel's being a metaphysician.) Accordingly, "the actual facts and events of social, legal, and political history" were conceived as manifestations of an "underlying reality." The Marxian dialectic "draws its necessity from the *hidden force* out of which it arises" (my italics).[130] Stumpf agrees: "Marx clearly expressed a metaphysical belief in the existence of a predetermined goal for all history."[131] All these opinions describe a supernatural cause-and-effect influence that charts the course of history in ways that no amount of human planning or accidents of history can alter.

Chapter 6

FALSE AND FUZZY
INTERPRETATIONS OF SPIRIT

In this chapter I will survey interpretations of *Phenomenology*, looking at the flaws in the interpretations of Hegel's Spirit. Excluded from coverage are many authors of books about Hegel who either focus on topics other than Spirit, have nothing intelligible to say, or aren't willing to commit themselves. I group the covered interpretations into five categories. The authors in the first category—Olson, Friedrich, Inwood, Singer, Plant, Fox, C. Taylor, Norman, Stern, Wallace, and Schlitt—offer panentheistic interpretations. These interpretations uphold, often with some uncertainty or reservations, the view that Spirit is both transcendent and immanent, that is, pan*ent*heistic. The next four interpreters—Kojève, Forster, McCarney, and Desmond— believe Spirit represents pantheism in the metaphysical sense of that term. A third group consists of Solomon, Beiser, and Tucker. They deny that Hegel believes in the supernatural; they offer God-is-nature-or-the-universe interpretations, but with heavy emphasis on humanity in Solomon's case. These God-is-nature interpretations, because they equate God with physical nature rather than with a metaphysical essence within nature, do not qualify Hegel as a pantheist, despite assertions of the first two authors to the contrary. The fourth category comprises Pinkard and M. Westphal. Their nonsupernaturalistic interpretations identify Spirit as society and social relationships. Finally, we have the noninterpretations of Findlay, Kaufmann, Rosen, Harris, and Franco. These are descriptions of Spirit that are so vague, superficial, inconsistent, and undeveloped, or in Harris's case incoherent, that Spirit remains an enigma.

PANENTHEISTIC INTERPRETATIONS

Eleven interpreters think Spirit either is or probably is panentheistic. They believe Spirit has an independent, transcendent mind, much like that of the Judeo-Christian God, in addition to being immanent, within everything in the universe. Unless "God" is watered down with qualifying statements that these interpreters seldom offer, panentheism portrays God as the traditional God with immanence grafted on.

Olson. Olson's interpretation is the most theologically oriented and the most naive; it could almost be classified as a theistic rather than a panentheistic interpretation. Olson identifies Hegel's Spirit with Christianity's Holy Spirit, and in the process of doing so he also identifies Spirit with God. According to Olson, "Holy Spirit and Absolute Spirit, for Hegel, are ultimately one and the same."[1] For emphasis, Olson subtitles his book *Philosophy as Pneumatology*, thereby describing *Phenomenology* as the study of the Holy Spirit, referred to in the New Testament by the Greek word *pneuma*. God's *pneuma* was God's inner self, his spirit or soul, separable from God's body, which was anthropomorphically conceived in biblical times and even today is so conceived by many Christians. In short, "Hegel's conception of Spirit . . . [is] directly inspired by and contiguous with Luther's understanding of Spirit."[2] And because the Holy Spirit, as God's inner self, is essentially a part of God, Olson can say that "Spirit . . . chooses, by its act of creation, to limit itself and become God—and not only in the abstract formal sense, but *materially* through incarnation."[3] Olson thus treats Spirit as the alter ego of God, the Judeo-Christian God responsible for the "act of creation." Hence "God, as the true infinite or Absolute Spirit, encompasses the ideas of limit and the unlimited."[4] The idea of limit or finitude alludes to the immanent side of Spirit, which Olson specifically describes as belonging to "metaphysics."[5] Although Olson definitely holds that Spirit participates in man, he fails to clarify whether Spirit also participates in the rest of the universe and thereby justifies the label panentheism.

Friedrich. Friedrich's interpretation is as forceful as Olson's in endorsing the idea that Spirit displays transcendence—independence of mind, existence above as well as within the universe. But Friedrich more clearly ascribes an immanent side to spirit. He writes:

Hegel was and wanted to be a Christian philosopher. To the end of his life he maintained that he considered himself a Lutheran. He rejected, in other words, those interpretations of his thought which put them into a [purely] pantheistic framework. He believed in a personal God whose spirit, the Holy Ghost of Christian doctrine, was at work shaping the destiny of man.[6]

That actually sounds not like panentheism but like out-and-out theism. Friedrich seems to have overlooked Hegel's demolition of theism and its "picture-thinking" God in *Phenomenology*'s section on "The Revealed Religion." Possibly, Friedrich would have been less inclined to accept Hegel's claim to be a Lutheran had Friedrich read Hegel's April 1795 letter to Schelling. In that letter, Hegel wrote, "Religion . . . has taught what despotism wanted to teach, contempt for humanity and the incapacity of man to achieve the good and to fulfill his essence through his own efforts."[7] Hegel was referring to German Protestantism, which Marcuse describes in these words: "Ever since the German Reformation, the masses had become used to the fact that, for them, liberty was an 'inner value,' which was compatible with every form of bondage, that due obedience to existing authority [the state] was a prerequisite to everlasting salvation, and that toil and poverty were a blessing in the eyes of the Lord."[8]

In another work, however, Friedrich retreats from pure theism and finds Hegel imputing immanence to Spirit. Friedrich refers to Hegel's "unquestioned pantheistic tendency which is sharply at variance with the orthodox Lutheran position."[9] This combining of transcendent theism with immanent pantheism gives us panentheism, although Friedrich doesn't use that word.

Inwood. Inwood is a third interpreter who leans heavily on theism. Like Friedrich, he naively takes Hegel at his word when Hegel claims to be a Lutheran believer: "He regarded himself as an *orthodox* Lutheran, reasserting the rationality of theism in the face of Kant's radical and influential attacks on it" (my italics).[10] Like many if not most of today's Christians, Hegel thought (according to Inwood) that God was essentially a mental entity, a "cosmic mind";[11] his God was not anthropomorphic. Indeed, the Hegelian God was metaphysical, for which reason Inwood writes, "I have preferred to stress the metaphysical elements of his thought."[12] To reiterate, Hegel was "a metaphysician."[13] This metaphysics reflects in the statement that "he saw the world [universe] as a whole on the model of a mind."[14] This statement amounts to the assertion that the "cosmic mind" that is God is, at the same time, "the world as a whole." God is thus immanent, a part of the world, as well as transcendent; hence we have another panentheistic interpretation.

Singer. Singer writes, "Not an orthodox theist, not a pantheist, not an atheist—what else is left?" Singer's tentative answer is panentheism. He finds panentheism "plausible." It is plausible "not only because it is consistent with what Hegel says specifically about God, but also because it makes sense of the dominant theme of his philosophy [God's being 'the ultimate reality of the universe']."[15]

Singer, however, provides no credible reason why pantheism—immanence alone—fails to make sense of Hegel's description of ultimate reality. He does say, "If reason is the essential medium of mind, it follows that mind is inherently universal." But that conclusion really doesn't "follow." Reason can just as easily come from human minds, which exist only on earth. Singer claims that what is "inherently universal" is "mind itself." Why should this be so? Why can't Spirit be universal—the physical universe—even though its mind, the collective mind of humans, is limited to finite humans? The only hint of an answer from Singer is that "the particular minds of individual human beings are linked because they share a common universal reason."[16] But it is more accurate to say that, in Hegel's philosophy, the human minds *produce* Spirit's reason. No transcendent mind is needed to inject reason into the minds of humans. Does Singer himself believe a transcendent mind is needed for human minds to express reason? Presumably not. Then why should Hegel believe it?

Plant. Plant thinks "Hegel's philosophy is best characterized by the term 'panentheism.'" His reasons are nebulous. Hegel's thought "is different from the pantheism of Spinoza . . . because for Hegel we cannot treat the given world as identical with God." Why not? Because our "knowledge of God is abstract without an understanding of the self-positing [self-recognition?] of God in the world which has to occur if God is . . . [both] consciousness [human] and Spirit [divine]." That seems to mean, if it means anything, nothing more than that Spirit must have a mind ("consciousness") in order to recognize that it is both human ("consciousness") and divine ("Spirit"). But whether Spirit has a mind isn't the issue. Why must God's—Spirit's—mind be a transcendent mind rather than the human mind? Plant doesn't say. The question doesn't even occur to him. Nonetheless, "what Hegel meant . . . [is] that God is immanent in the world but is more than the sum of the parts of the world."[17] The "more" is a mind that transcends—is not part of—the world.

Fox. Fox likewise holds that "Hegel's Absolute is *both transcendent* (greater than the world, inexhaustible) and *immanent* (at work in, and in some sense identical with, the rhythm of the world)."[18] It's unclear where Fox's idea that Spirit is transcendent comes from. His theory seems to be that God influences history and must therefore have an independent mind. Specifically, "his [Hegel's] panentheism introduces the additional element that all rivulets of change and development manifest the presence of the Absolute, the infinite energy coursing through the finite realm."[19] But, since Fox concedes that man is part of Spirit, we are left wondering why the part of Spirit that is man can't be responsible for those "rivulets of change and development" that constitute history. Or, to the extent that historical change follows dialectical patterns, why can't the change be directed by an impersonal metaphysical force, analogous to the Greek Logos? That force would eliminate the need for a transcendent mind, reducing the interpretation to pantheism. Fox has given us no reason to believe Spirit resembles God, a transcendent mind, with immanence attached as a secondary—or primary for that matter—feature. From all indications, Fox has simply been taken in by Hegel's many references to "God," hypocritical references designed by Hegel to convince his contemporaries that he was not an atheist.

C. Taylor. Charles Taylor (not to be confused with Mark Taylor) presents a far more detailed interpretation that is best described as a highly qualified form of panentheism. Taylor's description of Spirit displays considerable ambiguity, but Forster is certainly right in reading panentheism into Taylor's description. Forster says Taylor is "mistaken" when Taylor rejects the "anti-transcendent position."[20]

At first, Taylor seems headed toward that "antitranscendent" pantheistic interpretation: "Hegel's Spirit, . . . although he is often called 'God,' and although Hegel claimed to be clarifying Christian theology, is not the God of traditional theism; he is not a God who could exist quite independently of men, even if men did not exist, as the God of Abraham, Isaac and Jacob [existed] before the creation. On the contrary, he is a spirit who lives as spirit only through men." In short, unlike the traditional God, Spirit cannot exist independently of men, and he lives only through men. Not only that, what "Hegel understood as Spirit" is "that which underlies and manifests itself in all reality." Spirit's immanence is unmistakable: it is "a divine life flowing through everything" and "cannot exist separately from the universe." In fact, "this universe is his embodiment." Hence, "we can already see why Hegel had to suffer accusations of Spinozism or pantheism."[21]

"A divine life flowing through everything" and "cannot exist separately from the universe" leave no doubt that Taylor sees a strong immanent element in Hegel's Spirit. Taylor's saying that he "can already see why" Hegel was accused of pantheism strengthens the case for pantheism. Yet Taylor then says that "pantheism as this is generally understood will not do."[22] Spirit "has purposes and he realizes ends [goals] which cannot be attributed to finite spirits [humans] . . . , but on the contrary which finite spirits serve."[23] And Spirit is a "he," the conventional reference to a personal God, not an "it," the appropriate pronoun for Spirit. These descriptions remove all doubt that Taylor sees an element of transcendence situated alongside the immanence. But Taylor merely professes uncertainty: "It must already be clear that it is not easy (if indeed it is possible at all) to win through to a coherent view of a cosmic spirit on this model."[24]

Taylor nonetheless digs deeper. We next learn that, although "the universe is the embodiment of the totality of the 'life-functions' of God" (immanence), "it also is . . . something posited by God in order to manifest what he is."[25] Surely both "posited" and—once more—the "he' suggest transcendence. Furthermore, whereas "the accusation of pantheism . . . seems *at first* sight to fit him rather well," Hegel was not a person who "indiscriminately attributed divinity to finite things."[26] Again, "what distinguished Hegel's position from pantheism in his own mind" was that Spirit "determined its structure according to its own exigencies."[27] I'm not sure precisely what Taylor means here, but he seems to imply that Spirit is exercising the supernatural powers of a transcendent being. He certainly is questioning the pantheism interpretation. Yet Taylor turns around and questions panentheism too: "Hegel's theory has also been called by some 'panentheist'" but, whereas "there certainly are affinities," it is also true that "there is no exact parallel."[28] Panentheism, however, is not such a precise, narrowly defined concept that there can be an "exact parallel." Taylor's combining of transcendence with immanence boils down to panentheism, whether Taylor chooses to call it that or not.

Norman. No author better exemplifies the confusion resulting from Hegel's hypocritical use of the word "God" than does Norman. He can't decide whether Spirit is some vaguely defined "social" thinking of humans (human spirit, as it were) or, alternatively, a panentheistic being with a transcendent mind who created the world and controls the course of history. Norman looks first at *Phenomenology*, then at Hegel's lectures on history. The Spirit of *Phenomenology* might represent "a social theory of mind" and the idea that the world, rather than being the creation of God, can be interpreted with "concepts" and is, "in that sense, constituted by human [social] thought."[29] That unconscionably vague idea completely fails to say how or when such human thought overcomes self-estrangement and attains self-realization or Absolute Knowledge. Neither does it say what Absolute Knowledge is. This first alternative, social thinking, is almost devoid of recognizable content. The second alternative is that "the world is created by God, it is the product of divine reason, and human minds can understand that world because the reason which they employ is identical with the divine reason."[30] If this interpretation is correct, "Hegel's idealism would be a form of theism," and "Hegel would have to be interpreted as some kind of pantheist (or . . . what has been called a 'panentheist')."[31]

Turning to Hegel's philosophy of history, Norman argues that the panentheist interpretation "receives greater support from Hegel's later and posthumous works," such as *The Philosophy of History*—works "where Hegel slips into religious language much more readily."[32] Hegel's assertion that history is the work of reason might be interpreted, according to Norman, "as the claim that history . . . falls into a pattern" that human reason can discern. "But Hegel also seems committed to a stronger thesis, that the reason operative in history is a supra-human reason, akin to a divine providence [God]." In some passages, "Hegel . . . intimates that, because history reveals a rational development, it must be the work of a single *divine* mind."[33] Norman doesn't recognize that the "rational" progress of history can be supernatural without being the work of a personal mind, that of a panentheistic God: it can be the work of an impersonal Logos-like metaphysical force, a metaphysical Spirit, which forces history into dialectical patterns. So why does he rule out pantheism?

It turns out he doesn't. Despite having said that the "supra-human" interpretation positing a "divine mind" is the "stronger thesis," Norman remains somewhat open to the pantheism view. He first says, "'spirit' remains in the end ambiguous; it is not clear whether 'spirit' transcends the individual mind simply in the sense of being social [nonsupernatural] or in some much stronger sense which makes it akin to the traditional conception of God."[34] But then, referring to "the stronger and theistic form of idealism," Norman says, "I am reluctant to attribute such a position to Hegel."[35] Pantheism coming up? No. Comparing the "supra-human reason" interpretation, or transcendence, with the "pantheistic view," Norman says, "I have suggested that the former thesis (panentheism) is much more satisfactory than the latter."[36] The word "much" is, in my view, sufficient to put Norman in the panentheism camp.

Stern. Stern's *Hegel and the Phenomenology of Spirit* is a relatively short book (234 pages) that stands head and shoulders above all others that might be considered for use as a textbook for a course on Hegel's *Phenomenology*. (I exclude from this comparison longer, more analytical and interpretive works, particularly those of Solomon and Pinkard—the best of the longer books about *Phenomenology*.) Stern's book is one where the author tries to be impartial, perhaps to make the book more suitable for textbook use. Stern writes, "In the account I have offered . . . of the *Phenomenology*, I hope to have shown that it is possible to follow Hegel's text without any very rich conception of Spirit being required."[37] Stern has achieved his objective in admirable fashion.

Stern does, however, tentatively classify Hegel as a theist, albeit as a humanistic theist whose "theism" seems in some of Stern's remarks to amount to nothing more than pantheism. Referring to several Enlightenment thinkers, Stern says Hegel "shares none of their atheism."[38] That certainly means Hegel is a theist. Hegel nonetheless formulated "a revised conception of Christian doctrine" in which "his theism is designed to be compatible with the kind of humanism to which it [Christianity] is traditionally opposed."[39]

Moreover, "although he attempts to go beyond crude atheism, this does not make him a theist."[40] I'm not sure how we reconcile "none of their atheism" and "his theism" with "does not make him a theist." It may be that the answer can be found in this statement: "Hegel argues that Christianity ought to be a religion in which the divine is seen as living within the spiritual community, and thus as lacking any wholly transcendent element."[41] That sounds like the immanent God of pantheism. Then again, "living within the . . . community" is compatible with omnipresence, a characteristic of theism's God, who (in some versions) is everywhere at once yet not *within* his subjects. And "lacking any *wholly* transcendent element" is not the same as "wholly *lacking* any transcendent element." "Lacking any *wholly* transcendent element" seems to imply partial transcendence, or panentheism. Throw in "compatible with . . . humanism" and we seem to have a theistic God who is like the God of the Unitarians. The Unitarian God formulates no divine laws, issues no commands, bars no one from heaven, and (for most Unitarians) doesn't even have a heaven. On balance, and given those "his theism" and "none of their atheism" statements, Stern's interpretation amounts to panentheism.

Wallace. Wallace fairly early presents his belief that Spirit is not the traditional God, that it is a metaphysical entity. Acknowledging that Hegel's theology "is not a *traditional* Christian theology," Wallace counters that "neither is it a humanism with no serious metaphysical commitments." In fact, "Hegel is just as sincere in his objections to . . . atheism as he is in his objections to the traditional Christian theologies."[42] This is because Hegel's thought is something Wallace calls "Conceptual metaphysics."[43] Conceptual metaphysics is just another name for panentheism. Wallace thinks Spirit is transcendent but not wholly transcendent; it is also immanent. "What is false in traditional conceptions of transcendence and in traditional religion, Hegel brings out by criticizing a conception of God as *merely* 'transcendent'—as simply 'beyond.'" Hegel believes "the only *true* transcendence is one that includes the finite."[44] Wallace is saying that Hegel's God is immanent as well as transcendent; it is panentheistic.

Schlitt. The most recent panentheistic interpretation of Spirit comes from Schlitt. He argues that God is partly transcendent or infinite but that "for God to be truly infinite, [Hegel's] God had to include the finite or the human."[45] According to Schlitt, Hegel viewed religion as a relationship between the infinite and the finite, and more specifically as a relationship between divine consciousness and human consciousness. "Hegel did not envision this relationship as being one between two fully independent and fully separately existing realities. He insisted that God and finite consciousness were moments of one another."[46] We can see that Schlitt thinks Hegel's God, or Spirit, is a supernatural being resembling, but not the same as, the God of theism. But what are those divine and human "moments"? They are, says Schlitt, our old friends subject and object. Subject is "consciousness," which in Hegel's thought is a human or "finite" mind. And object is not any old thing perceived by the subject but is, in this case, God. "By implication, then, the subjective aspect is an essential moment of God."[47] Schlitt is saying that God is partially transcendent but also participates in human "consciousness," the human mind. And that means that Spirit, as interpreted by Schlitt, is a panentheistic God.

There is absolutely no room for doubt that Schlitt thinks he is interpreting a supernatural God, a God not too unlike the traditional God. "The consummate religion [of Hegel] is the religion of revelation. God reveals, and is revealed, as God really is."[48] This God bears a striking resemblance to the traditional God: it is a Trinity. "Hegel claims that God remains but an empty word if God is not grasped as triune."[49] (Schlitt is oblivious of the fact, explained in chapter 3, that Hegel's trinity is not that of Christianity but is instead a dialectical trinity wherein "Father" represents the *thesis* of potential unity, "Son" or God incarnate on earth represents the *antithesis* or actual separation, and the unifying "Spirit" represents the *synthesis*, actual unity.) Far from being an atheist, Hegel was—still according to Schlitt—concerned "that the orthodoxy of his day . . . tended to reduce God to an object and that its otherworldliness could lead to a this-worldly atheism."[50] Still, Hegel's God was not fully traditional, because Hegel saw religion as "a movement of the true infinite inclusive of finitude, God inclusive of the world."[51] That means God is immanent as well as transcendent. Once again we have the God of panentheism.

Problems Common to All Eleven Authors. It is apparent that all eleven of the "panentheism" authors have been seduced by Hegel's identifying Spirit with "God." Kaufmann, quoted earlier, was absolutely right when he said that Spirit's nontheistic character "should have caused no misunderstanding, had it not been for Hegel's occasional references to God."[52] Similarly, Findlay has pointed out that "Hegel often speaks the language of a metaphysical theology, but such language, it is plain, is a mere concession to the pictorial mode of religious expression."[53] To put it more bluntly, Hegel is equivocating—privately meaning one thing while trying to convey the impression that something else is meant.

The willingness of the eleven authors to take Hegel's references to "God" literally as references to a partially transcendent God ignores Hegel's powerful "Revealed Religion" attack on this God, a God Hegel says was created by "picture-thinking"—human imagination. The authors simply don't comprehend that Hegel is saying the transcendent God of theism is nothing more than imaginative thought, "picture-thinking." Neither do they realize that the death on the cross of this God is treated by Hegel as a symbol of the transfiguration of this God from one human (Jesus) to the whole universe of humans. "God" is Spirit, and Spirit is humanity—plus everything else in the universe. Taylor's concept of a personal God who can't exist without man and thus materializes only when man materializes out of nature reads into Hegel's thought something that isn't there. The only materializing of God that occurs is figurative, not literal: Spirit, which embraces all humanity (and more), materializes out of the Holy Spirit, which "possessed" only one human (Jesus), when God incarnate died on the cross. And that materialization is only symbolic; Spirit has really existed all along. Beyond these problems are the following:

1. The panentheism interpretations sink under the weight of their failure to acknowledge that Spirit undergoes a thesis stage of unconsciousness. How could a transcendent mind, essentially that of the God of theism, consciously create and shape the universe if that mind were unconscious until the arrival of man? Figuratively speaking, how could God say "Let there be light" if God were unconscious or even nonexistent (Taylor) when the universe, the solar system, earth, and man came into being? And if, as Fox claims, "*all* rivulets of change and development" reveal the presence of a transcendent God, how did God manage to produce those rivulets of change and development—evolution, for

example—in his unconscious state? Hegel's macrodialectic and its supporting evidence leave no reasonable room for doubt that Spirit went through that unconscious period before man arrived. Yet *"all rivulets of change"*—not just the later rivulets—means God was producing change even before he either woke up or was born. Not likely.

2. Presumably the eleven authors accept modern cosmological and evolution theories that attribute the universe to the big bang, the solar system to physical causes such as gravity and the accretion of matter, life to chemical processes, and man to evolution from primitive forms of life. Let us assume the authors think (correctly) that Hegel likewise accepted the idea that natural processes, the exact nature of which were unknown to him, can explain everything that happened before man arrived and began making history. The assumption then is that, in Hegel's thought, everything occurred naturally. But in that context of naturalism, how could Hegel explain the sudden arrival of transcendent supernaturalism? How could he provide a panentheistic explanation of the no-longer-eternal God and his transcendent mind suddenly emerging out of nowhere? How could supernaturalism suddenly pop up in a previously nonsupernatural universe, a universe not created by God? And where does Hegel even hint that such an absurd event occurred?

3. In embracing the panentheism interpretation, the eleven authors fail to even consider, much less answer, this vital question: if "God" includes man (is immanent), why can't man's mind be God's mind, as is actually the case in Hegel's philosophy? Why must God's mind be independent, transcendent? Why must God be schizophrenic, a being with two minds, a transcendent mind and the collective mind of man? I'm not arguing that Spirit is pantheistic; I'm saying that these interpreters have no valid reason for concluding that Spirit goes beyond pantheism by including a theistic mind. Man's mind not only can serve as Spirit's mind, it actually does.

4. Forster points out that Hegel "explicitly rejects the idea that, as he disparagingly puts it, 'God is *composed* [*zusammengesetzt*] of God and the world [*Encyclopedia*, para. 573].'"[54]

Many of Hegel's interpreters who have an opinion, including this interpreter, agree that Hegel was an atheist. Some think Hegel was a pantheist but still an atheist, a disbeliever in the God of theism. But pantheistic or not, Spirit is not partially transcendent. Spirit's Mind does not transcend the universe. The universe, or "all reality," is not just part of Spirit. It is *all* of Spirit. At any rate it is all of the physical side of Spirit; Spirit also has that mental side, the human mind. Hegel isn't saying a transcendent God existed in a mindless, noncreative state before man came along. He is saying that a purely conceptual "God" was unconscious—mindless—until man arrived on the planet. Man brought with him man's minds. Collectively, those minds are the Mind of Spirit. They are Spirit's only Mind. There is no transcendent, theistic mind.

PANTHEISTIC INTERPRETATIONS

Four authors of books about Hegel—Kojève, Forster, McCarney, and Desmond—think he is a pantheist in the metaphysical sense (as opposed to the mislabeled, actually nonpantheistic "God is nature" concept of pantheism). By metaphysical sense, I mean that true pantheism holds that God is not nature but is instead a metaphysical (hence supernatural) "substance" or "essence" hidden within everything natural. Three other authors (Solomon, Beiser, and Tucker), whom I review under the next heading, also identify Spirit with nature or the universe but treat nature, including humanity, as a nonsupernatural *definition* of Spirit rather than a metaphysical (supernatural) *belief*.

Kojève. Kojève's interpretation of Spirit comes from lectures delivered in the 1930s, then published as a French language book in 1947 and translated into English in 1969. Kojève is emphatic in stating that Hegel's God is not transcendent: "Never, at any moment of Time, is there a Spirit existing outside of the human historical World. Therefore, there is no transcendence."[55] To further emphasize this point, Kojève turns to the Schiller poem "Freundschaft" that Hegel uses in modified form to conclude *Phenomenology*. Hegel changes the words "das *ganze* Seelenreich" to "*dieses* Geisterreich." "By this change," says Kojève, "he means to exclude the angels of which Schiller speaks; he means to underline that eternal or infinite Being—that is, the absolute Spirit (which, in Schiller, is God)—arises solely from the totality of Human or historical existence."[56] Kojève's point here is that "the *Phenomenology* ends with a radical denial of all transcendence."[57]

In denying that Spirit is transcendent, Kojève is plainly signifying that Hegel's Spirit is not the God of panentheism. But is Spirit nonetheless supernatural, that is, metaphysical? The answer is apparently yes. "Hegel posits the principle of metaphysical 'realism.'"[58] Following a lengthy analysis of this Hegelian metaphysical realism, Kojève concludes that "Hegelian 'realism,' therefore, is not only ontological, but also metaphysical."[59] This Hegelian metaphysics is, however, a strange form of pantheism that seems to embrace only humanity. Kojève doesn't use the word pantheism and never addresses the question of just what this metaphysics is. But he seems to imply that Spirit is a metaphysical essence within humanity that somehow guides human history, much as the Logos of the Greeks did.

Forster. Forster's interpretation of Spirit begins with a quotation from *Phenomenology* in which Hegel says that "the True is . . . expressed in the representation of the Absolute as Spirit."[60] Forster says these words convey two meanings, both accurate. The first is that "the Absolute is itself essentially a self or person."[61] Hegel, he says, emphatically endorses this view. Here Forster seems unaware that the truth of this first meaning depends on the meaning of "essentially." Spirit is a self or person only in the figurative (metaphorical) sense that Hegel is treating Spirit as a Schelling-style living organism. It has a figurative Mind, but that Mind is the minds (plural) of humans. Figurative or not, Forster, in describing Spirit as God, plainly thinks the meaning is nonfigurative. The second meaning Forster gives to Hegel's quoted statement is "the Absolute is identical with, or has as an essential aspect, the *human* subject."[62] Now Forster is correct, provided we throw out "identical" and stick with "essential aspect." Humanity is Spirit's essential aspect because it is the mental side of the two-sided, physical-mental Spirit. Humanity provides Spirit's all-important Mind.

Humanity is also part of Spirit's physical side but just a minor part: Spirit's physical side is all reality.

Forster next turns to the question of whether Spirit, treated as God, is transcendent or merely immanent. He wisely rejects the transcendent view. He first says that both meanings of the Absolute as Spirit involve "a rejection of the traditional Judeo-Christian conception of God as *wholly* transcendent." But is God "partially transcendent" as in the "naturalistic reading"? The naturalistic reading, Forster says, "would be identifying God with man and nature outright." This is the reading Forster endorses. Referring to the traditional conception of God as a person, Forster argues that "without going beyond the sphere of man and nature you can find a quite sufficient basis for such a conception." That's good enough for Forster: "The *Phenomenology* shows a clear preference for the naturalistic over the partially transcendent option." Fortifying this opinion, he adds that "the *Phenomenology* is largely conceived as an attempt to dispel as an *illusion* the idea of a (partially) transcendent God and to show that, insofar as there is a God, he is to be found entirely at the level of man and his world."[63] "His world" is nature. Forster bolsters his position by quoting passages from *Phenomenology*'s "Unhappy Consciousness" and "Revealed Religion" discussions that show Hegel espousing the idea that *all* humans (not just Jesus) are incarnations of God.

Despite his rejecting the "partially transcendent" option, Forster holds firmly to the view that Hegel is some sort of supernaturalist. Forster thus writes: "Solomon goes too far when he argues . . . that 'Hegel was essentially an atheist . . . [that] There is no God, only man,' and that Hegel's 'Absolute is in no interesting sense God' (pp. 582, 630). . . . (Whether Hegel is really a *Christian* is another matter.)"[64] (In truth, Solomon is absolutely right; Forster is dead wrong.) Forster elaborates by saying Spirit is "a subject who [not which!] is over and above any particular human subject and who encompasses everything—and indeed also . . . is in a way both omniscient and omnipotent."[65] In denying that Hegel is an atheist and in attributing some sort of omniscience to Spirit, Forster is really describing the partially transcendent God of panentheism. I'll nevertheless let that contradiction ride and accept Forster's official position that the partially transcendent interpretation is an "illusion." It remains undeniable, though, that regardless of how the "in a way" phrase is meant to qualify "omniscient," Spirit's intelligence is far more than the collective intelligence of man. Forster's interpretation of Spirit is undeniably supernatural.

Forster has gone astray in accepting the idea that Hegel's "God" has any reality at all other than a definitional reality (Spirit *defined*, not believed in, as a four-part, physical-mental concept of the universe). But he has managed to take Spirit beyond the physical aspects of nature by underscoring the importance of man's mind. This is something the next interpreter, McCarney, doesn't quite manage to do.

McCarney. McCarney too considers both the transcendent God interpretation and the immanent God interpretation of Hegel's writing. He is not fully convinced that the latter is correct but decides that "the balance of argument, of considerations capable of determining an unbiased intellect, favours the immanent view."[66] McCarney begins with a compelling argument. Hegel's lectures on the philosophy of history were delivered during his tenure at the University of Berlin. There his enemies accused him of pantheism, a form of atheism. Were the charges to stick, Hegel would be out of a job. Hegel was forced to deny the charges. If he had believed in God (he didn't), all he had to do was to say so clearly, unambiguously, and forcefully. Instead, he used murky language that was far from convincing. McCarney puts it this way: "If . . . he really did believe in a transcendent personal deity, it seems almost inexplicable that he should lay an elaborate trail of materials for a radically non-theistic interpretation of his system. He might surely have been content to be the official philosopher, the Aquinas as it were, of Lutheranism."[67]

Instead of avowing theism, Hegel chose to deliver ambiguous and unconvincing disavowals of pantheism. McCarney describes one of Hegel's "conventional and unsatisfactory disavowals of pantheism" with these words: "As with similar attempts elsewhere, it conveys a sense of unease and misdirection, of an energetic assault on the wrong target and of punches being pulled when an appropriate one is in view. Pantheism is, we are told, the view that 'represents the universe as nature.' Such a view has, however, 'no content,' for in it 'God, the subject, disappears.'"[68] Hegel is leaving himself lots of wiggle room by using an ambiguous description of God. He is denying one form of pantheism while leaving open the door to another form. As it happens, his concept of

God is not pantheistic at all. But McCarney thinks this concept is compatible with a non-Spinozan pantheism. He says Hegel's denial "may have force against a pantheism such as that of Spinoza," where God is "substance," but it cannot have force where God is spirit.[69] (McCarney could have added that it cannot have force against a definition of pantheism that changes "nature" to "universe" and includes in the universe artificial as well as natural objects. Neither does Hegel's denial of pantheism have any force against Hegel's actual nonmetaphysical concept of Spirit.)

McCarney next brings out additional remarks by Hegel that purport to describe his system as something other than pantheism. Hegel refers "to what is offered as an alternative to pantheism but seems in truth to gesture towards a better understanding of its nature." What Hegel affirms is "the conception of 'the unity of God and the world.'"[70] McCarney misinterprets these words as a description of pantheism, which he thinks Hegel's thought constitutes. The words are actually sufficiently ambiguous to cover his real nonpantheistic concept of Spirit. But that's beside the point. What matters is that McCarney has presented another reason for not believing Hegel's disavowals of pantheism.

McCarney elaborates by reviewing Hegel's anti-Christian passages in *Phenomenology*'s discussion of "The Revealed Religion." Here McCarney spotlights what others have spotlighted: the fact that Hegel "conspicuously fails to endorse what is surely the simple essence of the matter for ordinary Christians, the unique status of Jesus as the incarnate second person of the Trinity."[71] McCarney is correct in his deduction that Hegel is an atheist and therefore not a panentheist. But he is incorrect in viewing pantheism as the only—or is it the only *convincing?*—alternative to panentheism.

Desmond. According to Desmond, "the central issue around which Hegel orbited" is "transcendence."[72] Desmond implicitly accepts the notion that Hegel's God is supernatural but rejects the belief that God's supernaturalism incorporates transcendence. "Let us be done with all weaseling that claims Hegel is a theist, even if substance [in the Spinozan sense] is replaced by Spirit—as it is. Not coincidentally, this is Hegel's own way of wiggling off the hook of pantheism—by denying that God is substance. Yet . . . the wiggling is disingenuous. We are always in the same circle of immanence."[73]

Hegel, says Desmond, equivocates by calling his nontheistic Spirit "God." This usage upsets Desmond, who calls Hegel's God "counterfeit" and a mere "double" for (imitation of) God. (He then loses grammatical control by drifting into a double negative, semi-sarcastically calling Spirit a "counterfeit double," which would mean not really a double for God.)

Although accusing Spirit of "immanence," the hallmark of pantheism (when immanence is not combined with transcendence to produce panentheism), Desmond seems to interpret Spirit's immanence as something confined to humanity. God is within man, and "humanity as *Geist* [Spirit] must struggle to make itself absolute." By making himself "the false double of God," man "thinks he is at last the true divinity."[74]

The Problem with "Pantheism" Interpretations. A basic fault of the pantheistic interpretations is that they fail to acknowledge that Spirit has a Mind. Were the "pantheism" authors to acknowledge that, they could easily be led in the wrong direction to the false conclusion that Hegel was a panentheist after all. What these authors don't recognize is that Hegel's atheism at least implies, even if it doesn't prove, that Hegel has designed a totally nonsupernaturalistic concept of Spirit. If Spirit has a Mind—Spirit's Mind happens to be the minds of individual humans—but if that Mind isn't the mind of a theistic God, then we should look not toward pantheism for answers but toward a nonsupernatural, nonmetaphysical interpretation of Spirit. The interpretations under the next two headings, though they are basically wrong, are right insofar as they recognize Hegel's uncompromising rejection of the supernatural.

Another basic flaw in the "pantheism" reading of Hegel is its failure to recognize that Hegel was not a supernaturalistic humanist but, rather, a humanist who unconditionally rejected supernaturalism. Those who consider Hegel a pantheist have overlooked his statement that the incarnate God's death on the cross represents not just the death of God's human or "natural" manifestation but also the death of his *supernatural* manifestation: "The death of the Mediator is the death not only of his *natural* aspect . . . but also of the *abstraction* of the divine Being."[75] The Mediator (between God and man) who dies is Jesus, God incarnate. God's "*natural* aspect" is the man Jesus, a natural human being, part of material nature. The "*abstraction* of the divine Being" is what Hegel calls the "picture-thinking" God, the nonmaterial, nonhuman God in the sky, the God created by the human imagination. Here Hegel is alluding to his natural-artificial dichotomy, discussed in chapter 4. Hegel is saying that it isn't just the *natural* God, the God in human form (Jesus), who has died; the imaginary, non-natural, man-made and therefore *artificial* God in heaven—God the Father—has also died. God, who lived only in man's imagination, is dead. There is no supernatural God. Spirit is not the alter ego of the supernatural God of theism. Spirit, whatever it is, is not a radically remodeled but still supernatural version of God.

Hegel also says this: "The *death* of the divine Man [Jesus] . . . becomes transfigured from its immediate meaning, viz. the non-being of this *particular* individual [Jesus], into the *universality* of the Spirit who dwells in His community, dies in it every day, and is daily resurrected."[76] Spirit's dying every day and being resurrected every day rules out the idea that Hegel is treating Spirit's omnipresence as theistic omnipresence—the idea that God dwells *among* rather than *within* humans. No omnipresent God of theism dies every day and is daily resurrected (in the form of newborn babies). It is humans who die and are born daily. Therefore Spirit must either be or include the humans: it is in human form—not as an extra person—that Spirit is living within the community. The transfiguration of particularity—Jesus, one "particular individual"—into "universality" solidifies the interpretation. Spirit, a.k.a. "God," universalizes itself from *one* incarnate divinity, Jesus, to an entire *universe* of incarnate divinities—all mankind.

NONSUPERNATURAL QUASI-PANTHEISTIC INTERPRETATIONS

Robert Solomon, Frederick Beiser, and Robert Tucker present God-is-nature interpretations, although with Solomon nature is just one of three possible interpretations—nature, humanity, and the "human spirit" (undefined). All three interpreters scrap the idea that Hegel was a supernaturalist. That should mean also scrapping the idea that he was a metaphysician, but Beiser chooses to embrace a strange concept of metaphysics that divorces metaphysics from any necessary connection to the supernatural. The Solomon and Beiser interpretations agree with the popular misconception of what pantheism is. So I'll begin with a review of my chapter 3 remarks about what pantheism means.

The Meaning of Pantheism. Whereas pantheism is popularly viewed as the belief that God is nature or the universe, this view is false. "God is nature" is a *definition*, not a belief. It is a definition of God used by atheists and near-atheist agnostics who, fearing social disapproval, wish to conceal their unbelief. The self-proclaimed "pantheist" does not believe in the existence of a rational, self-conscious, omniscient, omnipotent supernatural being who providentially watches over mankind and who (in the eyes of most believers, though not the nonreligious ones) appreciates being worshipped and praised. But the false pantheist is pretending to believe in something supernatural enough to be covered by society's tolerance for divergent religious beliefs. In some cases the "God is nature" philosophy may also be a halfway house for people who have ceased to believe in the God of theism but still have a lingering emotional attachment to religious thought patterns.

What pantheism really means is that God, rather than being physical nature, is an invisible, impersonal, metaphysical "substance" or "essence" *within* everything in nature. Spinoza's pantheism is the most widely used example. Spinoza believed, or pretended to believe, that within everything zzzzmystical "substance" that is God or the absolute. Tillich's definition of pantheism bears repeating:

> Pantheism does not mean, and never has meant, and never should mean that everything that is, is God. If God is identified with nature (*deus sive natura*), it is not the totality of natural objects which is called God but rather the creative power and unity of nature, the absolute substance which is present in everything. . . . Pantheism is the doctrine that God is the substance or essence of all things, not the meaningless assertion that God is the totality of all things.[77]

Previously quoted further words from Tillich also deserve an encore: "Wherever the concept of the world is complete without God [i.e., where no transcendent supernatural mind exists above the universe], God has become an empty name that one utters for the sake of religion, but which can be dispensed with completely, since it is all the same whether the universe is called 'matter' or 'spirit.'"[78]

I previously used "God is coffee," "God is honesty," and "God is Love" (Bishop Robinson's redefinition of God) as examples of "empty names that one utters for the sake of religion." These aren't beliefs. They are arbitrary, ambiguous, contrary-to-customary-usage redefinitions of God. Their only purpose is to mislead. "God is nature" falls into the same category when "nature" literally means nature and not an invisible metaphysical essence within nature. By metaphysical I mean supernatural but impersonal, nonrational, non-self-conscious, and nontheistic—more akin to the Greek Logos, astrological causation, or Marxian historical determinism than to God. I therefore strongly object to an interpreter's calling Hegel a pantheist when all the interpreter means is that Spirit is the physical universe ("matter" in the preceding Tillich quotation), not a metaphysical substance or essence within everything natural.

Solomon. Robert Solomon's *In the Spirit of Hegel* is the best of the many books interpreting *Phenomenology*. But Solomon denies the existence of the multitude of dialectics that give structure and meaning to—and are the very essence of—Hegel's work; consequently also misses the fundamentally important concepts of self-estrangement, self-realization, and separation and return; also, again consequently, overlooks the metaphorically "organic" structure of Spirit and Spirit's divine "life"; and, like everyone else, misinterprets Spirit. Still, on the plus side, Solomon is one of the authors who have correctly arrived at nonsupernaturalistic interpretations of Hegel.

Solomon presents a highly ambiguous and noticeably inconsistent pantheistic-but-maybe-not-pantheistic interpretation of Hegel. Solomon's interpretation, or at least one version of it, portrays Spirit as nature or the universe. This version thus agrees with the popular misconception that pantheism means God is nature or the universe rather than a hidden "substance" or "essence" within everything in the universe. But in another version, which really amounts to two other versions, Spirit is either (*a*) humanity, described as "us, nothing more," or (*b*) the "human spirit," a phrase that has no meaning other than its unmistakable connotation of nonsupernaturalism.

Early in his book, Solomon seems to deny that Hegel is a pantheist.

Though he later does call Hegel a pantheist, Solomon at first says Hegel "is the great anti-metaphysician, purging philosophy of every vestige of 'the thing in-itself,' the world behind, or beyond, the scenes."[79] Solomon is at this point challenging the belief that Hegel practices metaphysics, which is at the core of pantheism. If Hegel isn't practicing metaphysics, he isn't a pantheist. But Solomon views pantheism as *defining* God as nature rather than believing in an invisible "substance."

A few pages later, Solomon confirms his belief that Hegel opposes metaphysics. We are told that Hegel "is an anti-religious and *anti-metaphysical* proponent of the varieties of human experience, a conceptual anthropologist *rather than an ontologist*" (my italics).[80] Clear enough, one would think. Hegel's Spirit is not metaphysical; Hegel is not indulging in ontology, or speculation about a presumed impersonal metaphysical something or other called "being."[81] Yet, as Solomon later asserts, Spirit is pantheistic. This assertion makes it sound like Solomon is using the definition of pantheism that Tillich condemns: the definition asserting that God is the universe itself—the *visible* physical universe, what Tillich calls "matter"—not a hidden nonmaterial metaphysical "essence."

The last section in Solomon's penultimate chapter has the heading "Hegel's Humanism as a Species of Pantheism." Whoa! Pantheism is metaphysics. Didn't Solomon say earlier that Hegel rejected metaphysics? How can that be if Hegel's humanism (essentially a synonym for atheism in this context) is "a species of pantheism," which affirms metaphysics? Very quickly Solomon mentions that Stirling "admits that Hegel is a pantheist."[82] Now we can see the apparent contradiction between the earlier assertion that Hegel is "anti-metaphysical" and the new assertion that he is a pantheist. Pantheism is a form of metaphysics but, according to Solomon, Hegel is "anti-metaphysical."

On the next page, Solomon immediately seems to contradict what he just said. He now says this: "The view that Hegel's atheism is a form of pantheism raises two *insuperable* problems, however; first, Hegel vociferously denies he is a pantheist. Second, it may seriously be doubted that pantheism, the name aside, is a form of theism" (my italics).[83] Well, if those two problems are "insuperable," then Hegel can't be a pantheist, despite what Solomon said three sentences earlier. I must add that the two problems are far from insuperable.

Hegel's denials of pantheism *could* be construed as ambiguously attacking Spinozan pantheism while privately adhering to a different form of pantheism. (I'm not implying that Hegel actually is concealing a non-Spinozan form of pantheism.) As for Solomon's doubts that pantheism is a form of theism, of course pantheism is *not* a form of theism. But that proves absolutely nothing concerning whether Hegel is or isn't a pantheist; it is not even a problem, let alone an "insuperable" problem.

The plot thickens. One page later, having just said that calling Hegel a pantheist "raises . . . insuperable problems," Solomon again reverses course with a view that supersedes the "insuperable." Solomon explores a passage in Hegel's *Encyclopedia* where Hegel denies he is a pantheist. Hegel's denial, Solomon says, "turns on a small technical point" involving a distinction between two meanings of "everything." "What Hegel denies is that he has ever claimed that 'everything is God' in a certain first sense. But he clearly holds this view in a second sense," in which "everything" is "considered as a unity, a universe" and includes "a 'subject' [a human mind, intangible] as well as substance [physical matter, tangible]." Solomon then reaches a remarkable conclusion—remarkable because of his earlier denial that Hegel is a metaphysician and his previous-page assertion that calling Hegel a pantheist raises "insuperable problems." Solomon's conclusion: "Hegel's own position, that of God as Spirit and nothing but Spirit, places him in the pantheist camp without qualification."[84] Solomon is, of course, using the false definition of pantheism, the definition that flaunts the popular "God is nature" concept— the concept that Tillich rightly condemns.

Yet when we retreat four pages still another contradiction confounds the analysis. Now Solomon writes, "The point again and again becomes clear— there is no 'alien' God who reaches down to us; God is Spirit and Spirit is *us, nothing more*" (my italics).[85] Very interesting. If Spirit is "nothing more" than "us"—nothing more than human beings—then it isn't all of nature or the universe, and Hegel isn't a pantheist in any sense of the word. I suspect, though, that Solomon doesn't really mean what he says here. The words "nothing more" strike me as careless use of a widely used intensifier. Although we humans are by far Spirit's most important component (our bodies house Spirit's mind), Solomon's version of Spirit at this late point in his book seemingly does include a whole lot more than "us," the human race. It seems to include the entire universe.

And, yet again, if we retreat still farther, going way back to Solomon's Introduction, we find its first heading is "Hegel as Humanist."[86] Under this heading, Solomon says Hegel "sees God (insofar as we should use that word at all) as nothing more than human spirit writ large, or what Hegel calls *Geist*."[87] More problems. Because "God" is a synonym for Spirit and *Geist* also means Spirit, we are faced with a circular definition of Spirit: Hegel "sees Spirit . . . as nothing more than . . . what Hegel calls Spirit." Ignoring that problem, we must ask: what does "human spirit" mean? Whatever it means, it certainly doesn't mean "us," the humans. Humans are tangible, endowed with physical substance; spirit (lowercase) is intangible, whether conceived of as a supernatural soul, verve, feelings, moods, emotions, attitudes, aspirations, or something else. In a footnote, Solomon effectively abandons the "us" interpretation—the Spirit as humanity—and emphasizes the "human spirit" interpretation. He rejects Charles Taylor's belief that Spirit is "something other than or greater than the human spirit."[88]

Solomon's last sentence under the "Hegel as Humanist" heading amounts to his last word, even if his actual last words come near the end of the book. What Solomon says is, in effect, that he is unsure whether Spirit is limited to humanity or includes "everything." He writes: "Hegel's 'Spirit' is human spirit, and *if* it includes much more than just humanity (namely, everything) it is, nonetheless, a belligerently humanist demonstration that this is a human world in which all is but a stage for our own self-realization" (my italics).[89] Note the word "if" and the uncertainty it conveys. By "belligerently" Solomon means "virulently anti-theological, and more or less anti-Christian."[90] What Solomon is saying is that Hegel (1) *might* be a pantheist, in which case Spirit includes "everything" (apparently including artificial objects), (2) *might* instead be a narrowly defined humanist who defines Spirit as humanity and "nothing more," and (3) *might*, again instead, be a philosopher offering us a Spirit that is confined to humans without being humans per se, instead being some undefined quality called "human spirit." I have no idea what Solomon means by "human spirit" and, frankly, I don't think Solomon does either.

If, by chance, Solomon actually means Spirit is humanity or "human spirit" and "nothing more," then his interpretation is refuted by Hegel's portrayal of Spirit as an entity that existed in an unconscious—mindless—state of nature before humans arrived on earth. If Spirit is nothing more than humans or human spirit, how could Spirit exist before humans did? (The same problem shatters the societal interpretations of Pinkard and Westphal, coming up shortly.) The humanity and human spirit interpretations are additionally refuted by Hegel's two natural-and-artificial dialectics. These tell us that Spirit includes the artificial as well as the natural objects of the universe: "all reality" means *all* reality.

The humanity and human Spirit interpretations also founder in the quicksand of Hegel's concept of self-estrangement. Hegelian subject-object identity is not a purely humanistic concept. Hegel's many references to alien "objects" perceived by human "subjects"—human minds—permit no doubt that these objects are not always human beings. Indeed, an overwhelming majority of the objects are nonhuman. The objects include trees, houses, dogs, waterfalls, and stars, for example. When subject, a human's mind, doesn't recognize these "alien" objects as itself (both subject and objects are Spirit), how could the nonhuman objects be itself (subject) if only humans are Spirit? How could a tree be "itself," the observing subject?

Solomon's rendition of Spirit has still another problem. If Spirit is humanity, nature, or the universe—it doesn't matter which—then Spirit is a wasted word. "Humanity" or "universe," whichever applies, does the job much better. And if universe happens to be the intended meaning, we are saddled with that false connotation of metaphysical pantheism, whereas nothing genuinely metaphysical is meant. My own interpretation of Spirit avoids this problem. When Spirit is correctly understood as a more complicated concept than universe—that is, as a two-level, four-part concept that figuratively treats Spirit as a living organism with a dialectical "divine life"—then nobody is misled. The word Spirit is neither wasted nor misleading.

A final word: Lest there be any misunderstanding, I fully agree with Solomon's assertion that Hegel was a humanist. But let's be clear about what "humanist" means. It doesn't mean humanists are people who say God is humanity. Historically, the word "humanism" came into use during the Renaissance to refer to pursuits that reflected concern for secular rather than religious subjects. Humanism in painting was a shift away from Madonnas, Christs, angels, and the like to portraits, still life, landscapes, and other nonreligious subject matter. Nowadays "humanism" continues to have secular overtones but tends to be applied more narrowly to moral and ethical beliefs. A humanist is a person who disbelieves in any sort of divine law or commands and in the related concept of sin (violation of divine law). Humanists instead believe that all moral and ethical precepts come from, and should come from, the minds of human beings. Humanists include deists, pantheists, agnostics, atheists, and even liberal believers (especially Unitarians, Congregationalists, Quakers, and Reform Jews) who believe in God but don't believe in moral codes written among the stars. In the context of discussions of religion, humanism is usually a euphemism for atheism, used by nonbelievers who lack the courage of their convictions and who wish to avoid the social disapproval that often accompanies being identified as an atheist. All of us, except for those misguided souls who think Hegel was a pan*en*theist, should be able to agree that Hegel was a humanist. He believed neither in God nor in divine law. But that doesn't mean his Spirit is humanity or "human spirit."

Beiser. Tracing the evolution of Hegel's thought from concepts originating with Kant, Fichte, and Schelling—and to some extent originating with Hegel himself in collaboration with Schelling—Beiser reaches much the same conclusion as Solomon: Hegel's Spirit is the universe itself, not a metaphysical essence within it. Beiser's interpretation appears in his Introduction to *The Cambridge Companion to Hegel*, an essay collection he edited. Viewed as an investigation of the genesis of Hegel's concept of Spirit, the essay is outstanding. But in wrongly claiming to be a metaphysical interpretation of Spirit, and in describing Hegel's thought as a quest for "knowledge," the essay is deeply flawed.

On the second page, Beiser refers to "Hegel's metaphysics."[91] He soon adds that "even if Hegel avoided the term, he had a conception of philosophy that can only be described as 'metaphysical.'"[92] But, shortly thereafter we learn that Hegel's philosophy is metaphysical only in the sense that it deals with an "absolute," which happens to be *defined* as the universe. Hegel supposedly insisted, and Beiser agrees, that his "metaphysics has nothing to do with the supernatural."[93] But in that case it isn't metaphysics. The word "metaphysics" has always implied the existence of something supernatural but impersonal—something speculative, nonmaterial, intangible, and not amenable to observation, testing, or other forms of scientific inquiry. Ontology, philosophical inquiry concerning the possible existence and nature of a speculative supernatural entity called "being," is probably the best example. I'll have more to say about the meaning of metaphysics later in my analysis of Beiser's interpretation.

Beiser argues, persuasively, that Hegel inherited from Schelling an "organic conception of the absolute" having three salient features: (1) *defining* the absolute as the universe, (2) attributing "subject-object identity" to the universe-absolute, and (3) treating the absolute as a "living force."[94] Subject-object identity, of course, is what we find in Hegelian estrangement and self-realization: Spirit, using human minds (subjective, mental) as perceiving "subjects," sees external "objects" (objectively existing, physical) that are initially misconstrued as "alien"—things different from "subject"—but ultimately recognized as identical to subject (both are Spirit). The "living force" concept—this makes the absolute "organic"—is metaphorical. Spirit perceives, thinks, goes through many stages or "shapes" of consciousness, and finally arrives at self-realization—all through the minds of living human beings. The stages and shapes of consciousness are Spirit's "life." "Organic" and "life" are, of course, being used figuratively; Spirit is not really a living organism.

Beiser thinks Hegel believed he could "show" by his dialectic that "there can be a conceptual and demonstrative *knowledge* of the absolute" (my italics).[95] What? Surely Beiser can see that, if the absolute or Spirit is simply *defined* as the universe, then calling the absolute (or Spirit, or God) the "universe" or "all reality" is not a matter of knowledge. When Bishop Robinson defined God as Love, was he trying to bring knowledge to his readers? No, he was identifying a personal value, a quality or principle—actually just an emotion—he admired.

Another problem is that Beiser, although he attributes to Hegel the use of dialectics, has no idea what a Hegelian dialectic is. All he knows is that a dialectic is supposed to have three stages. Whereas Hegel's macrodialectic begins with unconsciousness, Beiser thinks it begins with consciousness: "Some finite concept, true of only a limited part of reality, would go beyond its limits in attempting to know all of reality."[96] What is that supposed to mean? A concept is not a mind; neither does it have a mind. How can a concept attempt to "know" anything? If "finite concept" is supposed to mean a human being—Hegel does call humans finite, and humans are "only a limited part of reality"—Beiser should say so in plain English instead of using highfalutin academic jargon. Humans are not concepts.

Meanwhile, if a human *is* what Beiser calls a "finite concept," what he thinks is Hegel's thesis is really Hegel's antithesis: humans don't exist in the thesis stage. And even in the antithesis, human minds are not attempting to "know" reality; they are just misinterpreting what they see. Likewise, if "go beyond its limits" means "misinterpret," Beiser should again say so in plain English. (How ironic it is that, earlier in his Introduction, Beiser mentions "the premium placed on clarity in contemporary philosophy."[97]) Beiser's description of the dialectic's second stage is without substance. He merely says, in effect, that the antithesis is the opposite of the thesis and, therefore, "depends for its meaning on some other concept."[98] That "other concept" would be whatever thesis concept the antithesis is the opposite of. Not even a hint about what the antithetical "concept" is. Beiser's synthesis has nothing specific to synthesize and thus fails to describe an actual synthesis. The fact is that, although Beiser is willing to use the words "thesis" and "antithesis" (but not "synthesis") in reference to Hegel's *Logic*, what he calls dialectics in *Phenomenology* is merely an amorphous "process of development involving conflicting [but not necessarily opposite] tendencies or forces."[99] He has the misconception that no resolution of "conflicting tendencies" occurs until, on the last page of *Phenomenology*, Spirit achieves self-realization, which Beiser misconstrues as the one and only resolution of the huge number of conflicting ideas or "tendencies" that have gone before. In short, he is reinterpreting dialectics as something other than true thesis-antithesis-synthesis dialectics.

Beiser's interpretation has other serious faults—beyond the misconceptions about metaphysics and Hegel's dialectics. The crucial fault is the same as that of Solomon's nonsupernaturalistic interpretation. If we go by the mislabeled pantheism version of Solomon's interpretation, Solomon's and Beiser's interpretations are pretty much the same. Both authors, when attributing pantheism to Hegel, treat Spirit as the physical universe, not an unseen metaphysical (hence supernatural) essence within everything in the universe. Therefore, the objections that apply to Solomon's interpretation apply with equal force to Beiser's.

Perhaps the biggest problem is that both Solomon and Beiser largely ignore the mental side of Spirit, the subjective element of subject-object (mental-physical) identity. Even less are they aware of the general-particular (universal-particular) dichotomy within Spirit's mental side. Hegel says Spirit is "supersensual." That might seem to mean Spirit cannot be perceived by the senses, but it actually means that (*a*) the *mental side* of Spirit—Spirit's Mind (man's minds)— cannot be perceived and (*b*) the mental *concept* of Spirit, which is the unseen universal "inner" of everything in the universe, cannot be perceived by the senses. Hegel draws an analogy between Spirit and a "force" such as gravity. That again means Spirit, viewed as either mind or a concept, cannot be seen. It is hidden. You must go "behind the curtain" to know what Spirit is. So how can "subject," a conscious human mind, not see Spirit when it sees an object if, as Beiser claims, Spirit is the physical object itself and nothing more (not also human minds)? If Spirit is nothing more than perceived physical objects that constitute the universe, it *can* be seen. It is supposedly not like gravity, which is invisible. By interpreting Spirit as the universe, Solomon and Beiser are missing half the story, the mental or "subject" half. The phrase "phenomenology of mind" refers to *mental* experience, not physical experience. Man's minds and their thoughts, not trees and houses, are traveling through history.

If Spirit is just the visible physical universe, why did Hegel choose the name *Geist*? *Geist* connotes something invisible. *Geist* is invisible regardless of whether it is interpreted as Mind (Baillie, Marcuse, Singer) or Spirit (Miller, Tillich, Findlay, Kaufmann, C. Taylor, Solomon, Beiser, Pinkard, Forster, Stern). Again, why does Beiser ignore Hegel's parallel distinctions between (*a*) inner and outer, (*b*) essence and existence, (*c*) divine and human, and (*d*) "in itself" (internal) and "for itself" (external)? In each of these pairs, the first member is invisible, intangible, as is a spirit. Why did Hegel also bring up phrenology, if not to make the point that something inner (a person's character or inclinations) and something outer (the person's face) are the same thing (as ultimately revealed in phrenology by the person's actions)? And, to repeat an earlier quotation from *Phenomenology*, why did Hegel write this: "Spirit is alone Reality. It is the *inner* being of the world" (my italics).[100] That quotation not only declares that Spirit has a hidden side; it also *emphasizes* the hidden side. The hidden side is (*a*) Spirit's mental side—the minds of man—in one sense and (*b*) Hegel's philosophical concept of a four-faceted Spirit in another sense. In the second sense, Spirit is not a metaphysical essence but a *concept* of Spirit that a human mind generates and projects into an external object it sees and correctly interprets as being, in essence, Spirit. When Hegel wrote that "Spirit . . . is the inner being of the world," he was emphasizing the mental concept of Spirit rather than Spirit's physical aspect.

In his chapter 3, "Force and the Understanding," Hegel develops the distinction between the world of appearance—the universe we see—and the hidden supersensible world, the world not perceived by the senses. Referring to "the world of appearance," Hegel says "we completely misunderstand . . . if we think that the supersensible world is . . . the sensuous world," the world of appearance. Why do we misunderstand? Because the true "world of appearance [the true universe] is, on the contrary, *not* the world of sense-knowledge [not the world we see] . . . but . . . an *inner* world" (Hegel's italics).[101] If Beiser is correct in implying that, for Hegel, there is no inner (mental, subjective) world, how does he explain Hegel's statement that there *is* an inner world? How does he explain Hegel's saying that the true universe is not the universe we see, the universe Beiser interprets as Spirit's meaning? If, as Beiser claims, Hegel thinks the observable physical universe is the only world there is, why does Hegel repeatedly refer to a supersensible world, a hidden "inner world" that is not observable? What does Beiser think this inner world is, if not something intangible, nonmaterial? If Spirit is nothing more than the physical universe that registers with our senses, why does Hegel say there is a metaphorical "curtain" whose role is "to conceal the inner world"?[102] Doesn't that mean there is a different world, a world we can't see, hidden behind the curtain?

There is a different "world," a world we can't see. It isn't a metaphysical world; it isn't supernatural. It is the *concept* of Spirit. Concepts are nonmaterial, nonphysical. They can't be seen. Spirit, as the hidden "inner" essence of everything in the universe, is simply a four-faceted mental image that Hegel projects into everything.

Beiser's version of "Hegel's God is the universe" is even weaker than Solomon's. With Solomon, the possibility exists that the universe includes artificial objects. Solomon doesn't commit himself but seems to imply that artificial objects are included; he says Spirit might include "more than just humanity (namely, everything)." "Everything" covers artificial as well as natural objects. But Beiser definitely maintains that artificial objects are *not* part of Spirit, defined as the universe: "Schelling and Hegel also insist that their metaphysics . . . [use a] conception of metaphysics [that is] indeed profoundly naturalistic. . . . They admired Spinoza precisely because of his thoroughgoing naturalism, . . . conceiving of God as nothing more than the *natura naturans*."[103] If that is the case, Beiser's interpretation is refuted by Hegel's two natural-artificial dialectics. Hegel makes it plain that Spirit is found in both natural and artificial objects; it is a synthesis of natural and artificial.

Another problem, one I have already touched on (maybe even belabored), involves the distinction between a definition and a fact or knowledge. According to Beiser, metaphysics can be defined as "the knowledge of the absolute."[104] The absolute is a term Hegel sometimes uses as a synonym for Spirit. Schelling and Hegel decided to equate "absolute" with Spinoza's concept of substance. Then, for philosophical purposes, they departed from Spinoza's concept of a supernatural substance hidden within natural objects. They *defined*—redefined, that is—substance as the physical universe, not its metaphysical inner reality. (Hegel later, after drifting apart from Schelling, substituted the name Spirit for substance and restored the "inner" quality by giving Spirit a mental side to complement Spirit's physical side.) Now, if Spirit's being the universe is just a matter of definition, why does Beiser repeatedly treat this as a matter of knowledge? When Bishop Robinson defined God as Love, was that knowledge? Or was it an arbitrary definition (not based on customary usage) that was neither true ("knowledge") nor false?

Beiser's discussion is full of words and phrases implying that Hegel was talking about something factual, or that might be factual. "Hegel," who (we are told) *defined* the absolute as the universe, "saw the purpose of philosophy as the rational *knowledge* of the absolute" (my italics).[105] Doesn't Beiser know the difference between an arbitrary definition and knowledge? "God is Love" isn't knowledge; it's a definition. So are "God is the universe" and "God is nature."

298 HEGEL'S UNDISCOVERED THESIS-ANTITHESIS-SYNTHESIS DIALECTICS

Beiser also says, "Hegel began to have serious *doubts* about some of Schelling's formulations of the nature of the absolute" (my italics).[106] If substance's or Spirit's being nature was just a definition, there was nothing factual to be doubted. Schelling and Hegel were "claiming that we can *know* nature as an organism" (my italics). Likewise, "Kant denies, and Hegel affirms, that we can *know* that nature is an organism" (my italics).[107] If "organism" is just a figure of speech—if "Spirit" is really just a made-up synonym for "universe"—how can we "know," or even mistakenly think, nature is an organism?

I am suggesting that, if Beiser is right in implying that Hegel merely defines Spirit (also called the absolute and substance) as the nonsupernatural *physical* universe, then he should know better than to assume he is talking about facts and knowledge. Why is Beiser assuming Hegel is discussing facts, whether real or hypothetical? As Tillich said, it is "all the same" whether the universe is called "matter" or "Spirit." And it is likewise all the same whether the universe is called "universe" or "God" or "substance." We aren't talking about facts or knowledge; we are just playing with words.

Part of the problem is that Beiser is confused about what metaphysics is. At best he is using an out-of-date concept. Beiser is certainly correct in saying metaphysics "is notoriously vague and ambiguous."[108] What he doesn't seem to grasp is that, in today's parlance, metaphysics deals with the supernatural. He does try to finesse this problem by offering a Kantian definition of metaphysics: "the attempt to know the unconditioned through pure reason."[109] But "the unconditioned" is every bit as vague and speculative as "substance." It isn't the subject of knowledge; it doesn't fall within the realm of science; it is supernaturalism, pure and simple, at least until it is given an explicit nonsupernatural definition.

Whatever metaphysics meant in the prescientific era of Aristotle, or even in Kant's day, it has come to mean speculation about or belief in a presumed impersonal (nontheistic, nondeistic) supernatural reality. I give examples in note 1 of chapter 3. The *American Heritage College Dictionary* gives four definitions of metaphysics, two of them figurative. The two nonfigurative definitions are (1) "the branch of philosophy that addresses questions about the ultimate composition of reality" and (2) "a priori speculation upon questions that are unanswerable to scientific observation, analysis, or experiment." In the first definition, "reality" has been construed as something intangible like the Logos, something assumed or believed to exist but not known to exist; it is essentially supernatural. In the second definition, the modern one, metaphysics is again "speculation" and is "a priori." That means it entails assumed or theoretical supernatural existence or causation rather than actual knowledge. The subject matter is supernaturalistic because it is "unanswerable to scientific observation, analysis, or experiment."

This second dictionary definition of metaphysics is essentially the same as the definition Beiser, in a later book, attributes to Kant. According to Beiser, "Kant saw metaphysics as speculation about *transcendent* entities, as a priori reasoning about objects lying beyond the sphere of experience." Remember, Beiser is trying to justify his calling Hegel's thought metaphysics by relying on Kant's concept of metaphysics. But now, in his later book, after restating Kant's concept, which is essentially the same as the second dictionary definition, Beiser says this: "In this [Kantian] sense Hegel cannot be a metaphysician at all, and for a very simple and compelling reason: he denied the existence of the transcendent, the purely noumenal or supernatural. If metaphysics consists in speculation about such a realm, then Hegel would be the first to condemn it as a pseudo-science."[110] My point exactly. So just what definition of metaphysics is Beiser using when he calls Hegel a metaphysician?

When Beiser describes metaphysics as concerning *knowledge* or things that we *know*, he is simply wrong. He is discussing something called an "absolute." An absolute is anything that is, in the eyes of a particular person and sometimes in a particular context, considered highest in importance or value. Typically it is a value, such as honesty or the environment or freedom; to a religious person it is apt to be God. In philosophy an absolute is a fundamental aspect of reality that is imagined but not known to exist, such as pantheism's "substance" or the Logos or, in ontology, "being." If the absolute is just a value like honesty or love, it is neither metaphysical nor in any other sense supernatural. If the absolute is God, it is supernatural but not metaphysical. Gods are rational and self-conscious—they have transcendent minds—whereas the characteristic that differentiates between gods and metaphysical entities is the latter's not being rational and self-conscious: astrological causation is not the product of a rational, self-conscious mind, and neither is bad luck that is caused by having a hotel room on the thirteenth floor.

Only if the absolute is an *imagined* or *theorized* or *assumed* supernatural but nonmental aspect of reality is it metaphysical. But Beiser correctly says Hegel simply *defines* the absolute—later renamed Spirit—as the universe; Beiser denies that Spirit is in any degree hidden, as the mind is. In that case, Spirit is not imaginary or theoretical, not "speculation," not something merely assumed to exist. It therefore is not metaphysical. It is, in fact, *physical.* In a similar vein, Beiser repeatedly refers to knowledge and to things that are known about the absolute. But if we know these things, the absolute is not something speculative or assumed. So, again, it is not metaphysical.

Beiser simply has not acknowledged the difference between reality and an arbitrary definition. He claims that, despite the fact that Hegel defines Spirit (the absolute) as the universe, whose existence is *known* and many of whose characteristics have been empirically verified, Spirit is metaphysical. That claim is both absurd and misleading. It is every bit as absurd as would be a claim that Bishop Robinson's *figurative* God, defined as Love, is something metaphysical and not just a human value or an emotion. We might just as well say that a fanatical chocoholic who defines chocolate as "the absolute" is a metaphysician. This is why I object to Beiser's saying that "Hegel . . . had a conception of philosophy that [although nonsupernaturalistic] can only be described as 'metaphysical.'"[111] Only? Hegel's concept, if it is what Beiser thinks it is (it isn't), is not metaphysical at all.

To sum up, when Beiser suggests that Spirit is neither supernatural nor speculative, that it is simply an arbitrary redefinition of God ("God is the universe"), his thesis collapses under the weight of the same problems that overwhelm Solomon's nearly identical thesis. In addition, the claims that this definition constitutes metaphysics and entails "knowledge" ("knowledge of the absolute") are utter nonsense. "God is Love" isn't knowledge. "God is humanity" isn't knowledge. And neither is "God is the universe."

Tucker. In an exceptionally well-written book about the philosophy of Karl Marx, Tucker devotes two chapters and part of a third to Hegel. In these chapters he does a far better job of summarizing Hegel's Phenomenology than most of the authors whose books are devoted exclusively to Hegel. Tucker's interpretation of Spirit is summarized in the following passage:

According to Hegel, God [Spirit] is . . . the whole of reality, the All (*daz Ganze*). He is all that ever has been and is, including nature spread out in space and civilization unfolding in historical time. Nature is god in his spatial extension; history is God in his temporal development. Beyond nature and history, nothing is. . . . For him, God and the world are one. . . . The two spheres of spirit's self-externalization are nature and history. It externalizes itself in space as the world of nature, and in time as the succession of civilizations or culture-worlds that rise and fall by human agency in the long sequence of history. . . . Nature and man are, therefore, two different grades of spirit.[112]

Tucker is off to a good start when he equates Spirit with "the whole of reality." At least by implication, and despite the emphasis on nature, he is including artificial objects in the concept of reality. But in further defining Spirit, Tucker introduces the wrong dichotomy: time and space. The correct dichotomy, as I explained in chapter 3, is physical and mental. Spirit does relate to time, but time is not a part of Spirit. Time or history, "the succession of civilizations or culture-worlds," is an aspect of the divine *life* of Spirit, not Spirit itself. That life includes the macrodialectic, the intermediate dialectics, and those twenty-two microdialectics, all of which belong to history. History is part of what Beiser insightfully describes as Hegel's adoption of Schelling's concept of the absolute as a living organism. Figuratively speaking, Spirit is an organism. It has a figurative life, which is all the thoughts and experiences and travails humans and their minds go through in *Phenomenology*. The humans are not all there is to Spirit; they are the mental side of Spirit, Spirit's mind.

In fairness to Tucker, I must acknowledge that in the same chapter Tucker accurately describes Spirit's travels through history as something tantamount to a life rather than being Spirit itself:

The final breakthrough to infinity occurs at the moment of the history of the world when "absolute knowledge" arises in the mind of the philosopher [Hegel] in the form of "philosophical science." On Hegel's postulate, spirit has now exhausted its creative possibilities of self-externalization [viewing itself as "other"]. It has assumed all the objective world-forms that it has the power to assume, and transcended them all in successive historic acts of knowing. Absolute knowledge, or "spirit knowing itself as spirit," is the world-self's knowledge of itself as absolute being. And absolute knowledge is embodied in Hegelianism, which comprises the scientific demonstration that the self is absolute being and comes to know itself as such in the history of the world.[113]

Here, you can see, Tucker is describing the history of Spirit, which is the same thing as the *life* of Spirit, not Spirit itself. Spirit is all those humans who have "assumed all the objective world forms" and the last of whom is Hegel.

By adopting Hegel's perspective, which treats Spirit as a living organism, Tucker at times seems to offer a metaphysical interpretation of Spirit. But Tucker makes it clear that Spirit exists only as a definition: Spirit "is an image of the self [conscious man] as God, and God, as we have seen, is *defined* by Hegel as . . . the whole of reality" (my italics).[114] All reality, of course, includes man.

Solomon, Beiser, and Tucker—I could almost add McCarney—are the interpreters who come closest to understanding Hegel's concept of Spirit. In Solomon's case, I refer only to the first of Solomon's three interpretations, wherein Spirit is the universe. The fundamental problem with these interpretations is that they fail to recognize (*a*) the two-level, physical-mental, universal-particular structure of Spirit and (*b*) the dialectical character of the divine life Spirit lives. In the process, they completely miss the macrodialectic and its thesis stage of unconsciousness—the first stage of Spirit's three-stage divine life.

NONSUPERNATURAL SOCIETAL INTERPRETATIONS

We are watching Spirit shrink. The first interpretations examined saw Spirit as a panentheistic entity; panentheism combines theism and pantheism. From there we went to pure pantheism, which shrinks Spirit by removing the transcendent mind while keeping the idea of an immanent God that participates in nature, hence includes man. Solomon, Beiser, and Tucker shrank Spirit still more by removing from nature that inner metaphysical essence, which is the immanent God and which Spinoza called substance. Terry Pinkard and Merold Westphal apply more shrinkage. They remove 99-plus percent of nature's content by limiting Spirit to the human race. Their interpretations assert that Spirit is either society or social relationships and other aspects of human society.

Pinkard. The first societal interpretation is that of Pinkard. In a major interpretive work, he asserts that Spirit "is not . . . some metaphysical supervisor directing the entire drama of history from off stage." Instead it is "just the human community taken as a whole, seen from the standpoint of humanity's gradually coming to terms with itself through its developing sets of social and political institutions."[115] As social communities develop, they accrue "shared social norms": folkways, mores, customs, standards, laws, other institutions, and other generally shared beliefs and values. Either society itself or these social norms, I'm not sure which, are what Pinkard calls Spirit.

Pinkard elaborates:

> Whenever there is mutual recognition among self-conscious subjects [humans] that is mediated by such a shared self-conscious understanding of what for them counts in general as an authoritative reason for belief and action . . . we have a relation of what Hegel calls *spirit*. Spirit—*Geist*—is a *self-conscious* form of life [humanity] . . . that has developed various social practices for reflecting on what it takes to be authoritative. . . . Spirit therefore denotes for Hegel not a metaphysical entity but a fundamental *relation* among persons that mediates their *self-consciousness*, a way in which people reflect on what they have come to take as authoritative for themselves."[116]

Spirit, in short, is nothing but (1) "the human community," (2) a "form of life," and (3) "a fundamental relation among persons."

I'm giving Pinkard a gold star for saying Spirit is "not a metaphysical entity" and thereby avoiding one of Beiser's mistakes. Hegel, says Pinkard, argues that "we must find a place for the divine within the concept of humanity."[117] That much is correct. But otherwise I find this interpretation highly inaccurate, completely untenable. It ignores all sorts of details of what Hegel says about Spirit. Pinkard himself admits his interpretation is unorthodox: "In the literature on Hegel, this characterization of spirit is, of course, controversial. The more traditional interpretation of spirit sees it as some metaphysical entity, a kind of grand mind of which human beings as particular minds are somehow parts."[118] Even these qualifying remarks display misunderstanding. Pinkard says traditional interpreters think human minds are "somehow" parts of the divine Mind. I gather that the word "somehow" applies also to his own interpretation. But why "somehow"? The "how" is obvious. Spirit, whether interpreted as the universe, nature, or society, includes human beings. Humans and their minds are either part or the whole of all three of these entities. So human minds are part of Spirit, the mental part. Human minds (lowercase) provide Spirit with its Mind (uppercase).

Seven objections to Pinkard's interpretation are especially telling:

1. Spirit has existed for as long as the universe has existed. Yet humans and their social relationships have not always existed. Humans have existed for only a tiny fraction of the life of the universe. As explained in chapter 3, Spirit undergoes a dialectical process of maturation. This maturation has a thesis stage, an antithesis stage, and a synthesis stage. In the thesis stage, Spirit is unconscious. It exists but has no Mind, because humans have not yet appeared on earth. Spirit does not acquire a mind until human minds, the Mind of Spirit, develop. Without humans, how could there be any societies, social norms and institutions, or a human "form of life" during Spirit's thesis stage? How would Pinkard explain the existence of Spirit, which he defines as "the human community," in the prehuman state of nature where no humans and no human community existed?

2. Pinkard effectively ignores what Hegel says about observed objects. Spirit's sorry state of self-estrangement during its antithesis stage of maturation is the most visible theme of *Phenomenology*. Self-estrangement, also called self-alienation, results because human minds (called "subject," "consciousness," and "the I" in various contexts) perceive external "objects." The objects are essentially identical to the human observers: both the observers and the objects observed are essentially Spirit. But the observers don't know this: Spirit, as

manifested in the observer, "does not recognize itself" in the observed object.[119] So humans become estranged or alienated from themselves; they perceive themselves as alien objects. More than 99.999 percent of the "alien" objects are nonhuman—things like raindrops, blackberry bushes, chimneys, and pork chops. How can Spirit be nothing more than human societies, customs, and institutions when Hegel plainly depicts Spirit as consisting mostly of nonhuman objects?

3. *Phenomenology's* Part A "Consciousness" dialectic, which revolves around objects, refutes Pinkard's interpretation. This dialectic is explained in my chapter 2 and consists of Hegel's headings I, Sense Certainty; II, Perception; and III, Force and the Understanding. The dialectical concepts behind those headings are universality (thesis); particularity (antithesis); and universe composed of particulars (synthesis). When consciousness perceives an object, "both are themselves the universal or the essence."[120] That is, both participate in Spirit—and in the universe, the physical side of Spirit. Discussing universality, Hegel gives three examples of perceived objects, which of course are particulars invisibly united by their participation in the universe. The examples are a tree, a house, and a bit of paper.[121] Notice that the last two are artificial, man-made. Later, discussing particularity, Hegel gives another example, salt. He also gives examples of characteristics that differentiate salt from other objects. The characteristics include white, tart, and cubical (an apparent reference to a block of salt).[122] It sure doesn't sound to me like humans are the only "objects" that "subject" or "consciousness" mistakes as alien.

4. Pinkard's interpretation also stumbles over the concept of self-estrangement in another way. To begin with, he doesn't understand the concept. He uses the word "alienation" in place of "estrangement" but fails to comprehend that Hegel's concept is *self*-alienation, or alienation from one's self. He speaks instead of man's alienation from "past forms of life" (political systems, customs, practices, medieval Catholicism) and, in the context of Unhappy Consciousness, from

306 HEGEL'S UNDISCOVERED THESIS-ANTITHESIS-SYNTHESIS DIALECTICS

his religion.[123] But under Hegel's real concept, self-alienation results from the failure of a human "subject" to recognize that the external humans and other "objects"—nonhuman objects—are really himself. The idea that Spirit's (Society's) self-alienation results from the failure of humans to recognize that all humans belong to society borders on absurdity. Every intelligent adult knows what society is and that he or she belongs to it. There can be no self-alienation of this type. Therefore, neither can there be any self-realization—realization by Hegel that he belongs to society.

5. Spirit doesn't mature, doesn't enter its synthesis stage, doesn't become *actual* rather than potential, until 1806. That is when Hegel wrote most of *Phenomenology* (published in 1807). And it is also when a human mind, Hegel's, finally recognized that it and everything else in the universe are essentially Spirit. Yet mature human societies with fully developed mores, norms, customs, attitudes, and institutions existed long before this. Remember, Pinkard isn't saying that Hegel's much-esteemed Germanic societies are the only manifestations of Spirit. *All* societies, according to Pinkard, are Spirit. Developed societies with folkways, customs, and shared beliefs, societies such as that of ancient Greece, existed long before 1806. How, then, can Pinkard explain Absolute Spirit's nonactuality (separation, Spirit's pre-self-realization status) before 1806?

6. While dissecting "The Revealed Religion," Hegel describes in previously quoted words how, when God (Jesus) dies, God "becomes transfigured" from particularity (one person, Jesus) into "universality" (all persons). God thus becomes "the Spirit who dwells in His community, dies in it every day, and is daily resurrected." Read those words carefully. Hegel isn't saying Spirit is the community, or society. He is saying Spirit is the living-and-dying human beings who *dwell* in the community. That doesn't mean, of course, that humanity is all there is to Spirit. Spirit is mostly nonhuman "objects." But it does mean that Hegel's references to the community depict Spirit not as

the community itself, or society, but as (in part) the individual humans who *dwell* in the community.

7. In *Phenomenology* Hegel plainly says in four different places that Spirit is "all reality."[124] To be sure, "all reality" is an oversimplification. Spirit does have that four-faceted structure described in chapter 3. But Spirit certainly does embrace all reality. How, then, can Pinkard say that Spirit is nothing but society or certain aspects of society? Society is just a tiny portion of all reality—of the universe. Society is not all there is to reality.

Any one of the seven objections is sufficient to disprove Pinkard's "sociality" interpretation of Spirit. The seven arguments taken together conclusively refute the interpretation.

Westphal. Merold Westphal (not to be confused with Kenneth Westphal) offers a similar nonmetaphysical, societal interpretation of Hegel's Spirit. This interpretation is somewhat opaque, however, and develops very slowly. Westphal begins with Hegel's first heading, "Consciousness," and makes virtually no progress. He does emphasize that Spirit is nonsupernatural: "Spirit is a social reality, a unity of individual human selves, not a timeless metaphysical reality . . . [and] not a supersensible beyond."[125] The nonmetaphysical point is clear enough, but "social reality" is so abstract as to be meaningless. There are literally thousands of "social realities"—opera, whist, foot racing, bullfighting, hide-and-seek, siestas, sailing, raising goats, merchandising, fishing, church dinners, crying babies, late deliveries, secret societies, social clubs, cults, sewing circles, fairs, circuses, piracy, fraud, celebrations, prejudice, love, hate, religion, atheism, self-flagellation, organized prayer, drunkenness, lice, barking dogs that keep people awake, children at play, marriage, funerals, murder, theft, adultery, charities, public officials, armies, taxes, measles, cholera, schools, dancing, folkways, customs, laws, and so on endlessly. "Social realities" everywhere. So what does "Spirit is a social reality" mean?

Spirit, Westphal says, is also "substance," but that doesn't mean physical substance; it means "permanence," "determinateness" (definiteness, which implies what?), and having "attributes" (which clarifies absolutely nothing).

And Spirit involves an attempt "to develop the concepts of love and life into fundamental philosophical categories," words that again clarify nothing.[126]

Farther along we learn that "transcendence" is one of Spirit's characteristics but that this transcendence is not "that of the theistic view." Then what is it? "The transcendence of Spirit is simply that of society to the individual."[127] It's beginning to sound like Spirit might be society. And forty-three unenlightening pages later, it develops that "society" is pretty close to the truth: "It is not difficult to recognize what Hegel intends by the notion of actual [self-realized] Spirit. It is the social reality which he calls the life of a people." This means, for reasons I can't comprehend, "that Spirit is the object of religious knowledge."[128] Why must "the life of a people" be "the object of religious knowledge"? The religious knowledge is untrue. We know this because Westphal previously said that "the divine is neither God in any traditional Judeo-Christian sense, nor the metaphysical absolute of the later so-called Hegelians."[129] So, Spirit is the "life of the people," and the life of the people (Spirit) is "the object of religious knowledge" and therefore the object of untrue knowledge. This "knowledge," whatever it is, has nothing to do with God or anything else supernatural. I hope you understand, because I don't.

We arrive at last at the final chapter, where Westphal tries with lots of stumbling but some success to resolve his earlier abstractions, ambiguities, etherealisms, and contradictions. The nonsupernaturalistic "religious knowledge" of which he spoke earlier is simply "recognizing the divine [Spirit] to be nothing beyond us but the social whole of which we are parts."[130] That doesn't quite square with Spirit's being the "*life* of the people." And can we reconcile "the social whole" with "the object of religious knowledge"? Frankly, I always thought that God, Jesus, Mary (in Catholicism), salvation, and providential divine intervention were the chief objects of religious knowledge. But at least (*a*) "life of the people," (*b*) the much earlier idea that society transcends the individual, and (*c*) "the social whole" point to society. Westphal seems to be saying, then, that Spirit is society, "the social whole of which we are parts." And society is about the same thing as what Pinkard says Spirit is: the human community, a form of life (the interaction of humans), and a fundamental relation among persons that involves customs, laws, practices, institutions, and the like. The difference, if there is one, is that Pinkard's identification of society and its traits is much clearer than Westphal's preliminary assertions that Spirit is something that has social reality, substance, permanence, determinateness, attributes, love, and life—possibly a herd of elephants.

The faults of Westphal's interpretation are the same as those of Pinkard's. These faults arise partly from failure to recognize that Spirit undergoes a prehuman, pre-societal stage of unconsciousness. First, the macrodialectic and its first stage—unconscious unity—contradict the notion that Spirit is society. How can Spirit be society if Spirit has existed for as long as the universe and nature have existed but society has existed only since the advent of man? Second, defining Spirit as society ignores what Hegel says about self-estrangement, or the failure of individuals to recognize nonhuman objects (as well as humans) as themselves, Spirit. How can Spirit be society when nonhuman "objects" such as mountains and carts constitute 99.999 percent of Spirit? On what basis does Westphal insist that, when Hegel speaks of a subject or consciousness perceiving external objects that are misconstrued as "alien," those objects can only be human beings? Third, Hegel specifically says the misinterpreted objects that are really Spirit include trees and paper. Fourth, if we apply Hegel's concept of self-alienation, society (Spirit) could be self-alienated only if individual "subject" members didn't recognize their "object" fellow citizens as being, like the subjects, members of society. But who doesn't know the everyone belongs to society? Fifth, Spirit does not achieve self-realization until Hegel writes *Phenomenology* in 1806. How can Spirit be society if societies existed in the ancient realms of China, Persia, India, Egypt, Judea, Greece, Rome, and North and South America? And if Westphal considers these older societies to be pre-self-realization societies, what is the difference (besides modernity) between those non-self-realized societies and self-realized societies? Sixth, when Hegel says the death of God transfigures God from particularity (one person, Jesus) to universality in the form of "the Spirit who dwells in His community, dies in it every day, and is daily resurrected," how can Westphal implicitly interpret that to mean that it is society that dies and is resurrected (born) daily? Hegel is obviously referring to individual *humans*. Seventh, Hegel says Spirit is "all reality." Society is not all there is to reality—far from it.

The conclusion is inescapable: The Pinkard-Westphal interpretation holding that Spirit is society, its customs, its social relationships, or some of society's other "attributes" is untenable. Both authors have misinterpreted Hegel's "Revealed Religion" statements about the dead God's being resurrected not as the one Jesus but the entire "community" (society) of humans. They think, mistakenly, that Hegel means this "community" is all there is to Spirit. But actually, the human community is just *part* of Spirit—by far the most important part (Spirit's Mind or "psychical nature") but nevertheless just a part. Spirit is the entire universe or "world"; it is the World-Spirit (*Weltgeist*). "World" is not just a metaphor for community or society. It isn't even just the earth. It is the entire physical universe, with its stars, planets, comets, and moons. Where physical nature is concerned, Hegel's *Philosophy of Nature* has detailed discussions of geological nature, plant nature, and animal nature; it also refers to the stars, the sun, and comets.[131] Physical nature is matter, and "matter is the form in which the self-externality of Nature achieves its first being-within-self, . . . which . . . brings the independent many into a universal being-for-self."[132] "Psychical nature" is, of course, man's mind.

FIVE NONINTERPRETATIONS

In the interest of providing reasonably complete coverage of the more prominent English-language interpretations of *Phenomenology* written since roughly 1950, I will comment on the works of five more authors: Findlay (1958), Kaufmann (1965), Rosen (1974), Harris (1995), and Franco (1999).[133] The 1950 cutoff date is not completely arbitrary. Kaufmann mentions that Findlay and Stace (1924) were, as of the 1965 date of Kaufmann's study, the two most widely read English studies of Hegel.[134] Stace's book is about Hegel's *Encyclopedia*, not *Phenomenology*. The prominent modern studies of Hegel thus begin with Findlay. What these last five studies have in common is that their authors have no discernible views on what Spirit means.

Findlay. Reading *The Philosophy of Hegel* in an effort to determine what Findlay thinks Spirit is is an exercise in frustration. The first two chapters, including one titled "The Notion of Spirit" (chapter 2), lead nowhere. They simply quote and paraphrase Hegel without interpreting or clarifying anything. Spirit is a "self-active Universal" and therefore can reasonably be called "infinite."[135] Do you understand? Findlay does manage to say what Spirit is not: it is not, for example, a metaphysical entity, because Hegel is not a "transcendent metaphysician, one who deals with objects or matters lying beyond our empirical ken." That statement at least affirms that Hegel is not a pantheist in the metaphysical sense of the term.

Findlay, like M. Westphal, spends a lot of time presenting vague generalities about Spirit without managing to strip away Hegel's ambiguity and mysticism. Try this: Spirit finds itself "encompassed and encircled by objects, things to which it cannot help attributing other-being, a being distinct from, and opposed to its own."[136] Those words do vaguely describe self-estrangement, but Findlay fails to state or even recognize this. He doesn't say the objects, unknown to Spirit, are itself. And even if he had clarified the significance of the objects, we still wouldn't know what Spirit is. All he has said is that Spirit, like everyone and everything else, exists in an environment containing other things besides itself. That again clarifies nothing.

Things do seem to be looking up when Findlay calls our attention to "the crowning point in the notion of Spirit." But the crowning point turns out to be meaningless: "Spirit . . . is, in a sense the *only* or the *absolute* reality, . . . what Hegel calls 'the True' or the 'Truth' of everything. By this Hegel means that one can only understand anything adequately in so far as it is seen as a stage towards, or as a condition of, the emergence of self-conscious Spirit."[137] Got that? Spirit is real. It is truth, the truth of everything. It is therefore the truth of the Tower of London, which is part of "everything." And it is the truth of the Duluth Public Library's copy of *Dracula*, the Amazon River, grandma's apron, and the Rock of Gibraltar. This paraphrasing without interpretation is nothing but inane blather.[138]

In mid-book Findlay presents this ambiguous statement: "The self-conscious Spirit which plays the part of God [replaces the God of theism] in his system is not the complex, existent person, but the impersonal, reasonable element in him, which, by a necessary process, more and more 'takes over' the individual, and becomes manifest and conscious in him."[139] So, Spirit is an "impersonal" and "reasonable" element of a person but is not a person. Does this mean that Spirit is certain unspecified but "reasonable" personality traits (wisdom? love? providence?) formerly attributed to the dead God of the human imagination? If so, and given that Spirit is "the Truth of everything," how can "reasonable" human personality traits, borrowed from Christianity's dead God, be the "truth," the invisible inner substance, of an erupting volcano, a dish of sauerkraut, a lilac bush, a lump of coal, an outhouse, or a lovely blue lake?

Findlay does say that philosophy "is the supreme form of Spirit" and that Spirit is "the principle of unity and universality."[140] But those two descriptions contradict each other: philosophy is a hotbed of disagreement, disunity, and particularity—a far cry from "unity and universality." And, when we consider that philosophers can't agree on what is true, how can philosophy be called the truth of everything? Findlay is going off in all directions.

The closest Findlay comes to giving Spirit any real substance is in the closing pages of the book. There Findlay reiterates that Hegel is anti-metaphysical, believes in no metaphysical Absolute, and believes in no God. The only Absolute compatible with Hegelianism is the one "that is revealed and known in certain experiences of individual human beings."[141] These words might be interpreted as suggesting that Spirit is nature, with which every human has had experiences (e.g., seeing birds, shoveling snow). The words could even point to good fortune, hard work, admiration of art and literature, pleasure, sadness, rectitude, deceit, interpersonal alienation, terror, or all of the foregoing; they all qualify as "experiences." But I interpret them as meaning that Findlay has no idea what Hegel means by Spirit. None of these things seems to qualify as the "truth" of the Tower of London, and the extreme variety of human experiences places the "experiences" interpretation in conflict with what Findlay said earlier about Spirit's being "the principle of unity and universality." Likewise, if philosophy (intangible, nonmaterial) is "the supreme form of Spirit," Spirit can't very well be nature (tangible, material). Findlay literally does not know what he is talking about.

Kaufmann. Looking at the subtitle of Kaufmann's *Hegel: A Reinterpretation*, you would think that the book contains an interpretation of Spirit. Not so. The book is probably the most readable piece that has been written about Hegel, it contains many insights (as well as misunderstandings), and it stresses that Hegel was not a supernaturalist; but it provides no comprehensible interpretation of Spirit.

If anything is clear in Kaufmann's "interpretation" it is that Spirit is not confined to humanity but is in some unexplained sense the universe. Kaufmann quotes with approval some lines written in 1857 by the German scholar Haym: "It [*Phenomenology*] is, I say, *the presentation of the universe as a beautiful, living cosmos*. After the manner of ancient Greek philosophy it wants to show how in the world as a whole all parts serve and unite into a harmonic whole."[142] Although Kaufmann doesn't say so, these words seem to echo Schelling's concept of the Absolute as nature, personified as a living organism.

Spirit's life, as described by Kaufmann, is a somewhat arbitrary collection of human experiences grabbed from history: "Hegel, like Goethe and Dante, created a world of his own, and instead of peopling it largely with figments of his imagination as many another writer [but not Goethe and Dante] has done, found places in it for the men and women and events he knew from history and literature, as well as a very few of his contemporaries. . . . A great deal is there because it happened just then to be of interest to the writer, and he was wondering where it belonged, how best to place it—how to fashion a cosmos out of the totality of his cultural experience without suppressing anything that seemed to matter."[143] Note that Kaufmann is now drifting away from Haym's meaning of "cosmos," the universe, and seems to be making "cultural experience" a metaphorical cosmos. If this is his meaning, Spirit is *not* the universe. Kaufmann later adds that "the framework of the book is loose enough to permit the introduction of all sorts of ideas for which the writer would like to find a place."[144] What Kaufmann seems to be saying is that Spirit is a nonsupernatural but figuratively living organism whose life is the thoughts, ideas, and events from many historical realms of human experience. Does this mean Spirit is history—"cultural experience"? Alternatively, is Spirit human culture?

Kaufmann has no answer. When he finally arrives at the end of *Phenomenology*, where Absolute Spirit comes into being, he can't say precisely what Absolute Spirit is. What he does say is that "the infinite spirit has to be found in the comprehension of this world, in the study of the [finite] spirits summoned in the *Phenomenology*."[145] The context these words refer to includes Hegel's last-paragraph references to history's "slow-moving succession of Spirits" in which "the realm of Spirits . . . constitutes a succession in Time in which one Spirit relieved another of its charge and each took over the empire of the world from its predecessor."[146] Here "Spirits," plural, refers to the real and fictitious humans—manifestations of the divine Spirit—who populate Hegel's dialectics. We know the plural Spirits are the humans because, in discussing Greek epics, Hegel says "the Minstrel [a human] is . . . [an] actual Spirit."[147] If the infinite Spirit has to be found in the study of humans, does this mean Spirit is humanity and nothing more, not all reality, not the literal "cosmos" that Haym equated with Spirit? Who knows?

Rosen. Stanley Rosen's interpretation of Spirit is a strange mixture of hints and vague ideas. Although Hegel was not an ontologist or any other sort of supernaturalist, Rosen makes him one. (This seems to be the reason Solomon sagely describes Rosen's book as "an intelligent but reactionary book" that attempts "to solve a series of ontological puzzles left unresolved by the ancient Greeks."[148]) Rosen thus tells us that "the emergence of Being [the Absolute of ontology] is for Hegel altogether intelligible" and that Hegel might have overlooked "the 'ontological difference' between the Absolute and its finite manifestations."[149] These words and those that give it context don't tell us what the Absolute or Being is, but we have learned that Rosen thinks Spirit is not only supernatural but the Absolute of ontological metaphysics.

Whether Spirit is also supernatural in a theistic sense is never clarified. But Rosen sometimes seems to lean toward theism, hence toward a pan*en*theistic concept of Spirit. "Hegel conceives of God or the Absolute as activity which, even though eternal and necessary, exhibits its essential nature in human history."[150] Does Rosen really mean Spirit is "activity," action rather than a thing, or is he just writing carelessly? Apparently he is just being careless: "Since the highest definition of the Absolute is *Spirit*, and since Spirit, as the identity of identity and non-identity, encompasses the three spheres of nature, self-consciousness, and conceptual knowledge, or the community of world, man, and God, it is evident that the term *Absolute* functions in Hegel as does the term *Whole* in classical thought."[151]

These words tell us that Spirit includes (1) the world, presumably meaning the universe, (2) man, which is a redundant detail already covered by "world," and (3) God. This is about as much detail as Rosen is willing to provide. Although Rosen avoids the words "panentheism," "transcendent," and "immanent," it sounds like he has that panentheistic conception of Spirit. Why else would (1) world and (3) God be treated as separate "spheres," parts of Spirit? And yet Rosen might simply be borrowing a loose or metaphorical usage of "God" from Hegel, who doesn't literally mean God. Rosen's earlier remarks about Being and ontology imply that "God" is really not like the Judeo-Christian God but is instead the mysterious impersonal Being of metaphysical philosophy. For this reason I hesitate to place Rosen's interpretation in the panentheism category.

The quoted statement also tells us that Spirit is "the identity of identity and non-identity." But, as Rosen's subsequent remarks show, he hasn't the faintest idea what that phrase means. He couldn't possibly understand, because understanding the phrase requires knowledge of Hegel's thesis-antithesis-synthesis dialectics, something Rosen lacks. (I explain the meaning of Hegel's phrase in chapter 4 in the last paragraph of my analysis of microdialectic 22.) So why does Rosen quote Hegel's phrase? What is his point?

If we fast-forward to Rosen's chapter 9, "The Absolute," we find him making one more attempt to explain what Hegel means in *Phenomenology*'s last chapter by "Absolute Knowledge" and "Absolute Spirit." But all he manages to say is that man is part of Spirit: Absolute Spirit is "the Whole of which man is the exhibiting [exhibited? meaning displayed or visible?] part."[152] If "exhibiting" means visible—what else can it mean?—that statement isn't even true. All nonhuman physical parts of reality—rivers, barns, the sun, buttons, and so on—are also displayed, hence visible. More important, the statement doesn't tell us what it is that man is a part of; "the Whole" is meaningless except for the implication that Spirit has parts.

In his next sentence Rosen, in a lame effort to clarify his meaning, provides us with a classic example of that lamentable perversion of English called gobbledygook: "Man is that part of the Whole which is able, under the form of time, to coincide with the Whole by way of achieving an equivalence between his self-consciousness and that of the Absolute, so as to transcend time, which continues in the modality of nature and finite or nonscientific spirit."[153] All this says, if it says anything, is that the Whole (Spirit) has parts other than man—but not "exhibiting" or visible parts—and that man "is able" over time to "transcend time" by turning his self-consciousness into that of Spirit. Well, it does say one other thing: "Man is *that* part [the only part] of the Whole which is able . . . to coincide with the Whole" (my italics). Wrong. The Whole is Spirit, and *all* parts of the Whole—all parts of the universe—"coincide with" (belong to) Spirit. We have now been told that (*a*) man is *the* (implicitly the *only*) "exhibiting" or visible part of Spirit, (*b*) Spirit's other parts are not "exhibiting," not visible, and (c) man's self-consciousness achieves "equivalence" with, but does not necessarily produce, Spirit's self-consciousness. Does that tell us what Spirit is? It doesn't. It doesn't even tell us whether man's "achieving an equivalence between his self-consciousness and that of the Absolute" means (*a*) that the Absolute is self-conscious all along and that man catches up, achieving equivalence with the Absolute, or (*b*) that man's self-consciousness *is* Spirit's, hence that the two become self-conscious simultaneously.

When on the next page Rosen says "Spirit becomes self-conscious of itself as the identity of subject and object only by temporality or the course of human history,"[154] he doesn't bother to say what subject and object mean. Rosen does add, in italics, that "*God becomes man in order to become God.*"[155] But that merely repeats the idea that man is part of God, part of "the Whole." And since Rosen has already told us that God is the metaphysical Being of classical ontology, it really isn't news that man is a part of Being. Rosen still hasn't said what Spirit, or Being, is.

Harris. Harris's concept of Spirit has content that is deliberately ambiguous, self-contradictory, and in some respects outlandish. Proceeding through *Phenomenology* in start-to-finish fashion, he provides no clues to Spirit's identity until he reaches Hegel's discussion of "inner" and "outer" in *Phenomenology*'s chapter on reason. There, discussing "inner," he relates this concept to an organism's "rational aspect" that "originates in the mind of a higher intelligence."[156] Does Harris mean this inner "rational aspect" exists only in humans, or are relatively intelligent nonhuman beings such as chimpanzees, dolphins, porpoises, and elephants also covered by "higher intelligence"? Harris might or might not even be hinting, but if so refusing to say, that Spirit is nothing more than human beings, or perhaps Pinkard's "society." Then again, the "higher intelligence" might be that of the God of theism, viewed metaphorically as an "organism." Is he suggesting that Spirit is the transcendent-and-immanent God of panentheism and that this God is the source of man's "rational aspect"?

Despite the thorough ambiguity of what he has said, and of what Hegel says, Harris reaches Hegel's next chapter, "Spirit," and begins acting coy. His outrageously unsupported, out-of-the-blue two opening sentences are these: "By now, it should be obvious that there is nothing mysterious (or mystical) about Hegel's concept of Spirit. Wherever two or more individuals can talk to one another successfully about some good of a non-instrumental kind that they have (or can hope to have) in common, there Spirit exists."[157] Problem 1: This doesn't say *what* Spirit is; it says *where* Spirit is. Problem 2: What is a non-instrumental good, and what is an instrumental good? Problem 3: What is it that exists when two people hold a conversation about a non-instrumental good they can agree on but does not exist when two people hold a conversation about either (*a*) something other than a "good" or (*b*) a good they can't agree on—or when they don't converse at all? Problem 4: Is Harris teasingly intimating that Spirit is humanity and, if so, why does he toss us red herrings suggesting that (*a*) Spirit isn't present until at least *two* humans are present, (*b*) the humans must be *conversing*, (*c*) the subject of the conversation must be a *good*, whatever that means, (*d*) the good must be *non-instrumental*, whatever that means, and (*e*) the humans must reach an *agreement*? Doesn't Harris know how to say "Spirit is humanity" or "Spirit is social interaction among human beings" or whatever he is implying?

A few lines later, Harris tosses us a totally different concept: "We already know that the *real* Spirit that exists and demands our recognition is 'the State'; in other words, it is the developed political community that maintains the school, and a great complex of other institutions which require our service and which protect or facilitate our free self-expression in a variety of ways."[158] Problem 5: Where on earth did he get that idea? If he got it from Hegel's *Philosophy of History* or *Philosophy of Right*, why does he imply in his "by now, it should be obvious" remark that the idea comes from the *Phenomenology* chapters that precede the "Spirit" chapter?[159] Problem 6a: How can Spirit be "the State" when Harris implied a moment ago that Spirit exists when two people sailing across the Atlantic or photographing penguins in Antarctica, places where no state exists, hold a conversation and agree about a non-instrumental good? Problem 6b: How does a political state materialize when two people get together and agree on something? Problem 7: How can Spirit be the state if Spirit existed in the prehuman period of nature, or for that matter in Marx's early hunter-gatherer societies, but no political state, schools, or "other institutions" did? Problem 8: How can Spirit be the state if Spirit has a Mind and the state doesn't? Problem 9: How can a state become self-alienated? Where in chapters 1 through 5 of *Phenomenology* does Hegel discuss civil war? Problem 10: How can a state undergo self-realization, given that Spirit already exists in non-self-realized status before achieving self-realization? Problem 11: If, by chance, Harris is confusing the state (general) with monarchy (particular) as the goal of Hegelian history, monarchy is not Spirit but, along with freedom, one of two *goals* of history. Problem 12: If, by further chance, Harris misspoke and really meant the state is not Spirit but Spirit's *goal*, how can the state be Spirit's goal, not realized until Hegel realizes he is Spirit, when governed states have existed for thousands of years? Problem 13: If Harris meant a unified *German* state (specifically, Prussia) is or was Spirit's goal, why didn't Harris say so instead of speaking abstractly of "the state" and omitting the vital detail that the state must unite previously autonomous political subdivisions? Problem 14: Where in chapters 1 through 5, the chapters leading up to "by now" (the beginning of chapter 6), does Hegel even mention the state?

Two sentences later we learn this: "Spirit is the unity of our world as we are conscious of it."[160] Problem 15: Conscious of what—Spirit, the unity, or the world? (Advice to Harris: Always make sure your pronouns have clear antecedents.) Problem 16: If Harris really means Spirit is "unified" (adjective), that it is the world perceived as one rather than as many, when he says "unity" (noun), Spirit is unified only in its thesis and synthesis stages; it is disunified—in a state of "actual separation"—until the very end of *Phenomenology*. Spirit displays *disunity*. And that antithesis-stage disunity includes chapter 6, "Spirit," where the "unity" remark appears. Only *Absolute* Spirit, which has not yet materialized at this point in Harris's discussion, displays unity. Problem 17: How can Spirit be an abstraction like unity and still (*a*) be the world itself or even just part of it, (*b*) be something that does not exist when two people have a conversation about something other than a good, (*c*) have a Mind, something "unity" doesn't have, and (*d*) be figuratively or literally a living organism? Problem 18: How can unity be self-alienated? Problem 19: How can unity undergo self-realization? That is, how can it change from disunity (conscious separation) to unity if it is already "unity," presumably meaning unified?

Next page: Harris refers to Objective Spirit, or Spirit in the form of an external object viewed by a subject, Subjective Spirit. Objective Spirit "becomes 'subject' [rather than an 'object'] as the self-conscious 'absolute' knowledge of every member of the community."[161] Problem 20: What is "absolute knowledge" and under what conditions is it "self-conscious"? We know the answer, but does Harris? Obviously, he does not. Problem 21: Knowledge cannot be self-conscious; only a human or other being can be self-conscious. Problem 22: "Subject" in Hegel's jargon refers to the mental side of a person; it is the mind, that which has and seeks knowledge, not the knowledge itself. Problem 23: How do we reconcile this latest description of Spirit with any of the preceding three? Problem 24: Contrary to what Harris implies, Spirit— its Mind, that is—is "subject" (the subjective side of Spirit) long before it achieves self-realization. Problem 25: How can "every member of the community" be conscious of itself as Spirit when Hegel plainly says that, even though the incarnate God has been "resurrected" as the humans of the human "community," "the community [except for Hegel] . . . does not [yet] possess the consciousness of what it is" and still "has those picture-thoughts" of God in the sky?[162]

I could go on with other examples of inane things Harris says, but you get the point. He is spouting nonsense. If he really thinks he knows what Spirit is—if he really thinks chapters 1 through 5 of *Phenomenology* make Spirit's identity "obvious"—he doesn't know how to put his thoughts into plain English and to make them consistent (*a*) with each other and (*b*) with certain things we know about Spirit (e.g., that Spirit existed before man, hence before any two people conversed; that Spirit has a Mind; that Spirit is self-alienated until the end of *Phenomenology*; that Spirit undergoes self-realization; and that Spirit's self-realization is the realization of a human mind—Hegel's—that it and everything else in the universe are, in essence, Spirit).

Franco. Paul Franco's interpretation of Spirit—it barely qualifies as an interpretation—agrees with those of other perceptive authors in asserting that Hegel is not a metaphysician. Regarding metaphysics, Franco begins by observing that Schelling had a "pantheistic conception" of the absolute, whereas Hegel's absolute, Spirit, "differs from Schelling's more metaphysical conception" and from "the romantic and untenable metaphysics of 'cosmic spirit' with which it has been frequently identified."[163] He adds that "it is not necessary to import into this concept [Spirit] any dubious metaphysical or cosmic connotations."[164]

So far, so good. Franco understands that Spirit is not metaphysical, not supernatural. But when we move from what Spirit isn't to what it is, the fog rolls in. In successive paragraphs, Franco states and then (for emphasis?) repeats in identical words his view that Spirit is "the essentially self-conscious and self-constituting character of human experience."[165] Franco doesn't tell us what "self-constituting" means, but he seems to be saying that human experience creates (constitutes) itself, a baffling and ultimately meaningless suggestion. Or is he saying that human experience constitutes (is) human experience, which is equally meaningless? If we remove the empty word "self-constituting," the definition boils down to the idea that human experience is self-conscious and that this self-consciousness *of experience* (not of people) is Spirit. I suspect that Franco was a bit tongue-tied when he said that. Experience is not a being, has no mind, and can't be self-conscious. Presumably, he really meant that Spirit is the self-consciousness that *humans* experience. And by "self-conscious" he meant that John Doe was aware that he, John Doe, exists; a human is aware of itself. Unfortunately for this definition, Spirit is not human self-consciousness. Moreover, although Spirit becomes Absolute Spirit when Spirit undergoes self-realization through the medium of a human mind (Hegel's), self-consciousness in that unorthodox sense is not the human's awareness of *itself*; it is the human's awareness that both (a) the human and (b) everything the human sees or otherwise senses are Spirit.

Franco later tries to clarify his earlier definition by saying that Spirit "simply refers to the realm of human awareness, doing, and understanding that Hegel counterposes to the unself-consciousness realm of nature."[166] This revised definition of Spirit takes us well beyond the earlier concept of self-awareness (self-consciousness) to *general* awareness, awareness of all sorts of things other than one's self, and to not only general awareness but understanding of whatever one is aware of. Now, it is certainly true that Spirit, seeing with the eyes of man, is aware of all sorts of things, things that are really itself but that it mistakes for alien "objects." But this awareness is not Spirit; Spirit, in its mental aspect, is the human minds (plural) that have the awareness. Another problem is that this revised definition seemingly excludes nature: we saw earlier that Franco contrasts Hegel's absolute with Schelling's pantheistic absolute. Hegel's real Spirit actually includes nature. Spirit becomes self-aware when a human mind realizes that not only the human but nature (not to mention other humans and artificial objects) is itself, Spirit.

Franco next says Spirit has a third and "more specific" meaning, namely, a "union of . . . universality and individuality, which is embodied in the ethical life of a people."[167] By this he seems to mean the combining of society's mores with personal moral opinions, as described in chapter 4's nineteenth microdialectic, "Duality." This idea abandons the earlier ideas that Spirit is self-conscious experience or, alternatively, human awareness of all sorts of things. The conflict among these three incompatible definitions of Spirit leaves us totally confused about what Franco thinks Spirit is. And it makes us ask: why arbitrarily choose a particular dialectic (the nineteenth microdialectic) and try to convert it into a definition of Spirit? We can also ask: when one person's moral opinions conflict with the moral consensus of society, how are the conflicting views combined to get Spirit? If I think abortion is moral but almost everyone else in my community (society) thinks it is immoral, where is this "union" of the "universal" (societal) ethics and my own "individual" (personal) ethical opinion? If everyone, including me, agrees to be tolerant and let each individual uphold his or her personal opinion about abortion, doesn't that set society's ethical consensus aside rather than bringing it into a "union" of universal (societal) and individual (personal) moral beliefs?

What is most significant, however, is that Franco is now, like Pinkard and Westphal, making Spirit a facet of society. Franco's final word on the subject is that "this unity of the particular [personal] will with the universal [societal] will in ethical life is 'spirit.'"[168] If that is what Franco thinks, his interpretation of Spirit faces most of the objections that I raised to the Pinkard and Westphal interpretations. Spirit existed in the unconscious state of nature before society and society's ethics came into existence, so Spirit cannot be society and cannot be derived from society's ethics. Again, the definition provides no clue as to how a combining of societal and personal ethics can be self-estranged. An ethical belief is not a self; it has no mind. Self-estrangement is meaningless in a context where there is no self, a self with a mind that can feel estranged or alienated from someone or something else. The same can be said of self-consciousness, self-awareness, and general awareness. How can a synthesis of universal and individual ethical beliefs be either self-conscious or conscious (aware) of anything else? Franco's final definition also ignores Hegel's repeated insistence that when a "subject" (person) views external "objects," including natural objects (nature), both subject and object are "itself," Spirit. Moreover, whereas Hegel clearly implies that Spirit includes nature, Franco says Spirit excludes nature. The plain truth is, Spirit is not whatever Franco thinks it is.

Chapter 7

SIDE ISSUES AND CONCLUSIONS

In this concluding chapter I will tie down three loose ends. First, what accounts for *Phenomenology*'s peculiar table-of-contents outline? More specifically, are several previous interpreters correct in theorizing that the headings AA (Reason), BB (Spirit), CC (Religion), and DD (Absolute Knowing) represent late amendments, and is Forster correct in theorizing that the amendments were designed to bring a triple perspective to history? Second, is Solomon correct in theorizing that Hegel's Beautiful Soul is Jesus? Third, how should we judge Hegel? Of what value are *Phenomenology* and *The Philosophy of History*?

FORSTER'S HYPOTHESIS OF LATE EXPANSION OF THE TEXT

Several interpreters have observed that *Phenomenology*'s weird table of contents displays confused organization. Forster attributes the confusion to a late change in plan that led Hegel to greatly expand the text from three main headings (A, B, and C) to six (A, B, C, [BB], [CC], and [DD], not counting [AA] because it duplicates C). Hegel's purpose, says Forster, was two-fold: (1) to provide a more complete introduction to his planned system, not just parts of it, and (2) to satisfy his growing interest in historical material, which he introduced in abundance in his added chapters. My own opinion is that Forster is right about the late change in plan but wrong about the reasons for it. The real reason for the change is that Hegel's mind shifted into high gear, coming up with all sorts of ideas for additional and more complicated (multilevel) dialectics beyond the originally planned ones.

Phenomenology's Table of Contents. Describing *Phenomenology*, Kaufmann comments that "some aspects of the conception are absurd, and some of the details are bizarre." He then adds that "the very table of contents of the *Phenomenology* may be said to mirror confusion."[1] After detailing some of this confusion, Kaufmann concludes, "The table of contents bears out that the work was not planned painstakingly before it was written, that parts V and VI (Reason and Spirit) grew beyond the bounds originally contemplated, and that Hegel himself was a little confused about what he had actually got when he was finished."[2] (As we shall see shortly, Forster disagrees that parts V and VI simply "grew"; he argues, and I agree, that they and part VII were added as afterthoughts.)

Solomon says this about *Phenomenology's* organization: "What is most striking about Hegel's *Phenomenology* is its structure, or apparent lack of it. Not only does it cover an enormous variety of topics. . . . It orders them in a peculiar, perhaps arbitrary way."[3] The table of contents inspires this remark: "The first point to make is obvious; the organization of this book is a mess." He then adds, "It is hard not to suspect from this, as several noted German scholars have argued in some detail, that Hegel changed his plan or got carried away with himself somewhere in the fifth chapter (on 'Reason') which presumably was to be the conclusion, . . . rather than the beginning of an entirely new set of sequences."[4]

Stern has similar observations. He says that "the haste in which the *Phenomenology* was written inevitably lends to the work an unconsidered and ungoverned quality (typified in confusions surrounding the title page, Preface, and table of contents)."[5] He later adds that "perhaps the greatest challenge to any reading of the *Phenomenology* is to show how it can be understood as a coherent and well-ordered work, and to fit its bewildering range of topics into a satisfactory and unified philosophical conception."[6]

The horribly disorganized structure of *Phenomenology's* table of contents can be seen in table 1, which omits Hegel's Preface and Introduction. Table 1 shows the first three levels of Hegel's outline and, under VI, the fourth level as well. Note the following problems:

Table 1

***Phenomenology*'s Table of Contents (Abbreviated)**

A. CONSCIOUSNESS

  I. SENSE-CERTAINTY: OR THE 'THIS' AND 'MEANING'

  II. PERCEPTION: OR THE THING AND DECEPTION

  III. FORCE AND THE UNDERSTANDING

B. SELF-CONSCIOUSNESS

  IV. THE TRUTH OF SELF-CERTAINTY

    A. Lordship and Bondage

    B. Stoicism, Scepticism, and the Unhappy Consciousness

C. (AA.) REASON

  V. THE CERTAINTY OF TRUTH AND REASON

    A. Observing Reason

    B. The Actualization of Rational Self-Consciousness

    C. Individuality Which Takes Itself to Be Real in and for Itself

(BB.) VI. SPIRIT

    A. The True Spirit: the Ethical Order

      a. The Ethical World

      b. Ethical Action

      c. Legal Status

    B. Self-Alienated Spirit: Culture

      I. The World of Self-Alienated Spirit

      II. The Enlightenment

      III. Absolute Freedom and Terror

    C. Spirit that is Certain of Itself: Morality

      a. The Moral View of the World

      b. Dissemblance or Duplicity

      c. Conscience: the 'Beautiful Soul,' Evil and its Forgiveness

(CC.) VII. RELIGION

    A. Natural Religion

    B. Religion in the Form of Art

    C. The Revealed Religion [Christianity]

(DD.) VIII. ABSOLUTE KNOWING

- The outline begins with A, B, and C as the primary-heading identifiers, associated with the large-type, all-caps main headings (CONSCIOUSNESS, SELF-CONSCIOUSNESS, REASON, SPIRIT, RELIGION, ABSOLUTE KNOWING). But for the last three main headings, the outline abruptly abandons the single capital letter identifiers.

- For heading C, REASON, the outline adds a duplicate main heading identifier, (AA), and the remaining three main headings—SPIRIT, RELIGION, and ABSOLUTE KNOWING—use this parenthetical two-letter system alone. In other words, half of the primary headings use A, B, and C; half of them use (BB), (CC), and (DD); and REASON uses both styles—C and (AA).

- Main heading A uses Roman numerals for the outline's second level, but starting with B the Roman numerals become, in effect, duplicate primary-heading identifiers—because the primary heading has no two-or-more-part breakdown at the Roman numeral level, and also because any genuine second-level Roman numerals would start with Roman numeral I for each new chapter or main heading.

- The ostensible third level of the outline uses A-B-C identifiers that duplicate the A-B-C style of the first three main-level identifiers—a naive practice when it comes to outlining and a source of confusion for the reader. (If the first-level A-B-C headings are retained, the third level should use Arabic numerals.)

- Carrying the duplicate-identifier problem to a ridiculous extreme, the REASON heading has *three* identifiers: C, (AA), and V. (V has expanded wording for the heading and is on a separate line, but it has the same content as C and (AA): V stands alone and thus does not represent a true subdivision of REASON. If it identified a subdivision, it would be subheading I and would be followed by at least subheading II.)

- As though the use of capital letters (A, B, C) for two different levels of the outline weren't stylistic duplication enough, Hegel repeats the use of Roman numerals at the ostensible fourth level under VI-B. (He should be using lowercase letters for the fourth level and lowercase Romans for the fifth.)

- The fourth-level identifiers use an inconsistent style: lowercase letters (a, b, c) in most instances but Roman numerals for heading VI-B.

- Lowercase letters represent the fourth level in most instances but represent the fifth level of the outline under heading VI-B. (Here space limitations don't permit showing the fifth level throughout table 1.)

Where style (contrasted with substance) is concerned, I doubt that there has ever been another so ungodly muddle of an outline in the entire history of scholarly books.

Forster's Analysis. For several reasons, Forster thinks Hegel's original plan for Phenomenology called for writing just the first three chapters: A. Consciousness, B. Self-Consciousness, and C. Reason. In support of this theory, he points out that two German authors, Haym and Haering (also cited by Solomon), reached the same conclusion. Haering, however, believes that Hegel originally intended to stop halfway through what became the Reason chapter.[7]

Forster adduces five reasons for his shift-in-plan hypothesis. I'll start with the fifth, because it is the most persuasive. As already noted, the first three chapters carry the identifiers A, B, and C; but the last three do not continue with D, E, and F. Instead, Hegel extends his Roman numeral series, begun under A (Consciousness) with I, II, and III, so that each chapter beyond the first has a Roman identifier. The result is that (*a*) each chapter beyond the first is given a single Roman numeral and (*b*) the second and third chapters—Self-Consciousness and Reason—have both a letter and a Roman numeral identifier. Forster is convinced, and I agree, that A, B, and C are the original system. This change-of-plan hypothesis, I should add, is rejected by Stewart, who believes that the Roman numeral headings are the original scheme and that both the A-B-C single-letter scheme and the (AA)-(BB)-(CC)-(DD) double-letter scheme were added when Hegel was reading the book's proofs.[8]

The lettering-numbering evidence that impresses me most—this is not mentioned by Forster—is that the first chapter, Consciousness, and only the first chapter, uses I, II, and III to label second-level headings. Without the A, Consciousness would have no first-level letter-or-number identifier to go with its title, Consciousness. Hegel would not have put a chapter without an outline identifier to go opposite its large-type heading in the table of contents. The A also serves a related purpose. As I explained in chapter 2, concepts hidden in chapter sections I, II, and III form the first of Hegel's four intermediate-level dialectics. In this particular dialectic the thesis (section I) is "universal," the antithesis (section II) is "particular," and the incipient synthesis (section III) is "universe composed of particulars"—Hegel's Spirit. Hegel approaches the synthesis but then, because he has decided not to reveal it yet, leaves it hidden "behind the so-called curtain." By "approaches the synthesis" I mean he repeatedly refers to an invisible entity, "force," which belongs to an invisible "supersensible world," a world beyond the senses. We know he is alluding to the presence of Spirit in every particular object in the universe; he just isn't ready to declare that Spirit is the supersensible force.

The extension of the Roman numeral series beyond the first chapter was introduced when Hegel later decided to write three more chapters. Why not label the later chapters D, E, and F? Forster's answer: "For some reason or other he felt a need to maintain a threefold division [the A, B, C chapters] (perhaps he had led his publisher to expect such a division, or perhaps his well-known liking for threefold divisions simply proved irresistible)."[9]

My own view is somewhat different. The titles of the last three chapters—Spirit, Religion, and Absolute Knowing—conceal the concepts used in the first of the three additional intermediate-level dialectics analyzed in my chapter 4. (The original intermediate dialectic is the I-II-III dialectic analyzed in chapter 2 under the "Part A: Consciousness" heading.) That first dialectic of the three additional intermediate ones is hidden in headings VI, VII, and VIII. Hegel wanted to separate these dialectical headings in his outline by placing them outside his A-B-C scheme. In doing so, he was creating a four-level hierarchy of dialectics with the macrodialectic at the top, two levels of intermediate dialectics below that, and the microdialectics as the fourth level.

Forster thinks Hegel "decided to effect a compromise with his original threefold [A, B, C] schema, by making *Reason* merely the first part of C instead of the whole of it, and accommodating *Spirit, Religion*, and *Absolute Knowing* as further parts [subheadings] of C."[10] But I disagree. The last three chapters are not intended as subheadings or "parts" of C. Hegel's real purpose in extending the series of Roman numeral headings was to provide an independent set of primary headings for his expanded outline while retaining the A-B-C headings for his original outline. Five considerations support my opinion:

1. An intent to create additional subheadings under Reason would require beginning a new I-II-III-IV Roman numeral series under C. Reason. The first member of a subdivision can't carry the numeral V or VI; it must begin a new series, starting with I.

2. Hegel's desire for a second, independent set of primary-heading identifiers explains why Roman headings IV (under B. Self-Consciousness) and V (under C. Reason) were added. They don't serve their ostensible purpose of identifying second-level subdivisions of B and C, because B and C have no Roman-numeral-level subdivisions. The purpose of IV and V is to independently number the second and third chapters. If the purpose of extending the Roman series were to make VI, VII, and VIII "further parts [subheadings] of C," why would Hegel add the meaningless IV under B?

3. If Spirit, Religion, and Absolute Knowing—the last three chapters— were intended to be subheadings under Reason, their headings would not use the same large type as the headings of the first three chapters, including the chapter titled Reason. Their type size and style clearly identify the last three chapters as main headings in the outline, not parts of Reason.

4. The last four chapters, beginning with Reason, have that duplicate set of primary heading identifiers: (AA), (BB), (CC), and (DD). If (BB) Spirit, (CC) Religion, and (DD) Absolute Knowing were intended as subheadings under (AA) Reason, they wouldn't use (AA)'s double-letter style for their outline identifiers.

5. Much of the material under Spirit and Religion doesn't agree with Hegel's concept of reason. For example, if the Unhappy Consciousness under primary heading B does not belong under Reason, why does "The Revealed Religion"—this covers much of the same ground, Christianity—belong under Reason? Reason is, in fact, the opposite of religion: Hegel sees nothing reasonable about religion, except where religious concepts can be used as the basis of antireligious analogies that redefine the concepts.

Let's backtrack now from the fifth reason to the first that Forster gives for his hypothesis. The hypothesis, once again, is that the originally planned work ended with the Reason chapter. Forster argues that *Phenomenology*'s Introduction suggests this: "The Introduction, the part of the work which was written first, characterizes the *Phenomenology* as an exposition just of a series of *shapes of consciousness*. . . . The Introduction knows nothing of any 'real Spirits' or 'shapes of a world' (the subject matter of the Spirit chapter)."[11] This reason has some validity, although it overstates the point. References to consciousness continue in the rest of the book. The later chapters are still about shapes of consciousness; the "shapes of a world" are simply particular types of shapes of consciousness. "World" is a reference to Spirit; Spirit is also called "world-Spirit,"[12] and the "shapes of a world" chapter is titled Spirit. Paragraphs 795–805 of the last chapter, "Absolute Knowing," has a protracted discussion of "shapes." This discussion includes four more specific references to "shapes of consciousness."[13] (These shapes are the theses, antitheses, and syntheses of the microdialectics; the shapes appear at "stations"—the dialectics—on "the path of the natural consciousness which presses forward to true knowledge."[14])

The next reason for Forster's change-of-plan hypothesis (reason 2 in Forster's sequence) again draws on the Introduction. The Introduction, written before Hegel decided to expand his book, "implies that the *Phenomenology* will contain just a single treatment of history, a history of the shapes of consciousness." But "the *Spirit* chapter contains a second treatment of history, dealing not with shapes of consciousness but with 'real Spirits' or 'shapes of a world,' and the chapters *Religion* and *Absolute Knowing* contain yet a third treatment of history, dealing not with shapes of consciousness but with 'shapes of religion.'"[15] The "second chronological history" deals with "social contexts" of consciousness; the "third chronological history" takes up "the conceptions of God."[16] I'll come back to this reason—it isn't valid—in a moment.

Two other pieces of evidence Forster presents in support of his theory cannot be summarized briefly and, in any case, are more conjectural. Readers interested in exploring this additional evidence should consult Forster's book.[17]

Forster next takes up the reasons Hegel had for adding the three additional chapters (VI, VII, and VIII). He thinks Hegel had two reasons. The first reason was to bring about correspondence between *Phenomenology* and related parts of the *Encyclopedia*:

> Hegel was of, or came to, the view that in order to be a satisfactory introduction to his system, the *Phenomenology* would have to give a provisional presentation of virtually *all contents* of the system. . . . But this required that it go beyond the originally planned chapters *Consciousness* through *Reason* dealing with the shapes of consciousness. For, although these chapters contained a sort of provisional presentation of the [1] Logic . . . , [2] the Philosophy of Nature . . . , and [3] one part of the Philosophy of Spirit . . . , they contained *no* provisional presentation of [4] other parts of the Philosophy of Spirit, in particular the parts dealing with [a] morality and ethical life . . . , and with [b] art, [c] religion, and [d] philosophy. . . . In order to make good this deficit Hegel had to add the remaining chapters of the *Phenomenology*.[18]

Hegel's second and "strongest" motive for adding the last three chapters, according to Forster, was a developing interest in history. While writing the originally planned first three chapters, "Hegel developed a strong *intrinsic*, as opposed to merely instrumental [needed for expository purposes], interest in the historical and historicist aspects of the account [of 'the chronological history of consciousness from ancient times up to his own age']. He saw the potential for developing these [aspects] into the sort of broader historical and historicist project which emerges with the addition of the new chapters."[19] This historicist motive ties in with one of Forster's reasons for believing the last three chapters were not part of Hegel's original plan. That reason, the third one presented above, was that Hegel wanted to present two more "treatments of history," one relating to Spirit—material "dealing with the social contexts"—and the other relating to religion.[20] Forster is arguing that both the material under Spirit and the material under Religion are arranged chronologically.

Flaws in the Chronology Argument. I have serious doubts about whether either of the two motives suggested by Forster, particularly the second, had much to do with Hegel's late-in-the-game decision to expand Phenomenology. That second motive, again, is that Hegel developed a stronger interest in history and decided to give history three chronological treatments instead of just the one originally planned—the history of "shapes of consciousness." This reason is weak. To begin with, that first "treatment of history," the "shapes of consciousness" treatment, is not organized chronologically and is therefore not a first treatment of history. In chapter 4, where history first appears, the discussion moves from (1) fable to (2) philosophy to (3) religion. That is not chronology. And under each of those three topics Hegel's material is organized dialectically—thesis first, antithesis second, synthesis third. As for chronology, under philosophy Hegel discusses Greco-Roman stoicism and skepticism. Then, as we move on to religion, we find Hegel retreating historically from Greece and Rome to ancient Judaism. In presenting the Unhappy Consciousness microdialectic in chapter 4, I showed how that dialectic advances from ancient Judaism (thesis) to Greek religion (antithesis) to medieval Christianity (synthesis). Here Hegel's subtopics go chronologically backward from stoicism and skepticism to early Jewish religion (bells and incense), then return to Greece (religious indifference), which has already been discussed in the philosophy context. That back-and-forth organization of material is definitely not chronological.

Chapter 5 continues the first alleged chronology. But the chapter's material has little to do with history. Its first microdialectic begins with natural laws (thesis) and psychological laws (antithesis), thoughts about which have no significant historical anchorage. The synthesis, phrenology and physiognomy, can be dated: Lavater's work on physiognomy was published in 1772, and Gall's work on phrenology has a 1796 date. But then we move on to *Faust*, which is not a historical episode. Hegel's treatment of Faust is based on Goethe's *Faust* fragment of 1790, but the *Faust* legend is much older and first appeared in a published version in 1587. We have moved backward from 1796 to 1790 and arguably to 1587. The rest of chapter 5's material—the law of the heart, the matter in hand, laws judged by reason and by tests—has no close historical ties and can't be dated. This isn't chronology. It is, for the most part, fables based on Hegel's observations and theories about human behavior. When, for example, Hegel writes about "the spiritual animal kingdom," he isn't talking about a time and place. Conclusion: the first "chronology" really isn't chronologically organized.

Forster argues that the Spirit and Religion chapters provide two more chronologies. The alleged new chronologies supposedly abandon the "shapes of consciousness" and replace it with chronologically organized "shapes of a world" and "shapes of religion" formats. But I disagree. Chapters 6 and 7 do add "shapes of a world" and "shapes of religion," but they continue to deal with "consciousness." Among the many references to consciousness in the Spirit chapter is this one: "Spirit is, in its simple truth, consciousness."[21] The first two paragraphs and various subsequent paragraphs of "The Revealed Religion" talk about consciousness. "Shapes of a world" and "shapes of religion" merely classify the "shapes of consciousness" into two broad subcategories. There is a loose chronological arrangement of material in each of the two chapters, but neither chapter amounts to a "treatment of history." What we really find is a *dialectical* arrangement of material (more on this point shortly).

I will concede that the material in the Spirit chapter is mostly—not entirely—chronological in its arrangement. Forster presents his interpretation of Hegel's "Spirit" chronology indirectly, but Hegel discusses his subtopics in the following order: (1) Greek morality, including that expressed in *Antigone*, (2) Rome, (3) Monarchy, (4) the Enlightenment, (5) the Reign of Terror, which came about fifty years after the Enlightenment began, (6) the moral ideas of the German philosophers Kant and Fichte, and (7) conscience. An immediate problem is that monarchy is older than the Greek and Roman topics Hegel discusses. For example, King Saul, the first king of Israel, was enthroned around 1047 BCE; *Antigone* was written around 442 BCE.

And if this is a chronological survey of the nonreligious aspects of human thought and social attitudes, why the big leap from even Roman imperial monarchy to the Enlightenment? What happened to the Renaissance thinkers? In particular, why does a review of ideas about morality avoid any mention of Machiavelli's *The Prince*, which recommends amoral empiricism as the road to successful governing? Beiser refers to Hegel's *Verfassungsschrift* essay (1799– 1800): "One of the most striking features of Hegel's tract is its outspoken defense of Machiavelli, who still had a terrible reputation in eighteenth-century Germany."[22] Emphasizing Machiavelli's importance to Hegel, Beiser remarks that "Hegel saw the force of Machiavelli's challenge: that moral principles cannot be applied to the political world because if people act according to them they destroy themselves."[23] It seems to me that if Hegel were at all concerned with providing a historical "treatment" of Spirit (chapter 6), and given his interest in Machiavelli, he would have found room for Machiavelli. I think Machiavelli was left out because Hegel couldn't come up with a Machiavelli dialectic. Also, inserting a discussion of Machiavelli would have crippled the VI-A, VI-B, VI-C (thesis, antithesis, synthesis) dialectic under VI Spirit.

Beyond the conspicuous Renaissance gap, the chronology particularly falters in the last two subtopics. The Reign of Terror took place in 1793–94, but Kant, whom Hegel discusses after discussing the Reign of Terror, did most of his writing before then. Kant's most important work, *Critique of Pure Reason*, was written in 1781, twelve years before the Reign of Terror began. As for the last item, conscience, Forster stretches his concept of chronology past the breaking point when he implies that human conscience didn't arrive until after Fichte, thereby completing history's trip "from ancient times up to the attainment of his [Hegel's] own standpoint in the modern age."[24] Surely Hegel couldn't have harbored the ethnocentric belief that conscience began with his generation of Germans and that societies preceding ancient Greece had no conscientious persons.

The fact is, the Spirit chapter's substance lies in primarily nonreligious ideas about morality and ethics—the realm of human thought or philosophy. Hegel is writing about these shapes of consciousness, not about history.

As for chapter 7, Religion, its material has a somewhat chronological arrangement at the natural-artificial level of the outline, although the Egyptian and Greek periods largely overlap. But under "Religion in the Form of Art," we encounter Homer. He dates back so far that historians aren't sure he was a real person. If he was real, he may have lived as early as 1000 BCE, which makes him older than most of the Greek statues covered in a preceding subsection on "The Abstract Work of Art." Meanwhile, if Hegel's intent in chapter 7 were to provide a chronological treatment of religion, how could he possibly have failed to cover Judaism, the religion from which Christianity (Hegel's main concern) evolved? Also, why did Hegel skip Islam, the most important post-Christian religious development?

Beyond these chronological flaws in Forster's "treatment of history" hypothesis as applied to the Religion chapter, we have this obvious fact: "The Revealed Religion," Christianity, had to be discussed last for nonhistorical reasons. Christianity is the first climax of a double climax Hegel has been building up to. (The second climax is Spirit's self-realization.) Christianity and the falseness of its theology is, in fact, the underlying theme of the entire book.[25] It *has* to come last in the Spirit chapter. The Christianity discussion is where Hegel declares in subtle language—too subtle for some interpreters—that man is God. This discussion is where Hegel reconceptualizes the Father, the Son, and the Holy Spirit. The Father is abstracted into divinity (and "artificial"); the Son is abstracted into humanity (and "natural"); and the Holy Spirit becomes Hegel's Spirit, which unites—combines—the divine and the human by declaring that the human *is* the divine (and that the artificial [God] = the natural [man]). As a concomitant of the Spirit's combining the divine and the human into one man-is-God entity, the Christianity discussion declares that the death on the cross of Jesus is the death not only of the incarnate God but of the "picture-thinking" (imaginary) Father in heaven too. And the resurrection becomes understood not as the resurrection of a unique human, Jesus, but as the *deification* of the entire human race. Surely Forster can't expect Hegel to retreat to discussions of Egyptian and Greek religion after his climactic discussion of Christianity! To repeat: climaxes come at the end.

Christianity is not just the substantive climax of the religion material. It is also the dialectical climax. It is the synthesis of the VII-A, VII-B, VII-C dialectic that proceeds from the thesis "natural" to the antithesis "artificial" to the synthesis "natural (man) = artificial (God)." The synthesis, "The Revealed Religion," has to come last—after natural religion (thesis) and artificial religion (antithesis). It has to come last not for reasons of chronology but because a synthesis must follow, not precede, the thesis and the antithesis.

I find myself in complete agreement with what Solomon says about Hegel's alleged historicism. "The *Phenomenology*," he writes, "is not a book about history, and its structure is not historical." He elaborates: "History does make its awaited appearance if rather late in the book (chapter 6 [*Spirit*]), but it, like everything else, consists of forms of consciousness which are not strictly historical and which are subjected to . . . conceptual demands."[26] Those conceptual demands, not described by Solomon, mainly entail (*a*) the need to put the climax, Christianity, at the end of the chapter and (*b*) the need to put the chapter's synthesis ("natural = artificial") after the thesis ("natural") and the antithesis ("artificial").

I also find myself basically in agreement with what Dudley says: "If the stages of the Spirit chapter of the *Phenomenology* are intended to parallel those of world history, and to provide a summary or provisional presentation of the corresponding sections of the *Encyclopedia*, then the fact that neither the parallel nor the correspondence is exact weakens the thesis. It is possible, as Forster suggests, that the thesis accurately characterizes intentions Hegel realized only imperfectly. But a more plausible explanation is that Hegel simply did not intend to organize the Spirit chapter chronologically."[27] (I disagree with the second quoted sentence but agree with the other two.)

Dialectical Motives. Beyond the extremely serious chronology problems of Forster's three-treatments-of-history hypothesis is an even more serious problem: dialectics. As I showed in chapter 4, and will discuss in more detail in a moment, Hegel's decision to create four outline levels of dialectics controls the organization of the last three chapters. The overarching macrodialectic is level one. The three primary headings of the "late expansion of text" material are (VI) Spirit (philosophy, human, many), (VII) Religion (theology, divine, one), and (VIII) Absolute Knowing (the synthesis: philosophical theology, human = divine, many = one). These headings form level two of the outline. Subheadings A, B, and C, found in both the Spirit chapter and the

Religion chapter, form level three. And at the outline's fourth level, Spirit offers seven microdialectics and Religion offers three more.

It seems clear to me that Hegel's real motive for expanding *Phenomenology* beyond its originally planned scope was dialectics, not history. Even the original plan was based on dialectics. The Absolute Knowing chapter, which has the macrodialectic's synthesis, was not supposed to be a separate chapter; Spirit's self-realization—the macrodialectic's synthesis—was to be the conclusion of the Reason chapter, chapter 5. This is why, early in chapter 5, Hegel anticipates Spirit's self-realization by writing, "Reason is the certainty of consciousness that it is all reality" and that "in the dialectical movement . . . otherness ['objects' perceived as persons or things *other* than the viewing 'subject'] . . . vanishes."[28] Repeat: otherness—separation—vanishes. The macrodialectic was thus to be completed at the end of chapter 5. Below the macrodialectic was the I-II-III dialectic (universal, particular, universe composed of particulars). Still within the scope of the original plan were the many smaller dialectics: the highly abstract and superficial one in the Preface (see chapter 2), the essence-existence dialectic in the Introduction (see chapter 2), and the first twelve of the twenty-two microdialectics (see chapter 4).

You can see that Hegel, even before inflating his book, was already enthralled by dialectics. Dialectics was his newfound "Science." He had picked up the thesis-antithesis-synthesis idea mostly from Fichte, who had refined the idea from the "theses" and "antitheses" of Kant. In the passage of *Phenomenology*'s Preface where Hegel praises dialectics, he first criticizes Kant for reducing the dialectical triad to "a lifeless schema." But in the next sentence he says that, since Kant, dialectics "has . . . been raised to its absolute significance" and has been given a "true form" in which "the Notion of Science has emerged."[29] Although, as I said in chapter 2, Hegel could be alluding to himself as the person who has raised dialectics to significance, thereby creating a science, Kaufmann believes Hegel is referring to Fichte. Dialectics, Kaufmann says, was "raised to 'absolute importance' ['absolute significance' in Miller's translation] by Fichte who made much of theses, antitheses, and syntheses."[30] It really doesn't matter whether Hegel is giving himself or Fichte credit for turning dialectics into a science. What does matter is that, as shown both by his praise of dialectics and by his heavy use of dialectics in the first three chapters, Hegel had become a dialectics enthusiast. Obviously impressed with the potentiality of dialectics, Hegel decided to expand his protest against Christianity into a dialectical revolution.

Hegel's passion for dialectics is nowhere better illustrated than in his phrenology dialectic. Why on earth would Hegel want to digress on phrenology while discussing the "shapes [thoughts] of consciousness"? Kaufmann observes that the first section of the third chapter "begins with over a hundred pages on theoretical reason" but "ends, rather oddly, with a discussion of phrenology."[31] He subsequently comments that Hegel "dwells at unnecessary length on irrelevancies."[32] And then he writes, "Hegel certainly did not manage to trace a necessary development from the unhappy consciousness to phrenology."[33] Solomon is likewise puzzled by the phrenology material. He says it "is universally recognized to be the oddest single section of the entire book."[34]

The reason—the only plausible reason—Hegel digressed far afield into phrenology was dialectics. Phrenology provided a splendid opportunity for another dialectic, one especially suited for Hegel's inner-outer dichotomy. Recall that "inner" refers to the inner "universality" or unity of Spirit, the *concept* that unites everything in the universe. "Inner" has as its antithesis "outer," which refers to the particularity of the antithesis stage. In the macrodialectic's antithesis, Spirit acquires a mind, which is "subject." "Subject" misconstrues particular external "objects" as things other than itself. (This is what Hegel means by "otherness.") But the inner essence of both is the concept of Spirit. The reason subject doesn't recognize its identity with objects is that subject sees only the visible or "outer" aspect of the objects. Phrenology mirrors the subject-object identity problem. In phrenology, one's inner tendencies or personality are supposedly mirrored in one's outer appearance, one's face. In Hegel's phrenology dialectic, the synthesis of inner and outer arrives when a person's inner tendency to murder and the facial characteristics that reveal that tendency are both revealed as Truth: the person actually murders someone. Voilà! Inner and outer are identical! Another dialectic! We see that, contrary to the belief that Hegel just wanted to get off his chest some ideas about phrenology, the dialectic was designed to reiterate a point: Absolute Spirit is a synthesis of inner (universality) and outer (particularity).

Chapter 7, Religion, is another example of Hegel's uncontrollable urge to cram more dialectics into his book. Solomon comments that this chapter looks superfluous: "The chapter on religion might seem well placed, but a quick examination of the sections that make it up and Hegel's introductory remarks on page 410 (and following) make it clear that this discussion too breaks the sequence of the book and introduces an apparently wholly extraneous discussion of the history of religion."[35] So why did Hegel write that chapter? Dialectics. Chapter 7's heading provides the antithesis of his new VI-VII-VIII intermediate dialectic, which moves from (VI) human reason to (VII) divine revelation to (VIII) divine reason, produced by the human God, man. Chapter 7's A-B-C subheadings develop a lower-level dialectic, the natural-artificial dialectic. And within A, B, and C are several new bottom-level dialectics.

As he worked on the first three chapters (A, B, and C) and created his early dialectics, Hegel apparently warmed up to his new tool, his "Science." He kept coming up with fresh ideas for dialectics, ideas he hadn't thought of when initially organizing his material. Maybe *Antigone* came to mind and he realized it could be transformed into a dialectic. While still thinking of Greek theater, he may have recognized that the actor who alternates between masked (divine) and unmasked (human) would make a nifty synthesis of the divine and the human. And somewhere along the way he realized he could introduce a higher order of dialectics by creating an extended outline having table-of-contents triads that formed dialectics. I believe the temptation to exploit dialectics to its fullest became irresistible. Hegel decided to add three more chapters—three because he needed that many to form the highest of his three new intermediate-level dialectics.

Now is the appropriate time to review the three new intermediate dialectics created by the addition of chapters 6, 7, and 8. At the beginning of this chapter (table 1), I presented in more detail Hegel's table-of-contents outline, part of which is reproduced in table 2.

Hegel's chapter 6, we saw, began with a statement about reason. Hegel had decided to continue his discussion of reason, begun in chapter 5. Reason is the tool of philosophy, revelation the tool of theology. So chapter 6 can be said to represent either philosophy or reason, both of which are the work of *humans*, who are *many*. Chapter 7, Religion, relates to theology and revelation, which is

Table 2

Hegel's Intermediate Dialectics

VI.   Spirit (human thought = Philosophy, reason, human, many)

        A.   The true Spirit: The Ethical Order (potential + union)

        B.   Self-Alienated Spirit: Culture (actual + separation)

        C.   Spirit that is certain of itself: Morality (actual + union)

VII.   Religion (God's thought = Theology, revelation, divine, one)

        A.   Natural Religion (Natural, alluding to man)

        B.   Religion in the form of art (Artificial, alluding to the man-made God)

        C.   The Revealed Religion (Natural = Artificial, or man = God)

VIII.   Absolute Knowing (revelation = reason, human = divine, many = one)

---

the word of the God, the divine, who (or which) is one. These concepts produce four variants of what is essentially one dialectic:

1. Thesis: philosophy (the thinking, ethics, and morality of humans)
   Antithesis: theology (the divinely conceived thoughts and morality of God)
   Synthesis: philosophical theology (rational theology emanating from man)

2. Thesis: reason (the product of humans)
   Antithesis: revelation (the product of the divine)
   Synthesis: Absolute Knowledge (human revelation from the true divinity, man)

3. Thesis: man (the source of human moral ideas)
   Antithesis: God (the source of divine moral ideas)
   Synthesis: man = God (the two sources are identical)

4. Thesis: many (humans)
   Antithesis: one (God)
   Synthesis: many = one (alternatively, one composed of many)

In the A-B-C dialectic under Spirit, (A) the "true" or essential Spirit is just one unified entity consisting of all the particulars of reality. It is a universal. But it does not yet recognize itself as such. The thesis is therefore "potential + union." (Refer to chapter 3 for details.) But (B) Spirit is "self-alienated," separated from itself. The antithesis is therefore actual + separation. Finally we get (C) "Spirit that is certain of itself," which means what the first sentence of chapter 6 says: "Reason is Spirit when its certainty of being all reality has been raised to *truth*" (my italics).[36] Note that the word "truth" is part of subheading A, "The true Spirit." We now have the synthesis: actual + union. This dialectic, we see, is identical to variation 2 of the macrodialectic explained in chapter 3. In summary form, the dialectic is

Thesis: potential + union
Antithesis: actual + separation
Synthesis: actual + union

In the A-B-C dialectic under Religion, we get that disguised dichotomy of (A) natural, the thesis, and (B) artificial, the antithesis. The disguise is the word "art." All art is man-made. And anything that is man-made rather than naturally occurring is artificial. The synthesis of natural and artificial is "the revealed religion," Christianity. ("Revealed religion" is ambiguous; it can also refer to Hegel's God = man "religion" in which the Holy Spirit is transfigured into Hegel's Absolute Spirit when man acquires Absolute Knowledge.) In Christianity, as viewed by Hegel, God is an artificial being, man-made, the product of human "picture-thinking." When God separates from himself and becomes incarnated as Jesus, we get a natural being: Jesus was a real, natural human being. The revealed religion's synthesis is the third member of the Trinity, the Holy Spirit. It unites God and Jesus—the artificial being and the natural being—when it settles on Jesus after Jesus is baptized. (After all, uniting God and man through spirit possession is the Holy Spirit's job, its raison d'être. Absent the Holy Spirit, people could not speak in tongues, disciples could not perform miracles, and virgins could not give birth.) In Hegel's philosophical theology, the Holy Spirit becomes just plain Spirit. It unites God and man through self-realization—through man's (Hegel's) realization that he and the divine (Spirit) are one. Man is God. In summary form, this dialectic is

> Thesis: natural (Jesus, the Son, a natural human being)
> Antithesis: artificial (God, the Father, an artificial being created by man)
> Synthesis: natural = artificial (the Holy Spirit unites Father and
>   Son in the Trinity)

Above the three new intermediate dialectics and spanning the entire length of the book, not just the three change-of-plan expansion chapters, is the macrodialectic:

> Thesis: unconscious + union
> Antithesis: conscious + separation
> Synthesis: conscious + union

And below the three new intermediate dialectics are ten more microdialectics, beyond the twelve presented in *Phenomenology*'s first three chapters. I won't review the ten new microdialectics here; they are in my chapter 4. Suffice it to say that *Phenomenology*'s last three chapters, the ones not in Hegel's original plan, add thirteen more dialectics. Three of these—the intermediate dialectics—introduce a new scheme: dialectics concealed in two lower levels of outline headings. These thirteen new dialectics are, in my opinion, the reason Hegel decided to add three more chapters to *Phenomenology*. Together with the overarching macrodialectic (the very top level), they provide a philosophical system with dialectics on four levels. That's what Hegel had in mind when he expanded his book.

SOLOMON'S BEAUTIFUL SOUL HYPOTHESIS

Microdialectic 19, Duality, has within it Hegel's remarks about the Beautiful Soul. This is a person of conscience who withholds moral judgment. Hegel says the Beautiful Soul "lacks the power to externalize itself" (i.e., to make its moral views known to outsiders); "it lives in dread of besmirching the splendour of its inner being [its conscience] by action," so "it flees from contact with the actual world, and persists in its self-willed impotence [inability] . . . to transform its thought into being [action]."[37] Stern's interpretation of these words is helpful: "The individual comes to see that the best way to secure his reputation for integrity in the eyes of others is to refrain from acting, as action might lead to a misinterpretation of his motives."[38]

One theory, so unconvincing as to be preposterous, is that the Beautiful Soul is Jesus. Solomon develops this theory.[39] After quoting Hegel's words about avoiding action and "flees from contact with the actual world," Solomon says this: "The beautiful soul abstains from moral judgment, places itself *above* such judgment, and ultimately amounts to a condemnation of moral concerns."[40] Jesus supposedly fits the description of the Beautiful Soul because Jesus allegedly (1) abstains from pressing his moral views on others, (2) refuses to judge others, and (3) refrains from taking action to advance his moral views. But I find that Jesus fails to display any of these three characteristics. He (1) advocates a host of moral rules, both his own and the Old Testament law, (2) is extremely judgmental, going so far as to endorse torture by fire of rule violators, and (3) takes violent action against those who offend his sense of morality.

Pressing Moral Views on Others. Apparently noting Hegel's statement that the Beautiful Soul "lacks the power to externalize itself,"[41] Solomon says that "many of Jesus' teachings were not moral exhortations but meta-moral preachings, attitudes to be taken toward moral laws and transgressions of laws rather than laws themselves."[42] I assume that "meta-moral preachings" means vacuous abstractions like "be good," "love thy neighbor," and "do unto others as you would have them do unto you." In other words, nothing specific. But I find in Jesus's preaching an abundance of very specific, concrete moral exhortations. Jesus inveighs against saying "you fool" (Mt. 5:21), divorce (Mk. 10:2–9), marrying a divorced woman (Mt. 5:32), accumulating material goods and riches (Mt. 6:19, 19:24), fornication (Mk. 7:21), theft (Mk. 7:21), murder (Mk. 7:21), adultery (Mk. 7:21), coveting (Mk. 7:21), slander (Mk. 7:21), and buying and selling in the Temple, in whose outer courtyards sacrificial lambs, oxen, and pigeons were sold—with priestly authorization—during Passover (Jn. 2:13–16; Mt. 20:12; Mk. 11:15–17).

Moreover, Jesus preached that the apocalypse—the horrifying, tumultuous end of earthly kingdoms and their replacement by God's kingdom on earth—was "at hand" (Mk. 1:14–15, 13:8, 24–27; Mt. 4:17, 24:7–8, 29–31; Lk. 17:29–30, 21:10–12, 25–26). Jesus believed God was about to descend from heaven to earth to rule in place of soon-to-be-deposed earthly kings. In this eschatological context, Jesus said, "Not an iota, not a dot, will pass from the law until all [the new kingdom of God] is accomplished." The "law" is Judaism's Old Testament religious law. It includes all sorts of prohibitions.

Among the Old Testament laws thus endorsed by Jesus are those calling for the death, typically by stoning, of (a) anyone who tries to convert a Jew to the worship of a god other than Yahweh (Deut. 13:1–5), (b) any child who curses or disobeys his father or mother (Ex. 21:17; Lev. 20:9), (c) any bride who is not a virgin (Deut. 22:13–21), (d) every witch and wizard (Ex. 22:18; Lev. 20:27, Deut. 18:10), and (e) anyone guilty of sodomy with animals (Ex. 22:19). Among numerous other Old Testament laws are those forbidding (f) making images or castings of other gods (Ex. 20:4–5, 23), (g) taking the Lord's name in vain (Ex. 20:7), (h) working on the Sabbath (Ex. 20:10), (i) killing (Ex. 21:14), (j) committing adultery (Ex. 20:14), (k) stealing (Ex. 20:15), (l) bearing false witness (Ex. 20:16), (m) eating hares and pigs (Lev. 11:4–8), (n) having homosexual intercourse (Lev. 18:22), (o) crossing two breeds of cattle (Lev. 19:19), (p) wearing garments made of two different materials (Lev. 19:19), (q) trimming beards (Lev. 19:27), (r) having tattoos (Lev. 19:28), (s) the wearing of male garments by women (Deut. 22:5), (t) a bastard's entering the house of the Lord (Deut. 23:2), (u) charging interest on loans to persons other than foreigners (Deut. 23:19–20), (v) carrying off a neighbor's grapes (Deut. 23:24), and (w) a wife's grabbing the testicles of a man who is beating her husband (Deut. 25:11–12). Solomon seems to have overlooked Jesus's endorsement of these laws. The laws are not mere "meta-moral preachings." They are clear and specific.

Jesus did not hide his moral views behind ambiguities, abstractions, and (to use Solomon's word) general "attitudes."

Judging People. Citing Jesus's "judge not that ye be not judged," Solomon argues that these words put Jesus in agreement with the fact that "the beautiful soul abstains from moral judgment."[43] But by "judge not" Jesus simply meant judging was a privilege he was reserving for himself. Jesus, like some other prophets of his time, was convinced that he was the Christ, or Messiah. What apparently convinced him was a mystical vision—a trancelike state of religious euphoria psychologists call "religious ecstasy"—that he experienced on the Mount of Transfiguration (Mt. 17:1–10; Mk. 9:2–9; Lk. 9. 28–36). Maurice Goguel, author of the definitive "life of Jesus," believes that Jesus's self-perception evolved from "a sense of a simple prophetic vocation" (proclaiming that the kingdom of God was "at hand") to "Messianic consciousness" when he began to suffer persecution and rejection during his ministry: "Jesus did not believe that he was the Messiah although he had to suffer; he believed that he was the Messiah because he had to suffer."[44] At one point, Jesus thus lamented, "Foxes have holes, and birds of the air have nests; but the Son of Man has nowhere to lay his head" (Lk. 9:58). Jesus's messianic delusions were responsible for his decision to enter Jerusalem riding an ass, an act that some Jews expected of the long-awaited Messiah (Mt. 21:1–7); the belief rested on a supposed prophecy in Zechariah 9:9. On several other occasions, Jesus directly acknowledged that he was the Christ (Mt. 16:13–20, 24:3–5; Mk. 13:8, 14:61–62; Lk. 9:18–22).

As the Messiah, whom he called the Son of man, Jesus expected that he, not God, would be the judge on Judgment Day, the climax of the apocalypse. He said that, when he returned on Judgment Day, he would personally judge both the living and the resurrected dead ("the quick and the dead" of the Apostles' Creed). He promised to separate the "sheep" from the "goats" and send to "the eternal fire"—unending torture—those people, the "goats," who did not follow his rules (Mt. 25:31–46). Underscoring his messianic consciousness by saying "I," Jesus elaborated: "On that day . . . will I declare to them, 'I never knew you; depart from me, you evildoers'" (Mt. 7:22–23). Jesus's proclivity to judge was so strong that he intended to relegate most of mankind to hell, everlasting torture by fire: "Enter through the narrow gate; for the gate is wide . . . that leads to destruction. . . . For many are called, but *few are chosen*" (Mt. 7:13, 22:14;

Lk. 13:23–24). None of this squares with Solomon's assertion that Jesus, as the Beautiful Soul, placed himself *"above* all such judgment."

And let us not overlook the cruel, inconsiderate, self-centered, vainglorious demands Jesus placed on his followers. One man who wished to join Jesus asked permission to first bury his father. Jesus's caustic, I-am-the-Messiah, me-before-your-father reply was: "Leave the dead to bury their own dead" (Lk. 9:59–60). Here the figuratively dead people Jesus says should do the burying are those who don't follow Jesus and who, for that reason, will be condemned by Jesus to hell on Judgment Day. That's why Jesus calls them "dead." Jesus is saying that those who don't follow him, or who even pause to meet family obligations, are condemned to hell! "Abstains from moral judgment"? Hardly.

That incident was not just an aberration in Jesus's behavior. Another man declared himself a willing follower of Jesus but then requested, "but let me first say farewell to those at my home." Jesus selfishly replied, "No one who puts his hand to the plow and looks back is fit for the kingdom of God" (Lk. 9:61–62). Translation: "If you pause to say good-bye to your family, I'll throw you into the eternal fire on Judgment Day." How much more judgmental can you get? Jesus's attitude was neither nonjudgmental nor forgiving; even less was it humane.

This messianic, ego-based propensity to judge was also expressed in favorable judgments extended to those who abandoned their parents or children to follow Jesus: "And everyone who has left . . . father or mother or children or lands, for my name's sake, will receive a hundredfold, and inherit eternal life" (Mt. 19:27–29; Mk. 10:28–31). Again, Jesus was judging.

Is it possible that Hegel was ignorant of this egocentric behavior, viewing instead an idealized picture of Jesus? It isn't. Hegel quotes the very passages I have quoted: "To a youth who wishes to delay the duties of discipleship till he has buried his father, Christ says: 'Let the dead bury their dead—follow thou me.' 'He that loveth father or mother more than me is not worthy of me.' . . . We may say that nowhere are to be found such revolutionary utterances as in the Gospels; for everything that has been respected, is treated as a matter of indifference—as worthy of no regard."[45] Jesus was judging. He was judging people as being worthy of either the kingdom of God or the eternal fire according to whether they did or didn't place Jesus above "everything that has been respected."

Ethics by Example. Solomon also says Jesus fits the model of "a beautiful soul' who teaches ethics by example"—by displaying good behavior.[46] But consider how Jesus taught "don't say 'you fool,'" "judge not," and "turn the other cheek" by example. Jesus did the following:

- judged the pharisees and scribes by calling them "fools," "vipers," and "serpents" (Mt. 23:17, 33),

- using a whip made of cords, and presumably backed by a somewhat riotous group of followers, drove from the Temple the sellers, their customers, and the animals being sold for ritualized Passover sacrifice (Jn. 2:15; Mk. 11:15–17; Lk. 19:45),

- overturned the tables of the money changers and the seats of the pigeon sellers (Jn. 2:13–15; Mt. 21:12; Mk. 11:15–17), and

- scattered the coins of the money changers (Jn. 2:15).

Here we have a highly judgmental man who swears at, behaves violently toward, and interferes with the Passover-sacrifice activities of people whose behavior he thinks is immoral. Is this "don't say 'you fool'"? Is this "do unto others as you would have them do unto you"? Is this "judge not"? Is this the Beautiful Soul? Do these actions agree with Solomon's statement that Jesus, as the Beautiful Soul, "refrains from action and moral judgment"? I think not.

It is this sort of megalomaniacal judgmentalism—Jesus's delusions of grandeur—and related arrogant behavior that led Albert Schweitzer to conclude, "There is nothing more negative than the result of the critical study of the Life of Jesus."[47] Schweitzer continued: "We must be prepared to find that the historical knowledge of the personality and life of Jesus will not be a help, but perhaps even an offence to religion."[48] In the same vein, Tillich said of Jesus: "Error is evident in his ancient conception of the universe [a flat earth; heaven in the sky above; hell below; the stars as small, nearby objects that would fall to earth during the apocalypse; the moon as an independent source of light; demons populating the earth and causing disease and insanity], *his judgments about men*, his interpretation of the historical moment [Mt. 16:28, 24:34], his eschatological imagination ['the Son of man coming on the clouds of heaven' (Mt. 24:30)]."[49]

Solomon's Jesus-was-Hegel's-Beautiful-Soul thesis does not pass muster. It doesn't even come close. Hegel was a seminary graduate and was thoroughly familiar with the New Testament gospels. He was not ignorant of or unimpressed by the details of Jesus's life, teachings, and behavior. Kaufmann remarks that Hegel, in his early religious writings, "considers Jesus by no means the most admirable teacher of virtue but inferior to Socrates and really rather unattractive," made more so by his "swaggering self-importance."[50]

What is more likely, however, is that the Beautiful Soul was simply an exaggerated hypothetical construct designed to reveal a weakness in philosophy's Romantic movement ideas. For a detailed discussion of the relationship between Romanticism and the Beautiful Soul, I recommend Pinkard's analysis.[51] My own view is that Hegel was criticizing people who have moral or ethical viewpoints but are unwilling to speak up in appropriate circumstances. This is not to say he was endorsing aggressive moralizing, proselytizing, or interfering with others who have different moral persuasions; it simply means than Hegel regarded as "a lost soul" anyone who was afraid to stand up for what he or she thinks is right.[52] At the same time, he was using the Beautiful Soul to bring the thesis stage of his Duality dialectic to its conclusion and to show why the antithesis, morality, needs to enter the scene. In this respect, the Beautiful Soul is just another example of Hegel's general procedure of finding problems with a micro-dialectic's thesis, problems that justify introducing the antithesis.

APPRAISING HEGEL'S THOUGHT

At this point in a work about Hegel's thought, if not earlier in a preface, it is customary to politely find something of value in that thought before launching into criticism. But I find it impossible to identify anything commendable in Hegel's thought. Not only is it outdated, even in its time it was without intellectual value. This conclusion applies to both *Phenomenology* and *The Philosophy of History*. I will discuss these two works separately. It is nonetheless conceivable that Hegel can be credited with having favorably influenced other thinkers, so I'll conclude my appraisal by tackling that issue.

Phenomenology of Spirit. Any appraisal of Hegel's philosophy must begin with an understanding of what its centerpiece, *Phenomenology of Spirit*, is. To begin with, it is a book Hegel felt compelled to write in order to advance his academic career. His friend and colleague, Schelling, had already written several books and, through them, had established a favorable academic reputation. Hegel needed to do the same. In his biography of Hegel, Pinkard describes Hegel's predicament in detail. At the University of Jena, as an unsalaried Privatdozent and subsisting on an evaporating inheritance, "Hegel was desperate for a position, and to get a position, he needed a book."[53]

But what to write about? Hegel, in his early writings, had always been concerned about religion, the Christian religion. More particularly, he had been concerned with criticizing Christianity, and his criticism had expressed his contempt for Christian supernaturalism. But he was embarking on a career as a philosopher, so he needed to write about philosophy. How could he combine his deep-seated negative interest in theology, and his desire to refute theology, with his need to write about—and his genuine interest in—philosophy? Hegel's solution was to write a philosophical theology, a synthesis of philosophy and theology.

As Solomon observes, "the ideal of a philosophical system was a pervasive demand among the post-Kantian philosophers."[54] Reinhold thus attempted to systematize Kant's philosophy, and Fichte regarded his own philosophy as a system based on Kant's philosophy. Obeying the then-current fad, Hegel decided that his philosophical theology would be systematic. The adjective "systematic," when applied to philosophy or theology, has no precise meaning but implies a well-defined methodology under which material is developed and presented with sufficient care that all assertions and conclusions are consistent. In a classification system, for example, categories should not overlap, and coverage should not have gaps. Tillich's definition of "systematic" is as good as any: "It is the function of the systematic form to guarantee the consistency of cognitive assertions in all realms of [the system's] methodological knowledge."[55] In Tillich's case, internal consistency of assertions was obtained by making all claims consistent with what Tillich called "the norm of systematic theology," namely, "Jesus as the Christ."[56] Jesus as the Christ is the incarnate God of mythology, contrasted with the real historical Jesus. The Christ was "fully God and fully man," a theological doctrine Tillich secretly but rationally reinterpreted to mean "God is humanity." Tillich made all his claims—essentially humanistic redefinitions of Christian concepts—consistent with his hidden criterion: God is man. For example, his covert redefinition of salvation (union with God) is becoming a humanist, a definition consistent with the idea that humanity is God. Tillich further systematized his theology, really a pseudotheology, by adopting Hegel's dialectics. Tillich's system also employed a device he called "the method of correlation," which I explain later in this chapter.

Hegel's system, the methodology Hegel uses to unite philosophy and theology, is pretty much the same as Tillich's. This is not surprising, given that Tillich's philosophical theology is based on Hegel's philosophical theology. Hegel's implicit "norm" amounts to Tillich's "God is man," except that, in Hegel's case, man is just the most important part of "God," or Spirit, which is the entire universe. Thesis-antithesis-synthesis dialectics, Tillich's second methodological tool, is also a tool of Hegel. And in Hegel's system, dialectics is really the more important tool. Since Hegel is synthesizing two disciplines, a system based on the concept of synthesis is a logical choice. Hegel's system has four features, not counting the obscurantist language used to conceal Hegel's atheism. The features:

1. Dialectical organization of the material.

2. Correlation of the theological concept of God with the philosophical concept of a metaphysical absolute.

3. Correlation of the theological concept of the Trinity with the philosophical concept of dialectics: Father, Son, Holy Spirit = thesis, antithesis, synthesis.

4. Correlation of God's Johannine "life" with Spirit's dialectical "life," the macrodialectic.

I discussed the first feature, dialectical organization of the material, earlier in this chapter under the "Dialectical Motives" subheading of my discussion of Forster's late-expansion-of-text hypothesis. To review briefly, Hegel's macrodialectic provides the first level of his outline. Two second-level intermediate dialectics cover most of the second level. The first intermediate dialectic is the part A "Consciousness" dialectic: "Sense-Certainty" (universality, the thesis), "Perception" (particularity, the antithesis), and "Force" (universe composed of particulars, the synthesis). The second intermediate dialectic is the highest late-expansion-of-text dialectic: VI. "Spirit" (philosophy or reason, the thesis), VII. "Religion" (theology or revelation, the antithesis), and VIII. "Absolute Knowledge" (philosophical theology or rational, man-made "revelation," the synthesis). The outline's third level, which applies only to the late-expansion-of-text material, is the A-B-C subheadings under both "Spirit" and "Religion." Under "Spirit," the subdialectic is potential union, the thesis; actual separation, the antithesis; and actual union, the synthesis. Under "Religion," the subdialectic is "natural" (Jesus as human, or "fully man"), the thesis; "artificial" (Jesus as God incarnate, or "fully God,"), the antithesis; and "natural = artificial" (man = God), the synthesis.

The second feature of Hegel's system is the correlation of theology's God with philosophy's "absolute." To be theology as well as philosophy, a philosophical theology needs a God. But the "divine" must be philosophical, a figurative God rather than a literal God. Hegel creates a philosophical God by correlating theology's concept of God with philosophy's concept of an absolute, a metaphysical something or other regarded as a highest reality under which everything else in the system is subsumed. To provide the necessary absolute, the philosophical analog of God, Hegel invents the absolute he calls Spirit. And to ensure that the correlation of theology's God with philosophy's absolute won't be missed by careful readers, he arranges for Spirit to graduate to the status of "*Absolute* Spirit" when Spirit achieves "*Absolute* Knowledge." Absolute Knowledge is nothing more than Spirit's eventual recognition that it is all reality, that all the external objects it sees (via a human mind, Hegel's) are essentially itself, Spirit. Everything that participates in reality is subsumed under Spirit.

Technically speaking, a philosophical absolute should be metaphysical, hence supernatural. Hegel's Spirit falls short by this criterion. But Hegel takes pains to mislead people into thinking it *is* supernatural, and maybe even theistic, by referring to Spirit as "God" and "He" and "His": "He [God] is immediately present as Spirit, . . . for He is Spirit,"[57] and Spirit is "the Spirit who dwells in His community."[58] So convincing is Hegel's pretend metaphysics that Pippin (who wasn't the least bit fooled) was able to write these perceptive remarks: "For many, Hegel is a speculative metaphysician and a failure, either an interesting failure . . . or simply a dismal failure. . . . For others, he is a speculative metaphysician of great note."[59] We thus have the fifteen interpreters from chapter 6 who consider Hegel a panentheist or pantheist, plus a sixteenth, S. Rosen, who offers a "fuzzy" interpretation that treats Hegel as a metaphysical ontologist and in one passage seems to imply panentheism.

The third feature of Hegel's system is the correlation of the theological concept of the Trinity with the philosophical concept of dialectics. Hegel correlates the three members of theology's Trinity—Father, Son, and Holy Spirit—with philosophy's thesis, antithesis, and synthesis. Father becomes the thesis, Son the antithesis, and Holy Spirit the synthesis. This threefold correlation is in turn based on theology's two separation-and-return myths—the Johannine incarnation myth and the Adam and Eve myth. Primarily, Hegel uses the Johannine myth. In it, God—the Father—starts out as one unified entity; the Father represents *union*. Then the God separates from himself, becoming two: the Father in heaven and the Son, God incarnate, on earth. The Son represents *separation*, God separated from himself. The third stage materializes when the Son is baptized and the Holy Spirit possesses him, uniting Father and Son through spirit possession; the Holy Spirit represents *reunion*, God reunited *with himself*.

In the parallel Adam and Eve myth, stage 1 finds Adam and Eve happily *united* with God in the Garden of Eden. Stage 2 has Adam and Eve *separated* from God—cast out of Eden for committing the original sin, eating the forbidden fruit from the tree of knowledge. Stage 3 arises when Jesus, through his sacrificial death on the cross, atones for the sins of mankind and thereby permits Adam and Eve (and all other minor-league sinners) to be *reunited* with God, not in Eden (on earth) but in heaven.

The fourth feature of Hegel's system, correlation of God's Johannine "life" with Spirit's dialectical "life," is intertwined with the third. Hegel reenacts the two separation-and-return stories with his macrodialectic. The macrodialectic depicts the "divine life" of Spirit, just as the Johannine myth depicts the divine life of God. The macrodialectic's three stages, once again, are (1) unconscious + *union*, the thesis, (2) conscious + *separation*, the antithesis, and (3) conscious + *union*, the synthesis. Spirit separates from and returns to union, the state of being unified, which is also the state of universality. The thesis, we can see, is the analog of the Johannine myth's Father stage, the state of union, or one unified God; the antithesis is the analog of the myth's Son stage, separation, or God separated *from himself*; and the synthesis is the analog of the myth's Holy Spirit stage, God reunited *with himself*.

In the macrodialectic, Spirit, as the reconstituted divinity, does the same thing God does in Christianity's Johannine myth. Spirit, when it achieves consciousness (that is, when man arrives on earth), first separates *from itself* by using human minds (collectively its own Mind) to perceive external "objects" that it misinterprets as "alien"—things other than itself. In Hegel's own words, "The object is revealed to it [Spirit] . . . and it does not recognize itself."[60] After proceeding through many intermediate dialectics and microdialectics and thereby becoming educated in the ways of dialectics,[61] Spirit, a slow learner, finally gets the point. It achieves self-realization or Absolute Knowledge, thereby becoming Absolute Spirit, by figuring out that the external "objects" it ("subject") sees are essentially *itself*. The explanation: everything in the universe has the *concept* of Spirit as its hidden inner essence. All objects, including all humans, are parts of all reality. The many are really one, Spirit.

Hegel uses his philosophical theology to formalize his original intellectual concern, attacking religion. Where Catholicism is concerned, Hegel attacks openly. He does this in his Unhappy Consciousness discussion. The attack isn't entirely limited to medieval Catholicism: Hegel's negative remarks about confession and absolution (priestly "mediation"), fasting, tithing, Latin services, and surrendering "its [consciousness's] right to decide for itself" also apply to the post-medieval Catholicism of his day. But where theology's fundamental belief in God is concerned, prudence forces Hegel to be subtle. God, after all, is a Protestant belief too. Hegel attacks God in his "Revealed Religion" discussion by guardedly declaring that (*a*) Jesus was not uniquely divine, not the *one* incarnate God of the Gospel of John, because *all* men are divine, (*b*) God is dead—the *supernatural* God of Christianity is dead—and (*c*) the true God is mankind.

Is there any value in this philosophical theology? In any such enterprise, the cards are stacked against the author. Theology, because it affirms and glorifies supernaturalism, which is always false no matter what its form, is an unpromising foundation on which to erect a system. Philosophy has the same weakness to an only slightly lesser degree. Much if not most pre-nineteenth-century philosophy revolves around such supernaturalistic concepts as the Logos, other metaphysical absolutes, natural law, and the divine right of kings. Aristotelian logic; ethics; and the empiricism of Machiavelli, Bacon, Locke, and Hume are the chief exceptions. Hegel avoids incorporating in *Phenomenology* any of these exceptions. Dialectics is not logical by any stretch of the imagination. Ethics? In discussing *Antigone*, as I have already observed, Hegel conspicuously avoids taking an ethical stand where he has good reason to. And, as noted in my criticism of Forster's three-chronologies theory, Hegel ignores Machiavelli despite the existence of a wide historical gap that Machiavelli could help fill. Hegel, in other words, was stuck with philosophy's supernaturalistic models. He did manage to dodge the supernaturalism missile by making his supernaturalism and his metaphysics (a form of supernaturalism) figurative. But by turning to metaphor, Hegel became mired in a different problem: fiction.

The simple truth is, *Phenomenology* is a piece of fiction. It isn't true. It isn't even true to life, or realistic. The whole thing is simply a product of Hegel's imagination. It is *deliberate* fiction masquerading as philosophical insight, "knowledge," and "truth." Apart from the overt criticism of religion in the Unhappy Consciousness material and the covert atheism of "The Revealed Religion" material with its ambiguous, pre-Nietzsche "God is Dead" remark,[62] the whole book is pure hokum. It's a gigantic put-on. And Hegel knows this. He knows Spirit doesn't exist and that God doesn't exist. He knows Spirit is just a creature he made up. He knows he is seeking to deceive an audience that is inclined to mistake obscurity, esoterica, and pseudometaphysics for profundity.[63] He invented Spirit because he needed something to write a book about. Spirit is just a philosophical construct Hegel created for the purpose of writing a book, a book about the three-stage life of a fictitious character named Spirit. For the same purpose Hegel further refined Fichte's previous refinement of dialectics. Just as Spirit is not a real entity, dialectics is not a real natural process of any sort; it is just a method of exposition—exposition of fiction.

Because it is fiction and is therefore untrue, *Phenomenology* cannot and does not contribute to man's knowledge. On the contrary, because some people take it seriously and believe it contains insights about reality, *Phenomenology* has undermined human knowledge. This is particularly true where the tendency of even some modern philosophers to entertain metaphysical and theological beliefs is concerned: knowledge of reality has been undermined by Hegel's ostensible endorsement of metaphysics and theological supernaturalism.

I'm not denying that fiction can have artistic or entertainment value or that it can be a useful vehicle for attacking baneful institutions (George Orwell's *Animal Farm*), presenting social philosophies (Harper Lee's *To Kill a Mockingbird*), or attacking religious superstition (Philip Pullman's allegorical *His Dark Materials* trilogy). But these purposes certainly don't apply to *Phenomenology*. Yes, Hegel is attacking the institution of Christianity, and he is presenting the hidden message that God is dead. But the language encrypting these tendentious elements of *Phenomenology* is far too hard to decipher for the limited serious content of Hegel's book to be of significant value. And, whereas we normally expect opinions embedded in fiction to be supported by *readable* and maybe even entertaining prose, *Phenomenology* exhibits what Pippin calls "the ugliest prose style in the history of the German language."[64]

Does anything in *Phenomenology* deserve credit? I could, I suppose, give Hegel credit for rejecting the supernatural and seeing how fatuous Christian superstition is. Even in today's world, where belief is much less commonplace (especially in Europe) than in Hegel's pre-Darwin world, not only ordinary persons but some highly intelligent ones continue to accept primitive Christian beliefs. These beliefs include belief in not only a concerned, benevolent God but in the prudence of kneeling and otherwise humbling one's self before God, God's egotistical craving for praise and veneration, the Holy Spirit, Satan, angels, demons, saints, heaven, hell, purgatory, limbo, miracles, exorcism, the power of prayer, divine creation, Adam and Eve, original sin and the inherent sinfulness of man, Mary's Immaculate Conception (her being born free from original sin), the bodily Assumption of Mary unto heaven, the Virgin Birth, the Incarnation, the Atonement, the Resurrection (of Jesus), the Second Coming of Jesus, the future resurrection of the dead on Judgment Day, divine law, sin as a violation of divine law, ritualized penance and absolution, baptism, the Bible's being the Word of God, God's having transformed Lot's wife into a pillar of salt, the Great Flood, ridiculous dress codes and vehicle codes, possession by the Holy Spirit, and other foolishness no intelligent person ought to accept. Hegel didn't believe these things. But unbelief was not rare among intellectuals, and much less was it original, even in Hegel's day. His antireligious ideas weren't seminal. So why compliment Hegel for rejecting superstitions that some other intelligent and sometimes famous men of his time and earlier—Spinoza, Bayle, Woolston, Tindal, Diderot, Voltaire, Hume, and Jefferson, for example—also rejected? Given that Hegel spoke freely of God, implying belief, and that he even claimed to be a Lutheran, I could just as well criticize him for hypocrisy. But I'll withhold that criticism, because I realize the man needed to keep his job.

Did Hegel produce any original and valid insights? The only elements of Hegel's thought that even approach originality are the concept of Spirit and the Hegelian dialectics. Let's take another look at Spirit. If Hegel's Spirit really exists, or ever did exist, it would definitely qualify as an original and valid insight. But it doesn't exist. It never did. It couldn't exist. Spirit "exists" only as a definition. Hegel defined Spirit (without telling us) as a physical-mental entity in which the physical side and the mental side each had two aspects, one universal (general) and the other particular. The physical side's universal aspect is our physical universe, all reality. The particular aspect is all the things, both natural and artificial, that constitute the universe. The mental side's universal aspect, or Mind (uppercase), is the collective Mind of all human beings—all human minds combined, including their thoughts. The mental side's particular aspect is particular human minds and their thoughts.

This four-part concept, Spirit, isn't anything that exists. Even less is it a metaphysical reality, an immanent God. It is only a mental construct that serves as a definition of Spirit. (The universe and its parts do exist, but Spirit is further defined as a partly mental entity with a divine life of separation and return.) Because Spirit is just an arbitrary, contrary-to-customary-usage redefinition of a word, God, that Hegel is redefining, Spirit is neither true nor false. To call Spirit an insight is like calling Bishop Robinson's redefinition of God as Love an insight, whereas "God is Love" is merely an eccentric definition. So Hegel's idea of Spirit does not qualify as an insight, a discovery, or even a hypothesis. Hegel has so far added nothing to human knowledge.

I should add that the core concept of Hegel's redefinition of God isn't even original. That concept is the idea that man is divine, or part of God, or partly Godlike. This idea appeared earlier in Schelling's philosophy, to some extent in Kant's, and even in Spinoza's. Where Schelling and Kant are concerned, and maybe or maybe not Spinoza (was his mysticism unadulterated antisupernaturalism in disguise?), the idea that man is part of God (or partly Godlike, as with Kant) is again just a definition. Man's godhood exists only by definition. Not only does Hegel's concept of man as the divine lack originality, it radiates absurdity when the divine—the Absolute Spirit produced by Absolute Knowledge—is identified with the absolutes of metaphysical philosophy and Christian theology. The absolute is a silly concept grounded in superstitious, prescientific approaches to understanding the universe. Hegel earns nothing but censure for making the concept of an absolute his plaything.

The second candidate for the role of an original insight in Hegel's thought is dialectics. Although Hegel's dialectics is original in some of its details, the underlying idea of a clash of opposites goes back to ancient Greek philosophy. And the more refined idea of thesis-antithesis-synthesis dialectics is borrowed largely from Fichte. Hegel's originality is limited to imaginative ways of coming up with syntheses. Foremost among these approaches to synthesis is the two-part synthesis that borrows one part from a two-part thesis and one from a two-part antithesis (e.g., potential + *one, actual* + many, *actual* + *one*). Another approach, wherein the synthesis is A = B, reveals that B is a disguised form of A. My favorite synthesis format is the one that uses a person as the synthesis. The person in one dialectic is Faust, who turns out to be both a predator (thesis) and a victim (antithesis). In another dialectic the person is the masked thespian from Greek comedy, who "drops the mask" of divinity and becomes human, thereby revealing that the divine (masked, thesis) is humanity (unmasked, antithesis).

Although Hegel's dialectics has this limited degree of originality, it does not lead to any fresh insights. In *Phenomenology*, dialectics leads to the conclusion that man is a part of God but that God is wholly nonsupernatural, not the God of theism or even the God of deism or pantheism. Hegel calls this conclusion "truth," but it isn't truth. It is just an arbitrary redefinition of God. Hegel has created that ersatz God which—not "who"—is no god at all. It is just a personal value. God, or Spirit, becomes something offered as a substitute for an ignoble value, Christianity's imaginary God. Crossing the dialectical ocean to the far shore of self-realized Spirit, Hegel not only dispatches Captain Yahweh en route but scuttles the Good Ship Christianity at the voyage's end. Both the Unhappy Consciousness dialectic and "The Revealed Religion" dialectic contribute to the scuttling. Again, however, Hegel's "Science" of dialectics has not led to fresh insight. Others recognized Christianity as a farrago of superstitions before Hegel did. (And if you should happen to be a Christian, you have all the more reason for concluding that Hegel's assault on Christianity did not produce any insight.)

Does anything remain in *Phenomenology* that might be admired or that could be considered a significant contribution to human thought? Let us stand back and view the book from afar. Our aim is to let the details fade into the background so as to achieve a better understanding of the whole. If we ignore *Phenomenology*'s dialectical structure (not seen from afar), we can see the book as a loosely structured, capriciously selective survey of human thought. This thought, the product of Spirit's Mind, meanders across a crazy quilt of topics that include philosophy, religion, literature, law, custom, morality, phrenology, conscience, theater, art, nature, the Enlightenment, the Reign of Terror, monarchic rule, and laissez-faire economics. And since (*a*) the meanderer is explicitly described as "consciousness" and (*b*) a pattern of randomness *seems* to characterize the meandering thoughts, nothing could be better qualified for the familiar label "stream of consciousness" than is Spirit's journey through time and space.

The various stops, called "shapes" and "stations," on Spirit's journey yield no discoveries and no original insights. For the most part, Hegel merely describes what happens in the places where Spirit pauses. Sometimes, as with *Antigone*, you expect Hegel to express an opinion but he doesn't—because the purpose of the stop is to create a beneath-the-surface dialectic (a step in Spirit's "education" in the "Science" of dialectics) rather than to criticize or praise some facet of the surface topic. Where he does express an opinion, as with the Unhappy Consciousness, he has nothing original, profound, or enlightening to say. On the core topic of religion, later writers—George Santayana, Walter Lippmann, H. L. Mencken, Homer Smith, and Richard Dawkins, for example—are far more readable, articulate, expansive, and persuasive in their attacks on religion.[65] And at the end of Spirit's journey, all we find is something that is not knowledge or the promised "truth" but an eccentric redefinition of God. Hegel is offering us that complicated ersatz God for which we have no need. He is telling us not to completely forsake religion. But why not?

The Philosophy of History. The next question is: Does Hegel's Philosophy of History have any value? Hegel's history dialectics lead to the conclusions that history's main goals are (1) freedom and (2) monarchy and that an important secondary goal is (3) the monarch's ruling over many political units. Are any of these goals worthy of praise?

History's first goal, freedom, seems to be the most important goal. Hegel writes, "Historical development . . . is . . . the production of an end . . . [that] is . . . the concept of freedom."[66] Freedom is a widely shared human value. Its worth is not something Hegel deserves credit for recognizing. Besides, questions exist as to just what sort of freedom Hegel was endorsing. Digging beneath the abstract concept of freedom to discern precisely what Hegel had in mind, I find it hard to formulate a compliment. If we take the word "freedom" at face value (a mistake), which to say if we too hastily assume Hegel is applauding sociopolitical freedom (human rights), Hegel's concept of freedom is too ambiguous and too limited to merit praise. Hegel made freedom a facet of the Prussian monarchy. Monarchy became a precondition of freedom. Not just any old monarchy but contemporary northern European monarchy. In Hegel's time, monarchy had been around for thousands of years: the early pharaohs of Egypt take us back to around 3000 BCE. Hegel wasn't praising Egyptian monarchy. The Prussian monarchy in which Hegel saw freedom's long-awaited realization was repressive. Though granting its citizens a large measure of personal freedom, Prussia's monarchy practiced censorship and denied the citizens the right to vote for legislators. Hegel endorsed these denials of freedom.

Not only was Hegelian freedom too circumscribed, it was too abstract to have much practical significance. The truth is, Hegel's concept of freedom has little to do with what the people of his day, like those of our day, regarded as human freedom or personal freedom. More specifically, the freedom of *The Philosophy of History* has four conceivable meanings. For reasons given in chapter 3, I am convinced that only the first is valid, but I shall discuss all four to cover interpretations that others might endorse. The four meanings:

1. Spirit achieves a purely philosophical state of freedom, a state having no practical application to human beings, when Spirit undergoes self-realization: "History," whose end is freedom, "has constituted the rational necessary course of the World-Spirit."[67] Spirit's self-realization, the synthesis of the macrodialectic, is Spirit's realization (via Hegel's mind) that it is all reality, including both natural and artificial "objects." Through the act of self-realization, Spirit escapes from the bondage of belief in God (the macrodialectic's antithesis) and thereby becomes free. Spirit's abstract escape symbolizes man's concrete escape from bondage to religious superstition: man stops believing in God. This meaning of freedom was developed in detail at the end of chapter 3, so I won't repeat the details here. What concerns us now is the lack of real-world substance in this philosophical state of freedom. Freedom in this ethereal sense occurs in 1807 and is explicitly described by Hegel as the "goal" of "History." History, according to this concept, is "the slow-moving succession of Spirits" (the humans, both real and fictional, who populate the intermediate dialectics and microdialectics) who have as "their goal" the "Absolute Knowledge" found at the end of Spirit's "path," the path that constitutes "History."[68] This clearly means that Spirit's freedom is one aspect—I believe the only aspect— of the concept of freedom that Hegel, in his *Philosophy of History*, says is the goal of history. And, as I said, this first meaning of freedom has no practical significance; it is just an element of Hegel's fictitious "life" of the fictitious Spirit. In fact, this release from "bondage" really amounts to nothing more than Hegel's own personal release from bondage to religious superstition (Tübingen, circa 1788–90).[69] There is no good

reason to think the freedom Hegel claims is achieved in his history synthesis is something more than the purely imaginary freedom that the fictional act of self-realization produces. But let's give Hegel the benefit of the doubt by examining the next three concepts.

2. Humans achieve a more practical, but somewhat narrow, form of freedom—religious freedom—when Protestantism arrives. Protestantism, in Hegel's eyes, gave humans freedom from the regimentation, persecution, and fear of medieval Catholicism. People became free to live according to their own beliefs rather than beliefs and practices (e.g., tithing, confession) dictated by the Catholic Church. Protestantism supposedly also gave man freedom of thought. But this freedom of thought existed only in a limited sphere, the sphere of religion. Men (but arguably not women) were now free to interpret the Bible for themselves and to reject some religious doctrines. On the other hand, German Protestant citizens were not free to profess atheism. Fichte found this out when he was falsely accused of atheism and discharged from his professorship at the University of Jena. Furthermore, Protestantism never meant unlimited religious freedom. That idealized Protestantism never existed—not in Hegel's day, not in our own day of fundamentalist attacks on freedom to reject religious beliefs that (*a*) abortion should be illegal, (*b*) evolution should not be taught in public school science classes, (*c*) the Ten Commandments should be posted in schools and courthouses, (*d*) atheists should be barred from holding public office, and (*e*) legislative sessions should begin with prayer.

3. Humans achieve another form of freedom, more practical but again narrow, when the Prussian state arrives and more or less completes the already well under way demise of feudalism. The Prussian monarch's authority replaces that of the petty princes and supposedly releases the serfs from subjugation. The practical significance of this type of freedom seems to arise largely from the removal of the impoverishing obligation of the serfs to share their crops and handicrafts with the feudal lords. But the extent to which this release actually eliminated

tenancy and land rent, and occurred *after* the formation of the Prussian monarchy, is an issue on which I am forced to defer to competent authorities on German feudalism and German history. I do, however, have my doubts about just how much the arrival of Frederick the Great's Prussia affected the condition of the serfs.

4. The fourth possible meaning of Hegelian freedom is the one to which all other interpreters seem to subscribe. This meaning is sociopolitical freedom in the broadest sense. Essentially, this is the concept of human rights, the attainment of a proper balance between the rights or powers of the state and the rights of the individual. But since "proper balance" is a highly subjective concept, this fourth meaning is riddled with ambiguity. The only thing that is clear is that, if we assume this meaning of freedom is the correct one, the proper balance is something very close to the balance found in Hegel's Prussian monarchy.

I am certain that the first concept of freedom—freedom from bondage to God and superstition—is the freedom that Hegel calls the goal of history. In other words, I think that all of the books and articles that have attempted to interpret Hegelian history's concept of freedom are way off base. Six considerations support my thesis that freedom from bondage to God is the only freedom Hegel applauds in his *Philosophy of History*.

The first consideration is the deceptive way Hegel introduces history's goal. He doesn't say history's "end" or goal is "freedom." He says history's end is "the *concept* of freedom." This particular concept is something that doesn't arrive until Germanic monarchy arrives, and with it a philosopher named Hegel, born in 1770 and a confirmed atheist by around 1788. Now, the *concept* of freedom in the usual sense of the word freedom was as old as political history when Hegel wrote. It is not something that arrived with Germanic monarchy. So when Hegel speaks of a *concept* that arrived with Germanic monarchy, either he is guilty of carelessly wording his statement or he is speaking of an idiosyncratic concept of freedom. Freedom in the sense of Spirit's release from bondage to religious superstition is such an idiosyncratic concept. If we assume that Hegel is not guilty of careless wording—that he really means not freedom per se but "the *concept* of freedom"—then we must conclude that Hegel is saying that the goal of history is Spirit's realization (self-realization) that it (essentially humanity) is the divine and that religion and all religious beliefs are superstition. The concept of freedom becomes the concept that there is no supernatural God, that the only "God" is a figurative God—the universe—and that Spirit's (Hegel's) realization that this is so releases Spirit from bondage to religious superstition. That is something that happens during the era of Germanic monarchy. To be specific, this concept of freedom arrives with the publication of *The Phenomenology of Spirit* in 1807.

A second consideration favoring the freedom-from-bondage-to-God interpretation is that the other interpretations fail to explain why Hegel keeps the meaning of freedom in the history context a secret. And he does keep it a secret. The meaning of freedom, discussed in detail only in *The Philosophy of Right*, is encoded there in the same abstract, ambiguous, equivocal, almost impenetrable, obscurantist language that Hegel uses in *Phenomenology* to hide the identity of Spirit and the meaning of the freedom that accompanies self-realization. Why? Hegel had good reason to keep the meaning of *Phenomenology*'s freedom a secret. Spelling out that meaning in lucid, unequivocal language would have identified Hegel as an atheist and rendered him unemployable in his chosen profession. But if history's freedom is some sort of sociopolitical freedom, why is Hegel unwilling to say precisely what this freedom is? For example, if this freedom is something that arises from the Prussian constitution, identifying that freedom as what it is would be complimenting the monarchy. Why keep a compliment a secret?

A third consideration is that sociopolitical freedom in any meaningful sense of the word did not really originate in Hegel's Prussia. What sort of sociopolitical freedom could Prussia boast of having that could not be found also, and earlier, in England and the United States? England's Parliament passed the Bill of Rights in 1689, roughly a hundred years before Hegel came of age. The US Constitution was ratified in 1788, the year Hegel turned eighteen; the Constitution's first ten amendments, known as America's Bill of Rights, followed in 1791, three years before Friedrich Wilhelm II introduced the liberal Prussian code of laws.

A fourth consideration is the weakness of the second and third interpretations. The second interpretation, which says that freedom means the arrival of Protestantism in Prussia, is especially weak. If Protestantism truly meant freedom, Hegel would have been free to declare openly both his atheism and his contempt for religious superstition. Instead, he was forced to hide his true beliefs in almost undecipherable language and in a "Science" of dialectics that has remained unexplained until now. The fact is, Hegel was not free to attack religion without losing his Berlin professorship. The third interpreta-tion of freedom, which emphasizes the Prussian state's freeing the serfs from exploitation by feudal lords, is highly implausible. This is a narrow concept of freedom that ignores other limitations on freedom that characterized Prussia. And if freedom from serfdom was what Hegel had in mind, why was he afraid to say so? Feudalism and its attendant serfdom were not favored by Hegel's sponsors in the Prussian hierarchy.

A fifth consideration supporting the first interpretation of history's version of freedom is the implausibleness of the fourth interpretation, socio-political freedom or human rights. Hegel repeatedly alludes in his later writ-ings and lectures on freedom to *Phenomenology*'s release-from-bondage-to-God concept of freedom. Cristi observes that "Hegel's most quoted definition of freedom appears in H. G. Hotho's lecture notes taken in 1822–3, two years after the *Philosophy of Right* appeared in print." Hegel initially describes a first "moment" and a second "moment" in the evolution of the will (meaning the evolution of Spirit and its Mind). Cristi doesn't recognize the thesis-antith-esis-synthesis language, which uses "moment" as a synonym for dialectical stage, but Hegel is obviously giving his macrodialectic a reprise. Cristi next quotes Hegel as saying, "Then the third moment is that 'I' ['consciousness' or 'subject,' a human mind] is [both] with itself . . . [and] in this other [an observed object]. . . . This, then, is the concrete concept of freedom" (my inter-polations).[70] The "third moment" is, of course, the dialectical synthesis. Hegel is describing Spirit's self-realization, the "conscious + union" event, which is also the "actual + freedom" event. Here Spirit, using Hegel's mind, real-izes that it is both the observing mind, or subject (the "I"), and the observed object (the "other"). Subject = object, because both are Spirit. And Spirit is all reality (including mental reality) but especially humanity and the human mind. So in the third moment Spirit is "with" (i.e., in) both the "I" (mind) and the "other" (matter); it is both mind and matter. According to the quotation (and according to *Phenomenology*), this "moment" of self-realization is where freedom materializes; "the concrete concept of freedom" is the outcome of the dialectic's third stage. As we saw in chapter 3, this macrodialectic concept of freedom is man's release from bondage to God and to religious superstition. It is what happens in the master-and-slave parable when the master (God) "let's the other again go free"[71]—releases the slave (man) from bondage. This release from bondage occurs when a human mind (Hegel's mind, part of Spirit's mind) finally realizes that *it*, not the imaginary supernatural being in heaven, is "God," the divine.

A sixth consideration further supports my belief that freedom from bondage to God and to religion is the meaning of freedom in the history context. I refer to a quotation from *The Philosophy of History* (previously cited in chapter 5): "The History of the world is none other than the progress of the *consciousness* of Freedom" (my italics).[72] Substitute "Spirit" for "world" in that quotation and you get a good description of Hegel's *Phenomenology of Spirit*. We saw in chapter 3 that *Phenomenology* is the history of the progress of Spirit's *consciousness*. Consciousness progresses from (1) a primordial, prehuman state of unconsciousness to (2) non-self-conscious consciousness—humans have arrived, giving Spirit a conscious Mind—in which Spirit is consciously aware of "objects," presumed to be things other than itself, to (3) self-consciousness, or self-realization, where Spirit finally becomes conscious that it is all reality, hence that those "alien" objects are really itself. A key external object in Spirit's non-self-conscious stage is God, believed during this stage to be a supernatural being living in the sky. Man submits to and becomes the slave of this supernatural God, the master. Master and slave. When self-realization occurs, man (Spirit's Mind) realizes that the most important "object," God, is really himself: there is no supernatural God. This realization releases man from bondage to the supernatural God and gives man what Hegel calls freedom—freedom from enslavement by God. Man has now progressed to consciousness of freedom. Hegel's quotation about *history's* being "the progress of the consciousness of Freedom" thus amounts to a rephrasing of *the history of Spirit's* being "the progress of the consciousness of Freedom."

The above paragraph focuses on the word "consciousness" in the quotation. Let's now shift our attention to the word "world." The quotation again: "The History of the *world* is none other than the progress of the consciousness of Freedom" (my italics). In *Phenomenology*, Hegel occasionally uses "God," "world," and "World-Spirit" (*Weltgeist*) as synonyms for Spirit. By "world" Hegel means the universe—Spirit—not just earth. Make no mistake: Hegel's "world" is Spirit. So in the quotation, "the history of the world" means the same thing as "the history of Spirit." Hegel is saying, in effect, that "the History of Spirit is none other than the progress of the consciousness of Freedom." The world's ultimately reaching consciousness of freedom is therefore the same thing as Spirit's ultimately reaching consciousness of freedom. And that freedom, the freedom discussed in *Phenomenology*, is not sociopolitical freedom, or human rights. That freedom—Spirit's ultimate freedom—is freedom from bondage to God and to derivative religious superstition.

In short, in saying that the concept of freedom is history's goal and has been achieved under Prussian monarchy, Hegel is equivocating. He seems to be saying that Prussia's monarchy brought social and political freedom. But he privately means that the twin concepts of Spirit and Spirit's self-realization arrived with Hegel during the period of the Prussian monarchy. Hegel is having his cake and eating it too—pleasing the monarch and attacking religion. This is hypocrisy. Hypocrisy can sometimes be condoned, but it is hardly something for which we should admire or praise Hegel.

Freedom is Hegel's first goal of history; monarchy is the second. Does Hegel's championing of monarchy deserve praise? Not according to my values. I don't believe monarchy is the best political system. Not that there is anything wrong with democratic, constitutional monarchies where the monarch is just a figurehead, as in the United Kingdom; I just happen to prefer the American system under which I live—republican government. So Hegel gets no compliment for treating monarchy as a goal, meaning a laudable goal, of history and as the highest form of government. To be more precise, he gets no compliment for *advocating* monarchy. He becomes even less deserving of credit when we recognize that the monarchy Hegel endorsed required a monarch with real, not just nominal, authority.

History's third goal, according to Hegel's history dialectics, is a state composed of many political units. Now, there is nothing wrong with a nation's having a multiplicity of subordinate units such as America's states, Canada's provinces, the United Kingdom's four countries, and Germany's *länder*. But neither is anything wrong with a nation's consisting of a single political unit (not counting towns, counties, and nongoverning electoral districts), as with Iceland, Luxembourg, and Sri Lanka. And neither is anything wrong with a nation's being small, too small to have subordinate governmental units. Accordingly, Hegel's advocacy of multiple political units, a characteristic of his Prussia, does not deserve praise.

Beyond the dubious nature of its conclusions, Hegel's philosophy of history's dialectical foundation is nothing but sand. In chapter 5 the picking-and-choosing character of Hegel's history dialectics was illustrated. Hegel's "Science" of dialectics is no science at all. Dialectics is a tool for shaping malleable conclusions—any preconceived conclusions the user wants to reach. Hegel used dialectics to reach the conclusion that monarchy was the goal of history. But Marx used dialectics to reach the conclusion that a stateless society was the goal of history. And in Tillich's dialectics, "the end [goal] of history is the end [vanishing] of religion."[73]

One other aspect of Hegel's version of history deserves attention. This is the ridiculous idea that history moves from east to west—from China to India to Persia to Greece (via Egypt!) to Rome to the "Germanic nations" of northern Europe. Since Prussia is the only Germanic nation fitting the dialectical prescription of monarchy combined with many partially autonomous subdivisions, that last stop is really Prussia. Hegel's east-to-west interpretation of history has no justification in scholarship. It instead reeks of ethnocentrism, although Hegel's desire to please his sponsors in the Prussian bureaucracy could be what we smell. In any case, even if a general east-to-west pattern could be established (it can't), Hegel has no good excuse for stopping at Prussia. If the pattern existed, why should it stop at Prussia? Why shouldn't history plod farther west to Great Britain, where a truly historic transformation of monarchy into democracy was taking place? And after Britain, why not go still farther west to the United States, where monarchy was entirely supplanted by democracy? We know the answer. Hegelian history stops at Prussia because there's no place like home, Hegel's home.

I am forced to conclude that, for anyone who seeks insight, edification, or knowledge, neither *Phenomenology* nor *The Philosophy of History* is worth reading. They offer nothing of value. Readers who believe in the God of theism will not be persuaded to abandon "Him." Readers who don't believe have no need for the substitute nonsupernatural "God," Spirit, that Hegel offers. They have their own value systems and will not be convinced that revering the universe has any practical applications. They might see practical applications for revering humanity, but such applications originate with opinions the readers already possess. This is not to say that persons with an academic interest in philosophy shouldn't read *Phenomenology* and *The Philosophy of History*. Acquiring knowledge of or insights into Hegel's thought is an entirely different matter. *Phenomenology* can also provide intellectual stimulation for persons like myself who enjoy the challenge of solving literary (and cinematic) puzzles, whether the puzzles be complex triple allegories or complex dialectical formulations describing mysterious gods (Hegel's and Tillich's). But don't turn to Hegel seeking wisdom. And above all, don't be seduced into believing that dialectics is a science rather than a peculiar literary tool.

Hegel's Influence on Other Thinkers. The lack of value in Hegel's thought does not necessarily mean the philosopher's thought is of no importance. It could be considered important for its direct or indirect influence on other thinkers or even on society, provided that it had such influence. Hegel did influence three other thinkers, but the practical effect of this influence might not amount to much. The three other thinkers are Ludwig Feuerbach, Karl Marx, and Paul Tillich. (I deliberately omit Emerson and Dewey, who were slightly influenced by Hegel—Dewey only temporarily—but whose Hegelian ideas lead nowhere.)

Feuerbach is the least important of the three. He took from Hegel the idea that man is a manifestation of God, an incarnation of sorts, and amplified this idea into the claim that man *is* God. According to Feuerbach, there is but one world, the material world; Hegel's supposed fanciful world of metaphysical neurosis, the world of Spirit and its delusional ideas, does not exist. Feuerbach, in turn, influenced Karl Marx. He convinced Marx that the real self-alienation was a quality of man. Marx, in this early writings, thus wrote: "Man, who has found in the fantastic reality of heaven, where he sought a supernatural being, only his own reflection, will no longer be tempted to find only the *semblance* of himself—a non-human being—where he seeks and must seek his true reality."[74]

In addition to indirectly influencing Marx via Feuerbach, Hegel directly influenced Marx. Pippin comments that "the mere mention of the name of Marx is sufficient to summarize Hegel's most visible influence on world history."[75] Hegel persuaded Marx that historical change occurred dialectically. Marx praised Hegel for his insight into dialectics even while accusing him of seeking dialectical change in the wrong place, in the nonmaterial world of ideas rather than in the material world of economic activity. The result was the Marxian history dialectics reviewed in chapter 5. Marx's dialectical synthesis, the goal of his dialectical history, was final communism. This goal was Marx's own original concept, not something he got from Hegel. Marx was a revolutionary and a vitriolic anticapitalist. The capitalist system, as he saw things, was oppressive and exploitive. It would be overthrown by a revolution of the exploited proletariat and replaced by world communism.

The revolution did occur, but in Russia, a country where capitalism had not even taken root. Stalin's dictatorship quickly ensued, along with state ownership of factories and farms. Then, after World War II, more than forty years of Cold War followed: the Soviet Union versus the West. If these developments could be attributed in part to Marx, Hegel could surely be said to have had a significant indirect influence on history. But what really inspired Russia's Bolshevik revolution of 1917 was czarist rule, not capitalism and not Marx's theories. Capitalism didn't exist in Russia to any significant extent. The revolutionaries did use Marx for doctrinal purposes, particularly where communism was concerned. But the revolution, with or without communism, would have occurred in the absence of Marx's philosophy. Even if someone could show that Marx's inspiration was necessary for the revolution's occurrence, that outcome could not be attributed even indirectly to Hegel. Marx's revolutionary ideas did not come from Hegel; only Marx's dialectics and his deification of man did. Neither did the advocacy of a Communist economic system come from Hegel.

The third and most important thinker Hegel influenced is philosopher-theologian Paul Tillich. Absolutely no room for doubt exists that Tillich, like Marx, understood Hegel's dialectics. Consider this evidence:

1. Tillich not only copied the idea of using dialectics from Hegel, he used three of Hegel's dialectical formats: (*a*) two-part syntheses that

combine one part of a two-part thesis with one part of a two-part antithesis, (*b*) the antithesis that is the thesis in disguise and that leads to an A = B synthesis, and (*c*) the "one composed of many" synthesis, which reveals that the divine (Hegel's Spirit, Tillich's humanity) is both one and many, one "universal" entity composed of many particulars. (Marx borrowed only Hegel's two-part formula.)

2. Tillich not only copied the related concept of separation and return from Hegel, he called attention to the concept by writing, "Obviously—and it was so intended by Hegel—his dialectics are the religious symbols of estrangement and reconciliation conceptualized and reduced to empirical descriptions."[76] In Tillich's pseudotheology, man separates from and returns to God—separates from belief in the God of theism and returns to belief in "the God above the God of theism," humanity. (In Marx's thought, man separates from primitive communism or gens, the wrong form of communism, and returns to a higher form of communism.)

3. As part of the separation-and-return concept, Tillich copied Hegel's concept of self-estrangement. In Tillich's thought, man becomes estranged from himself when he fails to recognize that the other persons he sees are essentially himself: both are humanity and, as such, both are God. (In Marx's thought, man becomes estranged from himself when he becomes separated from his essential self, a person who keeps what he produces.)

4. By surreptitiously defining God as humanity, Tillich borrowed from Hegel the essence of Hegel's Spirit, namely, the idea that man is divine. Man is by far the most important part of Hegel's Spirit; man is all there is to Tillich's "God above God."

5. Tillich borrowed from Hegel the concept describing what both men equivocally called "God" as a four-part, two-level entity that has (*a*) a physical or tangible side—all reality in Hegel's thought, all humanity

in Tillich's thought—(*b*) a mental or intangible side—mind for Hegel, "ultimate concern" for Tillich—(*c*) general and particular facets on both sides, and (*d*) a "divine life" in which the divinity separates from and returns to a state of union.

6. Tillich borrowed many of Hegel's dichotomies, including universal and particular, one and many, union and separation, essence and existence, divine and human, potential and actual, and unconscious (Tillich's "dreaming innocence") and conscious ("awakened").

7. Tillich borrowed Hegel's deliberately obscure, ambiguous, nearly incomprehensible style of writing and used it for the same purpose, concealing his atheism.

8. Tillich used the phrase "negation of the negation," used by Hegel to refer to a dialectical synthesis, to describe his own dialectical synthesis. (Marx likewise used "negation of the negation.")

German born and German educated, Tillich moved to the United States in 1933. He eventually became America's leading Protestant theologian, with the possible exception of Reinhold Niebuhr. Tillich's dialectical formats closely parallel those of Hegel, although Tillich does not claim that history unfolds dialectically. Tillich's definition of God as humanity—that's definition of, not belief in—comes only partly from Hegel. Tillich also found the idea, in one form or another, in the philosophies of Kant, Schelling (whose philosophy was the subject of Tillich's philosophy and divinity dissertations), Feuerbach, and Marx. His "God above the God of theism," as described in chapter 3, even has a "divine life" similar to Spirit's.

Like Hegel, Tillich had to conceal his atheism in order to keep his professor of theology positions and to retain his influence as a theologian. His American career consisted of professorships at Union Theological Seminary (1933–55), the Harvard Divinity School (1955–62), and the University of Chicago Divinity School (1962–65). The three volumes of his widely acclaimed and just as widely misunderstood *Systematic Theology* were published in 1951, 1957, and 1963. He deliberately added to the misunderstanding by describing his "Absolute" not only in theistic language as "God" and "He" but in ontological language as "being," "being-itself," and "the ground of being." (Being-itself is human being itself, and the ground of our being is humanity, the "ground" from which all humans sprout.)

Tillich's identifying God with being is part of his so-called "method of correlation." This method, which is based on Hegel's similar correlations, correlates analogous theological and philosophical concepts that jointly symbolize analogous humanistic concepts. The result is triangular analogies: the first two concepts symbolize both each other and the humanistic concept. God and being thus jointly symbolize humanity: "The religious and the philosophical Absolutes, *Deus* and esse, cannot be unconnected!"[77] Why not? Because there exists "the correlation of . . . being and God."[78] Tillich also employs the following correlations (the concept symbolized is in parentheses):

- the correlation of reason and revelation" (the realization that God is humanity)[79]

- the correlation of the Trinity and dialectics (the three-stage "divine life" of man, which goes from Yes to the God of theism to No to the God of theism to Yes to "the God above the God of theism")

- the correlation of Father and thesis (potential unity of humanity and man)

- the correlation of Son and antithesis (actual separation of humanity and man)
- the correlation of Holy Spirit and synthesis (actual union of humanity and man)

- the correlation of innocence and potential essence (potential union with "the God above the God of theism")

- the correlation of sin and estrangement (actual separation from "the God above God")

- the correlation of salvation and realized essence (actual union with "the God above God")

- the correlation of the Fall and the transition from essence to existence (man's "fall" from theism to atheism in his divine life)

- the correlation of resurrection and the transition from existence to realized essence (man's conversion to humanism, the realization that God is man)

- the correlation of the Kingdom of God and philosophy's utopias, particularly Hegel's Germanic monarchy and Marx's final communism (an idealized "all in all" situation wherein *all* men recognize *all* humanity as God)

- the correlation of theology and philosophy (humanism)

You can see that Tillich's method of correlation partially copies and then extrapolates Hegel's correlations. Hegel correlated thesis, antithesis, and synthesis with Father, Son, and Holy Spirit, and he correlated theology's God with philosophy's absolute.

Almost no one understood what Tillich was talking about when he spoke of "God" or one of God's alter egos (e.g., "being-itself"). But those who read closely and paid attention to his words could see that Tillich left absolutely no room for doubt that his God was not Christianity's God. He said, "If 'existence' refers to something which can be found within the whole of reality, no divine being exists."[80] He also said this: "Ordinary theism has made God a heavenly, completely perfect person who resides above the world and mankind. The protest of atheism against such a highest person is correct. There is no evidence for his existence, nor is he a matter of ultimate concern."[81] And this: "God is the basic and universal *symbol* for what concerns us ultimately. . . . Everything we say about being-itself, the ground and abyss of being, must be *symbolic*. . . . Therefore it cannot be used in its literal sense. To say anything about God in the literal sense of the words used means to say something false about Him" (my italics).[82] Removing all doubt, he identified a feature "that is fundamental to *all* my thinking—the antisupernaturalistic attitude" (my italics). He added that "in the first volume of my *Systematic Theology*, where I deal extensively with miracles, inspiration, ecstasy, and all these concepts, . . . [I] try to interpret them in a nonsupernaturalistic—and that would also mean a nonsuperstitious—way."[83]

Tillich even more openly attacked the myths of Adam and Eve, the fall, Noah and the flood, the virgin birth, Jesus's divinity, Jesus's miracles, Jesus's resurrection, the ascension, the Second Coming, future resurrection of the dead, salvation, heaven, hell, divine law, sin, the Holy Spirit, and the Trinity. Example: "If the Christ—a transcendent, divine being—appears in the fullness of time, lives, dies and is resurrected, this is an historical myth."[84] Likewise, the belief in immortality is a "popular superstition."[85] Salvation "is certainly not what popular imagination has made of it, escaping from hell and being received in heaven, in what is badly called 'the life hereafter.'"[86] Instead, salvation is recognizing humanity, the God above the God of theism, as one's ultimate concern. The Holy Spirit? "As for the mythology concerning the third person of the Trinity coming down from heaven—forget all about it!"[87]

Tillich may not have converted many of his students to atheism, given that divinity students have strong religious inclinations, but he surely must have helped a fair number of them to liberalize their thinking and to jettison at least some of their supernatural loads. A second audience, the readers of his many books, was probably more receptive. Known for his liberal views—at Harvard he was considered a de facto Unitarian—Tillich probably attracted predominantly liberal readers. Tillich must have helped some of these readers to confirm existing doubts and particularly to strengthen doubts about God's existence.

Tillich's influence brings us back to Hegel. Hegel does deserve partial credit for whatever influence Tillich wielded. I don't think Tillich's drift into doubt during his divinity student days can be attributed to Hegel's influence. Instead, Tillich reacted to the same influences Hegel reacted to. Both men were indoctrinated in Lutheranism as children—Tillich's father was a Lutheran minister in Germany—and both began to question the popular superstitions when they achieved adult intelligence. In college, removed from the influence of small-town parochialism and exposed to a more cosmopolitan atmosphere and to atheistic philosophy, Tillich reacted the way many other intelligent students have reacted: he first questioned and then abandoned his early religious beliefs.

It was when Tillich began writing theology that Hegel's thought came into play. Tillich needed a framework on which to attach his ideas while concealing the full extent of his atheism. Hegelian dialectics, the Hegelian God minus its nonhuman particulars, and Hegelian obscurantist obliqueness of presentation provided that framework. Onto this framework Tillich attached the original elements of his theology: (1) the method of correlation, (2) the related idea that all traditional religious concepts should be converted to symbols for atheistic God-is-man concepts, (3) the idea that "Jesus as the Christ"—fully God yet fully man—should be the "norm" for theology, and (4) the transformation of the mental side of God from universal and particular minds to universal and particular "ultimate concerns."

I seriously doubt that, absent Hegel's framework, Tillich could have constructed an imaginative and adequate theological framework of his own design. Without *Phenomenology*, Tillich's thought would in all likelihood be just an asterisk in the history of theology. Hegel, not in Germany and not in his own time but in mid-twentieth-century America, indirectly helped thinking adults shake off the fetters of religious superstition.

NOTES

CHAPTER 1

1. Donald P. Verene, *Hegel's Absolute: An Introduction to Reading the* Phenomenology of Spirit (Albany: State University of New York Press, 2007), p. 18.

2. Robert Stern, *Hegel and the* Phenomenology of Spirit (Abingdon, UK: Routledge, 2002), pp. xiii–xv, 15–16, 20, 23, 26, 41–42, 109, 196, 201.

3. Williams asserts that over ten thousand books and articles about Hegel's thought have been written. See Robert R. Williams, *Hegel's Ethics of Recognition* (Berkeley: University of California Press, 1997), p. xi.

4. J. N. Findlay, "Analysis of Text," in G. W. F. Hegel, *Phenomenology of Spirit*, trans. A. V. Miller (Oxford: Oxford University Press, 1977), p. 591.

5. Gustav E. Mueller, "The Hegel Legend of 'Thesis-Antithesis-Synthesis,'" *Journal of the History of Ideas* 19, no. 3 (1958): 411–14; Walter Kaufmann, *Hegel: A Reinterpretation* (New York: Doubleday Anchor Books, 1966); William Young, *Hegel's Dialectical Method: Its Origins and Religious Significance* (Nutley, NJ: Craig Press, 1972); Burleigh Taylor Wilkins, *Hegel's Philosophy of History* (Ithaca, NY, and London: Cornell University Press, 1974); William Maker, "Does Hegel Have a 'Dialectical Method'?" *Southern Journal of Philosophy* 20 (1982): 75–96; Robert C. Solomon, *In the Spirit of Hegel: A Study of G. W. F. Hegel's* Phenomenology of Spirit (New York: Oxford University Press, 1983); Allen W. Wood, *Hegel's Ethical Thought* (Cambridge: Cambridge University Press, 1990); Terry Pinkard, *Hegel's Phenomenology: The Sociality of Reason* (Cambridge: Cambridge University Press, 1994); Kenley R. Dove, "Hegel's Phenomenological Method," in *The* Phenomenology of Spirit *Reader*, ed. Jon Stewart (Albany: State University of New York Press, 1998), pp. 52–75; Stephen Crites, *Dialectic and Gospel in the Development of Hegel's Thinking* (University Park: Pennsylvania State Press, 1998); Michael Allen Fox, *The Accessible Hegel* (Amherst, NY: Humanity Books, 2005); Frederick Beiser, *Hegel* (New York: Routledge, 2005); and Verene, *Hegel's Absolute*.

6. Michael Forster, "Hegel's Dialectical Method," in Frederick C. Beiser, ed., *The Cambridge Companion to Hegel* (Cambridge: Cambridge University Press, 1993), pp. 130–70.

7. Mueller, "Legend," pp. 411–14.

8. Kaufmann, *Hegel*, pp. 154–55.

9. Ibid., p. 158.

10. Ibid., p. 173.

11. Ibid., p. 160.

12. Young, *Dialectical Method*, p. 9.

13. G. W. F. Hegel, *Phenomenology of Spirit*, trans. A. V. Miller (Oxford: Oxford University Press, 1977), para. 50.

14. Wilkins, *Hegel's Philosophy of History*, pp. 16–17.

15. Maker, "Dialectical Method," p. 76.

16. Ibid.

17. Solomon, *Spirit of Hegel*, pp. 21–22.

18. Ibid., p. 23.

19. Ibid., p. 269.

20. Ibid., p. 476.

21. Ibid., p. 477.

22. Ibid., p. 148.

23. Wood, *Ethical Thought*, pp. 3–4.

24. Pinkard, *Sociality*, p. 17.

25. Ibid., p. 12.

26. Dove, "Hegel's Phenomenological Method," p. 52.

27. Ibid., p. 71, n. 1.

28. Crites, *Dialectic and Gospel*, p. xv.

29. Ibid., p. 134.

30. Ibid., p. 446.

31. Fox, *Accessible Hegel*, p. 43.

32. Ibid., p. 52.

33. Hegel, *Phenomenology*, trans. Miller, para. 50.

34. Beiser, *Hegel*, pp. 160, 161.

35. Verene, *Hegel's Absolute*, p. 18.

36. Ibid., pp. 20–21.

37. Ibid., pp. 34–35.

38. Ibid., p. 105.

39. Beiser, *Hegel*, p. 185; Crites, *Dialectic and Gospel*, p. 322; J. N. Findlay, *The Philosophy of Hegel: An Introduction and Re-Examination* (New York: Collier, 1958), pp. 95–96; Fox, *Accessible Hegel*, pp. 120, 126, 127; Hans-Georg Gadamer, *Hegel's Dialectic: Five Hermeneutical Studies* (New Haven, CT, and London: Yale University Press, 1971), p. 67; Jean Hyppolite, *Genesis and Structure of Hegel's* Phenomenology of Spirit (Evanston, IL: Northwestern University Press, 1974), pp. 1970–72; Howard P.

Kainz, *Hegel's* Phenomenology, Part I, *Analysis and Commentary* (Tuscaloosa: University of Alabama Press, 1976), pp. 85, 87; George Armstrong Kelly, "Notes on Hegel's 'Lordship and Bondage," in Alasdair MacIntyre, ed., *Hegel: A Collection of Critical Essays* (Garden City, NY: Doubleday, 1972), p. 210; Quentin Lauer, *A Reading of Hegel's* Phenomenology of Spirit (New York: Fordham University Press, 1993), pp. 124, 130; Paul S. Miklowitz, *Metaphysics to Metafictions: Hegel, Nietzsche, and the End of Philosophy* (Albany: State University of New York Press, 1994), pp. 43, 49; Patricia Jagentowicz Mills, *Feminist Interpretations of G. W. F. Hegel* (University Park: Pennsylvania State University Press, 1996), p. 4; Frederick Neuhouser, "Desire, Recognition, and the Relation between Bondsman and Lord," in Kenneth R. Westphal, ed., *The Blackwell Guide to Hegel's* Phenomenology of Spirit (Malden, MA, Wiley-Blackwell, 2009), pp. 49, 53; Pinkard, *Sociality*, p. 53; Robert B. Pippin, *Hegel's Practical Philosophy: Rational Agency as Ethical Life* (Cambridge and New York: Cambridge University Press, 2008), pp. 161, 214; Charles Taylor, *Hegel* (Cambridge and New York: Cambridge University Press, 1975), p. 152; and Verene, *Hegel's Absolute*, p. 57.

40. Beiser, *Hegel*, pp. 186–91.

41. John McCumber, *The Company of Words: Hegel, Language, and Systematic Philosophy* (Evanston, IL: Northwestern University Press, 1993), p. 123.

42. Nectarios G. Limnatis, *The Dimensions of Hegel's Dialectic* (London and New York: Continuum, 2010), p. 1.

43. Klaus Brinkmann, "The Dialectic of the Inverted World and the Meaning of *Aufhebung*," in ibid., pp. 131–36. The errors in Brinkmann's belief about what Hegelian dialectics is will become more apparent as my explanation of dialectics unfolds and I present examples from the thought of Hegel, Marx, and Tillich.

44. Hegel, *Phenomenology*, trans. Miller, para. 107; G. W. F. Hegel, *Science of Logic*, trans. A. V. Miller (Atlantic Highlands, NJ: Humanities Press International, 1989), pp. 115, 116, 137, 178, 500, 603; G. W. F. Hegel, *Logic* (*Encyclopaedia*, Pt. 1), trans. William Wallace (Oxford: Clarendon, 1975), p. 138.

45. Karl Marx, *Capital*, trans. Samuel Moore and Edward Aveling (New York: Modern Library, undated reprint of 1906 Charles H. Kerr ed.), chap. 32, para. 3; Karl Marx and Friedrich Engels, *Historisch-Kritische Gesamtausgabe, Erste Abteilung*, vol. 3, ed. D. Rjazanov and V. Adoratski (Berlin: Marx-Engels Verlag, 1927–32), pp. 126, 134, cited in Robert Tucker, *Philosophy and Myth in Karl Marx* (London: Cambridge University Press, 1961), pp. 154, 160.

46. Frederick Engels, *Herr Edugen Dühring's Revolution in Science (Anti Dühring)*, trans. Emile Burns (New York: International Publishers, 1939), pp. 142, 143, 144, 145, 147, 148, 149, 152, 154, 155, 156.

47. Paul Tillich, *Systematic Theology*, vol. 3 (Chicago: University of Chicago Press, 1963), pp. 403, 406; Paul Tillich, *The Courage to Be* (New Haven, CT: Yale University Press, 1952), p. 179.

48. Klaus Hartmann, "Hegel, A Non-Metaphysical View," in Alasdair MacIntyre, ed., *Hegel: A Collection of Essays* (Garden City, NY: Doubleday, 1972), pp. 101–25.

49. Michael Forster, "Hegel's Dialectical Method," in Beiser, *Cambridge Companion*, pp. 130–70.

50. W. T. Stace, *The Philosophy of Hegel* (New York: Dover, 1955), p. 97; J. N. Findlay, *The Philosophy of Hegel: An Introduction and Re-Examination* (New York: Collier, 1958), pp. 69–72.

51. John M. E. McTaggart, *Studies in the Hegelian Dialectic* (Cambridge: Cambridge University Press, 1896), pp. 2, 104; Findlay, *Philosophy of Hegel* (New York: Collier, 1958), pp. 156–57; Charles Taylor, *Hegel* (Cambridge: Cambridge University Press, 1975), p. 232; Michael Forster, "Hegel's Dialectical Method," in Frederick C. Beiser, ed., *The Cambridge Companion to Hegel* (Cambridge: Cambridge University Press, 1993), pp. 131, 133; Peter Singer, *Hegel: A Very Short Introduction* (Oxford: Oxford University Press, 2001), p. 103; David James, *Hegel: A Guide for the Perplexed* (London: Continuum, 2007), pp. 126–31.

52. Lee Cameron McDonald, *Western Political Theory, Part 3: Nineteenth and Twentieth Centuries* (New York: Harcourt Brace Jovanovich, 1968), pp. 471–76.

53. Findlay, *Philosophy of Hegel*, p. 68.

54. Hegel, *Phenomenology*, trans. Miller, para. 232.

55. Ibid., para. 233; cf. para. 438.

56. Singer, *Hegel*, pp. 100–102.

57. Ibid., p. 102.

58. G. W. F. Hegel, "The Philosophy of History," trans. Carl J. Friedrich and Paul W. Friedrich, in *The Philosophy of Hegel*, ed. Carl J. Friedrich (New York: Modern Library, 1953), p. 144.

59. Paul Strathern, *Hegel in 90 Minutes* (Chicago: Ivan R. Dee, 1997), p. 32.

60. Hegel, *Science of Logic*, pp. 603–605, 612.

61. Strathern might argue that I am misinterpreting what Hegel means by individuality. In reply, I would assert that Hegel's strange descriptions of various concepts in his *Logic* are not adequate to create legitimate dialectics—a dialectic with a legitimate synthesis in this instance—especially where the antitheses are arbitrarily chosen concepts instead of true opposites of the theses. Moreover, Strathern does not offer any eccentric definition of individuality; he presents individuality to his readers as a concept that can be taken at face value. Taken at face value, individuality means particularity.

62. Tucker, *Karl Marx*, p. 46.

63. Ibid., pp. 48–49.

64. Ibid., p. 60.

65. Paul Tillich, *The Protestant Era*, abridged ed., trans. James Luther Adams (Chicago: University of Chicago Press, 1957), p. xxiv; Paul Tillich, *Systematic Theology*, vol. 1 (Chicago: University of Chicago Press, 1951), p. 234; cf. Paul Tillich, *Systematic Theology*, vol. 2 (Chicago: University of Chicago Press, 1957), pp. 90–91, and *Courage*, p. 88.

66. Tillich, *Systematic Theology*, vol. 1, 234; cf. *Courage*, p. 180, *Protestant Era*, p. ix, and *The New Being* (New York: Charles Scribner's Sons, 1955), p. 102.

67. Tillich, *Courage*, pp. 182–90; cf. 39.

68. Leonard F. Wheat, *Paul Tillich's Dialectical Humanism: Unmasking the God Above God* (Baltimore: Johns Hopkins Press, 1970).

69. Tillich, *Systematic Theology*, vol. 1, p. 101.

70. Tillich, *New Being*, p. 102.

CHAPTER 2

1. Paul Tillich, *Perspectives on Nineteenth and Twentieth Century Protestant Theology*, ed. Carl E. Braaten (London: SCM, 1967), p. 122.

2. Robert Tucker, *Philosophy and Myth in Karl Marx* (Cambridge: Cambridge University Press, 1961), p. 57.

3. G. W. F. Hegel, *Phenomenology of Spirit*, trans. A. V. Miller (Oxford: Oxford University Press, 1977), para. 233.

4. Ibid., para. 438.

5. J. B. Baillie, "Translator's Introduction," in G. W. F. Hegel, *The Phenomenology of Mind*, trans. J. B. Baillie (New York: Harper Torchbooks, 1967), p. 37.

6. Hegel, *Phenomenology*, trans. Miller, para. 216.

7. Paul Tillich, *Systematic Theology*, vol. 2 (Chicago: University of Chicago Press, 1957), p. 45.

8. Paul Tillich, *Systematic Theology*, vol. 1 (Chicago: University of Chicago Press, 1951), p. 66.

9. Hegel, *Phenomenology*, trans. Miller, para. 207 (my italics).

10. Ibid., para. 37.

11. Hegel, *Phenomenology*, trans. Baillie, p. 86. Miller's translation of the same passage reads: "The spiritual alone is the *actual*; it is essence, or that which is *being in itself*" (para. 25).

12. Hegel, *Phenomenology*, trans. Miller, para. 309.

13. Ibid.

14. Tillich, *Systematic Theology*, vol. 1, pp. 164–65.

15. Michael N. Forster, *Hegel's Idea of a Phenomenology of Spirit* (Chicago: University of Chicago Press, 1998), p. 194, n. 2.

16. Frederick Beiser, *Hegel* (New York: Routledge, 2005), p. 81.

17. Ibid.

18. Baillie, "Introduction," pp. 37–39.

19. Hegel, *Phenomenology*, trans. Miller, paras. 793, 794 (Hegel's italics).

20. Paul Tillich, *Systematic Theology*, vol. 3 (Chicago: University of Chicago Press, 1963), p. 129.

21. Tillich, *Systematic Theology*, vol. 1, p. 206.

22. Baillie, "Introduction," p. 33.

23. Hegel, *Phenomenology*, trans. Miller, para. 33.

24. Walter Kaufmann, *Hegel: A Reinterpretation* (Garden City, NY: Doubleday Anchor Books, 1966), p. 154.

25. *Phenomenology* is peppered with the word "antithesis." But in almost all cases Hegel is referring to the opposition or contrast—the antithesis—between two concepts (usually not a thesis and an antithesis) and not to the second stage of a dialectic.

26. Kaufmann, *Hegel*, p. 273.

27. Ibid., p. 124.

28. John Edward Toews, in his book *Hegelianism: The Path Toward Dialectical Humanism, 1805–1841* (Cambridge: Cambridge University Press, 1980), p. 95, introduces his chapter 5 with a gloriously comical quotation from a former student of Hegel's, Heinrich Heine: "Occasionally I observed how he [Hegel] looked about in fear that he might have been understood." From Heinrich Heine, *Sämtliche Werke*, ed. O. Walzel, vol. 9, 10 vols. (Leipzig: 1911–15), p. 484.

29. Robert C. Solomon, *In the Spirit of Hegel* (New York and Oxford: Oxford University Press, 1983), p. 582.

30. Robert C. Solomon, *From Hegel to Existentialism* (New York and Oxford: Oxford University Press, 1987), p. 57.

31. Hegel, *Phenomenology*, trans. Miller, para. 50.

32. J. N. Findlay, "Analysis of the Text," in Hegel, *Phenomenology*, trans. Miller, p. 501.

33. Walter Kaufmann, *Hegel: Texts and Commentary* (Garden City, NY: Anchor Books, 1966), pp. 75, 77.

34. Norman agrees that Hegel delivers high praise for dialectics, though in another

context. See Richard Norman, *Hegel's Phenomenology: A Philosophical Introduction* (East Sussex, UK: Sussex University Press, 1976), pp. 25–26. Norman turns to another quotation cited by Kaufmann, a quotation from Hegel's *History of Philosophy*. After showing that Hegel, in the material cited by Kaufmann, says Kant has "correctly" explained and differentiated between thesis, antithesis, and synthesis, Norman comments: "If this is how Hegel 'reproaches' [Kaufmann's word], his praise must be lavish indeed!" Norman, it is true, construes Hegel's dialectics not as thesis, antithesis, and synthesis but as "the problem of *opposites* and their reconciliation" (p. 26). But that misconception or, I could say, overly loose and vague conception, in no way invalidates his opinion that Hegel praises dialectics.

35. Frederick Beiser, *Hegel* (New York: Routledge, 2005), p. 161.

36. Kaufmann, *Texts and Commentary*, p. 75.

37. Kaufmann, *Hegel*, p. 154.

38. J. N. Findlay, *The Philosophy of Hegel: An Introduction and Re-Examination* (New York: Collier, 1958), pp. 66–67.

39. Hegel, *Phenomenology*, trans. Miller, para. 36.

40. Ibid., p. 53.

41. Ibid.

42. Ibid.

43. Ibid.

44. G. W. F. Hegel, *The Philosophy of History*, trans. J. Sibree (New York: Dover, 1956), p. 1.

45. Hegel, *Phenomenology*, trans. Baillie, p. 111.

46. Kaufmann, *Texts and Commentary*, p. 80.

47. Ibid., p. 81, n. 20. Kaufmann is quoting from Hermann Glockner's German work, *Hegel*, vol. 2 (publisher not named, 1940).

48. Hegel, *Phenomenology*, trans. Miller, para. 71.

49. Ibid., para. 89.

50. Ibid.

51. Ibid.

52. Hegel, *Phenomenology*, trans. Baillie, p. 37.

53. Ibid., p. 38.

54. Hegel, *Phenomenology*, trans. Miller, para. 86.

55. Ibid., para. 87.

56. Ibid.

57. Ibid.

58. Ibid.

59. Ibid.

60. Ibid.

61. Ibid.

62. Ibid.

63. Ibid.

64. Ibid., para. 33.

65. Karl Popper, *Conjectures and Refutations: The Growth of Scientific Knowledge* (New York: Routledge, 1963), p. 94.

66. Ibid., p. 95.

67. Kaufmann, *Hegel*, p. 155.

68. Hegel, *Phenomenology*, trans. Miller, para. 203.

69. Ibid., para. 96.

70. Ibid., para. 110.

71. Ibid., para. 90

72. Ibid., para. 91.

73. Ibid., para. 110.

74. Ibid., para. 131.

75. G. W. F. Hegel, *Logic: Encyclopaedia of the Philosophical Sciences, Part One*, trans. William Wallace (Oxford: Oxford University Press, 1975), p. 280.

76. G. W. F. Hegel, *Philosophy of Nature*, trans. A. V. Miller (Oxford: Oxford University Press: 1970), p. 277.

77. Ibid., p. 282.

78. W. T. Stace, *The Philosophy of Hegel* (New York: Dover, 1955), pp. 330–31.

79. Ibid., p. 329.

80. Baillie, "Introduction," p. 52, n. 1 (my italics).

81. Hegel, *Phenomenology*, trans. Miller, para. 125.

82. Ibid., para. 125.

83. Ibid., p. 131.

84. Solomon, *Spirit of Hegel*, p. 367.

85. Hegel, *Phenomenology*, trans. Miller, para. 132.

86. Solomon argues, in substance, that "conditioned" means influenced or determined by the historical and social context. "The truths of particular activities are 'conditioned' by their contexts; for example, what counts as 'art' or 'good art' (or as 'bad art' or as *Kitsch*) at any given time is 'conditioned' by the art world, by the current canons of aesthetic taste, by the art market [and so on]" (Solomon, *Spirit of Hegel*, p. 179). But "influenced" is only remotely related to what Hegel means by the implicit concept

of "conditioned" when Hegel speaks of the "unconditioned universal." Though it is true that this concept is strictly Hegel's and thus is not influenced by the tastes or opinions of anyone else, that isn't Hegel's point. When Hegel says "consciousness does not recognize itself" as "the unconditioned universal," the unconditioned universal is obviously Spirit. We know this because we know that consciousness is a manifestation of Spirit and the "itself" it doesn't recognize is an "object" perceived by consciousness, an object that is also Spirit. In what sense is Spirit, in its guise as the perceived object ("itself") conditioned? The answer is clear: Spirit is *not subject to the limiting condition* that applied to "the This" and "the Things" discussed in the preceding two sections of text—"Sense Certainty" and "Perception." To be specific, Spirit is not subject to the condition that what consciousness perceives must be something material (matter, contrasted with an *idea* or *concept*, the product of a mind). In other words, Spirit is not subject to the condition that it must be visible, audible, or otherwise perceivable by the senses. Hegel is implying that the "unconditioned universal," Spirit, is spiritual (nonmaterial) and invisible.

87. Hegel, *Phenomenology*, trans. Miller, para. 141.

88. Ibid.

89. Ibid., para. 89.

90. Ibid., para. 144.

91. Ibid., para. 161.

92. Ibid.

93. Ibid., para.162.

94. Ibid., para. 161.

95. Ibid., para. 162.

96. Ibid.

97. Ibid., para. 808.

98. Ibid., para. 165.

99. Ibid.

CHAPTER 3

1. The term "metaphysical" as I use it refers to any supernatural entity, power, force, or causal influence that lacks an *independent*, self-conscious mind akin to the mind of a god, a ghost, or a spirit. The Greek Logos is an example of a metaphysical entity. Spinoza's supernatural "substance" within everything in nature is a second example.

(Most interpreters assume that Spinoza's mysterious substance is supernatural, but I suspect it was a nonsupernatural concept in disguise, intended to suggest just enough supernaturalism to hide the full extent of Spinoza's obvious atheism.) Magic is a third example of metaphysics, provided that the magic does not require support from a rational, self-conscious god. Bad luck caused by taking a hotel room on the thirteenth floor is a fourth example. Astrological determinism is a fifth example. Historical predestination controlled not by God but by an impersonal force that causes history to advance according to a Marxian thesis-antithesis-synthesis pattern in history is a sixth example. Telekinesis is a seventh example. Psychics and fortune-tellers are an eighth example.

2. Paul Tillich, *Systematic Theology*, vol. 1 (Chicago: University of Chicago Press, 1951), pp. 233–34. Beiser uses almost the same wording to define pantheism: "The pantheist holds that God is the *substance* or *essence* of all finite things, which are only appearances of it." Frederick Beiser, *Hegel* (New York and London: Routledge, 2005), p. 143.

3. Paul Tillich, *What Is Religion?* trans. James Luther Adams (New York: Harper & Row, 1969), p. 126. In the same vein, Solomon accurately informs us that "pantheism . . . is no more than pious atheism" (Robert C. Solomon, *In the Spirit of Hegel* [New York and Oxford: Oxford University Press, 1983], p. 633).

4. Tillich, *Systematic Theology*, vol. 1, pp. 237–38.

5. Leonard F. Wheat, *Paul Tillich's Dialectical Humanism: Unmasking the God above God* (Baltimore: Johns Hopkins Press, 1970), pp. 30–38.

6. Ibid., pp. 40–41.

7. Ibid., pp. 41–45.

8. Paul Tillich, *Ultimate Concern: Tillich in Dialogue*, ed. D. MacKenzie Brown (New York: Harper & Row, 1948), p. 158 (my italics).

9. John A. T. Robinson, *Honest to God* (Philadelphia: Westminster, 1963), pp. 49, 53, 63, 75, 105, 115, 116, 127, 130.

10. Frederick C. Beiser, "Introduction: Hegel and the Problem of Metaphysics," in Frederick C. Beiser, ed., *The Cambridge Companion to Hegel* (Cambridge: Cambridge University Press, 1993), p. 4.

11. Ibid., p. 5. For elaboration on the connection between metaphysics and supernaturalism, see note 1 above.

12. Robert Tucker, *Philosophy and Myth in Karl Marx* (Cambridge: Cambridge University Press, 1961), p. 43.

13. Ibid., p. 66.

14. Ibid., p. 47.

15. Joseph McCarney, *Hegel on History* (London and New York: Routledge, 2000), pp. 47–48.

16. Solomon, *Spirit of Hegel*, p. 466.

17. Ibid., p. 626.

18. Ibid., p. 630.

19. Robert C. Solomon, *From Hegel to Existentialism* (New York and Oxford: Oxford University Press, 1987), p. 67.

20. G. W. F. Hegel, *Phenomenology of Spirit*, trans. A. V. Miller (Oxford and New York: Oxford University Press, 1977), para. 784.

21. Ibid.

22. Jean Hyppolite, *Genesis and Structure of Hegel's* Phenomenology of Spirit, trans. Samuel Cherniak and John Heckman (Evanston, IL: Northwestern University Press, 1974), p. 567.

23. J. N. Findlay, *The Philosophy of Hegel: An Introduction and Re-Examination* (New York: Collier, 1958), p. 353.

24. Ibid., p. 359.

25. Walter Kaufmann, *Hegel: A Reinterpretation* (Garden City, NY: Doubleday Anchor Books, 1966), p. 273.

26. Ibid., pp. 147–48.

27. Ibid., p. 273.

28. Paul Tillich, *Dynamics of Faith* (New York: Harper & Row, 1957), p. 63.

29. Hegel, *Phenomenology*, trans. Miller, para. 49.

30. Beiser, "Introduction," pp. 5–7.

31. Hegel, *Phenomenology*, trans. Miller, paras. 233, 235, 394, 438.

32. McCarney, *Hegel on History*, p. 42.

33. Solomon, *Spirit of Hegel*, p. 582.

34. Ibid., p. 10.

35. Quoted in Paul Tillich, *Gesammelte Werke*, I (Stuttgart, Germany: Evangelisches Verlagswerk, 1959), p. 96; cited in David Hopper, *Tillich: A Theological Portrait* (New York: J. B. Lippincott, 1968), p. 124.

36. Richard Kroner, "Introduction," in G. W. F. Hegel, *On Christianity: Early Theological Writings*, trans. T. M. Knox (New York: Harper Torchbooks, 1961), p. 22.

37. Ibid., p. 24.

38. Hegel, *Phenomenology*, trans. Miller, para. 77.

39. Paul Tillich, *Systematic Theology*, vol. 3 (Chicago: University of Chicago Press, 1963), p. 329.

40. Tillich, *Systematic Theology*, vol. 1, p. 56.

41. G. W. F. Hegel, "The Preface to the *Phenomenology*," trans. Walter Kaufmann, in *Hegel: Texts and Commentary* (Garden City, NY: Anchor Books, 1966), p. 56; cf.

Hegel, *Phenomenology*, trans. Miller, para. 36, and G. W. F. Hegel, *The Phenomenology of Mind*, trans. J. B. Baillie (New York: Harper Torchbooks, 1967), p. 96.

42. Hegel, *Phenomenology*, trans. Baillie, p. 555. Cf. Miller, para. 532, where "moment" is used as a poor substitute for "stage" (of a dialectic).

43. Tillich, *Systematic Theology*, vol. 1, p. 206.

44. Paul Tillich, *Systematic Theology*, vol. 2 (Chicago: University of Chicago Press, 1957), p. 29.

45. Ibid., pp. 29, 30.

46. Matthew 3:16–17, Mark 1:9–11, Luke 3:21–22, John 1:29–34.

47. Paul Tillich, *Ultimate Concern: Tillich in Dialogue*, ed. D. MacKenzie Brown (New York: Harper & Row, 1965), p. 47.

48. Hegel, *Phenomenology*, trans. Miller, para. 758.

49. Ibid., para. 762.

50. Ibid.

51. Ibid., para. 763.

52. Ibid.

53. Ibid., para. 765.

54. Ibid., para. 767.

55. Ibid.

56. Ibid., para. 771.

57. Ibid., para. 780.

58. Ibid., para. 781.

59. Ibid., para. 784.

60. Ibid., para. 776.

61. Ibid., para. 785.

62. Ibid., para. 786.

63. Ibid., para. 787.

64. Ibid.

65. Ibid., para. 773.

66. Ibid., para. 774.

67. Ibid., para. 780.

68. Tucker, *Karl Marx*, p. 46.

69. Ibid., p. 60.

70. Robert C. Pippin, "You Can't Get There from Here: Transition Problems in Hegel's *Phenomenology of Spirit*," in Beiser, ed., *Cambridge Companion*, p. 78.

71. Cf. Tillich, *Systematic Theology*, vol. 1, p. 206; vol. 2, pp. 9, 20, 21, 22, 33,

35, 67, 148; and vol. 3, p. 129; and J. B. Baillie, "Translator's Introduction," p. 33, in Hegel, *Phenomenology*, trans. Baillie. Baillie is unaware that potentiality refers to a dialectic's thesis, the unconsciousness stage; he thinks potentiality is the state of estrangement. But he does recognize that self-realization progresses from potentiality to actuality, even while remaining unaware that actuality first arises in the antithesis stage of *actual* separation.

72. Hegel, "Preface," trans. Kaufmann, p. 56.

73. Hegel, *Phenomenology*, trans. Miller, para. 673 (my italics).

74. G. W. F. Hegel, *The Philosophy of History*, trans. J. Sibree (New York: Dover, 1956), pp. 323–24 (my italics).

75. Hegel, "Preface," trans. Kaufmann, p. 42.

76. Hegel, *Phenomenology*, trans. Miller, para. 27.

77. Hegel, *Phenomenology*, trans. Baillie, p. 88.

78. G. W. F. Hegel, "Lectures on the Philosophy of History," in *Reason in History*, trans. Robert S. Hartman (New York: Bobbs-Merrill, 1953), p. 70.

79. G. W. F. Hegel, *Philosophy of Nature* (*Encyclopaedia*, Pt. 2), trans. A. V. Miller (Oxford: Clarendon, 1970), pp. 281–84.

80. Hegel, "Philosophy of History," trans. Hartman, p. 20; G. W. F. Hegel, "The Philosophy of History," in *The Philosophy of Hegel*, trans. Carl J. Friedrich and Paul W. Friedrich (New York: Modern Library, 1953), p. 12.

81. Hegel, *Nature*, trans. Miller, p. 277.

82. Ibid., p. 282.

83. Ibid.

84. Tillich, *Systematic Theology*, vol. 1, p. 234.

85. Paul Tillich, *Theology of Culture*, ed. Robert C. Kimball (New York: Oxford University Press, 1964), p. 156; Tillich, *Systematic Theology*, vol. 1, p. 259; vol. 2, pp. 33–36, 128; vol. 3, p. 129.

86. Tillich, *Culture*, p. 156.

87. Tillich, *Systematic Theology*, vol. 2, p. 33.

88. Paul Tillich, *Perspectives on 19th and 20th Century Protestant Theology*, ed. Carl E. Braaten (London: SCM, 1967), pp. 145–46 (my italics).

89. Terry Pinkard, *Hegel: A Biography* (Cambridge: Cambridge University Press, 2000), p. 580.

90. Hegel, *Phenomenology*, trans. Miller, para. 771.

91. Ibid., paras. 144, 222; cf. Hegel, *Phenomenology*, trans. Baillie, p. 656.

92. Hegel, *Phenomenology*, trans. Miller, para. 167.

93. Tillich, *Perspectives*, p. 144 (my italics).

94. Tillich, *Systematic Theology*, vol. 2, p. 45.

95. Hegel, *Phenomenology*, trans. Baillie, p. 511; Hegel, *Phenomenology*, trans. Miller, para. 486. Tillich writes: "In my opinion the two words ['alienation' and 'estrangement'] mean the same thing, but I know that some philosophers prefer the word 'alienation,' perhaps because it is a bit more abstract. I myself have preferred to use the word 'estrangement' because it contains the imagery of the stranger and the *separation* of people who once loved each other and belong *essentially* to each other" (my italics). (Tillich, *Perspectives*, p. 124.)

96. Hegel, *Phenomenology*, trans. Baillie, p. 220.

97. Hegel, *Phenomenology*, trans. Miller, para. 167.

98. Hegel, *Phenomenology*, trans. Baillie, p. 555; cf. Hegel, *Phenomenology*, trans. Miller, para. 532.

99. Hegel, *Phenomenology*, trans. Miller, para. 808; cf. Hegel, *Phenomenology*, trans. Baillie, p. 808. Miller's last paragraph and Baillie's last page have the same number—a coincidence.

100. Hegel, *Phenomenology*, trans. Baillie, p. 808; cf. Hegel, *Phenomenology*, trans. Miller, para. 808.

101. Hegel, *Phenomenology*, trans. Miller, para. 785.

102. Ibid., p. 784.

103. Solomon, *Spirit of Hegel*, p. 584.

104. Tucker, *Karl Marx*, p. 43.

105. Ibid.

106. Tillich, *Perspectives*, p. 245.

107. Hegel, *Phenomenology*, trans. Miller, para. 33.

108. Ibid., para. 89.

109. Ibid., para. 62.

110. Ibid., para. 780.

111. Ibid., para. 804.

112. Ibid., para. 805.

113. Ibid.

114. Ibid., para. 806.

115. Ibid., para. 190.

116. G. W. F. Hegel, *The Philosophy of History*, trans. J. Sibree (New York: Dover, 1956), p. 413.

117. G. W. F. Hegel, "Lectures on the Philosophy of Religion," in *On Art, Religion, Philosophy: Introductory Lectures to the Realm of Absolute Spirit*, ed. J. Glenn Gray (New York: Harper Torchbooks, 1970), p. 182.

118. G. W. F. Hegel, *Phenomenology*, trans. Miller, para. 189.

119. Ibid., para. 193.

120. Ibid., para. 195.

121. Ibid., para. 196.

122. Ibid., para. 808 (my italics).

123. Kaufmann, p. 147.

124. Ibid., pp. 147, 148. My interpretation of Hegel's Schiller adaptation is based on Kaufmann's, which I regard as immune to challenges.

125. The US Census Bureau has compiled world population estimates for 1800 from six sources. The estimates range from 0.813 billion to 1.125 billion, averaging close to 1 billion. See http://www.census.gov/ipc/www/worldhis.html.

126. Hegel, "The Philosophy of History," trans. Friedrich and Friedrich, pp. 16–17.

127. Renato Cristi, *Hegel on Freedom and Authority* (Cardiff: University of Wales Press, 2005); Paul Franco, *Hegel's Philosophy of Freedom* (New Haven, CT: Yale University Press, 1999); Axel Honneth, *The Pathologies of Individual Freedom* (Princeton, NJ, and Oxford: Princeton University Press, 2001); Stephan Houlgate, *An Introduction to Hegel: Freedom, Truth and History*, 2nd ed. (Oxford: Blackwell, 2005); Dudley Knowles, *Hegel and the* Philosophy of Right (London and New York: Routledge, 2002); Joseph McCarney, *Hegel on History* (London and New York: Routledge, 2000), chap. 5, pp. 65–82; Alan Patten, *Hegel's Idea of Freedom* (Oxford: Oxford University Press, 1999); Richard L. Schacht, "Hegel on Freedom," in Alasdair MacIntyre, ed., *Hegel: A Collection of Critical Essays* (Garden City, NY: Doubleday, 1972); Robert M. Wallace, *Hegel's Philosophy of Reality, Freedom, and God* (Cambridge: Cambridge University Press, 2005); and Richard Dien Winfield, "The Theory and Practice of the History of Freedom: On the Right of History in Hegel's *Philosophy of Right*," in Robert L. Perkins, ed., *History and System: Hegel's Philosophy of History* (Proceedings of the 1982 Sessions of the Hegel Society of America) (Albany: State University of New York Press, 1984), pp. 123–44.

128. McCarney, *Hegel on History*, p. 67.

129. Knowles, *Hegel and the* Philosophy of Right, pp. 56–58.

130. Patten, *Hegel's Idea of Freedom*, p. 163.

131. Wallace, *Reality, Freedom, and God*.

CHAPTER 4

1. G. W. F. Hegel, *Phenomenology of Spirit*, trans. A. V. Miller (Oxford: Oxford University Press, 1977), para. 438.

2. Sidney Hook, *Hegel to Marx* (Ann Arbor: University of Michigan Press, 1962), p. 20.

3. Michael N. Forster, *Hegel's Idea of a* Phenomenology of Spirit (Chicago: University of Chicago Press, 1998), pp. 505–10. Also see my chapter 7, first heading.

4. Hegel, *Phenomenology of Spirit*, trans. Miller, para. 808.

5. Ibid., para. 80.

6. Ibid., para. 78.

7. Ibid., para. 808.

8. Ibid., paras. 182, 189, 190, 192, 193, 195.

9. Robert C. Solomon, *In the Spirit of Hegel* (Oxford: Oxford University Press, 1983), p. 20.

10. Hegel, *Phenomenology*, trans. Miller, para. 228.

11. Ibid., para. 181.

12. Ibid., para. 182.

13. Ibid., para. 186.

14. Ibid., para. 807.

15. Ibid., p. 197.

16. Solomon, *Spirit of Hegel*, p. 455.

17. Hegel, *Phenomenology*, trans. Miller, para. 199.

18. Ibid., para. 200.

19. Ibid., para. 201.

20. Ibid.

21. Ibid., p. 202.

22. Ibid., p. 203.

23. Ibid., para. 205.

24. Ibid., para. 206.

25. Ibid., paras. 214, 217.

26. Ibid., para. 222.

27. G. W. F. Hegel, *The Philosophy of History*, trans. J. Sibree (New York: Dover, 1956), p. 378.

28. Hegel, *Phenomenology*, trans. Miller, para. 225.

29. Hegel, *History*, trans. Sibree, p. 379.

30. Hegel, *Phenomenology*, trans. Miller, paras. 228, 229.

31. J. B. Baillie, translator's notes, in G. W. F. Hegel, *Phenomenology of Mind*, trans. J. B. Baillie (New York: Harper Torchbooks, 1967), p. 241.

32. J. N. Findlay, *The Philosophy of Hegel* (New York: Collier, 1958), p. 98.

33. Walter Kaufmann, *Hegel: A Reinterpretation* (Garden City, NY: Doubleday Anchor Books, 1966), p. 140.

34. Richard J. Norman, *Hegel's Phenomenology: A Philosophical Introduction* (Hampshire, UK: Gregg Revivals, 1991 [orig. pub. Sussex University Press, 1976]), p. 60.

35. Solomon, *Spirit of Hegel*, p. 616.

36. Ibid., p. 618.

37. Terry Pinkard, *Hegel's Phenomenology: The Sociality of Reason* (Cambridge: Cambridge University Press, 1994), p. 73.

38. Forster, *Hegel's Idea*, pp. 324–25; cf. 326.

39. Robert Stern, *Hegel and the* Phenomenology of Spirit (Abingdon, UK: Routledge, 2002), pp. 92–93.

40. John W. Burbidge, "'Unhappy Consciousness' in Hegel: An Analysis of Medieval Catholicism?" in Jon Stewart, ed., *The* Phenomenology of Spirit *Reader* (Albany: State University of New York Press, 1998), pp. 192–209.

41. Mark C. Taylor, *Journeys to Selfhood: Hegel & Kierkegaard* (Berkeley: University of California Press, 1980), pp. 108–109.

42. Stanley Rosen, *G. W. F. Hegel: An Introduction to the Science of Wisdom* (South Bend, IN: St. Augustine's, 2000), p. 169.

43. Hegel, *Phenomenology*, trans. Miller, para. 217.

44. Jean Hyppolite, *Genesis and Structure of Hegel's* Phenomenology of Spirit, trans. Samuel Cherniak and John Heckman (Evanston, IL: Northwestern University Press, 1974), p. 191.

45. Hegel, *Phenomenology*, trans. Miller, para. 217.

46. Ibid., p. 218.

47. Hegel, *History*, trans. Sibree, p. 219.

48. Hegel, *Phenomenology*, trans. Miller, paras. 251, 253.

49. Ibid., para. 438.

50. Alasdair MacIntyre, "Hegel on Faces and Skulls," in Stewart, ed., *Reader*, pp. 213–24; cf. Michael Quante, "'Reason . . . Apprehended Irrationally': Hegel's Critique of Observing Reason," in Dean Moyer and Michael Quante, eds., *Hegel's* Phenomenology of Spirit: *A Critical Guide* (Cambridge: Cambridge University Press, 2008), pp. 91–111.

51. Solomon, *Spirit of Hegel*, p. 412.

52. Hegel, *Phenomenology*, trans. Miller, para. 365.

53. Ibid.

54. Ibid., para. 362.

55. Ibid., para. 808.

56. Ibid., para. 369.

57. Ibid., para. 373.

58. Ibid., paras. 374, 375.

59. Ibid., para. 381.

60. Ibid., paras. 410–20.

61. Ibid., para. 420.

62. Ibid., para. 437.

63. Hegel, *Phenomenology*, trans. Baillie, p. 482; cf. Miller's translation, para. 463. An earlier reference to "the dutiful reverence of husband and wife towards each other" (para. 456) reinforces the other quotation.

64. Hegel, *Phenomenology*, trans. Baillie, p. 482.

65. Pinkard, *Sociality*, p. 144.

66. Stern, *Hegel*, pp. 140–41.

67. Hegel, *Phenomenology*, trans. Miller, para. 78.

68. Ibid., p. 481.

69. Ibid., paras. 481, 482.

70. If you are interested in these "real world" tribulations, an excellent summary is available in Stern, *Hegel*, pp. 147–51. Unfortunately, Stern misses Hegel's essential point, which concerns alienation.

71. Hegel, *Phenomenology*, trans. Miller, paras. 511, 512.

72. Ibid., para. 528.

73. Ibid., para. 581.

74. Ibid., para. 584.

75. Ibid., para 585.

76. Ibid., para. 591.

77. Ibid., para. 600.

78. Ibid., para. 617.

79. Ibid., para. 631.

80. Ibid., para. 659.

81. Ibid., para 671.

82. See John 1:7–9; 3:19–21; 8:12, 23; 11:9–10; 12:35–36, 46. John's famous passage "you will know the truth, and the truth will make you free" (8:32) alludes to gnosis, the secret knowledge (in effect, passwords) that would allow Gnostic converts

to sneak past the evil archons guarding a series of concentric aeons surrounding the world so as to reach the remote God of light.

83. Hegel, *Phenomenology*, trans. Miller, para. 686.

84. Ibid., para. 689.

85. In his allegorical film classic *2001: A Space Odyssey*, Stanley Kubrick used four domino-shaped black monoliths to represent seven—*many*—different things: the human attributes of intelligence, superstition, and power (from "the will to power"), derived from Nietzsche's *Thus Spake Zarathustra* (allegory number one); Odysseus's Great Bow, the Trojan Horse, and the Sirens, taken from Homer's *The Odyssey* (allegory number two); and milestones in evolution, from an original man-machine symbiosis tale (allegory number three). See Leonard F. Wheat, *Kubrick's 2001: A Triple Allegory* (Lanham, MD: Scarecrow, 2000), pp. 92–93; also pp. 42–44, 49–50, 54–55, 60, 65, 114–16.

86. Hegel, *Phenomenology*, trans. Miller, para. 707.

87. Ibid.

88. Ibid., para. 723 (italics added).

89. Ibid.

90. Ibid., para. 729.

91. Ibid., para. 730.

92. Ibid., para. 733.

93. Ibid., para. 744.

94. Ibid., para. 787 (Hegel's italics).

95. Ibid., para. 785.

96. The highly anthropomorphic God of early Christianity, who remains the God of many of today's Christians, had a head (Rev. 22:4), arms, and legs; he and man shared the same image (Gen. 1:27). God sat on a throne in heaven, with Jesus sitting at his right hand (Apostles' Creed and Rev. 22:1, 3). Back when God was a manlike being, it made a certain degree of sense for him to have a soul (*pneuma*, spirit), just like mortal men. God's soul or spirit was the Holy Spirit. Its job was to depart from God's physical body and go down to earth to possess people (spirit possession). For example, it possessed the Virgin Mary, causing her to conceive Jesus (Mt. 1:18, 20; Lk. 1:34, 35). It gave the disciples the power to work miracles after Jesus's departure (Acts 1:8; 5:12–16). It also caused—and still causes—people to "speak in tongues," or to participate in the frenzied glossolalia of today's Pentecostal sects (Acts 2:4; 10:44–46). Nowadays, most Christians, particularly the better-educated ones, think of God himself as a spirit—noncorporeal, invisible, shapeless, and even omnipresent, not spatially localized (not on a throne in the sky). It makes no sense for a spirit (God) to

have its own spirit. This is why virtually none of today's Christians comprehends the idea of the Holy Spirit. And it is presumably why Tillich refers to "the fading of the symbol 'Holy Spirit' from the living consciousness of Christianity" (Tillich, *Systematic Theology*, vol. 3, p. 22).

97. Stanley Rosen, *G. W. F. Hegel: An Introduction to the Science of Wisdom* (South Bend, IN: St. Augustine's, 2000), p. 36; cf. Hegel, *Phenomenology*, trans. Miller, para. 780.

98. Michael N. Forster, *Hegel's Idea of a* Phenomenology of Spirit (Chicago: University of Chicago Press, 1998), p. 79, n. 160; p. 195, n. 6; pp. 199–204.

99. Hegel, *Phenomenology*, trans. Miller, para. 78.

100. Peter Singer, *Hegel: A Very Short Introduction* (Oxford: Oxford University Press, 2001), pp. 100, 102; cf. Hook, *Hegel to Marx*, p. 20.

101. Hegel, *Phenomenology*, trans. Miller, paras. 233, 235, 438.

CHAPTER 5

1. G. W. F. Hegel, *The Philosophy of History*, trans. J. Sibree (New York: Dover, 1956), p. 10.

2. Ibid.

3. Walter Kaufmann, *Hegel: A Reinterpretation* (Garden City, NY: Doubleday Anchor Books, 1966), p. 249; cf. Hegel, *History*, trans. Sibree, pp. 18, 104.

4. Hegel, *History*, trans. Sibree, p. 19.

5. Carl J. Friedrich, "Introduction to Dover Edition," in Hegel, *History*, trans. Sibree, second page (unpaginated).

6. Hegel, *History*, trans. Sibree, p. 63.

7. Paul Tillich, *Systematic Theology*, vol. 2 (Chicago: University of Chicago Press, 1957), p. 24.

8. Hegel, *History*, trans. Sibree, p. 18.

9. Ibid., p. 105.

10. Ibid., p. 104.

11. G. W. F. Hegel, *Reason in History: A General Introduction to the Philosophy of History*, trans. Robert S. Hartman (New York: Bobbs-Merrill, 1953), p. 55.

12. Hegel, *History*, trans. Sibree, p. 105.

13. Ibid., p. 112.

14. Ibid., p. 113.

15. G. W. F. Hegel, "The Philosophy of History," trans. Carl J. Friedrich and

Paul W. Friedrich, in Carl J. Friedrich, ed., *The Philosophy of Hegel* (New York: Modern Library, 1953), p. 44.

16. Hegel, *History*, trans. Sibree, p. 111.

17. Ibid., p. 104.

18. Ibid., p. 18.

19. Ibid., pp. 254–55.

20. Ibid., p. 312.

21. Joseph McCarney, *Hegel on History* (London and New York: Routledge, 2000), pp. 146–47.

22. Hegel, *History*, trans. Sibree, p. 18.

23. McCarney, *History*, p. 147.

24. Hegel, *History*, trans. Sibree, pp. 417–18.

25. Hegel claimed, "I am a Lutheran and will remain the same," but the claim was sheer hypocrisy. (G. W. F. Hegel, "Lectures 'On Philosophy,'" trans. E. S. Haldane, in *G. W. F. Hegel on Art, Religion, Philosophy: Introductory Lectures to the Realm of Absolute Spirit*, ed. J. Glenn Gray [New York: Harper Torchbooks, 1970], p. 277.)

26. Hegel, *History*, trans. Sibree, pp. 18, 104.

27. Ibid., p. 44.

28. Ibid., p. 109.

29. Ibid., p. 456.

30. Karl R. Popper, *The Open Society and Its Enemies*, vol. 2, *The High Tide of Prophecy: Hegel, Marx, and the Aftermath* (New York: Harper Torchbooks, 1967; first published 1945), pp. 32–33.

31. Ibid., p. 33.

32. Hegel, *History*, trans. Sibree, p. 412.

33. Popper, *Open Society*, p. 49.

34. Hegel, *History*, trans. Sibree, p. 412.

35. Ibid., p. 442.

36. Charles Taylor, *Hegel* (Cambridge: Cambridge University Press, 1975), p. 442.

37. Ibid., p. 445.

38. Peter Singer, *Hegel: A Very Short Introduction* (Oxford and New York: Oxford University Press, 2001), pp. 54–59.

39. Shlomo Avineri, *Hegel's Theory of the Modern State* (Cambridge: Cambridge University Press, 1972), p. 177.

40. Robert C. Solomon, *In the Spirit of Hegel* (New York and Oxford: Oxford University Press, 1983), p. 18.

41. George H. Sabine, *A History of Political Theory*, rev. ed. (New York: Henry Holt, 1950), p. 633.

42. Michael Allen Fox, *The Accessible Hegel* (Amherst, NY: Prometheus Books, 2005), p. 134. Hegel's quoted words are from *Elements of the Philosophy of Right*, ed. Allen W. Wood, trans. H. B. Nisbet (Cambridge: Cambridge University Press, 1991), p. 240.

43. Terry Pinkard, *Hegel: A Biography* (Cambridge: Cambridge University Press, 2000), p. ix.

44. Pinkard's assertion that there exists a belief that Hegel "glorified the Prussian state" can be supported not only by citing Popper but by citing none other than Karl Marx. Marx wrote that "dialectic became the fashion in Germany, because it seemed to transfigure and to glorify the existing state of things." See Karl Marx, *Capital: A Critique of Political Economy*, ed. Frederick Engels (New York: Modern Library, n.d.; first published 1906), p. 25.

45. Hegel, *History*, trans. Sibree, p. 103.

46. Ibid., p. 112.

47. Hegel, "Philosophy of History," trans. Friedrich and Friedrich, p. 81.

48. Hegel, *History*, trans. Sibree, p. 295.

49. Hegel, "Philosophy of History," p. 113; cf. ibid., p. 399.

50. Hegel, *History*, trans. Sibree, p. 255.

51. Ibid., p. 455.

52. Ibid., pp. 281–83, 306, 314.

53. Ibid., p. 296.

54. Hegel, *Reason in History*, trans. Hartman, p. 39.

55. Hegel, *History*, trans. Sibree, p. 282.

56. Ibid., p. 341; Hegel, "Philosophy of History," trans. Friedrich and Friedrich, p. 88. Hartman's translation is not based on the same German text but does refer to "the Germanic peoples" (Hegel, *Reason in History*, trans. Hartman, p. 24).

57. Hegel, *History*, trans. Sibree, p. 343; cf. Friedrich trans., p. 91: "A union thus arose between the spiritual and secular."

58. Hegel, "Philosophy of History," trans. Friedrich and Friedrich, p. 99.

59. Ibid.

60. Ibid., p. 107.

61. Ibid., p. 91.

62. Solomon, *Spirit of Hegel*, p. 466.

63. Hegel, "Philosophy of History," trans. Friedrich and Friedrich, pp. 92, 104, 108, 117.

64. Ibid., p. 108.

65. Ibid., pp. 107–108.

66. Ibid., pp. 92, 118; cf. Hegel, *History*, trans. Sibree, p. 379.

67. Hegel, "Philosophy of History," trans. Friedrich and Friedrich, p. 92.

68. Ibid., pp. 145, 157.

69. Hegel, *History*, trans. Sibree, p. 165.

70. Ibid., p. 187.

71. Hegel, "Philosophy of History," trans. Friedrich and Friedrich, p. 47.

72. Hegel, *History*, trans. Sibree, p. 198.

73. Ibid., p. 208.

74. Ibid., p. 212.

75. Ibid., p. 214.

76. Ibid., pp. 241–56. The subjective work of art and the objective work of art form an obvious subject-object, or thesis-antithesis, dichotomy and thereby point to what amounts to an eleventh history dialectic. Because this fourth-level dialectic, or sub-sub-subdialectic, is not part of a consistent pattern of fourth-level dialectics, and because the dialectic is so flimsy, I'm not going to count it; but it does need to be acknowledged. The subjective work of art is the beautiful bodies of Greek athletes and maidens who participate in "games and aesthetic displays" (p. 243). Here "the human being elaborates his physical being, in free, beautiful movement and agile vigor, to a work of art" (p. 242). The objective work of art is "the gods of the Greeks" (p. 244). Calling the humans subjects and the divinities objects strikes me as arbitrary. In *Phenomenology* Hegel, in effect, claims that gods are subjective—"picture-thinking" creations that exist only in the human imagination. Humans, on the other hand, objectively exist as real, tangible, physical beings. But it is nevertheless apparent that Hegel's purpose is to create the philosophical dichotomy of subject and object that was popular in his day; he wants to work it in somewhere. For a synthesis, Hegel really has to strain: "The State unites the two phases just considered, viz., the Subjective and the Objective Work of Art. In the State, Spirit is not a mere Object, like the deities, nor, on the other hand, is it merely subjectively developed to a beautiful physique" (p. 250). In other words the state is a dialectical synthesis of subject and object for no other reason than that the humans and the gods are both associated with Greek city-states.

77. Ibid., p. 256.

78. Ibid., p. 275.

79. Ibid., p. 277.

80. Ibid., pp. 285, 290, 296.

81. Ibid., p. 298.

82. Ibid., p. 350 (Sibree's Gemüth interpolation).

83. Ibid., p. 355 (Hegel's italics).

84. Ibid., p. 356.

85. Ibid., p. 389.

86. Ibid., p. 392.

87. Ibid., p. 389.

88. Ibid., p. 366.

89. Ibid., p. 410.

90. Ibid., p. 424.

91. Ibid., p. 425.

92. Ibid., pp. 426, 427.

93. Ibid., p. 454.

94. Ibid., p. 456.

95. Ibid., p. 447.

96. McCarney, *Hegel on History*, p. 82.

97. Hegel, *History*, trans. Sibree, pp. 446–47.

98. Sabine, *Political Theory*, p. 644. Sabine is using an abstract concept of dialectics; he is not referring to the concrete dialectics I have described and of which Sabine is unaware.

99. Bertrand Russell, *A History of Western Philosophy* (New York: Simon & Schuster, 1945), p. 735.

100. Marx, *Capital*, p. 25.

101. James D. White, *Karl Marx and the Intellectual Origins of Dialectical Materialism* (London and New York: Macmillan and St. Martin's Press, 1996), pp. 26–27, 324–26.

102. Marx, *Capital*, p. 22.

103. A. J. P. Taylor, "Introduction," in Karl Marx and Friedrich Engels, *The Communist Manifesto*, trans. Samuel Moore (London: Penguin, 1985), p. 11.

104. Karl Marx and Frederick Engels, *The German Ideology*, ed. C. J. Arthur, with translations by W. Lough, C. Dutt, and C. P. Magill (New York: International Publishers, 1970), p. 44.

105. Marx and Engels, *German Ideology*, pp. 43–44; Frederick Engels, *Anti-Dühring: Herr Eugen Dühring's Revolution in Science*, trans. Emile Burns (New York: International Publishers, 1939), pp. 164, 178–80, 194, 197–99.

106. Engels, *Anti-Dühring*, p. 199.

107. Marx and Engels, *German Ideology*, pp. 45–46.

108. Marx, *Capital*, p. 353.

109. Ibid., pp. 368–69.

110. Ibid., p. 837.

111. Robert Tucker, *Philosophy and Myth in Karl Marx* (Cambridge: Cambridge University Press, 1961) and M. M. Bober, *Karl Marx's Interpretation of History*, 2nd ed., rev. (Cambridge: Harvard University Press, 1950).

112. Tucker, *Karl Marx*, pp. 117–18, 123–61.

113. Bober, *Marx's History*, p. 386.

114. Ibid., pp. 383–85.

115. Marx and Engels, *Manifesto*, p. 88.

116. Marx, *Capital*, p. 837.

117. Engels, *Anti-Dühring*, p. 200.

118. Bober, *Marx's History*, p. 386; cf. Henry J. Koren, *Marx and the Authentic Man* (Pittsburgh: Duquesne University Press, 1967), pp. 27–28.

119. Marx, *Capital*, p. 837.

120. Ibid.

121. Ibid., p. 835.

122. Bober, *Marx's History*, p. 54.

123. Marx, *Capital*, p. 835.

124. Ibid.

125. Ibid., p. 836.

126. For elaboration on this point, see James Farr, "Science: Realism, Criticism, History," in Terrell Carver, ed., *The Cambridge Companion to Marx* (Cambridge: Cambridge University Press, 1991), pp. 106–123.

127. Tucker, *Karl Marx*, p. 227.

128. Ibid., p. 230.

129. Popper, *Open Society*, p. 108.

130. Sabine, *Political Theory*, p. 763.

131. Samuel Enoch Stumpf, *Philosophy: History & Problems*, 5th ed. (New York: McGraw-Hill, 1994), p. 417.

CHAPTER 6

1. Alan M. Olson, *Hegel and the Spirit: Philosophy as Pneumatology* (Princeton, NJ: Princeton University Press, 1992), p. 148.

2. Ibid., p. 5.

3. Ibid., p. 142.

4. Ibid., p. 144.

5. Ibid., p. 142.

6. Carl J. Friedrich, "Introduction to Dover Edition," in G. W. F. Hegel, *The Philosophy of History*, trans. J. Sibree (New York: Dover, 1956), third page (unpaginated).

7. Quoted in Herbert Marcuse, *Reason and Revolution: Hegel and the Rise of Social Theory* (Boston: Beacon, 1960 [repr. of original New York: Oxford University Press, 1941]), p. 12. Marcuse is quoting from Karl Hegel, ed., *Briefe von und an Hegel* (Leipzig, 1887).

8. Marcuse, *Reason and Revolution*, p. 14.

9. Carl J. Friedrich, *The Philosophy of Hegel* (New York: Modern Library, 1953), p. xxxii.

10. Michael J. Inwood, *Hegel* (London: Routledge, 1983), p. 2.

11. Ibid., p. 1.

12. Ibid.

13. Ibid., p. 2.

14. Ibid., p. 1.

15. Peter Singer, *Hegel: A Very Short Introduction* (Oxford: Oxford University Press, 2001), pp. 106, 108.

16. Ibid., p. 89.

17. Raymond Plant, *Hegel* (New York: Routledge. 1999), pp. 51–52.

18. Michael Allen Fox, *The Accessible Hegel* (Amherst, NY: Prometheus Books, 2005), p. 88.

19. Ibid., p. 95.

20. Michael N. Forster, *Hegel's Idea of a Phenomenology of Spirit* (Chicago: University of Chicago Press, 1998), p. 199, n. 14.

21. Charles Taylor, *Hegel* (Cambridge: Cambridge University Press, 1975), pp. 44–45, 87.

22. Ibid., p. 43.

23. Ibid., p. 45.

24. Ibid.

25. Ibid., p. 88.

26. Ibid., p. 102.

27. Ibid.

28. Ibid.

29. Richard J. Norman, *Hegel's Phenomenology: A Philosophical Introduction* (Hampshire, UK: Gregg Revivals, 1991 [orig. pub. Sussex University Press, 1976]), p. 112.

30. Ibid., pp. 112–13.

31. Ibid., p. 113.

32. Ibid.

33. Ibid., pp. 114–15.

34. Ibid., p. 113.

35. Ibid., p. 114.

36. Ibid., p. 115.

37. Robert Stern, *Hegel and the* Phenomenology of Spirit (Abingdon, UK: Routledge, 2002), p. 199.

38. Ibid., p. xiii.

39. Ibid., p. xiv.

40. Ibid.

41. Ibid., pp. 193–94.

42. Robert M. Wallace, *Hegel's Philosophy of Reality, Freedom, and God* (Cambridge and New York: Cambridge University Press, 2005), p. 44.

43. Ibid., p. 315.

44. Ibid., p. 98.

45. Dale M. Schlitt, *Divine Subjectivity: Understanding Hegel's Philosophy of Religion* (Scranton and London: University of Scranton Press, 2009), p. xvii.

46. Ibid., p. 31.

47. Ibid., p. 43.

48. Ibid., p. 104.

49. Ibid., p. 174.

50. Ibid., p. 175.

51. Ibid., p. 299.

52. Walter Kaufmann, *Hegel: A Reinterpretation* (Garden City, NY: Doubleday Anchor Books, 1966), p. 273.

53. Findlay, *Philosophy of Hegel*, p. 353.

54. Forster, *Hegel's Idea*, p. 200.

55. Alexandre Kojève, *Introduction to the Reading of Hegel* (Ithaca and London: Cornell University Press, 1980), pp. 161–62.

56. Ibid., p. 167. I have added the closing dash to correct a punctuation error and to thereby clarify the quotation.

57. Ibid.

58. Ibid., p. 151.

59. Ibid., p. 158.

60. G. W. F. Hegel, *Phenomenology of Spirit*, trans. A. V. Miller (Oxford: Oxford University Press, 1977), para. 25.

61. Forster, *Hegel's Idea*, p. 194.

62. Ibid., p. 196.

63. Ibid., pp. 197–98.

64. Ibid., p. 198, n. 11.

65. Ibid.

66. Joseph McCarney, *Hegel on History* (London: Routledge, 2000), p. 41.

67. Ibid., p. 43.

68. Ibid., p. 46.

69. Ibid.

70. Ibid., p. 47.

71. Ibid.

72. William Desmond, *Hegel's God: A Counterfeit Double?* (Aldershot, UK, and Burlington, VT: Ashgate, 2003), p. 1.

73. Ibid., p. 179.

74. Ibid.

75. Hegel, *Phenomenology*, trans. Miller, para. 785.

76. Ibid., p. 784.

77. Paul Tillich, *Systematic Theology*, vol. 1 (Chicago: University of Chicago Press, 1951), pp. 233–34.

78. Paul Tillich, *What Is Religion?* trans. James Luther Adams (New York: Harper & Row, 1969), p. 126.

79. Robert C. Solomon, *In the Spirit of Hegel: A Study of G. W. F. Hegel's Phenomenology of Spirit* (New York: Oxford University Press, 1983), p. 8.

80. Ibid., p. 27.

81. Tillich disdainfully calls the traditional concept of ontology (contrasted with his own nonsupernatural "ontology") "a speculative-fantastic attempt to establish a world behind the world"—almost identical in phrasing to Solomon's "world behind the scenes." See Tillich, *Systematic Theology*, vol. 1, p. 20.

82. Solomon, *Spirit of Hegel*, p. 631.

83. Ibid., p. 632.

84. Ibid., p. 633.

85. Ibid., p. 629.

86. Ibid., p. 5.

87. Ibid., pp. 5–6.

88. Ibid., p. 6, n. 11.

89. Ibid., p. 7.

90. Ibid., p. 5.

91. Frederick C. Beiser, "Introduction: Hegel and the Problem of Metaphysics," in Frederick C. Beiser, ed., *The Cambridge Companion to Hegel* (Cambridge: Cambridge University Press, 1993), p. 2.

92. Ibid., p. 4. Beiser subsequently, in his book *Hegel* (New York: Routledge, 2005), repeats his claim that Hegel practices metaphysics ("a strictly *immanent* metaphysics") when he says that "Hegel's strategy [is] to resurrect metaphysics on the basis of the Kantian critique of knowledge" (p. 170) and "Our only point now is to stress one fundamental aim of the *Phenomenology*: its attempt to provide a critical foundation for metaphysics" (pp. 172–73).

93. Ibid., p. 5.

94. Ibid., pp. 5–6.

95. Ibid., p. 18.

96. Ibid., p. 19.

97. Ibid., p. 2.

98. Ibid., p. 19.

99. Beiser, *Hegel*, p. 317.

100. G. W. F. Hegel, *The Phenomenology of Mind*, trans. J. B. Baillie (New York: Harper Torchbooks, 1967), p. 86.

101. Hegel, *Phenomenology*, trans. Miller, para. 147.

102. Ibid., para. 165.

103. Beiser, "Introduction," p. 5.

104. Ibid., p. 4.

105. Ibid.

106. Ibid., p. 6.

107. Ibid., p. 9.

108. Ibid., p. 3.

109. Ibid., p. 4.

110. Beiser, *Hegel*, p. 55.

111. Ibid., p. 4.

112. Robert Tucker, *Philosophy and Myth in Karl Marx* (Cambridge: Cambridge University Press, 1961), pp. 47–48.

113. Ibid., p. 55.

114. Ibid., p. 52.

115. Terry Pinkard, *Hegel's Phenomenology: The Sociality of Reason* (Cambridge: Cambridge University Press, 1994), p. 335.

116. Ibid., pp. 8–9.

117. Ibid., p. 254.

118. Ibid., p. 347, n. 14.

119. Hegel, *Phenomenology*, trans. Miller, para. 771.

120. Ibid., para. 111.

121. Ibid., paras. 98, 101, 110.

122. Ibid., para. 113.

123. Pinkard, *Sociality*, pp. 274, 336.

124. Hegel, *Phenomenology*, trans. Miller, paras. 233, 235, 394, 438.

125. Merold Westphal, *History & Truth in Hegel's* Phenomenology, 3rd ed. (Bloomington: Indiana University Press, 1998), p. 129.

126. Ibid., p. 130.

127. Ibid., pp. 144–45.

128. Ibid., p. 188.

129. Ibid., p. 145.

130. Ibid., p. 211.

131. G. W. F. Hegel, *Philosophy of Nature*, trans. A. V. Miller (Oxford: Oxford University Press, 1970), pp. 26, 273–445.

132. Ibid., p. 26.

133. The original publication dates in this sentence sometimes differ from the dates in subsequent endnotes. This is because some of the quotations are from later editions that I own.

134. Kaufmann, *Hegel*, p. xi.

135. J. N. Findlay, *The Philosophy of Hegel: An Introduction and Re-Examination* (New York: Collier, 1958), p. 39.

136. Ibid., pp. 41–42.

137. Ibid., p. 43.

138. Kaufmann, referring to efforts to interpret "Hegelian jargon," mentions "the tradition of paraphrasing obscure texts and, when the original becomes too dark for paraphrase, taking refuge in quotations." Walter Kaufmann, "Foreword," in Ivan Soll, *An Introduction to Hegel's Metaphysics* (Chicago: University of Chicago Press, 1969), p. xi. I strongly suspect that Kaufmann had Findlay's book in mind.

139. Ibid., p. 143.

140. Ibid., pp. 53, 54.

141. Ibid., p. 353.

142. Kaufmann, *Hegel*, p. 112.

143. Ibid., p. 119.

144. Ibid., p. 142.

145. Ibid., p. 148.

146. Hegel, *Phenomenology*, trans. Miller, para. 808.

147. Ibid., para. 729.

148. Solomon, *Spirit of Hegel*, p. 8, note 15.

149. Stanley Rosen, *G. W. F. Hegel: An Introduction to the Science of Wisdom* (South Bend, IN: St. Augustine's, 2000), p. 34 (first published by Yale University Press in 1974.)

150. Ibid., p. 33.

151. Ibid., p. 36.

152. Ibid., p. 233.

153. Ibid.

154. Ibid., p. 234.

155. Ibid.

156. H. S. Harris, *Hegel: Phenomenology and System* (Indianapolis: Hackett, 1995), p. 50.

157. Ibid., p. 61.

158. Ibid.

159. In discussing Hegel's "Reason as lawgiver" and "Reason as testing laws" sections (the topics of microdialectic 13, "Morality")—two pages before his "By now, it should be obvious" remark—Harris does interpret Hegel's moral law example, "Love thy neighbor," as meaning this: "I can do *no* good for my neighbour (or myself) unless we are participants in the great common good that we call 'the State'" (p. 59). But "the State" is a reckless and wholly untenable corruption of Hegel's meaning; Hegel isn't implying anything about states. Harris's injecting states into the discussion is totally at odds with what Hegel says. Hegel isn't even discussing *how* to do good (participating in a state); he is discussing *what* is good in the sense of being moral. The laws tested in Hegel's discussion of "testing laws" require no human participation in a state. They are not promulgated by states; they are moral laws upheld by participants in *society*. Hegel expressly says that "we cannot ask for their origin" and that each such law is "the law within itself," residing within "self-consciousness" (Hegel, *Phenomenology*, trans. Miller, paras. 421, 422). The moral laws are valid, according to Hegel, not because they are reasonable or pass tests—they flunk the tests—but because everybody accepts them as valid. These laws can exist in a tribal society, where there is no state, or in a feudal fiefdom that has not

yet been incorporated into a united Prussia or any other state. All that is required is a community of humans, not necessarily participants in a state. So *Phenomenology*'s earlier discussion of moral laws provides no basis for Harris's preposterous claim that "the *real* Spirit . . . is 'the State.'"

160. Harris, *Hegel*, p. 61.

161. Ibid., p. 62.

162. Hegel, *Phenomenology*, trans. Miller, para. 787.

163. Paul Franco, *Hegel's Philosophy of Freedom* (New Haven, CT: Yale University Press, 1999), p. 83.

164. Ibid., p. 84.

165. Ibid., pp. 83–84.

166. Ibid., p. 102.

167. Ibid.

168. Ibid., p. 229.

CHAPTER 7

1. Walter Kaufmann, *Hegel: A Reinterpretation* (New York: Doubleday Anchor Books, 1966), p. 133.

2. Ibid., p. 135.

3. Robert C. Solomon, *In the Spirit of Hegel* (Oxford: Oxford University Press, 1983), p. 211.

4. Ibid., pp. 213–14.

5. Robert Stern, *Hegel and the* Phenomenology of Spirit (London: Routledge, 2002), p. 9.

6. Ibid., p. 10.

7. Michael N. Forster, *Hegel's Idea of a* Phenomenology of Spirit (Chicago: University of Chicago Press, 1998), p. 501.

8. Jon Stewart, "The Architectonic of Hegel's *Phenomenology of Spirit*," in Jon Stewart, ed., *The* Phenomenology of Spirit *Reader: Critical and Interpretive Essays* (Albany: State University of New York Press, 1998), pp. 444–77, esp. pp. 447–50.

9. Forster, *Hegel's Idea*, p. 509.

10. Ibid., pp. 509–10.

11. Ibid., p. 505.

12. G. W. F. Hegel, *Phenomenology of Spirit*, trans. A. V. Miller (Oxford: Oxford University Press, 1977), para. 802.

13. Hegel, *Phenomenology*, trans. Miller, paras. 794, 795, 797, 805.

14. Ibid., paras. 77, 80.

15. Forster, *Hegel's Idea*, p. 506.

16. Ibid., p. 537.

17. Ibid., pp. 507–509.

18. Ibid., p. 541.

19. Ibid., p. 543.

20. Ibid., p. 537.

21. Hegel, *Phenomenology*, trans. Miller, para. 444.

22. Frederick Beiser, *Hegel* (New York: Routledge, 2005), p. 216.

23. Ibid., p. 214.

24. Forster, *Hegel's Idea*, pp. 536–37.

25. Solomon, though not explicitly asserting that the falseness of Christianity is the theme of *Phenomenology*, comes close to saying just that in his astute analysis of Hegel's atheism (Solomon, *Spirit of Hegel*, pp. 580–84).

26. Ibid., p. 211.

27. Will Dudley, "Ethical Life, Morality, and the Role of Spirit in the *Phenomenology of Spirit*," in Dean Moyer and Michael Quante, eds., *Hegel's* Phenomenology of Spirit: *A Critical Guide* (Cambridge: Cambridge University Press, 2008), p. 136.

28. Hegel, *Phenomenology*, trans. Miller, para. 233.

29. Ibid., para. 50.

30. Walter Kaufmann, *Hegel: Texts and Commentary* (Garden City, NY: Anchor Books, 1966), p. 75.

31. Kaufmann, *Reinterpretation*, p. 135.

32. Ibid., p. 141.

33. Ibid., p. 142.

34. Solomon, *Spirit of Hegel*, p. 412.

35. Ibid., p. 214.

36. Hegel, *Phenomenology*, trans. Miller, para. 438.

37. Ibid., para. 658.

38. Robert Stern, *Hegel*, p. 180.

39. Solomon, *Spirit of Hegel*, pp. 578, 622–25.

40. Ibid., p. 623.

41. Hegel, *Phenomenology*, trans. Miller, para. 658.

42. Solomon, *Spirit of Hegel*, p. 623.

43. Ibid.

44. Maurice Goguel, *Jesus and the Origins of Christianity*, vol. 2, *The Life of Jesus*, trans. Olive Wyon (New York: Harper Torchbooks, 1960), p. 392.

45. G. W. F. Hegel, *The Philosophy of History*, trans. J. Sibree (New York: Dover, 1956), pp. 327–28. The differences in phrasing between my and Hegel's quotations of the same sayings of Jesus result from two factors: (1) I am quoting the Revised Standard Version of the Bible whereas Hegel is using a much earlier German translation, probably Martin Luther's, and (2) Hegel's quotation may have been further altered by German-to-English translation.

46. Solomon, *Spirit of Hegel*, p. 622.

47. Albert Schweitzer, *The Quest of the Historical Jesus*, trans. W. Montgomery (New York: Macmillan, 1961), p. 398.

48. Ibid., p. 401.

49. Paul Tillich, *Systematic Theology*, vol. 2 (Chicago: University of Chicago Press, 1957), p. 131 (my italics).

50. Walter Kaufmann, *Hegel*, pp. 32, 33.

51. Terry Pinkard, *Hegel's Phenomenology: The Sociality of Reason* (Cambridge: Cambridge University Press, 1994), pp. 207–20.

52. Hegel, *Phenomenology*, trans. Miller, para. 658.

53. Terry Pinkard, *Hegel: A Biography* (Cambridge and New York: Cambridge University Press, 2000), p. 224.

54. Solomon, *Spirit of Hegel*, p. 284.

55. Paul Tillich, *Systematic Theology*, vol. 1 (Chicago: University of Chicago Press, 1951), p. 58.

56. Ibid., p. 50.

57. Hegel, *Phenomenology*, trans. Miller, para. 761.

58. Ibid., para. 784.

59. Robert B. Pippin, *Hegel's Idealism: The Satisfactions of Self-Consciousness* (Cambridge: Cambridge University Press), 1989, pp. 4–5.

60. Hegel, *Phenomenology*, trans. Miller, para. 771.

61. An earlier quotation referring to the microdialectics as "education" is worth repeating: "The series of configurations [dialectics] which consciousness goes through along this road is, in reality, the detailed history of the *education* of consciousness itself to the standpoint of Science [dialectics]" (Hegel's italics). Ibid., para. 78.

62. Ibid., para. 752.

63. Solomon comments: "Hegel discovered, like hundreds of academic hopefuls before him and since, that obscurity and profundity are easily confused, that the smaller

the audience, the more academically acceptable one is likely to be, and that the harder one is to understand, the less likely one is to be refuted" (*Spirit of Hegel*, p. 170).

64. Pippin, *Hegel's Idealism*, p. 5.

65. See George Santayana, *Reason in Religion* (New York: Collier, 1962), vol. 3 of *The Life of Reason* (1906); Walter Lippmann, *A Preface to Morals* (Boston: Beacon, 1960), first published in 1929; H. L. Mencken, *Treatise on the Gods* (New York: Vintage Books, 1963), first published in 1930; Homer W. Smith, *Man and His Gods* (New York: Grosset & Dunlap, 1952); and Richard Dawkins, *The God Delusion* (Boston: Houghton Mifflin, 2006).

66. G. W. F. Hegel, "The Philosophy of History," trans. Carl J. Friedrich and Paul W. Friedrich, in Carl J. Friedrich, ed., *The Philosophy of Hegel* (New York: Modern Library, 1953), pp. 16–17.

67. G. W. F. Hegel, *The Philosophy of History*, trans. J. Sibree (New York: Dover, 1956), p. 10.

68. Hegel, *Phenomenology*, trans. Miller, para. 808.

69. See Pinkard, *Hegel* (2000), pp. 16–22, 25–26. Hegel, born August 27, 1770, was eighteen when he enrolled at the Tübingen seminary in the winter of 1788. This is the approximate age when human intelligence reaches its plateau. At this age, if not earlier among precocious children such as Hegel, people who ultimately abandon their childhood beliefs in religious supernaturalism often begin and sometimes complete their drift into doubt. An away-from-home environment and rebellious friends— Hegel's Tübingen situation—facilitates the switch to atheism. And we know that by 1790 Hegel and his closest friends, Hölderlin and Schelling, had "resolved not to become pastors" (ibid., p. 21). In fact, Hegel tried after completing the first two years of his studies at Tübingen (a two-year program of general and philosophical studies that preceded a three-year program of theological studies) to switch to the law program, but his father blocked the change (ibid., p. 28). Solomon refers to "the cynicism of his theological studies at the *Stift* [Tübingen]" (Solomon, *Spirit of Hegel*, p. 588). We also know that Hegel's religious writings of the 1790s reveal a strong antipathy toward religion. Hegel's unpublished Tübingen essay, written in 1793 while Hegel was still a seminary student, accuses Christianity of "human degradation" (ibid., p. 585). It therefore seems likely that agnosticism infiltrated Hegel's mind even before his seminary days and that, in any case, Hegel's atheism reached fruition sometime during his first two seminary years. Since Hegel's mind is the mind through which Spirit achieves self-realization, and since atheism is the essence (not the detailed content) of self-realization, and since there is no evidence that any other human has subsequently realized that he

or she is Spirit (as defined by Hegel), we can interpret Spirit's release from bondage to superstition as Hegel's personal conversion to atheism. Hegel's "realization" that he is "God" becomes Spirit's achievement of "freedom." So, by this interpretation of freedom, Hegelian freedom is simply Hegel's conversion to atheism. This conversion occurred during the period of Germanic monarchy. It may be all there is to the freedom that Hegel claims arrived during the Germanic period.

70. Renato Cristi, *Hegel on Freedom and Authority* (Cardiff: University of Wales Press, 2005), p. 46.

71. Hegel, *Phenomenology*, trans. Miller, para. 181.

72. Hegel, *Philosophy of History*, trans. Sibree, p. 19.

73. Paul Tillich, *Systematic Theology*, vol. 3 (Chicago: University of Chicago Press, 1963), p. 403.

74. Karl Marx, *Early Writings*, trans. and ed. T. B. Bottomore (London: C. A. Watts, 1963), p. 43.

75. Pippin, *Hegel's Idealism*, p. 3.

76. Tillich, *Systematic Theology*, vol. 3, p. 329.

77. Paul Tillich, *Theology of Culture*, ed. Robert C. Kimball (New York: Oxford University Press, 1959), p. 12.

78. Tillich, *Systematic Theology*, vol. 1, p. 163.

79. Ibid.

80. Paul Tillich, *Dynamics of Faith* (New York: Harper & Row, 1957), p. 47.

81. Tillich, *Systematic Theology*, vol. 1, p. 245.

82. Paul Tillich, *Love, Power, and Justice* (New York: Oxford University Press, 1954), p. 109.

83. Paul Tillich, *Ultimate Concern: Tillich in Dialogue*, ed. D. MacKenzie Brown (New York: Harper & Row, 1965), p. 158.

84. Tillich, *Dynamics*, p. 5.

85. Tillich, *Systematic Theology*, vol. 3, pp. 409–410.

86. Paul Tillich, *The Eternal Now* (New York: Charles Scribner's Sons, 1956), p. 114.

87. Tillich, *Ultimate Concern*, p. 77; cf. *Systematic Theology*, vol. 1, p. 56.

TRANSLATIONS USED FOR WORKS BY HEGEL

TRANSLATIONS OF *PHENOMENOLOGY*

The Phenomenology of Mind. Translated by J. B. Baillie. New York: Harper Torchbooks, 1967. First published 1910.

Phenomenology of Spirit. Translated by A. V. Miller. Oxford: Clarendon, 1977.

Preface to Phenomenology of Spirit. Translated by Walter Kaufmann. In *Hegel: Texts and Commentary*. Garden City, NY: Anchor Books, 1966.

TRANSLATIONS OF THE *PHILOSOPHY OF HISTORY*

"The Philosophy of History" (abridged). Translated by Carl J. Friedrich and Paul W. Friedrich. In *The Philosophy of Hegel*, edited by Carl Friedrich, pp. 1–158. New York: Modern Library, 1953.

The Philosophy of History. Translated by J. Sibree. New York: Dover, 1956.

Reason in History. Translated by Robert S. Hartman. New York: Bobbs-Merrill, 1953.

TRANSLATIONS OF OTHER WORKS BY HEGEL

On Christianity: Early Theological Writings. Translated by T. M. Knox. New York: Harper Torchbooks, 1961. First published 1948.

Hegel's Logic: Being Part One of the Encyclopaedia of the Philosophical Sciences. Translated by William Wallace. Oxford: Clarendon, 1975. First published 1873.

Hegel's Philosophy of Nature: Being Part Two of the Encyclopaedia of the Philosophical Sciences. Translated by A. V. Miller. Oxford: Clarendon, 1970.

Hegel's Science of Logic. Translated by A. V. Miller. Atlantic Highlands, NJ: Humanities Press International, 1989. First published 1969.

"The History of Philosophy" (abridged). Translated by Carl J. Friedrich. In Friedrich, *Philosophy of Hegel*, pp. 159–73.

Lecture "On Art." Translated by Bernard Bosanquet. In *On Art, Religion, Philosophy: Introductory Lectures to the Realm of Absolute Spirit*, edited by J. Glenn Gray. New York, Harper Torchbooks, 1970.

Lecture "On Philosophy." Translated by E. S. Haldane. In Gray, *Introductory Lectures*.

Lecture "On Religion." Translated by E. B. Speirs and J. Burdon Sanderson. In Gray, *Introductory Lectures*.

"Lectures on Aesthetics" (abridged). Translated by E. Bosanquet and W. M. Bryant. In Friedrich, *Philosophy of Hegel*, pp. 331–95.

"Philosophy of Right and Law, or Natural Law and Political Science Outlined" (abridged). Translated by J. M. Sterrett and Carl J. Friedrich. In Friedrich, *Philosophy of Hegel*, pp. 219–329.

"The Science of Logic" (abridged). Translated by W. H. Johnston and L. C. Struthers. In Friedrich, *Philosophy of Hegel*, pp. 174–217.

TRANSLATIONS USED FOR WORKS BY MARX AND ENGELS

Engels, Friedrich. Anti-Dühring: *Herr Eugen Dühring's Revolution in Science.* Translated by Emile Burns. New York: International Publishers, 1939.

———. *The German Ideology, Part One with Selections from Parts Two and Three and Supplementary Texts.* Edited and introduction by C. J. Arthur. New York: International Publishers, 1970.

Marx, Karl. *Capital: A Critique of Political Economy.* Volume 1. Translated by Samuel Moore and Edward Aveling. New York: Modern Library, n.d. First published 1906.

Marx, Karl, and Friedrich Engels. *The Communist Manifesto.* Translated by Samuel Moore. Introduction and notes by A. J. P. Taylor. London and New York: Penguin Books, 1985; Moore trans. first published 1888.

Marx, Karl, and Friedrich Engels. *A Contribution to the Critique of Political Economy.* Translated by S. W. Ryazanskaya. Introduction by Maurice Dobb. New York: International Publishers, 1970.

BIBLIOGRAPHY

246 AUTHORS OF WORKS ON HEGEL, MARX, OR BOTH WHO EITHER DENY THAT HEGEL USES THESIS-ANTITHESIS-SYNTHESIS DIALECTICS, REDEFINE DIALECTICS, FAIL TO PROVIDE ACCURATE EXAMPLES, OR IGNORE THE TOPIC

(Authors with More Than One Listed Work Are Counted Only Once)

190 AUTHORS WRITING ABOUT HEGEL OR BOTH HEGEL AND MARX

Acton, H. B. "Hegel, Georg Wilhelm Friedrich." In *The Encyclopedia of Philosophy*. Volume 3. New York: Macmillan and Free Press, 1967.

Adelman, Howard. "Of Human Bondage: Labor, Bondage, and Freedom in *Phenomenology*." In *The* Phenomenology of Spirit *Reader: Critical and Interpretive Essays*, edited by Jon Stewart, pp. 155–71. Albany: State University of New York Press, 1998.

Ahlers, Rolf. "The Dialectic in Hegel's Philosophy of History." In *History and System: Hegel's Philosophy of History* (Proceedings of the 1982 Sessions of the Hegel Society of America), edited by Robert L. Perkins, pp. 149–66. Albany: State University of New York Press, 1984.

Arthur, Christopher J. "Hegel as Lord and Master." In *Socialism, Feminism and Philosophy: A Radical Philosophy Reader*, edited by Sean Sayers and Peter Osborne, pp. 27–45. London and New York: Routledge, 1990.

Avineri, Shlomo. "Consciousness and History." In *New Studies in Hegel's Philosophy*, edited by Warren E. Steinkraus, pp. 108–18. New York: Holt, Rinehart and Winston, 1971.

————. "The Fossil and the Phoenix: Hegel and Krochmal on the Jewish Volkgeist." In Perkins, *History and System*, pp. 47–63.

————. "Hegel Revisited." In *Hegel: A Collection of Critical Essays*, edited by Alasdair MacIntyre, pp. 329–48. Garden City, NY: Doubleday, 1972.

————. *Hegel's Theory of the Modern State*. Cambridge and New York: Cambridge University Press, 1972.

Baillie, J. B. "Translator's Introduction." In G. W. F. Hegel, *The Phenomenology of Mind*. Translated by J. B. Baillie, pp. 21–64. New York: Harper Torchbooks, 1967.

Beiser, Frederick C., ed. *The Cambridge Companion to Hegel*. Cambridge and New York: Cambridge University Press, 1993.

————. *Hegel*. New York and London: Routledge, 2005.

————. "Hegel's Historicism." In Beiser, *Cambridge Companion*, pp. 270–300.

————. "Introduction: Hegel and the Problem of Metaphysics." In Beiser, *Cambridge Companion*, pp. 1–24.

————. "'Morality' in Hegel's *Phenomenology of Spirit*." In *The Blackwell Guide to Hegel's* Phenomenology of Spirit, edited by K. Westphal, pp. 209–25. Malden, MA: Wiley-Blackwell, 2009.

Bencivenga, Ermanno. *Hegel's Dialectical Logic*. Oxford and New York: Oxford University Press, 2000.

Benhabib, Seyla. "On Hegel, Women, and Irony." In *Feminist Interpretations of G. W. F. Hegel*, edited by Patricia Jagentowicz Mills, pp. 25–43. University Park: Pennsylvania State University Press, 1996.

Bosteels, Bruno. "Hegel in America." In *Hegel and the Infinite: Religion, Politics, and Dialectic*, edited by Slavoj Žižek et al., pp. 67–90. New York: Columbia University Press, 2011.

Brinkmann, Klaus. "The Dialectic of the Inverted World and the Meaning of *Aufhebung*." In *The Dimensions of Hegel's Dialectic*, edited by Nectarios G. Limnatis, pp. 123–39. London and New York: Continuum, 2010.

Bronowski, J., and Bruce Mazlish. *The Western Intellectual Tradition: From Leonardo to Hegel*. New York: Dorset, 1986.

Brown, Alison L. "Hegelian Silences and the Politics of Communication: A Feminist Appropriation." In Mills, *Feminist Interpretations*, pp. 299–319.

————. *On Hegel*. Belmont, CA: Wadsworth, 2001.

Burbidge, John. "Hegel's Conception of Logic." In Beiser, *Cambridge Companion*, pp. 86–101.

Bykova, Marina F. "Spirit and Concrete Subjectivity in Hegel's *Phenomenology of Spirit*." In K. Westphal, *Blackwell Guide*, pp. 265–95.

———. "'Unhappy Consciousness' in Hegel: An Analysis of Medieval Catholicism?" In Stewart, Spirit *Reader*, pp. 192–209.

Caputo, John D. "The Perversity of the Absolute, the Perverse Core of Hegel, and the Possibility of Radical Theology." In Žižek et al., *Hegel & the Infinite*, pp. 47–66.

Clarke, Eric O. "Fetal Attraction: Hegel's An-aesthetics of Gender." In Mills, *Feminist Interpretations*, pp. 151–75.

Collingwood, R. G. *The Idea of History*. New York: Oxford University Press, 1956. First published 1946.

Copleston, Frederick C. "Hegel and the Rationalization of Mysticism." In Steinkraus, *Hegel's Philosophy*, pp. 187–200.

Cristi, Renato. *Hegel on Freedom and Authority*. Cardiff: University of Wales Press, 2005.

Crites, Stephen. *Dialectic and Gospel in the Development of Hegel's Thinking*. University Park: Pennsylvania State Press, 1998.

Crockett, Clayton, and Creston Davis. "Introduction: Risking Hegel: A New Reading for the Twenty-First Century." In Žižek et al., *Hegel & the Infinite*, pp. 1–18.

De Nys, Martin J. *Hegel and Theology*. London and New York: T & T Clark, 2009.

———. "Mediation and Negativity in Hegel's Phenomenology of Christian Consciousness." In Stewart, Spirit *Reader*, pp. 401–423.

De Laurentiis, Allegra. "Absolute Knowing." In K. Westphal, *Blackwell Guide*, pp. 246–64.

Desmond, William. "Between Finitude and Infinity: On Hegel's Sublationary Infinitism." In Žižek et al., *Hegel & the Infinite*, pp. 115–40.

———. "Hegel, Art, and History. In Perkins, *History and System*, pp. 173–84.

———. *Hegel's God: A Counterfeit Double?* Aldershot, UK, and Burlington, VT: Ashgate, 2003.

Devi, B. Nirmala. *A Study of the Dialectic of Hegel*. Dehli: Eastern Book Linkers, 1995.

Devries, Willem A. "Sense Certainty and the 'This-Such.'" In *Hegel's* Phenomenology of Spirit: *A Critical Guide*, edited by Dean Moyar and Michael Quante, pp. 63–75. Cambridge: Cambridge University Press, 2008.

Dickey, Laurence. "Hegel on Religion and Philosophy." In Beiser, *Cambridge Companion*, pp. 301–47.

———. "Religion, History, and Spirit in Hegel's *Phenomenology of Spirit*." In K. Westphal, *Blackwell Guide*, pp. 226–45.

Dove, Kenley R. "Hegel's Phenomenological Method." In Stewart, Spirit *Reader*, pp. 52–75. Also in Steinkraus, *Hegel's Philosophy*, pp. 34–56.

Dudley, Will. "Ethical Life, Morality, and the Role of Spirit in the *Phenomenology of Spirit*." In Moyar and Quante, *Hegel's* Phenomenology, pp. 130–49.

Dulckeit, Katharina. "Can Hegel Refer to Particulars?" In Stewart, Spirit *Reader*, pp. 105–21.

Düsing, Klaus. "Ontology and Dialectic in Hegel's Thought." In Limnatis, *Hegel's Dialectic*, pp. 97–122.

Ferrini, Cinzia. "The Challenge of Reason: From Certainty to Truth." In K. Westphal, *Blackwell Guide*, pp. 72–91.

———. "Reason Observing Nature." In K. Westphal, *Blackwell Guide*, pp. 92–135.

Findlay, J. N. "The Contemporary Relevance of Hegel." In MacIntyre, *Hegel Essays*, pp. 1–20.

———. "Hegel's Use of Teleology." In Steinkraus, *Hegel's Philosophy*, pp. 92–107.

———. *The Philosophy of Hegel: An Introduction and Re-Examination*. New York: Collier, 1958.

Flay, Joseph C. "Hegel's 'Inverted World,'" In Stewart, Spirit *Reader*, pp. 138–52.

Forster, Michael N. "Hegel's Dialectical Method." In Beiser, *Cambridge Companion*, pp. 130–70.

———. *Hegel's Idea of a Phenomenology of Spirit*. Chicago: University of Chicago Press, 1998.

Fox, Michael Allen. *The Accessible Hegel*. Amherst, NY: Prometheus Books, 2005.

Franco, Paul, *Hegel's Philosophy of Freedom*. New Haven, CT: Yale University Press, 1999.

Friedrich, Carl J., ed. and intro. *The Philosophy of Hegel*. New York: Modern Library, 1953.

Fulda, Hans-Friedrich. "Science of the *Phenomenology of Spirit*: Hegel's Program and Its Implementation." In Moyar and Quante, *Hegel's* Phenomenology, pp. 21–42.

Gabriel, Marcus. "The Dialectic of the Absolute: Hegel's Critique of Transcendent Metaphysics." In Limnatis, *Hegel's Dialectic*, pp. 76–96.

Gadamer, Hans-Georg. *Hegel's Dialectic: Five Hermeneutical Studies*. New Haven, CT, and London: Yale University Press, 1971.

Godfrey, F. La T. "Hegel's Absolute and Theism." In Steinkraus, *Hegel's Philosophy*, pp. 167–86.

Gram, Moltke S. "Moral and Literary Ideals in Hegel's Critique of "The Moral World-View.'" In Stewart, Spirit *Reader*, pp. 307–33.

Gray, J. Glenn. "Introduction: Hegel's Understanding of Absolute Spirit." In G. W. F. Hegel, *On Art, Religion, Philosophy*. Translated by J. Glenn Gray. New York: Harper Torchbooks, 1970.

Guyer, Paul. "Thought and Being: Hegel's Critique of Kant's Theological Philosophy." In Beiser, *Cambridge Companion*, pp. 171–210.

Hardimon, Michael O. *Hegel's Social Philosophy: The Project of Reconciliation*. Cambridge: Cambridge University Press, 1994.

Harris, Errol E. "Hegel's Theory of Feeling." In Steinkraus, *Hegel's Philosophy*, pp. 71–91.

Harris, H. S. *Hegel: Phenomenology and System*. Indianapolis: Hackett, 1996.

———. "Hegel's Intellectual Development to 1807." In Beiser, *Cambridge Companion*, pp. 25–51.

———. "Hegel's Phenomenology of Religion." In *Thought and Faith in the Philosophy of Hegel*, by John Walker, pp. 89–111. Dordrecht, Netherlands: Kluwer Academic, 1991.

Hartman, Robert S. "Introduction." In G. W. F. Hegel, *Reason in History*, trans. Robert S. Hartman New York: Bobbs-Merrill, 1953.

Hartmann, Klaus. "Hegel: A Non-Metaphysical View." In MacIntyre, *Hegel Essays*, pp. 101–124.

Hartnack, Justus. "Kierkegaard's Attack on Hegel." In Walker, *Thought and Faith*, pp. 121–32.

Heidegger, Martin, *Hegel's Phenomenology of Spirit*. Bloomington: Indiana University Press, 1988.

Heidemann, Dietmar H. "Doubt and Dialectic: Hegel on Logic, Metaphysics, and Skepticism." In Limnatis, *Hegel's Dialectic*, pp. 157–72.

———. "Substance, Subject, System: The Justification of Science in Hegel's *Phenomenology of Spirit*." In Moyar and Quante, *Hegel's* Phenomenology, pp. 1–20.

Heiss, Robert. *Hegel Kierkegaard Marx: Three Great Philosophers Whose Ideas Changed the Course of Civilization*. Translated by E. B. Garside. New York: Delacorte, 1975.

Honneth, Axel. "From Desire to Recognition: Hegel's Account of Human Sociality." In Moyar and Quante, *Hegel's* Phenomenology, pp. 76–90.

———. *The Pathologies of Individual Freedom*. Princeton, NJ, and Oxford: Princeton University Press, 2001.

Hook, Sidney. *From Hegel to Marx*. Ann Arbor: University of Michigan Press, 1962.

Horstmann, Rolf-Peter. "The *Phenomenology of Spirit* as a 'Transcendentalistic" Argument for a Monistic Ontology." In Moyar and Quante, *Hegel's* Phenomenology, pp. 43–62.

Hösle, Vittoria. "What Can We Learn from Hegel's Objective-Idealist Theory of the Concept that Goes Beyond the Theories of Sellars, McDowell, and Brandom?" In Limnatis, *Hegel's Dialectic*, pp. 216–36.

Houlgate, Stephen. *An Introduction to Hegel: Freedom, Truth and History*. 2nd ed. Oxford: Blackwell, 2005.

Hoy, David Couzens. "The Ethics of Freedom: Hegel on Reason as Law-Giving and Law-Testing." In K. Westphal, *Blackwell Guide*, pp. 153–71.

———. "Hegel, *Antigone*, and Feminist Critique: The Spirit of Ancient Greece." In K. Westphal, *Blackwell Guide*, pp. 172–89.

Hylton, Peter. "Hegel and Analytic Philosophy." In Beiser, *Cambridge Companion*, pp. 445–85.

Hyppolite, Jean. *Genesis and Structure of Hegel's* Phenomenology of Spirit. Evanston, IL: Northwestern University Press, 1974.

———. "Hegel's Phenomenology and Psychoanalysis." In Steinkraus, *Hegel's Philosophy*, pp. 57–70.

Inwood, Michael J. *Hegel*. London: Routledge, 1983.

Irigarahy, Luce. "The Eternal Irony of the Community." In Mills, *Feminist Interpretations*, pp. 45–57.

Jaeschke, Walter. "World History and the History of the Absolute Spirit." In Perkins, *History and System*, pp. 101–15; also in Walker, *Thought and Faith*, pp. 9–27.

James, David. *Hegel: A Guide for the Perplexed*. London: Continuum, 2007.

Jameson, Fredric. *The Hegel Variations: On the Phenomenology of the Spirit*. New York: Verso, 2010.

Jamros, Daniel P. "'The Appearing God' in Hegel's *Phenomenology of Spirit*." In Stewart, Spirit *Reader*, pp. 334–47.

Johnston, Adrian. "The Weakness of Nature: Hegel, Freud, Lacan, and Negativity Materialized." In Žižek et al., *Hegel & the Infinite*, pp. 159–80.

Kainz, Howard P. *Hegel's* Phenomenology, Part I: *Analysis and Commentary*. Tuscaloosa: University of Alabama Press, 1976.

———. *Hegel's* Phenomenology, Part II: *The Evolution of Ethical and Religious Consciousness to the Dialectical Standpoint*. Athens: Ohio University Press, 1983.

Kaufmann, Walter. "Foreword." In *An Introduction to Hegel's Metaphysics*, by Ivan Soll. Chicago: University of Chicago Press, 1969.

———. *Hegel: A Reinterpretation*. Garden City, NY: Doubleday Anchor Books, 1966.

———. "The Hegel Myth and Its Method." In MacIntyre, *Hegel Essays*, pp. 21–60.

———. "Hegel's Ideas about Tragedy." In Steinkraus, *Hegel's Philosophy*, pp. 201–20.

———. *Hegel: Texts and Commentary*. Garden City, NY: Doubleday, 1966.

———. "The Young Hegel and Religion." In MacIntyre, *Hegel Essays*, pp. 61–100.

Kelly, George Armstrong. "Notes on Hegel's 'Lordship and Bondage.'" In Stewart, Spirit *Reader*, pp. 172–91, and in MacIntyre, *Hegel Essays*, pp. 189–219.

Knowles, Dudley. *Hegel and the* Philosophy of Right. London and New York: Routledge, 2002.

Knox, T. Malcolm. "A Plea for Hegel." In Steinkraus, *Hegel's Philosophy*, pp. 1–17.

Knox, T. Malcolm, and Mario Rossi. "Hegel and Hegelianism." In *The New Encyclopedia Britannica, Macropedia*, Volume 20, pp. 487–97. Chicago: Encyclopedia Britannica, 2007.

Kojève, Alexandre. *Introduction to the Reading of Hegel*. Ithaca, NY: Cornell University Press, 1980.

Kosok, Michael. "The Formalization of Hegel's Dialectical Logic." In MacIntyre, *Hegel Essays*, pp. 237–88.

Krasnoff, Larry. *Hegel's* Phenomenology of Spirit. Cambridge: Cambridge University Press, 2008.

Krell, David Farrell. "Lucinde's Shame: Hegel, Sensuous Woman, and the Law." In Mills, *Feminist Interpretations*, pp. 89–117.

Kroner, Richard. "Introduction." In G. W. F. Hegel, *On Christianity: Early Theological Writings*. Translated by T. M. Knox, pp. 1–66. New York: Harper Torchbooks, 1961. First published 1948.

Lauer, Quentin. "Hegel as Poet." In Perkins, *History and System*, pp. 1–14.

———. *A Reading of Hegel's* Phenomenology of Spirit. New York: Fordham University Press, 1993.

Leidecker, Kurt F. "Hegel and the Orientals." In Steinkraus, *Hegel's Philosophy*, pp. 156–66.

Lewis, Thomas A. "Finite Representation, Spontaneous Thought, and the Politics of an Open- Ended Consummation." In Žižek et al., *Hegel & the Infinite*, pp. 199–220.

———. "Religion and Demythologization in Hegel's *Phenomenology of Spirit*. In Moyar and Quante, *Hegel's* Phenomenology, pp. 192–209.

Lichthem, George. "Introduction to the Torchbook Edition." In G. W. F. Hegel, *The Phenomenology of Mind*. Translated by J. B. Baillie, pp. xv–xxxii. New York: Harper Torchbooks, 1967.

Limnatis, Nectarios G., ed. "The Dialectic of Subjectivity, Intersubjectivity, and Objectivity." In Limnatus, *Hegel's Dialectic*, pp. 173–92.

———. *The Dimensions of Hegel's Dialectic*. London and New York: Continuum, 2010.

Loewenberg, Jacob. *Hegel's Phenomenology: Dialogues on the Life of Mind*. La Salle, IL: Open Court, 1965.

Lombardi, Franco. "After Hegel." In Steinkraus, *Hegel's Philosophy*, pp. 221–52.

Lonzi, Carla. "Let's Spit on Hegel." In Mills, *Feminist Interpretations*, pp. 275–97.

Löwith, Karl. *From Hegel to Nietzsche: The Revolution in Nineteenth-Century Thought*. Translated by David E. Green. Garden City, NY: Doubleday, 1967.

————. "Mediation and Immediacy in Hegel, Marx and Feuerbach." In Steinkraus, *Hegel's Philosophy*, pp. 119–41.

MacIntyre, Alasdair. *Hegel: A Collection of Critical Essays*. Garden City, NY: Doubleday, 1972.

————. "Hegel on Faces and Skulls." In MacIntyre, *Hegel Essays*, pp. 219–36, and in Stewart, Spirit *Reader*, pp. 213–24.

Magnus, Kathleen Dow. *Hegel and the Symbolic Mediation of Spirit*. Albany: State University of New York Press, 2001.

Maker, William. "Does Hegel Have a 'Dialectical Method'?" *Southern Journal of Philosophy* 20 (1982): 75–96.

Malabou, Catherine. "Is Confession the Accomplishment of Recognition? Rousseau and the Unthought of Religion in the *Phenomenology of Spirit*." In Žižek et al., *Hegel & the Infinite*, pp. 19–30.

Marcuse, Herbert. *Reason and Revolution: Hegel and the Rise of Social Theory*. Boston: Beacon Press, 1970.

Margolis, Joseph. "The Greening of Hegel's Dialectical Logic." In Limnatis, *The Dimensions of Hegel's Dialectic*," pp. 193–215.

Matarrese, Craig B. *Starting with Hegel*. London and New York: Continuum, 2010.

McCarney, Joseph. *Hegel on History*. London and New York: Routledge, 2000.

McCumber, John. *The Company of Words: Hegel, Language, and Systematic Philosophy*. Evanston, IL: Northwestern University Press, 1993.

McDonald, Lee Cameron. *Western Political Theory, Part 3: Nineteenth and Twentieth Centuries*. New York: Harcourt Brace Jovanovich, 1968.

McTaggart, John M. E. *Studies in the Hegelian Dialectic*. Cambridge: Cambridge University Press, 1896.

Meist, Kurt Rainer. "'Absolute' and 'Consummate' Religion: The Foundations of Hegel's Comparison of Christianity and the Non-Christian Religions in His Philosophy of History." In Walker, *Thought and Faith*, pp. 39–71.

Miklowitz, Paul S. *Metaphysics to Metafictions: Hegel, Nietzsche, and the End of Philosophy* Albany: State University of New York Press, 1994.

Millán, Elizabeth. "From Hegel's Dialectical Trappings to Romantic Nets: An Examination of Progress in Philosophy." In Limnatis, *Hegel's Dialectic*, pp. 237–51.

Miller, Mitchell H., Jr. "The Attainment of the Absolute Standpoint in Hegel's *Phenomenology*." In Stewart, Spirit *Reader*, pp. 427–43.

Mills, Patricia Jagentowicz, ed. *Feminist Interpretations of G. W. F. Hegel*. University Park: Pennsylvania State University Press, 1996.

————. "Hegel's *Antigone*." In Stewart, Spirit *Reader*, pp. 243–71.

————. "Introduction." In Mills, *Feminist Interpretations*, pp. 1–24.

Moyar, Dean, and Michael Quante. *Hegel's* Phenomenology of Spirit: *A Critical Guide.* Cambridge: Cambridge University Press, 2008.

————. "Self-Completing Alienation: Hegel's Argument for Transparent Conditions of Free Agency." In Moyar and Quante, *Hegel's* Phenomenology, pp. 72, 150.

Mueller, Gustav E. "The Hegel Legend of 'Thesis-Antithesis-Synthesis.'" *Journal of the History of Ideas* 19, no. 3 (1958): 411–14.

————. "The Interdependence of the *Phenomenology*, *Logic*, and *Encyclopedia*," In Steinkraus, *Hegel's Philosophy*, pp. 17–33.

Negri, Antonio. "Rereading Hegel: The Philosopher of Right." In Žižek et al., *Hegel & the Infinite*, pp. 31–46.

Neuhouser, Frederick. "Desire, Recognition, and the Relation between Bondsman and Lord." In K. Westphal, *Blackwell Guide*, pp. 37–54.

Norman, Richard J. *Hegel's Phenomenology: A Philosophical Introduction.* Hampshire, UK: Gregg Revivals, 1991.

Norman, Richard J., and Sean Sayers. *Hegel, Marx and Dialectic: A Debate.* Sussex, UK: Harvester, 1980.

Nusser, Karlheinz. "The French Revolution and Hegel's *Phenomenology of Spirit*. In Stewart, Spirit *Reader*, pp. 282–306.

Nuzzo, Angelica. "Dialectic, Understanding, and Reason: How Does Hegel's *Logic* Begin?" In Limnatis, *Hegel's Dialectic*, pp. 12–30.

O'Brien, George D., *Hegel on Reason and History: A Contemporary Interpretation.* Chicago: University of Chicago Press, 1975.

O'Brien, Mary. "Hegel: Man, Physiology, and Fate." In Mills, *Feminist Interpretations*, pp. 177–207.

Olson, Alan M. *Hegel and the Spirit: Philosophy as Pneumatology.* Princeton, NJ: Princeton University Press, 1992.

Pahl, Katrin. "The Way of Despair." In Žižek et al., *Hegel & the Infinite*, pp. 141–58.

Pateman, Carole. "Hegel, Marriage, and the Standpoint of Contract." In Mills, *Feminist Interpretations*, pp. 209–23.

Patten, Alan. *Hegel's Idea of Freedom.* Oxford and New York: Oxford University Press, 1999.

Perkins, Robert L., ed. *History and System: Hegel's Philosophy of History* (Proceedings of the 1982 Sessions of the Hegel Society of America). Albany: State University of New York Press, 1984.

Pinkard, Terry. *Hegel: A Biography*. Cambridge and New York: Cambridge University Press, 2000.

———. *Hegel's Phenomenology: The Sociality of Reason*. Cambridge and New York: Cambridge University Press, 1994.

———. "Shapes of Active Reason: The Law of the Heart, Retrieved Virtue, and What Really Matters." In K. Westphal, *Blackwell Guide*, pp. 136–52.

———. "What Is a 'Shape of Spirit'?" In Moyar and Quante, *Hegel's* Phenomenology, pp. 112–29.

Pippin, Robert B. *Hegel on Self-Consciousness: Desire and Death in* The Phenomenology of Spirit. Princeton, NJ, and Oxford: Princeton University Press, 2011.

———. *Hegel's Idealism: The Satisfactions of Self-Consciousness*. Cambridge and New York: Cambridge University Press, 1989.

———. *Hegel's Practical Philosophy: Rational Agency as Ethical Life*. Cambridge and New York: Cambridge University Press, 2008.

———. "The 'Logic of Experience' as 'Absolute Knowledge' in Hegel's *Phenomenology of Spirit*." In Moyar and Quante, *Hegel's* Phenomenology, pp. 210–27.

———. "You Can't Get There from Here: Transition Problems in Hegel's *Phenomenology of Spirit*." In Beiser, *Cambridge Companion*, pp. 52–85.

Plant, Raymond. *Hegel*. New York: Routledge, 1999.

Popper, Karl R. *The Open Society and Its Enemies*, vol. 2, *The High Tide of Prophecy: Hegel, Marx, and the Aftermath*. New York: Harper Torchbooks, 1967. First published 1945.

Price, David W. "Hegel's Intertextual Dialectic: Diderot's *Le Neveu Rameau* in the *Phenomenology of Spirit*." In Stewart, Spirit *Reader*, pp. 272–81.

Prokopczyk, Czeslaw. *Truth and Reality in Marx and Hegel: A Reassessment*. Amherst: University of Massachusetts Press, 1980.

Quante, Michael. "'Reason . . . Apprehended Irrationally': Hegel's Critique of Observing Reason." In Moyar and Quante, *Hegel's* Phenomenology, pp. 91–111.

Rauch, Leo, and David Sherman. *Hegel's Phenomenology of Self-Consciousness: Text and Commentary*. Albany: State University of New York Press, 1999.

Ravven, Heidi M. "Has Hegel Anything to Say to Feminists?" In Mills, *Feminist Interpretations*, pp. 225–53.

Redding, Paul. *Analytic Philosophy and the Return of Hegelian Thought*. Cambridge and New York: Cambridge University Press, 2007.

Roberts, Julian. *German Philosophy: An Introduction*. Atlantic Highlands, NJ: Humanities Press International, 1988.

Robinson, Daniel N. *Toward a Science of Human Nature: Essays on the Psychologies of Mill, Hegel, Wundt, and James*. New York: Columbia University Press, 1982.

Rockmore, Tom. *Before and After Hegel: A Historical Introduction to Hegel's Thought.* Berkeley: University of California Press, 1993.

————. "Dialectic and Circularity: Is Hegel's Circularity a New Copernican Revolution?" In Limnatis, *Hegel's Dialectic*, pp. 55–75.

Rosen, Michael. *Hegel's Dialectic and Its Criticism.* Cambridge: Cambridge University Press, 1982.

Rosen, Stanley. *G. W. F. Hegel: An Introduction to the Science of Wisdom.* South Bend, IN: St. Augustine's, 2000.

Russell, Bertrand. *A History of Western Philosophy.* New York: Simon & Schuster, 1945.

Russon, John. *Reading Hegel's Phenomenology.* Bloomington: Indiana University Press, 2004.

Sabine, George H. *A History of Political Theory.* Rev. ed. New York: Henry Holt, 1950.

Sallis, John. "Hegel's Concept of Presentation: Its Determination in the Preface to the *Phenomenology of Spirit*." In Stewart, Spirit *Reader*, pp. 25–51.

Sayers, Sean, and Richard Norman. *Hegel, Marx and Dialectic: A Debate.* Sussex, UK: Harvester, 1980.

Schacht, Richard L. "Hegel on Freedom." In MacIntyre, *Hegel Essays*, pp. 289–328.

Schlitt, Dale M. *Divine Subjectivity: Understanding Hegel's Philosophy of Religion.* Scranton, PA, and London: University of Scranton Press, 2009.

Schöndorf, Harald. "The Othering Becoming Other and Reconciliation of God in Hegel's *Phenomenology of Spirit*. In Stewart, Spirit *Reader*, pp. 375–400.

Schor, Naomi. "Reading in Detail: Hegel's *Aesthetics* and the Feminine." In Mills, *Feminist Interpretations*, pp. 119–47.

Shapiro, Gary. "Notes on the Animal Kingdom of the Spirit." In Stewart, Spirit *Reader*, pp. 225–39.

Siebert, Rudolf J. *Hegel's Philosophy of History: Theological, Humanistic, and Scientific Elements.* Washington, DC: University Press of America, 1979.

Siep, Ludwig. "Practical Reason and Spirit in Hegel's Phenomenology of Spirit." In Moyar and Quante, Hegel's Phenomenology, pp. 173–91.

Simpson, Peter. *Hegel's Transcendental Induction.* Albany: State University of New York Press, 1998.

Singer, Peter. *Hegel: A Very Short Introduction.* Oxford and New York: Oxford University Press, 2001.

Soll, Ivan. *An Introduction to Hegel's Metaphysics.* Chicago: University of Chicago Press, 1969.

Solomon, Robert C. *From Hegel to Existentialism.* New York and Oxford: Oxford University Press, 1987.

————. "Hegel's Concept of '*Geist*.'" In MacIntyre, Spirit Essays, pp. 125–50.

————. *In the Spirit of Hegel*. New York and Oxford: Oxford University Press, 1983.

Speight, Allen. "Skepticism, Modernity, and the Origins of Hegelian Dialectic." In Limnatis, *Hegel's Dialectic*, pp. 140–56.

Stace, W. T. *The Philosophy of Hegel*. New York: Dover, 1955.

Starrett, Shari Neller. "Critical Relations in Hegel: Woman, Family, and the Divine." In Mills, *Feminist Interpretations*, pp. 253–73.

Steinkraus, Warren E., ed. *New Studies in Hegel's Philosophy*. New York: Holt, Rinehart and Winston, 1971.

Stern, Robert. *Hegel and the Phenomenology of Spirit*. Abingdon and New York: Routledge, 2002.

Stewart, Jon. "The Architectonic of Hegel's *Phenomenology of Spirit*." In Steward, Spirit Reader, pp. 444–77.

————. ed. *The Phenomenology of Spirit Reader: Critical and Interpretive Essays*. Albany: State University of New York Press, 1998.

Stolzenberg, Jürgen. "Hegel's Critique of the Enlightenment in 'The Struggle of the Enlightenment with Superstition.'" In K. Westphal, pp. 190–208.

Strathern, Paul. *Hegel in 90 Minutes*. Chicago: Ivan R. Dee, 1997.

Stumpf, Samuel Enoch. *Philosophy: History & Problems*. 5th ed. New York: McGraw-Hill, 1994.

Taylor, Charles. "The Opening Arguments of the *Phenomenology*." In MacIntyre, Hegel Essays, pp. 151–88.

————. *Hegel*. Cambridge and New York: Cambridge University Press, 1975.

Taylor, Mark C. "Infinite Restlessness." In Žižek et al., *Hegel & the Infinite*, 91–114.

————. *Journeys to Selfhood: Hegel & Kierkegaard*. Berkeley: University of California Press, 1980.

Thalheimer, August. *Introduction to Dialectical Materialism: The Marxist World-View*. Translated by George Simpson and George Weltner. New York: Covici-Friede, 1936.

Toews, John Edward. *Hegelianism: The Path toward Dialectical Humanism, 1805–1841*. Cambridge and New York: Cambridge University Press, 1980.

————. "Transformations of Hegelianism, 1805–1846." In Beiser, *Cambridge Companion*, pp. 378–413.

Tucker, Robert. *Philosophy and Myth in Karl Marx*. Cambridge and New York: Cambridge University Press, 1961.

Tunick, Mark. *Hegel's Political Philosophy: Interpreting the Practice of Legal Punishment*. Princeton, NJ: Princeton University Press, 1992.

Verene, Donald Phillip. *Hegel's Absolute: An Introduction to Reading the* Phenomenology of Spirit. Albany: State University of New York Press, 2007.

Vieillard-Baron, Jean-Louis. "Natural Religion: An Investigation of Hegel's *Phenomenology of Spirit.*" In Stewart, Spirit *Reader*, pp. 351–74.

Walker, John, ed. "Absolute Knowledge and the Experience of Faith: The Relevance of the Religious Dimension in Hegel's Thought." In Walker, *Thought and Faith*, pp. 151–68.

———. *Thought and Faith in the Philosophy of Hegel*. Dordrecht, Netherlands: Kluwer Academic, 1991.

Wallace, Robert M. *Hegel's Philosophy of Reality, Freedom, and God*. Cambridge: Cambridge University Press, 2005.

Walsh, David. "The Historical Dialectic of Spirit: Jacob Boehme's Influence on Hegel." In Perkins, *History and System*, pp. 15–35.

Wandschneider, Dieter. "Dialectic as the 'Self-Fulfillment' of Logic." In Limnatis, *Hegel's Dialectic*, pp. 31–54.

Wartenberg, Thomas E. "Hegel's Idealism: The Logic of Conceptuality." In Beiser, *Cambridge Companion*, pp. 102–29.

Werkmeister, William H. "Hegel and Heidegger." In Steinkraus, *Hegel's Philosophy*, pp. 142–55.

Westphal, Kenneth. "The Basic Context and Structure of Hegel's *Philosophy of Right.*" In Beiser, *Cambridge Companion*, pp. 234–69.

———. ed. *The Blackwell Guide to Hegel's* Phenomenology of Spirit. Malden, MA: Wiley-Blackwell, 2009.

———. *Hegel's Epistemology: A Philosophical Introduction to the* Phenomenology of Spirit. Indianapolis: Hackett, 2003.

———. "Hegel's Phenomenological Method and Analysis of Consciousness." In K. Westphal, *Blackwell Guide*, pp. 1–36.

———. "Hegel's Solution to the Dilemma of the Criterion." In Stewart, Spirit *Reader*, pp. 76–101.

Westphal, Merold. "Hegel and the Reformation." In Perkins, *History and System*, pp. 73–92.

———. "Hegel's Phenomenology of Perception." In Stewart, Spirit *Reader*, pp. 122–37.

———. *History and Truth in Hegel's* Phenomenology. Bloomington: Indiana University Press, 1979.

White, Alan. *Absolute Knowledge: Hegel and the Problem of Metaphysics*. Athens: Ohio University Press, 1983.

Wicks, Robert. "Hegel's Esthetics: An Overview." In Beiser, *Cambridge Companion*, pp. 348–77.

Wiedmann, Franz. *Hegel: An Illustrated Biography*. New York: Pegasus, 1968.

Wilkins, Burleigh Taylor. *Hegel's Philosophy of History*. Ithaca, NY, and London: Cornell University Press, 1974.

Williams, Robert R. *Hegel's Ethics of Recognition*. Berkeley: University of California Press, 1997.

Williamson, Raymond K. *Introduction to Hegel's Philosophy of Religion*. Albany: State University of New York Press, 1984.

Winfield, Richard Dien. "Hegel's Challenge to the Modern Economy." In Perkins, *History and System*, pp. 219–53.

———. *Hegel's Ethical Thought*. Cambridge and New York: Cambridge University Press, 1990.

———. "Hegel's Ethics." In Beiser, *Cambridge Companion*, 211–233.

———. "The Theory and Practice of the History of Freedom: On the Right of History in Hegel's *Philosophy of Right*." In Perkins, *History and System*, pp. 123–44.

Wood, Allen. "Hegel and Marxism." In Beiser, *Cambridge Companion*, pp. 414–44.

Wyschogrod, Edith. "Disrupting Reason: Art and Madness in Hegel and Van Gogh, In Žižek et al., *Hegel & the Infinite*, pp. 181–98.

Young, William. *Hegel's Dialectical Method*. Nutley, NJ: Craig, 1972.

Žižek, Slavoj, Clayton Crockett, and Creston Davis. "Hegel and Shitting: The Idea's Constipation." In Žižek et al., *Hegel & the Infinite*, pp. 224–32.

———. *Hegel & the Infinite: Religion, Politics, and Dialectic*. New York: Columbia University Press, 2011.

56 Authors Writing about Marx Alone

Adams, William. "Aesthetics: Liberating the Senses." In *The Cambridge Companion to Marx*, edited by Terrell Carver, pp. 246–74. Cambridge: Cambridge University Press, 1991.

Afanasyev, V. G. *Dialectical Materialism*. New York: International Publishers, 1987.

Althusser, Louis. *For Marx*. Translated by Ben Brewster. London and New York: Verso, 2005.

Ball, Terence. "History: Critique and Irony." In Carver, *Cambridge Companion*, pp. 124–42.

Barnett, Vincent. *Marx*. Abingdon, UK: Routledge, 2009.

Beehler, Rodger. *The Theory, Not the Theorist: The Case of Karl Marx*. Lanham, MD: University Press of America, 2006.

Berlin, Isaiah. *Karl Marx*. New York: Time, 1963.

Bober, M. M. *Karl Marx's Interpretation of History*. Cambridge: Harvard University Press, 1950.

Carver, Terrell, ed. *The Cambridge Companion to Marx*. Cambridge: Cambridge University Press, 1991.

———. "Reading Marx: Life and Works." In Carver, *Cambridge Companion*, pp. 1–22.

Cohen, G. A. *Karl Marx's Theory of History: A Defence*. Princeton: Princeton University Press, 1978.

Cornforth, Maurice. *Materialism and the Dialectical Method*. 4th rev. ed. New York: International Publishers, 1968.

De George, Richard T. *Patterns of Soviet Thought: The Origins and Development of Dialectical and Historical Materialism*. Ann Arbor: University of Michigan Press, 1966.

Desai, Meghnad. *Marx's Revenge: The Resurgence of Capitalism and the Death of Statist Socialism*. London and New York: Verso, 2002.

Eagleton, Terry. *Marx*. London: Phoenix, 1997.

Elster, Jon. *Making Sense of Marx*. Cambridge: Cambridge University Press, 1985.

Farr, James. "Science: Realism, Criticism, History." In Carver, *Cambridge Companion*, pp. 106–23.

Feinberg, Barbara Silberdick. *Marx and Marxism*. New York: Franklin Watts, 1985.

Fine, Ben. *Marx's Capital*. London: Macmillan, 1975.

Gilbert, Alan. "Political Philosophy: Marx and Radical Democracy." In Carver, *Cambridge Companion*, pp. 168–95.

Guest, David. *A Textbook of Dialectical Materialism.* New York: International Publishers, 1939.

Hearn, Jeff. "Gender: Biology, Nature, and Capitalism." In Carver, *Cambridge Companion*, pp. 222–45.

Heilbroner, Robert L. *Marxism: For and Against.* New York and London: W. W. Norton, 1980.

———. *The Worldly Philosophers.* New York: Simon & Schuster, 1953.

Hilferding, Rudolf. "Böhm-Bawerk's Criticism of Marx." In Sweezy, *Böhm-Bawerk's Criticism of Marx*, pp. 121–96.

Himmelweit, Susan. "Reproduction and the Materialist Conception of History: A Feminist Critique." In Carver, *Cambridge Companion*, pp. 196–221.

Howard, Dick. *The Development of the Marxian Dialectic.* Carbondale: Southern Illinois University Press, 1972.

Hunt, E. K. *History of Economic Thought: A Critical Perspective.* 2nd ed. New York: Harper Collins, 1992.

Koren, Henry J. *Marx and the Authentic Man: A First Introduction to the Philosophy of Karl Marx.* Pittsburgh: Duquesne University Press, 1967.

Krapivin, V. *What Is Dialectical Materialism?* Translated by Galina Sdobnikova. Moscow: Progress, 1985.

Landreth, Harry, and David C. Colander. *History of Economic Thought.* 3rd ed. Boston: Houghton Mifflin, 1993.

Lee, Wendy Lynne. *On Marx.* Belmont, CA: Wadsworth, 2002.

Lefebvre, Henri. *Dialectical Materialism.* Translated by John Sturrock. London: Jonathan Cape, 1968.

Lindsay, A. D. *Karl Marx's Capital: An Introductory Essay.* London: Oxford University Press, 1925.

Mayo, Henry B. *Introduction to Marxist Theory.* New York: Oxford University Press, 1960.

Mazlish, Bruce. *The Meaning of Karl Marx.* Oxford: Oxford University Press, 1984.

McLellan, David. *Karl Marx.* New York: Viking, 1975.

McMurtry, John. *The Structure of Marx's World-View.* Princeton: Princeton University Press, 1978.

Meikle, Scott. "History of Philosophy: The Metaphysics of Substance in Marx." In Carver, *Cambridge Companion*, pp. 296–319.

Miller, Richard. "Social and Political Theory: Class, State, and Revolution." In Carver, *Cambridge Companion*, pp. 55–105.

Ollman, Bertell. *Dance of the Dialectic: Steps in Marx's Method.* Urbana: University of Illinois Press, 2003.

Rader, Melvin. *Marx's Interpretation of History.* New York: Oxford University Press, 1979.

Reiman, Jeffrey. "Moral Philosophy: The Critique of Capitalism and the Problem of Ideology." In Carver, *Cambridge Companion*, pp. 143–67.

Robinson, Joan. *An Essay on Marxian Economics.* London: Macmillan, 1942.

Rubel, Maximilien, and Margaret Manale. *Marx without Myth: A Chronological Study of His Life and Work.* New York: Harper Torchbooks, 1975.

*Sayers, Sean. "Marxism and the Dialectical Method: A Critique of G. A. Cohen." In *Socialism, Feminism and Philosophy: A Radical Philosophy Reader*, edited by Sean Sayers and Peter Osborne, pp. 140–68. London and New York: Routledge, 1990.

Shaw, William H. *Marx's Theory of History.* Stanford: Stanford University Press, 1978.

*Singer, Peter. *Marx: A Very Short Introduction.* Oxford: Oxford University Press, 1980.

Staley, Charles E. *A History of Economic Thought: From Aristotle to Arrow.* Cambridge, MA, and Oxford: Blackwell, 1989.

Thomas, Paul. "Critical Reception: Marx Then and Now." In Carver, *Cambridge Companion*, pp. 23–54.

Turner, Denys. "Religion: Illusions and Liberation." In Carver, *Cambridge Companion*, pp. 20– 337.

von Böhm-Bawerk, Eugen. "Karl Marx and the Close of His System." In *Karl Marx and the Close of His System & Böhm-Bawerk's Criticism of Marx*, edited by Paul M. Sweezy, pp. 3–118. New York: Augustus M. Kelley, 1949.

Walker, Angus. *Marx: His Theory and Its Context.* New York: Longman, 1978.

Wetter, Gustav A. *Dialectical Materialism: A Historical and Systematic Survey of Philosophy in the Soviet Union.* Translated by Peter Heath. New York: Praeger, 1958.

White, James D. *Karl Marx and the Intellectual Origins of Dialectical Materialism.* London and New York: Macmillan and St. Martin's, 1996.

Wilde, Lawrence. "Logic: Dialectic and Contradiction." In Carver, *Cambridge Companion*, pp. 275–95.

Wolff, Robert P. *Understanding Marx: A Reconstruction and Critique of* Capital. Princeton. NJ: Princeton University Press, 1984.

Wolfson, Murray. *Karl Marx.* New York: Columbia University Press, 1971.

*Wood, Allen W. *Karl Marx.* London and Boston: Routledge & Kegan Paul, 1981.

Worsley, Peter. *Marx and Marxism.* London and New York: Routledge, 1989.

* Author not counted because counted previously on the Hegel list.

Note: Some of the Hegel authors are not discussing topics relating to *Phenomenology* or to *The Philosophy of History*. But, given that Hegel's using thesis-antithesis-synthesis dialectics has evolved into a revolutionary idea, no longer accepted by scholars, the authors writing about unrelated topics would surely be anxious and able to relate their topics to dialectics if they had hitherto unrevealed insights into dialectics at their disposal. And, given that nobody has previously revealed Marx's thesis-antithesis-synthesis dialectics, any Marx author with knowledge of Marx's Hegelian dialectics could hardly avoid bending his or her topic (if necessary) to place it in its dialectical setting.

INDEX